Schools opened as social centers, Rochester, Ne[w]
gress of Pl[ay]

Schools made available for recreation, Gary, Indiana.	*1908*
NORMAL COURSE IN PLAY first published by Playground Association of America.	*1909*
Boy Scouts of America—American Camping Association—Camp Fire Girls established.	*1910*
National Federation of Settlements and Neighborhood Centers established.	*1911*
U.S. Children's Bureau established. Girl Scouts of America established.	*1912*
U.S. Agricultural Extension Service and National Association of College Unions established.	*1914*
National Park Service established (U.S. Department of Interior).	*1916*
War Camp Community Service and other national private agency programs for military established. New Jersey passed enabling law. National Committee on Women's Athletics organized.	*1917*
Community Chests and Councils of America established.	*1918*
National Parks Association established.	*1919*
National Conference on State Parks established.	*1921*
Conference on Outdoor Recreation met at the White House.	*1924*
National Recreation School organized.	*1926*
Playground and Recreation Association of America changed name to National Recreation Association.	*1930*
First International Recreation Congress, Los Angeles.	*1932*
National Park Service, National Parks and Monuments, National Military Parks, National Battlefield Parks and Sites, National Memorials, and National Capital Parks consolidated into National Parks Service.	*1933*
Establishment of Emergency Services of Federal Government during the Depression and provision for recreation services and facili-	*1933-1936*

Continued on back cover

Community Recreation

A Guide to Its Organization

Fourth Edition

HAROLD D. MEYER

CHARLES K. BRIGHTBILL

H. DOUGLAS SESSOMS

Prentice-Hall, Inc., Englewood Cliffs, N.J.

13-153155-7

LIBRARY OF CONGRESS CATALOG CARD NUMBER: 74-76297

Printed in the United States of America

Current printing (last digit):

10   9   8   7   6   5   4

PRENTICE-HALL INTERNATIONAL, INC., *London*
PRENTICE-HALL OF AUSTRALIA, PTY. LTD., *Sydney*
PRENTICE-HALL OF CANADA, LTD., *Toronto*
PRENTICE-HALL OF INDIA PRIVATE LTD., *New Delhi*
PRENTICE-HALL OF JAPAN, INC., *Tokyo*

Preface

Since the first edition of *Community Recreation* was published in 1948, the recreation movement has advanced rapidly in this country and throughout the world. Every indication notes that its progress will be even more rapid and widespread in the future. While the philosophy and principles of community recreation remain basically as they were, the conditions, approaches, methods, and contents change with changing times and a changing culture. This fourth edition of what has become a standard text in the study of community recreation recognizes these changes and provides information which the authors hope will be helpful to the reader. And while the wealth of new material which has been added is applicable to the immediate present, it has also been weighed with an eye to the future.

The responsibility for organized recreation rests in the local community. Here recreation under public, private, and commercial auspices has its roots. In neighborhoods, villages, towns, cities, districts, and counties, organized recreation is closely associated with the people. Community planning and action are the order of the day. Community recreation is not spontaneous; it requires planning, organization, administration, development, and intelligent evaluation.

It has been demonstrated repeatedly that community recreation, adequately and properly organized, contributes to the building of sound physical and mental health, to the molding of democratic citizenship and character, to the amelioration of delinquency and crime and other aspects of social pathology, and, in general, to the promotion of social well-being. Significantly, organized recreation has become a strong factor in our national life by making communities more attractive and desirable for home-makers, business investors, and industrialists, and by creating wider markets for capital and consumer goods, for services, and for jobs. Year by year, recreation assumes a more important place in the social and economic life of the people.

Community Recreation provides an introduction to the study of organized recreation in the United States and a general guide for professional recreation personnel, a reference and source book for community and civic leaders, groups, and organizations of all types, including volunteer leaders, members of boards and commissions, club leaders, study groups, and planning committees. The volume provides a basis for the understanding of the structure of organized recreation and its further development.

Recreation is treated and interpreted in its broadest possible sense; however, the breadth and flexibility of approach have not prevented the authors from arriving at definite, concrete conclusions. A short historical sketch and a general theoretical interpretation of organized recreation are included, along with some of the philosophical "why," a portion of the statistical "what," and much of the practical "how." The authors recognize the many forces, resources, and interests which are required to provide total community recreation coverage. Although the whole story of organized recreation cannot be presented within the covers of this work, the more important aspects of recreation techniques and experiences in the field are stressed. The chief contribution is that the book opens doors to effective thought, planning, and action for the advance of the place of recreation in our contemporary society.

The fact that the emphasis on problems of organization is given to local public recreation agencies is no indication that the role of private and commercial groups, or recreation in other settings, is less important. All are fully recognized, but the authors deliberately stress local community recreation because of the growing and widespread interest in it. Moreover, the principles which apply to local recreation, with few exceptions, apply to other situations.

Each chapter includes a "workshop" which suggests further study and research and gives the reader an opportunity to apply the contents of each chapter to practical situations. The authors have chosen to carefully select a few outstanding volumes, past and present, pertinent to the chapter subject. No bulletin, magazine, article, or paragraph excerpt is included. It is suggested that each agency or individual develop a scrapbook of leading topics, a filing system of subject matter, or an agency library. The "Comment" feature of the references should be helpful in finding additional resources, printed and otherwise, and in proposing additional study and investigation. The authors have included an appendix listing the chief recreation agencies and organizations in the organized movement in the United States. A glossary also provides a list of terms used in the field of recreation. A suggested listing of films relating to recreation has been included in the appendix.

The authors wish to acknowledge their indebtedness to all those who advised them, who shared their material, and who allowed quotations from their works. Special thanks go to those who worked on the details of typing, arrangements, and reading of proof.

The authors especially thank the following for services to this revision:

Sal J. Prezioso, Executive Vice President of the National Recreation and Park Association and members of his staff for suggestions about professional organizations; James S. Stevens, Jr., and Robert Buckner of the North Carolina Recreation Commission staff for work on the chapters relating to government and recreation; Thomas A. Stein and Mary E. Fortune of the Curriculum in Recreation Administration at the University of North Carolina for updating material on the family and on the ill and disabled; Don Neer, Executive Director of the National Industrial Recreation Association for suggestions about employee recreation; Wesley H. Wallace, head of the Department of Television, Radio, and Motion Pictures at UNC for updating material about radio and television; Lt. Colonel Ingle of Special Services in the Department of Defense for assistance relative to the Armed Services; and H. Harold Hipps, Board of Education of the Methodist Church.

The secretaries of the North Carolina Recreation Commission—Miss Myrtle Raines, Mrs. Judy Brown, and Mrs. Brenda Parker, and the secretaries of the Curriculum in Recreation Administration at UNC—Mrs. Dahlia Crim and Mrs. Shannon Grisham for valuable services in typing manuscript material.

The staff of Prentice-Hall, Inc. for guidance in bringing this fourth edition through the stages of publication and to the many individuals who, through the years, have made suggestions and given constructive ideas for the enrichment of the volume.

This major revision of *Community Recreation* is timely. With complete faith in the increasingly rich contribution that recreation will make to democratic living, the authors hope that this book will continue to encourage the high aims and ideas of the recreation profession.

Harold D. Meyer
H. Douglas Sessoms

TO

The National Recreation and Park Association whose membership forms the professional and lay leadership of the recreation and park movement in the United States and whose services offer to the nation opportunities for more abundant and wholesome recreation in this, the leisure age.

ABOUT THE AUTHORS

Harold D. Meyer is Chairman Emeritus of the Curriculum in Recreation Administration, University of North Carolina, and Consultant to the North Carolina Recreation Commission

The late Charles K. Brightbill was the Head of the Department of Recreation and Municipal Park Administration, University of Illinois

H. Douglas Sessoms is Head of the Curriculum in Recreation Administration, University of North Carolina

Contents

I

Background

Above: Aquatic recreation
—frogman style. Right:
Artist at work. Below: Recreation dollars afloat.

Left: An essential in modern real estate. Directly below: Vacation in the saddle.
Below: Not *always* an
adult's world.

1

History of Early and Modern Recreation and Leisure

LEISURE AND RECREATION IN EARLY TIMES

Ancient Civilization

Man has had leisure in some form since the dawn of history—even though precious little of it at first.

Man's initial struggle, of course, was to survive. He had to find and grow food, provide shelter and clothing, and protect himself from his enemies. Beyond these, however, he has always had some time "on his own."

There is no better marked trail of the development of leisure, and the desire of man for self-expression, than in the rise of the arts. Although records have been found which date primitive forms of art back to *Paleolithic* man, the arts first found an important place in western culture in the ancient civilizations of Egypt, Babylonia, and Crete. Pottery-making and sculpture were among the early arts in many parts of the ancient world. To be sure, the potter's wheel and the loom had as their first purpose the making of *useful* things. But the decorative refinement of the products turned out on these early devices shows that man was interested in more than usefulness. The seeking of beauty, the desire to express, and the wish to create have all developed concurrently through the centuries with the growth of leisure. Painting, music, literature, the dance, drama, and games and sports are all traceable to early civilizations and, either directly or indirectly, to the hours during which man was temporarily liberated from daily toil.

Painting

Painting goes back to the Stone Age when pictures were painted on the walls of caves and engravings were made on bone. Later paintings in the tombs of the Egyptian Pharaohs depicting daily life among the early people along the Nile are well known. The more natural and realistic classical paintings of the Greeks and Romans who followed illustrate the progress which civilization made and the culture which was reflected through the work and leisure of those peoples.

Music

Music was probably the first of the arts because music is rhythm, which is a part of life itself. Music has played an important role in every stage during the history of man, from the clapping of hands and stamping of feet through the boom of crude drums and the sounding of trumpets as knights rode into battle. The Egyptians not only had large pyramids and temples; their orchestras and choruses were large, too. Composing music was a favorite pastime of the Athenians who knew well how to use their newly-earned leisure, and employed music during their great dramatic, religious, and sports festivals. Although the Romans were more interested in playing than composing music, they, too, were devoted to music. Every school child knows the story of how Nero fiddled while Rome burned.

Literature

From ancient civilizations come some of the great literary works of all time. These range from the Old Testament of the Hebrews to the great comedies, tragedies, and philosophical writings of the Greeks. Writing and reading were related in many ways to work, government, and religion, but in countless instances they were also born of leisure time.

Dance

Just as early men and women gave expression to their rhythmic feelings through music, so also have they done so through the dance. The ancient dance may have been tied to man's interest in religion and magic, but if any of the arts can be closely associated with the "after work" and festive hours of man, it is surely dancing. Dancing in Egypt was a favorite interest of the lower classes, and was also performed widely for exhibition.

As was true of their interest in most of the arts, the interest of the Greeks in dancing had its inspiration in religion; yet Greece, too, had its troupes of educational and acrobatic dancers, its warrior dances, and theatrical dances, which served the pleasures of Spartan and Athenian families alike. The Romans did comparatively little dancing themselves, but they imported professional dancers for their leisure entertainment.

Drama

Drama has often been looked upon as a mirror of living, reflecting the hopes, fears, habits, customs, conquests, and problems of people. A search of the past reveals that drama, as we know it today, also had its beginnings in the region of the Nile. Its dual purposes have been to educate and to entertain. Its reputation for the latter does not necessarily discount its social or educational influences upon the generations. Early Grecian drama also built upon the religious instincts of the people. The Greek theater, with its first dramatist, Thespis (from whom comes our term, Thespian), brought with it great outdoor theaters to which the Greeks thronged to be entertained and inspired. Roman drama, which drew its pattern from the Grecian stage, was important in the lives of the Romans. Its emphasis, however, was upon comedy, which catered to the whims and fancies of a people who preferred to be amused. To identify the major emphasis of drama in Rome with anything other than the entertainment of idle people would be to stretch the imagination.

Games and Sports

Games are as old as civilization itself. For centuries games and sports of all kinds have been a powerful and lasting force in our culture. It is not easy to follow, from the obscure past, the origins of particular games and sports. Nevertheless, we can be sure that these physical pursuits sprang from events in the lives of the people—some tragic, some happy, and some commonplace. Many grew out of mythology, folk customs, and social habits. The basic skills of these early activities can be detected in the games and sports of today, even though we know them in different form.

We also know that these early games and sports grew out of things which men, in early times, had to do to survive. Running, jumping, throwing, hunting, and the like were required to find food and escape from or pursue the enemy. Games and sports also were related closely to the religious interests of man—as were dancing, music, and other forms of the arts—but the time came, even in ancient civilization, when there was purposefulness in the games just for their amusement or exhibition value, or, as we say today—"just for the sport of it."

Homer's *Iliad* gives an early account of the athlete's action related to his physical strength. The athletics and games of both the Greeks and the Romans often had as an incentive the preparation for warfare. The Grecian athlete, particularly, saw his efforts as pleasing to the gods. The Olympic Games had their origin in Olympia, Greece, which was a center for religion and athletics. Here were the temples of Zeus and Hera, as well as the Palestra (wrestling and boxing school), and the Hippodrome, where chariot races were held. The fifth century B.C. even had its professional athlete, or "pot hunter," who traveled from town to town, displaying his athletic prowess at festivals.

The Romans, too, had their facilities for the entertainment and relaxation of their people. Slaves worked so that their Roman masters might be free to use baths, forums, circuses, and amphitheaters. The Romans favored strenuous exercise, but they also had gardens which were the forerunners of our parks.[1]

Rome

Unfortunately, the ways in which Romans spent their leisure contributed to the degeneration of the Empire, along with slavery, graft, nepotism, and unsavory morals. For the leisure activities of Rome were not creative, constructive, or uplifting. Rather, they were bloody and barbarous pastimes, enervating forms of amusement, and frenzied, profane exhibitions. The play and recreation habits of the Romans stand as a fine example of a civilization on the wane.

The East

If space permitted, a review of ancient history in Asia, particularly China, would also reveal a strong relationship between the culture and the play and creative efforts of the people. The history of Chinese literature starts early and includes no Dark Ages. Poetry and philosophy have been a part of the Chinese culture for hundreds of years. The simple lines of Chinese painting have been a highly respected form of art for more than two thousand years. Oriental dancing is of even greater age and the stringed instruments and cymbals of Chinese music came with its early civilization. For hundreds of years, the world has admired the skill of the Chinese craftsman as he has produced lovely and valuable projects of metal, stone, ivory, and paper. Almost any event—births, weddings, har-

---

[1] The hunting preserves of the Egyptians, or even Nebuchadnezzar's Hanging Gardens of Babylon, long before Rome, might be considered the first signs of man's interest in setting aside a part of the outdoors for his personal enjoyment—exactly the purpose of the modern park.

vest time—was the occasion for a celebration by the ancient Chinese, and these customs persist today.

The Middle Ages

The leisure or recreation aspects of culture cannot be clearly separated from the economic and political characteristics of an era, for these have a strong bearing upon the former. The Middle Ages, which began with the fall of the Roman Empire, and which lasted approximately one thousand years, were largely agricultural and feudal. These times found the masses working long and hard amidst great danger, in the absence of police protection as we have it today. There were mainly three classes of people—the clergy, the lords and knights, and the workers.

The church had a powerful influence on the people during this period and its rules were many and rigid. These rules, combined with the daily toil of the serfs, left little opportunity for the working people to enjoy any kind of pleasure beyond the telling of stories, the singing of songs, and, occasionally, taking part in folk games and dances. Literature, drama, dancing, and the like were reserved for the leisure class.

There was great sport and fighting, however, among the knights. Sports attained a certain prominence from the tenth to the fourteenth century—the period of chivalry. Contests and tournaments with such combative sports as archery, fencing, and jousting were much in flower. Riding, hawking, and falconry were equally popular sports in the Middle Ages. Some authorities believe that such games and sports as bowls, nine pins, and bait-casting were practiced as early as the thirteenth century. Certainly the shooting of wildlife was both enjoyed and controlled during the reign of feudalism.

It must be emphasized, nevertheless, that for the great majority of people in the Middle Ages, there was little opportunity for personal enjoyment. Pleasure, when one had the leisure to pursue it, was impeded by lack of education and a general attitude of restraint which was placed upon the population by religious interests. After chores, boys were trained to hunt and fight. After the spinning, weaving, and sewing were finished, the girls had some, but not much, opportunity to listen to the songs and poems of the wandering singers and troubadours. Knowledge of the outside world came mainly from the tales of battle described by the knights and squires.

The Modern Era

Both the attitudes toward and opportunities for play, recreation, and leisure changed considerably in the modern period. Although agriculture remained a large part of the economy, men no longer hesitated to break away from the soil and their masters. Political, religious, social, and economic changes came about, along with a gradual reshaping of the play factor in the lives of western people. The Renaissance, the Reformation, and the Industrial Revolution made colossal impacts upon the manner of living.

Renaissance

The Renaissance resulted in refinements of various after-work pleasures. Sports and games became less brutal, even though many remained forms of combat in more highly civilized guise. New interest and new styles developed in the arts, particularly in painting, sculpture, and architecture. This period was one of slow but certain enlightenment, an occurrence which in itself was to help lead toward the new leisure. With the beginning of modern science in this period, man began to understand the world and its resources better and began to learn how science could help improve the lot of humanity. The opening of trade to the Orient gave early Europeans a taste of rare luxury goods but at the same time exposed them to a philosophy which put less of a premium upon material things. The Renaissance opened the door to new learning and was a departure from ignorance and superstition.

Renaissance and Reformation

The Renaissance was a period of reaction against the stifling influence of a corrupt church. The balance of power and wealth gradually shifted from church to state and people were freed from economic and political intolerance as well as religious dogma. During these two centuries, feudalism came to an end, modern science had its beginnings, and trade became worldwide. Neoclassic schools replaced the parochial and, above all, there were great literary and artistic achievements. The guiding philosophy of the period was Humanism, emphasizing the dignity of man and his achievements.

The Reformation reasserted the importance of religion in response to the worldliness and impiety of the Renaissance man. The teachings of the reformer Calvin, and the discipline he espoused, were to leave their impression upon the minds and habits of men for a long time. These views held little place for frivolity and amusement and implied that there was something sinful in those who took time out for pleasure. The attitude of the Puritans, later in America, that idleness and play were the tools of Satan, was ascribable to much of the philosophy which prevailed during the Reformation. But changes did take place which led to more widespread recreation. Some religious reformers even openly recognized the value of games and athletics, as well as of music and other arts.

Industrial Revolution

Prior to the Industrial Revolution, man earned his living largely through agriculture and trade. It was through inventions of countless kinds and industrial progress over a long period of years that leisure in increasingly large quantities was provided.

The effect of inventions upon opportunities for leisure is too vast to calculate. Starting with the invention of movable printing type in the fifteenth century, and progressing to the steam and gas engines of the 1700's, and, later, electric power, up to our present-day inventions—the results are a higher standard of living, more leisure, and a more abundant life.

THE EARLY DAYS OF RECREATION IN THE UNITED STATES

The growth of recreation in the United States is the result of a number of developments—technological and industrial progress, the advance of science and medicine, more widespread education, and changing social attitudes. From the end of the eighteenth century to the middle of the twentieth century, the United States moved from a pioneer, agriculural land to a highly industrialized nation with many large centers of population. Urbanization took place. People moved in large numbers to the cities and suburbs. In California, for example, as the sixth decade of the twentieth century opened, 89 per cent of the people were living on 5 per cent of the land. During this same period, Americans benefited from many new labor-saving devices, which gave them more free time, and medical discoveries, which not only prolonged life but also made it more healthful and enjoyable. Public education took hold of the people and helped to cultivate tastes and desires for recreation. The attitude toward recreation underwent such a drastic change that activities that were once scorned became not only acceptable, but actually socially desirable.

There were other significant changes. Parks, for example, which have always represented man's wish to bring country living to the city, moved from the status of the cow pasture, to the commons for drilling the militia, to the formal garden—"keep-off-the-grass"—park, to the outdoor recreation center where nature in all of its beauty can be enjoyed, and physical as well as social expression exercised by the people. Great changes also came about in the home, which was the first recreation center. Often, in the early days, it was difficult to distinguish between work and play in the home. Craftsmanship was enjoyed, but it was also necessary to sustain life. The church, too, was subject to change. Its attitude toward recreation has constantly become more liberal. It would be difficult to find any part of American culture which did not change and which did not in one way or another have a sharp influence upon the leisure and recreation of the people.

Recreation in Colonial America was not held in high esteem. Idleness was thought to be associated with evil, loose morals, and personal degeneration. Strict Calvinist doctrine was, in great part, responsible for this attitude, but there was also little place for leisure in a land of pioneers who had to make their way in the world. In any event, public opinion, particularly in Colonial New England, New York, and Pennsylvania, was against leisure and play. Efforts were made to control "such foolishness" by law. The Continental Congress discouraged horse racing, cock fighting, gambling, and the like. Pennsylvania passed "Blue Laws" which even today control certain forms of amusement there on the Sabbath. Despite the prevalence of unfavorable public opinion, however, people did manage to find recreation in Colonial America. The English game of cricket was played at Dartmouth College in the eighteenth century, and the game of golf was played by a few in New York in the seventeenth century. A more tolerant attitude toward leisurely pursuits was evident in the South. Visitors in Colonial times to Williamsburg, Virginia, compared its elegant social season to that of London. Men gathered in the taverns to discuss politics and the events of the day, boys and girls played tag in the streets, and the ladies often assembled to converse and do needlework.

With the opening of the frontiers and the rise of cities in the nineteenth century, recreation took on many interesting forms. This was the period in which American folklore had its real beginning. Social dancing in the East and square dancing in the West became more popular. The waltz, polka, and quadrille, restrained as they were, flourished—even though many thought that the placing of one's arm around a young lady's waist was immoral. There were sleigh rides and skating in the winter and excursions to the beaches for "bathing" in the summer. Travel to Europe, for those who could afford it, increased during this period. Gentlemen's clubs were organized in the large eastern cities, with members asserting reasons of health to justify their action. The newly created legitimate theatres in Boston, Philadelphia, and New York competed with the lyceums and lecture halls for popular support. Minstrel and variety shows found their way into the smaller hamlets. Although greatly ridiculed, billiard rooms and pool halls were opened, and well-patronized country sports engaged the interest of males in different sections of the nation. Hunting and fishing (with the wilderness as a game paradise) were made spectacular through such events as turkey shoots, buffalo hunts, and fish fries. People took a real interest in outdoor activity. But interest in games, athletics, and sports was not by any means confined to the country or outing activities. Professional prizefighting, although often broken up by police raids, and other more acceptable forms of athletics came into being. The National Professional Baseball League was organized in 1876, and football was started in colleges in the 1880's. About this same time, many Americans—young and old—took to wheels with the velocipede, the bicycle, and the bicycle "built for two." Other sports were practiced in the United States at about the following times: Baseball, 1845; Basketball, 1891; Birling, 1840; Billiards, 1845; Gliding, 1885; Field Hockey, 1875; Rodeo, 1850; Softball, 1887; Table Tennis, 1895; Volleyball, 1893.

The church backed into the effort by sponsoring camp meetings, which served both religious and social purposes. Even the rural families managed to find recreation at harvest time by getting together to work and play. Quilting bees, barn raisings, and husking contests were among the events which were well attended by those whose homes were in the farming areas.

Toward the end of the nineteenth century, with transportation more easily available, amusement parks sprang up in the outlying districts of cities. By this time the penny arcade, the travelling medicine show, and the annual visit of the circus "big top" had become popular. Band concerts in the parks, huge holiday celebrations with fireworks on the Fourth of July, and "taffy pulls" in the homes were known in small and large towns across the nation.

Public recreation in the cities, particularly the large metropolitan centers, began to take shape. The movement started with sand gardens and model playgrounds, first without and later with leadership. As the twentieth century opened, small parks began to dot communities; settlement houses were established, and the American people entered an era of new social consciousness—a period which was to raise the curtain, in the new century, on recreation for all of the people as no people in history had known it before.

TWENTIETH CENTURY HIGHLIGHTS

Opening Years of the Century (1900–1914)

The nineteenth century gave the twentieth many sound foundations upon which to build. It fought the battles of intolerance, taboos, "sinful" interpretations, and "waste of time" concepts, and gradually broke through Victorian prejudices to provide the new century with a challenging future. It supplied the basis for an awakened interest in all the potential values of recreation to community life.

Among the early beginnings of community action were the opening of the South Park Playgrounds in Chicago in 1903 under public auspices, the establishment of the first playground commission within municipal government by Los Angeles in 1904, the organization by Ernest Thompson Seton in 1902 of the Woodcraft Indians, which stimulated outdoor activities and formed the basis of many boys' and girls' club programs, the first public school athletic league, founded by Luther Gulick in New York in 1903, together with the daring steps taken by Pittsburgh in broadening the sphere of play activities so as to include many things formerly not listed in the category of play.

The year 1906 is perhaps the most significant of this period, marking the birthday of the Playground and Recreation Association of America, a service organization which was supported by voluntary contributions. For more than a half century it stood at the forefront of community recreation development. Its field staff and special workers went from place to place stimulating recreation organization, giving consultation service, and cooperating in arranging conferences, institutes, and workshops. It published much practical and informative material on recreation and offered a continuous community recreation service.[2]

In 1907 Rochester, New York, gave to the nation the first practical demonstration of the use of the school building as a community center. This beginning has had far-reaching effects on the general use of the school for community purposes. In 1908 Gary, Indiana, stressed the use of the school plant for recreation services. The National Education Association in 1911 approved the use of school buildings and grounds for recreation. Since these first steps, many important advances have been made, including the valuable contribution of the extracurricular school program.

The years 1910 and 1912 are significant for community recreation, as they witnessed the organization of three outstanding youth-serving agencies: the Boy Scouts of America in 1910 and the Camp Fire Girls and Girl Scouts in 1912. These organizations have grown extensively and continue to offer important services to community recreation.

The period from 1910 to 1914 was also characterized by a marked expansion in the camping movement. Private camps and youth-service agency camps increased in large numbers.

College and high school athletics advanced, with better facilities available, larger numbers participating, and more effective administration and control. The intramural program gained a sound foothold about 1914 and made steady progress.

[2] This organization became the National Recreation Association and in 1965 merged with other professional groups to form the National Recreation and Park Association.

World War I (1914–1918)

Although the United States did not enter the war until the spring of 1917, the war in Europe influenced the social behavior of our democracy. The steady march of normalcy which characterized the opening of the century had already determined the trend of organized recreation. Attention was centered on neighborhood and community interests, and recreation molded into a sound pattern to benefit these two types of group living. The war period greatly strengthened this movement.

Rainwater referred to the 1915–1918 period as the "neighborhood organization" stage of the play movement in the United States. He said these years were characterized by the development of self-supported, self-governed, decentralized play activities in the neighborhoods. It was in this period that school buildings, field houses and community properties became recreation centers, funds were solicited for their operation, and the need for recreation opportunities was recognized on a more rational and less sentimental basis.[3]

With the entrance of the United States into World War I and the establishment of a universal draft system for the enlistment of military personnel, there was a drastic social upheaval in practically every community of the nation. This was especially true in communities adjacent to army cantonments, naval bases, and training stations, and in places where industrial war production created unusual population problems. Camp towns and industrial areas increased in population from fifty to one hundred per cent or more.

All of these abnormal conditions provoked a demand for adequate recreation facilities and opportunities. To meet these needs, War Camp Community Service (W.C.C.S.) was organized. The leadership in this movement was the former Playground and Recreation Association of America. It proposed a plan which was essentially one of neighborhood organization to the Council of National Defense, and the plan was readily accepted.

The war was of short duration, yet during the war W.C.C.S. organized over 600 communities adjacent to military posts and over 50 industrial districts. Over 2700 leaders were employed, and 60,000 volunteers rendered services of all types.

On the military posts, in addition to the meager programs operated at that time by the Army and Navy, an extensive program was operated by the Young Men's Christian Association. This program was approved by the War and Navy departments. The Knights of Columbus, the Salva-

---

[3] Rainwater, Clarence E., *The Play Movement in the United States* (The University of Chicago Press, 1922).

tion Army, and the Friends Service Committee of the Quakers had programs, too. The National Travelers Aid Association set up services in transportation centers. These programs were not exclusively for recreation. There was an emphasis on religious activities and social welfare services of all types.

The agencies were not operated jointly, but functioned under a coordinating board. They served wherever the armed forces were stationed. They functioned during the period of demobilization and made many contributions to the work of reclamation and rehabilitation of human resources. With the advent of peace, the agencies returned to their community tasks throughout the nation.

At the close of the war, the W.C.C.S. became "Community Service, Incorporated." The importance of its work continued throughout the country.

A Decade of Expansion (1920–1930)

The years following World War I saw extensive expansion of all types of recreation activities. The rapidity of this growth had a marked effect on community recreation and stimulated community acceptance of responsibility to provide and promote recreation programs.

The rising tide of industry, and its accompanying factors of machine tools, shorter hours, and monotony of work, the rapid growth of cities, and the inadequacy of traditional rural amusements, the growing demands for proper satisfaction in leisure hours through pleasurable pursuits, brought a tremendous awakening in recreation.

Stimulating these factors was the possession by the people of the United States of purchasing power beyond that required for the mere necessities of life. The decade developed a higher standard of living than that of any previous period. More people had more leisure and more wealth. Automobiles, radios, mammoth sports events, motion pictures, tourist travel, and a host of other opportunities came within the reach of many people as surplus purchasing power increased. There was also a marked trend away from the more simple ways of recreation to pleasures that required increased expenditures for facilities and participation.

With these forces came an awareness of the value of recreation to individual and social well-being. The statistics from the draft boards showing the nation's physical and mental fitness, the significance of recreation as a morale builder, and its growth as a preventive and cure of social ills brought a finer appreciation of the arts of leisure. Recreation was established as a force for molding character, developing physical and mental health, and giving man a finer environment in which to dwell.

A list of some of the developments of this decade provides a background for interpreting the total significance of these forces on community recreation.

Recreation for adults gained wide popularity. The number of women participating in recreation increased markedly.

Mass production of automobiles brought mobility to the people and gave impetus to vacation travel. The tourist age arrived.

Broadcasting became an actuality, and the millions of radios in urban and rural homes brought enjoyment to as many families.

Fads in recreation reflecting the great American bandwagon habit swept the country. Mahjong, crossword puzzles, miniature golf, dance marathons, bathing beauty contests, flagpole sitting, and many others had their day. Some disappeared and others persisted.

Contract bridge came into its own and spread into every section of the country.

Sound became a feature of motion pictures and assured their continued popularity as a form of recreation.

Football became outstanding in the field of spectator sports. Baseball became the "national game." Prize-fighting was at its height. This was the era of the first million-dollar "gate."

Races of all types had phenomenal growth—automobile races, horse races, and dog races.

Sports participation broke all previous records in the fields of golf, tennis, softball, and winter sports.

There was ever-increasing popularity of water sports, sun bathing, swimming, yachting, motorboating, sailboating, rowboating, and canoeing.

The legitimate stage had a rebirth, and all forms of drama gained in popularity.

State fairs, county fairs, lyceum and Chautauqua courses, little theater leagues, school entertainments and benefits, and civic club activities flourished.

Commercial recreation facilities were used more than ever before. These included amusement parks, resorts, billiard parlors, bowling alleys, and dance halls.

Lighter books and periodicals flooded the market for the reading public.

Manufacturers and suppliers of recreation materials enjoyed a big expansion in production and sales. Musical instruments, games of all types, and sporting goods and equipment led the field.

The Period of Depression (1930–1941)

After the economic cycle moved from World War I into a period of wild extravagance and inflation, there followed a period of depression greater and more widespread than in any similar period in the nation's history. Prior to 1935, the general public solution of industrial unemployment was the dole system and unemployment insurance—remedies which kept people alive but left them still unemployed.

The establishment of New Deal agencies to curb the depression brought forth the most extensive public recreation program ever to be attempted up to that time. The approach was based on the principle that work, any kind of work, was better than idleness, and that it was the duty and responsibility of government to furnish work when private enterprise found itself incapable of so doing. Work projects were established, and among them was a project in the field of community public recreation.

These "make work" programs of the federal government advanced recreation 25 years. They served to stimulate mass recognition of and action in community recreation. Practically every state possessed a state-wide program of recreation with many specialized features.

The Federal Emergency Relief Administration. The Federal Emergency Relief Administration was created during the third year of the depression. Its primary purpose was to give employment. Of necessity, new vocations were evolved. At the same time, problems of recreation grew serious, and demands came from all sections of the country for recreation leadership. Here was an opportunity to meet the challenges of leisure as applied to the masses, to put people, especially those of the white-collar class, to work, and at the same time create a leadership supply to meet an urgent need.

There were two approaches to recreation by the F.E.R.A.: (1) the construction of facilities, and (2) the development of recreation programs and activities under trained leadership. Today, these work projects are permanent monuments to better recreation facilities.

The Works Progress Administration. The Works Progress Administration, later changed to the Work Projects Administration, enlarged these opportunities and enhanced their value to community and individual life.

Along with the construction of areas and facilities, many recreation programs were developed. Because of their permanent social value, these projects were placed on an equal footing with construction. They touched on all phases of life, supplementing existing facilities, expanding old services, and providing new activities. These services were first rendered through the Division of Professional and Service Projects in cooperation with the National Youth Administration. Later the Division was known as the Division of Women's and Professional Service Projects. A part of this division was the Community Organization for Leisure Section. It was in this unit that recreation advanced steadily. So rapid was the growth and popularity of this program that the W.P.A. established a Division of Recreation Projects in August, 1936.

Prior to 1933, small towns and municipalities continued to struggle without assistance, as they had done for a quarter of a century, to meet the increasing demands for recreation leaders and programs. It is estimated that in 1930, 22,000 volunteers and professionals were engaged in the field of recreation, only 2500 of these being employed full time. Within three years after the inauguration of a "white collar" works program, approximately 45,000 full-time workers were added to the field by the Work Projects Administration to meet this community need.

Reports from all over the country showed that governmental agencies, including boards, commissions, departments, and divisions were created by cities and states in order that recreation activities and facilities might be maintained. In some instances, defunct agencies were reestablished. Approximately 27,000 volunteers serving on local advisory committees interpreted the emergency recreation program and local needs to officials and the public.

The W.P.A. training program for recreation workers was one of the most intensive attempted by any of the emergency agencies. An overwhelming majority of the 45,000 recreation workers spent at least two hours each week in some type of in-service training.

In order to give employment to thousands of manual workers throughout the country, and to fill a need felt by local communities for more adequate recreation facilities, thousands of recreation areas and facilities were constructed through the various work relief agencies.

The demand arose for recreation leaders to man new facilities, to supplement the work of agencies already established in the field, and to provide adequately directed programs. Work Projects Administration leaders worked under supervision of such local tax-supported units as recreation departments, park boards, planning boards, departments of education, and welfare boards. Their work was often integrated into the recreation program of the local community, which came to depend upon their services. From time to time, relief personnel was transferred to the pay rolls of local sponsoring agencies, thus assuring permanent and adequate program direction.

Under the direction of the W.P.A. recreation leadership, another milestone was added to the growing interest in professional preparation for the field. The first College Conference on Training Recreation Leaders was held at the University of Minnesota in 1937. Subsequent conferences were held at the University of North Carolina in 1939 and at New York University in 1941 and 1948.

In addition to the Division of Recreation of the Work Projects Administration, other divisions of W.P.A. and other relief agencies of the government functioned in recreation. A brief account of each agency follows:

The Civilian Conservation Corps. The Civilian Conservation Corps, created to give employment and vocational training to unemployed young men, came into existence by executive order in April, 1933. The Corps consisted of unmarried young men between the ages of 17 and 28, several thousand Indians, and a few thousand local men enrolled regardless of age because of their needed experience. In addition, about one-sixth of the Corps were World War I veterans. From 1933 to 1942, when the Corps was dissolved, about 3,500,000 young men benefited by the program.

The Corps built roads, picnic areas, camp grounds, cabins, hiking and riding trails, swimming and boating facilities, and scores of special types of recreation facilities under the supervision of sponsoring agencies such as the National Park Service, U.S. Forest Service, and W.P.A.

Under the direction of company commanders, educational advisors developed and supervised the education-recreation program in the camps. The Corps considered recreation a definite part of the educational program. The program consisted of arts and crafts, drama and music, athletics and social activities, and indoor and outdoor games and activities of all types.

The National Youth Administration. The National Youth Administration was established by executive order in June, 1935, within the W.P.A. Its Projects Division offered part-time employment of needy youths to help in recreation programs and in construction of recreation facilities in communities. It also assisted in organizing local recreation training institutes. The Division of Student Aid gave grants-in-aid to schools to establish and operate recreation projects.

The Public Works Administration. The Public Works Administration was limited entirely to construction, especially of the larger facilities. It took the lead in building recreation facilities of many kinds.

During this same period, the need to organize a professional group became clear. As a result, the Society of Recreation Workers of America was established.

Although it was not a part of the emergency efforts of the government in any way, the society multiplied the number of people in the United States who were at work professionally in recreation.

World War II (1941-1945)

The nation was recovering from the depression when threatening events in Europe cast a shadow over the future. The war in Europe began in 1939, and while everything possible was done to keep the United States out of the conflict, events made entrance almost inevitable. The war spread rapidly in all directions, and with the attack on Pearl Harbor by the Japanese in December, 1941, this country entered the struggle.

For the next four years the nation was in an "all out" war. The government geared the nation to the gigantic task; never in its history was there such unity of purpose and complete cooperation and participation on the part of the citizenry. The threatened necessity of carrying on defensive warfare on this continent demanded that every community unite for the common welfare.

Recreation went to war. It served close to the battle fronts, in the convalescent areas and rest centers, on troop trains, ships, and airplanes, at embarkation stations, in training camps, in communities adjacent to encampments, in industrial centers geared to high-power, mass production by war contracts, and in every hamlet of the nation where people were working to produce for war, learning the tactics of home defense, and endeavoring to keep up a stable morale. Recreation was an ally of every segment of the war effort. It was accepted by all authorities from the Commander in Chief to the block warden.

It brought cheer to the men at the fronts, was recognized as a part of building a fighting force, and served to bring contentment and enjoyment to war workers gathered in congested quarters. It relieved tension and lessened the worry of the millions of citizens in the thousands of communities throughout the nation. Recreation was now becoming accepted as an essential force in the total pattern of living.

A number of programs should be mentioned as affording major contributions during this period:

The Armed Forces (Now the Department of Defense). In the Army the Special Service Division had the responsibility for providing facilities and programs for recreation and entertainment on the various military posts. Some 12,000 special service officers, several times that number of enlisted men, and thousands of volunteers manned the program. Hundreds of millions of dollars were spent to provide areas, facilities, and equipment, and millions of dollars were invested in the highest type of entertainment.

In the Navy the recreation program functioned through the Welfare and Recreation Section of the Bureau of Naval Personnel. Approximately 1500 officers were assigned to recreation service. The program had as its chief objective wholesome recreation activities for the entire personnel in off-duty time on ship and on land stations.

The Coast Guard, the Marines, and the Seabees functioned as a part of the Navy, but in 1945 the Marines established their own recreation service.

Never in the history of the armed forces was so much attention given to recreation as a functional part of the total military operation. While the program of activities accentuated athletics, sports, and games, every major field of recreation was included, with special emphasis on social and entertainment features. A volume should be written on the contribution of recreation to the war effort. It would make a vivid and stimulating story.

The U.S.O. (United Service Organizations). The six private organizations forming the U.S.O.—The Jewish Welfare Board, The Salvation
Army, the National Catholic Community Service, the National Travelers
Aid Association, the Young Men's Christian Association, and the Young
Women's Christian Association—made a magnificent contribution. It is
well known that the U.S.O., through its constituent agencies of different
faiths and backgrounds, was a real partnership and a most successful ex-
periment in joint action. It is not generally known, however, that it was
also in partnership with the United States government through the Federal Security Agency. To the millions of men and women who served
in the armed forces, U.S.O. meant "a billion touches of home—an infinite
variety of personal services ranging from the routine provision of writing
paper to convalescent care." It was charged with the responsibility of providing adequate recreation, social, and spiritual activities for men of the
armed services when they were off duty or on leave. It functioned in continental United States and in other locations of the western hemisphere,
outside of camps, in clubs, station lounges, hostels, mobile units, and information centers. U.S.O. Camp Shows, Inc., was recognized as the sole
agency for the procurement of professional theatrical talent for entertainment of troops overseas, performing on military posts, in war theaters,
and in many Veterans Administration hospitals.

Through public subscription drives, U.S.O. received more than $200,-
000,000, and at its peak it served one million people a day in over 3000
operations. Camp Shows put on 700 performances each day.

The American National Red Cross. At the request of what was then the
War Department, the American National Red Cross accepted the responsibility of providing recreation facilities and opportunities in leave areas
overseas, on posts anywhere in the world when it was requested to do so
by the armed forces, and for programs in hospitals, both overseas and at
home.

The American National Red Cross established approximately 750 clubs
in all theaters of operation, and approximately 250 mobile units, with
some 4000 workers, and had more than 1500 hospital recreators. It was
recognized as the sole agency to operate with an expeditionary force. Its
program was well balanced in offering opportunities in all the fields of
recreation, with special emphasis on social events and recreation of therapeutic value.

United Seamen's Service. The responsibility for providing off-duty recreation opportunities for merchant seamen was given to the United Seamen's Service. Its programs were operated both in this country and overseas. It had 130 locations in 72 different ports.

*The Federal Security Agency (Now the Department of Health, Educa-
tion, and Welfare).* During the war the Federal Security Agency had an
Office of Community War Services, and in this office a Division of Recrea-

tion was established which was responsible for helping communities affected by war to organize, develop, and maintain adequate recreation programs. It assisted communities adjacent to military posts, those swollen by industrial plants and geared to war production, and those affected by all kinds of war tensions.

Through 65 field representatives these communities received advice on organization and development of programs, the best use of facilities and funds, and the employment and training of leaders. The division made an excellent contribution to community recreation throughout the entire nation and demonstrated the need for permanent federal recreation services.

In addition to doing its primary war recreation job of meeting military and industrial recreation needs in more than 2500 communities throughout the United States, the Recreation Division was directly responsible for helping establish from 250 to 300 permanent, local, tax-supported recreation systems in the United States. The division did a fine job, helping the towns and cities and their leaders to grow in professional stature. Its work, by design, was little publicized—full credit going to the towns. Among other things, it served as a liaison with the Army and Navy and certified the need for Lanham-Act funds for recreation facilities (460 buildings) and programs. It acted as agent for the War Production Board, the Office of Defense Transportation, the War Man-Power Commission, the Office of Price Administration, and other war agencies in matters pertaining to recreation.

Above all, the Federal Security Agency took the lead in driving for expanded and strengthened permanent state recreation services. Its publications, statements, and field service left an indelible and significant mark on recreation in the United States.

The Federal Works Agency. This agency had the responsibility of building the large number of recreation centers that were used during the war by the U.S.O. and many communities. These federal buildings were constructed in cooperation with the local communities. They were located adjacent to military posts and centers of industrial war production. At the close of operations under war pressure, most of these buildings were purchased by the local communities for community recreation use. The Federal Works Agency also administered millions of dollars of Lanham-Act funds for maintenance and operation of recreation projects.

Community Services. The communities of the country gave their full weight of recreation leadership to both the armed forces and the civilian population. Public and private forces joined hands in providing recreation opportunities to the best of existing facilities and leadership. The Office of Civilian Defense, in cooperation with the Recreation Division of the Federal Security Agency, established many state and local recreation committees to provide activities.

AFTER WORLD WAR II

In many respects, the progress of the recreation movement became even more pronounced after World War II than at any time before it—despite the international tensions which continued to persist and multiply.

Following World War II dozens of small towns and large cities constructed "living" war memorials in the form of community centers, swimming pools, playgrounds, athletic and play fields. Tax-supported public recreation systems increased in number, and the states gave greater attention to establishing programs to improve recreation facilities and services. New state recreation commissions and boards, state youth authorities, and state inter-agency recreation committees were established. Many of the "old line" departments of state government such as education, parks, welfare, and highways moved to strengthen their recreation services to the people. In this same period the interest in and development of recreation in hospitals was greatly advanced, particularly in armed forces hospitals, veterans hospitals, state neuropsychiatric hospitals, and children's hospitals.

With the Korean conflict interest in recreation for the armed forces and defense industrial workers and their families was revived. The President's Committee on Religion and Welfare in the Armed Forces issued its study on "Free Time in the Armed Forces." United Service Organizations, Inc., was reactivated and a new organization, United Defense Community Services, concentrating on the needs of defense workers, was created. Because of a temporary shortage of critical materials, the construction of recreation facilities for the civilian population was retarded for about two years. Two factors—increase of public interest in recreation and inflation—nevertheless resulted in heavily increased expenditures for recreation on all fronts. More money was being spent for commercial recreation as well as community recreation. There were now 42,000,000 people in the United States enjoying paid vacations. The suggested standard for per capita expenditure in public recreation was first doubled—from three to six dollars, and then continued to increase with the spiraling inflation.

The Second Half of the Century

The Mid-Century White House Conference on Children and Youth gave much attention to recreation and the growing amounts of leisure. Institutions of higher learning established and expanded their curricula for professional preparation in recreation. Academic degrees were now available not only for undergraduates but also for those competent to study at the master and doctoral level.

But if the need for professional preparation was recognized in colleges and universities, it was also reflected in the in-service training and staff development programs of already operating agencies. It was in the early '50s that national workshops on recreation and allied fields were undertaken, and underwritten by the Athletic Institute. The First National Recreation Workshop was held in Jackson's Mill, West Virginia, in 1952.

The '50s brought forth a tremendous expansion of recreation on *all* fronts: public recreation, voluntary agency recreation, employee recreation, armed forces recreation (on a "cold war" basis), commercial recreation, and recreation for the ill and handicapped. The last of these received support from the medical profession, as psychiatrists and physical medicine specialists, in particular, became interested in the potentials of recreation for helping in the treatment and rehabilitation of the ill and injured. It was in this period that the Council for the Advancement of Hospital Recreation was organized.

Not the least of the developments during this period, which had far reaching implications for recreation, was the decision of the United States Supreme Court which ruled as unconstitutional race segregation on public playgrounds and parks.

With the rapidly increasing number of elderly citizens, new attention was given to the role recreation could play in brightening the enforced hours of leisure among the aged population. The White House Conference on the Aging in 1961 placed much emphasis on recreation.

It was natural, too, that politics and economics on an international scale should encourage recreation planning on the international level. Professional recreation personnel from the United States went to other lands, under the auspices of the U.S. Department of State, to help establish recreation services. The International Office of Labor, which had had a long-standing interest in the leisure problems and challenges of the working man, stepped up its interest. The United Nations, concerned with the problems of the Western powers and the Soviet bloc, acknowledged the importance of recreation, although its resources were turned toward more troublesome issues. The National Recreation Association established an international office, and the International Recreation Association was organized. Significantly, a European Recreation Society was created. Vast increases in international travel also occurred during this period.

There were other significant developments. With more people, more leisure, and greater mobility, more use was made of public lands. The struggle for space—not only to acquire it, but also to retain and protect it—loomed as a new challenge on the planning horizon.

The scope of the encroachment threat is attested to by a nation-wide survey (concluded in 1961) by the National Committee on Encroachment of Recreation Lands and Waters. The survey indicated that within a ten-year period, 2687 acres of recreation land were lost in 257 areas recording encroachment. The estimated land value in 44 of these areas alone was nearly nine million dollars. Millions of dollars of irreplaceable park lands and open spaces slipped away from public recreation use, into the path of highways, commercial and industrial enterprises, schools, community buildings, and housing developments.

The recreation explosion was five times as large as the population explosion. The National Park Service started its Mission 66 to improve and develop the national parks, and the United States Forest Service inaugurated a similar program in the forests with its Operation Outdoors. Congress established the Outdoor Recreation Resources Review Commission and asked it for an estimate of needs for outdoor recreation space in the year 2000. Shortly thereafter, in 1963, Congress created the Bureau of Outdoor Recreation. What was true of open space needs far from home was also true of space needs close to home. Consequently, recreation needs played a part in the problems of urban planning and development. The Housing and Urban Development Department was established as an agency to serve urban areas, metropolitan centers and the large cities of the nation. The Administration on Aging was established in 1965 and is a part of the Social and Rehabilitation Services of the Department of Health, Education, and Welfare.

Probably the most paradoxical of all the recreation developments at this time was the emphasis which national leaders, including the President (who established the Council on Youth Fitness), placed upon the importance of young people being fit, while some education authorities eliminated physical education as a curriculum requirement.

This was also a period in which positions in professional recreation enterprises multiplied over and over again. The demand for recreators was far greater than the supply. Programs for recruiting young people for the field were initiated. Great expansion occurred in the numbers and kinds of recreation opportunities available to more and more people. The quantity of literature increased. The beginning of scientific research in the field emerged, and the use of leisure for recreation touched the interests of many disciplines, particularly the behavioral sciences.

THE WORKSHOP

1. Discuss the play habits and customs of ancient civilizations with a historian.
2. Interview a clergyman and get his reactions to the changing attitude of the church toward recreation through the years.

3. Study the customs of early Oriental people to learn of their games and amusements.
4. Compare amateurism and professionalism in the days of Athens and Sparta with current practices.
5. Study the influence of the Renaissance and Reformation upon people's attitudes toward leisure and recreation.
6. Compare forms of commercial and community recreation in the United States during the nineteenth century.
7. Compare the recreation services in World War I with those of World War II.
8. Make a list of combative sports in the Middle Ages and compare with those of today.
9. Prepare a statement which shows convincingly the historical influence of leisure upon our culture.
10. Compare the development of public education and public recreation since 1880.

REFERENCES

Burns, C. Delisle. *Leisure in the Modern World*. The Century Company, 1932.

De Grazia, Sebastian, *Of Time, Work, and Leisure*. New York: The Twentieth Century Fund, 1962.

Denney, Reuel, *The Astonished Muse*. Chicago: The University of Chicago Press, 1957.

Doell, Charles F., and Gerald B. Fitzgerald, *A Brief History of Parks and Recreation in the United States*. Chicago: The Athletic Institute, 1954.

Dulles, Foster Rhea. *America Learns to Play*. New York: Appleton-Century-Crofts, Second Edition, 1965.

Gardiner, Edward N., *Athletics of the Ancient World*. New York: Oxford University Press, 1930.

Gross, Karl. *The Play of Animals*, 1889 and *The Play of Man*, 1901. New York: Appleton-Century-Crofts.

Huizinga, Johan. *Homo Ludens—A Study of the Play Elements in Culture*. New York: The Beacon Press, 1955.

Lindeman, Edward C. *Leisure, A National Issue*. New York: Association Press, 1939.

Michael, Donald N. *The Next Generation*. New York: Random House, Inc., 1965.

Rainwater, C. E. *The Play Movement in the United States*. Chicago: University of Chicago Press, 1922.

Steiner, Jesse F., *Americans at Play*. New York: McGraw-Hill Book Company, 1933.

Toynbee, Arnold. *Civilization on Trial*. Cleveland: Meridian Books, 1958.

Comments

History related to recreation, play, and leisure can be noted in the great books of general history—the histories of sports, of the arts, and of religions. Readers should also explore back issues of *Recreation Magazine* and our periodicals featuring recreation activities. Publications of the United States government relating to recreation may be located in Agency documents.

Some of the references here have copyright dates of years ago, but since this is a chapter on history these books are important to the subject and they do not have to be of current dates to be worthy.

Many of the books dealing with the general recreation movement have one or more chapters portraying the historical significance of the movement which are similar to Chapter 1.

The reader will do well to check with local historians about his local recreation development as it is important to link the present achievements with the area's past.

The story of the progress of recreation and parks in the United States is continued. As we enter the "Leisure Age" we readily witness the significance of recreation in contemporary society and note its dramatic prophecies for the years ahead.

Chapters of the book (especially Chapter 24) portray "The Future."

2

The Theory, Philosophy, and Principles of Leisure, Play, and Recreation— Recreation as a Social Force

LEISURE

The word *leisure* derives from the Latin *licere*, meaning "to be permitted" and is defined in the dictionary as free, unoccupied time during which a person may indulge in rest, recreation, and the like. Leisure is a "block of time" and is often referred to as unobligated time, spare time, or free time, time when one is relatively free to do what he chooses. Leisure is *time beyond* that which is required for *existence*, the things which we must do, biologically, to stay alive (e.g. eat, sleep, eliminate, etc.), and *subsistence*, the things we must do to make a living, as in work, or prepare to make a living, as in school. Leisure is time in which our feelings of compulsion *should be* minimal. It is *discretionary* time, time to be used according to our own judgment or choice.

If time were to be divided into the major uses made of it, it might appear as follows:

TIME

Type of Time	How Used
I. Existence	Eat
	Sleep
	Bodily care
II. Subsistence	Work
III. Leisure	Play—Recreation
	Rest

While these three types of time are vastly different from the standpoint of how they are used, they also have certain characteristics in common. For example, each area is highly flexible and may be increased or decreased depending upon various circumstances. Also, none of these areas can necessarily be defined in terms of what is *good* or what is *bad*. One may have bad habits in his leisure, in his choices of recreation. But one may also have undesirable habits in his work, or in his eating and sleeping.

Just as there are different kinds of time, there are two types of leisure—*true* leisure and *enforced* leisure. *True* leisure is the kind of leisure which is not imposed upon the individual. *Enforced* leisure, however, is not the leisure which people seek or want. It is the time one has on his hands when he is unemployed, ill, or made to retire from his work when he wants to continue.

As indicated earlier, true leisure is used either for rest or for play and recreation.

THEORIES

Many attempts have been made to explain satisfactorily the meaning and purpose of play and recreation. These explanations have multiplied and expanded as interest in the subject has broadened. At first, attention was given to the study of play as it occurred in animals, then play in children, and, finally, recreation in the daily living of all people. As society became increasingly interested in play and recreation, greater efforts were made to explain them philosophically and scientifically. Biologists, physiologists, psychologists, and sociologists, as well as educators and persons identified with the recreation profession, have drawn inferences from principles based upon systematic study of data on play and recreation.

The term *play* (from the Anglo-Saxon, *plegian, plegan,* to play, and akin to the German, *pflegen,* meaning to take care of, to bestir oneself) often refers to the free, happy, and natural expression of people. To many it means to frolic or amuse one's self. Reference is made to it in connection with the spontaneous diversion of children, or perhaps small animals, although the word also finds its way into the vocabulary of adults. Grownups go to see a "play," men and women "play" musical instruments, the neighbors are invited in to "play" a game of cards, and so forth. As the importance of "play" has come to be better understood, and as the concept of satisfactory and wise use of leisure has become more widely accepted, more frequent reference is made to the term *recreation* (from the Latin, *recreare*), particularly where it refers to the activity of young people and adults. The line which distinguishes *play* from *recreation* is, indeed, thin. Recreation might well be considered less frivolous, although this is not always true. In this book it is viewed as *activity voluntarily engaged in during leisure and primarily motivated by the satisfaction or pleasure derived from it.* For purposes of examining the theories and philosophy of *play* and *recreation,* the terms are considered synonymously.

These theories or explanations of play and recreation may not be completely convincing, but they are provocative. There remains some doubt as to whether any of the theories provided offers a completely satisfactory explanation. This is not to imply that they are incorrect, but rather inadequate or incomplete. A brief explanation of some of the more widely known theories follows: [1]

Theory	Proponent(s)	Essence	Comment
Surplus energy	Schiller, Spencer	That energy not needed by the playing animal to stay alive and perpetuate the species (or in other words, excess energy) finds its outlet in play.	Views play as aimless, which is questionable. Does not account for playing to the point of exhaustion. Offers no explanation of the differences in forms of play among the various species of animal life.
Preparation for life	Groos, et al.	That play is instinctive and is a part of the animal's educational experience. Through play the animal practices those things which he must follow later in life. It is, in a sense, preparation for living and a hereditary trait.	Attempts to explain the form which play takes, but leaves no explanation of adult play.
Recapitulation	Hall	That the animal repeats through play the activities his ancestors experienced (running, jumping, throwing, and the like); heredity is a large factor.	Does not explain progression in play and tends to ignore or refute the new forms which are taken by play. Contributes to the attempt to classify culture by cycles or eras, which is debatable.
Instinct	James, McDougall, et al.	That play is wholly instinctive and based on automatic impulses, a result of a drive, appetite, and inner urge; play instinct common among humans and perhaps other forms of animal life.	There is disagreement as to what constitutes an instinct in human beings. How can one distinguish the acquired from the innate? How can one distinguish between instinct and impulses or reflexes?

[1] For more detailed explanation of the theories of play and recreation refer to Allen V. Sapora and Elmer D. Mitchell, *The Theory of Play and Recreation,* 3rd ed. (New York: The Ronald Press Company, 1961), Chapters IV–IX.

Theory	Proponent(s)	Essence	Comment
Relaxation	Patrick	That play is pleasurable and sought for its own sake; that it is a release from work, compulsion, and the struggle to live; that play results in its own satisfactions; play relieves stresses and strains of the individual. NOTE: The catharsis explanation of play—that play is an outlet for pent-up emotions—is closely related to the theory of relaxation.	Applies mainly to play and recreation of adults, but inadequate in explaining the play of children.
Recreation	Kames, Muths	That play is the natural change-over from work and refreshes, replenishes, and restores energy. In this respect, it is quite as essential as rest.	Enlightening in relation to the function of play, but not in relation to its nature and characteristics.
Catharsis	Aristotle	That play is an outlet for confined emotions, a release for feelings which might otherwise remain suppressed and harmful.	Leaves unanswered the same kinds of questions as does the Surplus Energy Theory.
Self-Expression	Mitchell, Mason (since modified and refined by others)	That play is the natural urge for action. Recognizes the nature and capacity of man, his anatomical and physiological structure, his psychological inclinations, and his desire for self-expression. Sees self-expression as man's supreme need.	Widely accepted and seemingly plausible theory, but provides no explanation of or accounting for play other than that the organism is present.

It should be noted that while there are a number of differences in these theories, there are also points of agreement. For example, all of the theories conceive play to be an "action," rather than idleness. This does not necessarily mean vigorous action or muscle activity. It may be passive in nature, but nevertheless, it is an action. Apparent, too, is the fact that the theories do not limit the forms which play and recreation take. Play can be physical, mental, or, as is almost always the case, a combination of both of these.

The earlier theories set forth above constitute the nucleus of thinking for more modern explanations of play and recreation.

PHILOSOPHIES

John Dewey, the eminent philosopher of education, recognized the importance of play and recreation. He held that play was an attitude of mind which was attainable in any situation. Clarence Rainwater, who contributed so much to the history of the play movement in the United States, believed play and recreation to be pleasurable behavior patterns undertaken for no reward and conditioned by social attitude. Joseph Lee, often referred to as the "Father of Playgrounds," saw play as a factor in the growth of the individual. He decided that play was "nature's prescribed course of education" and observed that if a child were denied the opportunity for play, he would not grow up—at least emotionally and intellectually. Howard Braucher said simply, "The heart's desire is for play."

Johan Huizinga contends that play is something more than biological —that it serves a social and cultural purpose. This view is also held by Roger Caillois, his thesis being that the games of a society reflect the development of its culture and indicates the degree of civilization which it has obtained. Games of chance and competition, he writes, are more characteristic of high civilizations than are those which stress mimicry and vertigo.

Lawrence Jack, an English educator and author, stresses the importance of recreation as a vitalizing element in the process of education. Social philosopher, Edward C. Lindeman, also thought of recreation as an opportunity for education, but he looked at it, too, as a means of participating in civic affairs, in esthetic endeavors, in developing skills, and enjoying nature. George Herbert Mead considers it basic to the socialization of man, stating that play joins language as a basic vehicle for the shaping of the attitudes and behavior of children and adults. Through play they develop and accept the morale of the society.

Psychologists Eric Erikson and Jean Piaget conclude that play is basic to the development of intelligence and the strengthening of the ego. Random and symbolic play serve to develop the sensory and intellectual skills while games with rules increase the opportunity for social interaction and provide a means for the nurturing of the social self. Both conclude there are developmental stages of play, a conclusion also shared by Fritz Reidel and William Wattenburg.

Jay Nash says that play is any act other than survival activities which carries its own drive and which the individual enters without feeling an outer compulsion. He refers to recreation as a use of leisure on a qualitative scale, with *participating* in a *creative* way at the top of the scale, watching others perform in the middle, and "getting in trouble" at the bottom.

Sociologists Martin and Esther Neumeyer have stressed the social interpretations and cultural implications of play and recreation. They have pointed out how the social processes are involved in recreation, how group stimulation and behavior influence and stimulate recreation pursuits, and how recreation is a form of social behavior. Ott Romney says that recreation "is not a matter of motions—but rather emotions." He believes it is a "personal response" and "a way of life."

As there are ideas in common among the play theories, so are there similar strains of thought among the philosophies of recreation. For example, all of them, Brightbill, de Grazia, Gulick, Cutten, Pack, Braucher and others look upon recreation as an *integral,* self-perpetuating part of the human mechanism and the *whole* person. They also seem to recognize the extremely close relationship between recreation and education. Also, although the contribution which recreation can make to the development of the rich personality is implied in these philosophies (only Nash says so outright), no attempt is made to interpret recreation in terms of what is *good* or what is *bad.* Finally, all of these philosophers seem to believe in the creative potentials of recreation, even though they do not make clear what constitutes *creativeness.*

Many behavioral scientists believe that all human behavior is motivated by desires to serve, to gain, or to express and create. Recreation appears to be a satisfactory outlet for all of these desires. Life itself is an active experience. The physiological and psychological structure of man constantly leads to expression in many forms. The form which such expression takes is conditioned by cultural environment, by physical and intellectual capabilities, by attitudes and habits, and by social influences and interactions. Recreation provides the opportunity for free expression and thus gives the best chance for creative living, which is its own reward.

CHARACTERISTICS

Recreation can be identified by its many basic characteristics. Among them are:

1. *Recreation involves activity.* As mentioned previously in discussing the nature of play, recreation always consists of *activity* of some kind. The action may be physical, mental, or emotional, but there is always activity. It is action as distinguished from rest. In one way or another recreation involves the exertion of powers and forces even though these actions may not always be visible externally. It is easy to see how action is involved when a person plays golf, swims across a lake, or climbs a mountain. It is not as easy to detect action by observing a person reading

a book, listening to a concert, or watching birds. The action, nevertheless, is there. Leisure may result in rest or idleness, but recreation, which often absorbs the lion's share of leisure, involves action and activity.

2. *Recreation has no single form.* This flexibility, in itself, gives to recreation its depth and breadth, even though as a result its identity is often difficult to define and its role not easy to interpret. If a dozen persons were asked to explain what they mean by recreation, they would give a dozen different definitions. This is because the desires, wishes, and tastes of people vary so greatly concerning things which are enjoyable and satisfying. The range of activities which people enjoy during leisure is endless. It is a great error to attempt to define recreation as a given list of activities. To do so is like trying to catch a rainbow in a landing net. The boundaries of recreation cannot be circumscribed. The fact that there is an endless variety of choice in things enjoyable for humans can be traced to another factor—*motivation.*

3. *Recreation is determined by motivation.* That which determines the choice or moves the will of a person to take a certain action is motivation. Whether or not an activity is recreation depends upon the motive or incentive of the participant. If he is motivated by the desire to enjoy and/or the realization that the result of such participation will be personally satisfying to him, the action is likely to be *recreation.* The enjoyment and satisfaction which result from activity are the only rewards sought. Although the degree of enjoyment and satisfaction may be influenced by the emotional and physical condition of the participant, the motive that prompts him to take the action is the overriding influence. Recreation is actually an attitude of mind toward or about an action in leisure.

It is the motivation factor that makes a given activity recreation for one person and work for another. A hike along the banks of a river where plant and animal life can be enjoyed may be recreation to the tourist but work for the park naturalist who makes the trip daily with groups of visitors. Having a major role in the short play of the local little theater may be lots of fun and recreation to the housewife, but it probably would be hard work to a Broadway star who performs professionally night after night. This does not mean, of course, that one's work cannot be enjoyable. Again, depending upon motive, an activity can be both work and recreation to a person at different times under different conditions.

When recreation is organized and involves recreation leadership, there may be more than one motivation to consider. There is first the motivation of the participant—which always remains the same—the seeking of enjoyment and personal satisfactions, and then the motivation of the leader, or organizer, who may or may not be motivated by the same considerations. For example, while the participant seeks enjoyment in the activity, the leader of the playground, community center, or camp may be concerned that such activity will provide experiences for the participants which will help make them better citizens or keep them out of trouble. Or the hospital recreator may encourage patients to participate because he believes, with good reason, that the outcome will help make the ill and disabled more receptive to medical treatment, aid them in recovering their health, and contribute to their rehabilitation. Again, in industry, while the production line worker plays on the company team because he enjoys it, the industrial recreator may be motivated by the fact that the opportunity for recreation may help decrease labor turnover, reduce absenteeism, or build better industrial relations. Such dual motivations are not necessarily in conflict with each other. Competent recreation leadership makes them a single blend.

It may be correctly assumed from the above that even though the factor which motivates people to pursue recreation is personal enjoyment, recreation of a wholesome kind has countless by-products which often translate themselves into richer personalities, better health, improved citizenship, and even economic as well as spiritual, intellectual, and physical advantages.

4. *Recreation occurs in unobligated time.* Time which is required to make a living, prepare to make a living, or take actions which one is compelled to take for one reason or another, may be thought of as *work*. Much of what is work does not always involve monetary compensation. Where time is unobligated, and one is free to do what he pleases, how he pleases, and with whom he pleases, it is *leisure*. To say that recreation, which is personally enjoyable and satisfying, always takes place in leisure is not to deny that certain personal satisfactions can also be derived from work. But the fact that work is enjoyable does not make it recreation—so long at least as the element of compulsion is present in work.

5. *Engagement in recreation is entirely voluntary.* Recreation must be sought and accepted voluntarily. It cannot be superimposed upon personalities nor cast over a group as one would cast a blanket over a bed. At the moment participation becomes compulsory, the activity ceases to be recreation to the one under compulsion. To hope for recreation to flourish under such circumstances would be to display the attitude of the scoutmaster who admonished his scouts in the middle of a hike, "Boys, this is the hour for rest and relaxation, and I do not want any shirking." Recreation is the open road to opportunities for self-discovery, self-expression, creativity, and recreativity, none of which finds satisfactory outlets in a cloak of obligation or compulsion. Opportunities for recreation can be provided and activities even planned and organized, but *complete freedom of choice and action must be preserved.*

6. *Recreation is universally practiced and sought.* Recreation is a physiological and psychological expression of the human mechanism.

Play is evident in lower forms of animal life, too. A kitten, a dog, a colt, and many different kinds of birds have been observed playing. The preschool age child, the adolescent, the youth, the adult, and the older person express themselves in countless ways through play and recreation. Recreation has never known limitations of time, place, or people. While some people hesitate to admit that they find time for recreation—at least their concept of recreation—a close examination of their habits and experiences will reveal the opposite to be true. Recreation, in one form or another, is so ingrained a mode of individual expression that, paradoxically, some mistakenly think it superfluous and even deny its existence. One has only to imagine the absence of recreation in the world to understand how drab and dull affairs could be without it.

7. *Recreation is serious and purposeful.* The fact that recreation is always an enjoyable experience would seem to deny its seriousness and purposefulness. Humans are never more serious, however, than when they are absorbed in activities from which they secure satisfactions and pleasure. A fair way to test this contention is to interrupt or molest an individual when he is busily engaged in his favorite recreation or hobby. It will be seen quickly that such intrusion is not welcome. Joseph Lee observed the seriousness of children at play and commented, "What a boy lies awake about is probably not his spelling or arithmetic, but his chance of getting on the team." Boys playing sandlot baseball have little patience with other players who commit errors; adults, too, approach their recreation with a high degree of seriousness and absorption. Once a person has taken a fancy to some form of recreation—reading, fishing, or playing the piano—it is not at all a matter of secondary importance. Instances of persons neglecting other obligatory duties and chores for the sake of pursuing a favorite hobby are legion in the American household. These folks are not "playing," in the frivolous sense of the word. They are engaged in all seriousness in something which is an integral part of their living diet. Recreation, to many, may be an avenue of escape from the things they must do to stay alive, but even in this light it is essential to the growth, development, and well-being of the human organism. It is likely that the very educational values—coming to appreciate beauty, sharpening skills, delving into the world of the unknown, achieving emotional stability and maturity, discovering talents heretofore unknown—which grow out of an absorbing interest in recreation contribute to its purposefulness.

8. *Recreation is flexible.* Recreation cannot be identified by the environment, auspices, or conditions under which it occurs. It can be found in countless settings. Recreation can be organized or unorganized. For most people recreation is not organized any more than is their education in its broadest sense. The degree of systematic arrangement of recreation also varies greatly. It can range from simply providing recreation facilities

for people to enjoy, such as making beaches, picnic areas, hiking trails, tennis courts, and the like, available to the citizenry, to actually providing the money, facilities, equipment, planning, and direction for an enterprise.

Recreation can be enjoyed alone or in groups. It can be participated in by large numbers of people—even crowds. If organized, recreation can be found under the auspices of public, tax-supported departments, voluntarily-supported social agencies, miscellaneous clubs, associations, and organizations, or industry, commerce, and trade.

9. *Recreation has by-products.* It may be assumed from the above that even though the factor which motivates people to participate in recreation is personal enjoyment and satisfaction, recreation can have countless by-products. It can reward the participant in terms of intellectual, physical, and social growth, better health, improved citizenship, and in other qualities of personality development. But pursuit of undesirable forms of recreation can contribute to the disintegration, degradation, and de-generation of personality. Recreation's by-products can help build, but they can also help destroy. It is these dual possibilities and by-products which make the element of choice—the right choice—so important in recreation.

RECREATION VALUES AND THE INDIVIDUAL

Each person has a distinct personality. Each personality is unique in itself. All individuals have ideals, hopes, fears, beliefs, and attitudes, just as all persons have purposes, habits, interests, and desires. But these elements of personality are not all present in equal degree or form among all people, nor are they arranged exactly alike in any two persons. A rich personality has many purposes, interests, and desires, and knows how to enjoy and make the most of new experiences. When the various personal elements fit together nicely, the well-integrated personality results. The physical factors that serve as the springboard to personality may be inherited, but experts seem to agree that much of personality is also acquired. However personality is formed, there is no such thing as a "trivial" personality to the person who owns it. This is why the relationship of recreation to personality is so important.

Recreation has a direct influence upon those factors which create personality.

Happiness. If recreation has any purpose, it is the enjoyment it can produce and the happiness it can help achieve. This sense of enjoyment is not necessarily feeling cheerful, glad, or gleeful, although it may include them. It refers, rather, to the kind of feeling you get inside when you feel that an experience has been enriching and abundant, when you feel "good" about having expressed yourself in a certain way.

Satisfactions. Related to the objective of *happiness* are the satisfactions which contribute to it. These include feeling secure, being recognized, belonging, accomplishing, and creating, as well as experiencing new adventures. Many of these are served through recreation. If an individual is a fine tennis player, an excellent swimmer, or performs well in the arts, he draws the admiration and often the plaudits of others. When he is a member of a team he knows that he is accepted and wanted. The world of recreation is an open-ended concourse for "satisfying" experiences of many kinds.

Balanced Growth. Scientists believe that the human organism needs balance and that when there is not physiological and psychological balance, tensions and conflicts arise. It is also true that people need to achieve a balance between inner desires and outer pressures—to achieve some kind of harmony or balance with their environment. Recreation often affords the opportunity for the individual to approach, if not attain, such balances. The chances to do so in other aspects of living, including work, are not always present.

Creativeness. Modern culture, with its patterns of conformity and regimentation of communication and education, tends to stifle our creative desires and limit opportunities for creativeness. Manual skills are lost, and the opportunity for uninhibited expression, upon which creativeness thrives, is diminished. Here again recreation makes it possible to exercise our creative talents in countless ways—not only in the arts and crafts, but in motor expression and communication.

Competition. Everyone desires to achieve or to excel. Man is a competitive being. Life with his fellows or with nature finds him in competition. In recreation there is full opportunity to satisfy this urge. One may compete with himself or against others. To weave a better garment, to use fewer strokes on the putting green, to throw the ball with greater accuracy, and to lure the fish to the hook are displays of competitive spirit. The team winning the game, the chorus which is judged the champion, and the group winning the treasure hunt at a party are examples of the competitive spirit.

Competition under control and in balance is most important in fulfilling man's desires, and it flourishes in recreation.

Character. Nobody can participate in various forms of wholesome recreation without being influenced for good. When a child in a competitive game, for example, learns to win modestly and lose without bitterness, he has moved closer to a higher ethical and moral plane of living. If you observe what another person does with his leisure, when he is free to do what he wishes, how he wishes, with whom he wishes, a clue is given to the nature and level of his character. It is often during time which rests heavily upon your hands, in the absence of something absorbing and constructive to do, that many social ills occur. Recreation, however, provides the chance for people to develop good habits—integrity, honesty, and reliability, and perhaps such qualities as unselfishness, courtesy, friendliness, and courage. Through the creative and recreative use of the hands and mind, an appreciation and better understanding of nature develops, with positive influences upon character and elevation of ideals and even spiritual interests.

Recreation leaders everywhere can relate incidents illustrating how different kinds of recreation have helped teach the ways of democratic living, giving to young people an understanding of the obligations as well as the privileges which democracy brings forth.

Mental Capacity and Learning. Opportunities for broadening knowledge and skills in recreation are unlimited. Skills developed through recreation come faster and seem to remain longer because the knowledge and skills are sought and pursued—not imposed. At an art contest for students at a midwestern university most of the awards went to college students who painted as a hobby, although they were in competition with those who were preparing to be professional artists. Many amateur scientists, athletes, musicians, gardeners, and sportsmen possess knowledge and skill which tax the imagination. Countless forms of recreation and avocational pursuits have been the forerunners of distinguished professional careers. We have seen junior high school lads in recreation clubs making model airplanes of which an aeronautical engineer would be proud.

The educational values of recreation cannot be passed over lightly. The real test of education lies in the type of personality it develops. By this test, is not recreation an adventure in education? It is if recreation offers a cafeteria of interests and attractions to the mind. It is if recreation helps open the door to the cultural arts. It is if recreation helps to develop constructive skills. Does not rich experience many times grow out of the things we do, not because we *must* do them, but just because we *want* to do them? If it is the objective of education to teach the ways of democratic living, and understanding and enjoyment of the arts, to develop constructive skills, to stimulate intellectual, personal, and social growth, and to help the individual attain health and emotional stability, then the educational values of recreation are enormous.

Freedom. The greatest contribution which recreation makes to personality development is the chance it provides for a person to be completely free. Recreation appears to be man's best chance of escape from the standardization which a complex society forces upon him. Regimentation, intolerance, obligation, coercion, compulsion, and rejection are terms unfamiliar to the world of recreation. It is axiomatic that the flourishing personality depends upon preserving and strengthening the dignity of the individual. Such dignity hinges heavily upon the freedom which surrounds it, and recreation is a strong pillar in the full exercise of freedom.

Physical Condition. A large part of recreation is of a physical nature. All forms of games, sports, and athletics fall into this category. In these situations recreation provides the opportunity to achieve better coordination and motor development. Physical recreation, undertaken with common sense and good judgment, is absolutely essential to good health. It becomes the opportunity for developing one's muscles, for stimulating the circulatory system, for increasing respiratory capacity, for aiding the digestive system, and for helping improve the nervous system. The importance of physical recreation, particularly for children out of doors, and for adults, too, has long been recognized by the medical profession. Such healthful participation in physical recreation has its beneficial effects upon physical condition and appearance.

Social Condition. Social drives and social expression are just as important as any other traits in shaping personality. The opportunities which recreation opens for expressing social interests are one of its major benefits. Modern living is group living. Today a person is seldom alone, and complete privacy is difficult to find—assuming that people want it occasionally. Some groups are *primary* in nature (people are involved in face-to-face contacts); others are *secondary* (people have a common bond, but their association does not necessarily involve face-to-face contacts). In either group—and most recreation groups are of the primary type—the social drives, expressions, actions, and interactions of the group and individual are expressed. Social expression is an important factor in the development of personality. Recreation affords a chance for such expression.

Social contact in recreation is likely to be an enjoyable experience, because participation is voluntary. The recreation group duplicates for a person the modern group-living experience, except that it takes place under conditions pleasing to that person, otherwise he would not be there of his own volition. Under such circumstances there is unlimited opportunity for social desires and needs to be satisfied. Here one person has an influence upon the other. People must adjust, at least to some small degree, to one another. Sometimes there is competition and even conflict. If all of the participants are to be accommodated, some may be forced to give up something for the benefit of all. The stronger personalities may influence the weaker ones, with the latter trying to emulate as many of the other's qualities as they consider acceptable and worthwhile. Certainly such group association in recreation requires cooperation, and may or may not involve competition. It is the good feeling of sociability which grows out of recreation that makes it indispensable in the development of character.

Attitude. If anything, recreation is really an attitude toward, and a way of, life. As the late Justice Oliver Wendell Holmes said, "The superfluous is the necessary . . . to make life livable. . . ." There is evidence to support the fact that recreation grows out of our deepest emotional drives. Man is a gregarious animal; he hungers for pleasant associations with other men and searches for opportunities to be sociable. He looks for and expects affection, acceptance, and security. He must also have opportunity to release his physical and emotional energies in creative, expressive ways which, in turn, give him a sense of power, achievement, and the joy of mastering something. Each of us wants the chance to escape from himself occasionally and experience those things which do not always result from work—the urge for an adventuresome, zestful existence. Man also strives to be organically healthy and, above all, free. These needs are met by recreation. The problem of keeping the mind and body creatively occupied may be the greatest challenge of our times.

The nature, purpose, and value of recreation are perhaps best understood when we examine the results that it has upon people's lives. Therefore, it is appropriate to consider its potential in personality growth and development.

Emotional Stability

Recreation is often the chief form of relaxation for both young and old. It is a means of establishing a world apart from the things one must do to stay alive. The pressing and serious problems of growing up and making one's way in life can be lost in the world of recreation. Recreation becomes an ideal way for people to reconcile their lives with their dreams, because it simultaneously releases and disciplines the imagination. However, relaxation does not mean loafing; it is often said, "It is difficult to rest if you are doing nothing." The desire for acceptance, recognition, and self-realization—all ingredients of a healthy personality—come to fruition in play and recreation. The individual who enjoys a well-balanced diet of recreation, incorporating in it a variety of avocational pursuits, finds his life full and his existence a refreshing, ever-changing multiplication of human delights. The establishment of emotional balance, the chance to express, the ability to respond realistically to environment, and the ability to live creatively are enhanced through recreation.

As indicated earlier, each culture inflicts its own demands upon its people. Often these outer pressures are in conflict with the innate desires and impulses of the individual. We need internal physiological and psychological balance, but no less do we need balance with our environment. Recreation is often the means of helping resolve these conflicts of inner desires and outer pressures, especially in today's highly structured societies. Psychiatrists also believe that recreation aids in sustaining sound health by changing our daily patterns and encouraging self-identification. Add these findings to the opportunities recreation provides for the individual to adjust to social situations and to cultivate tolerance and understanding, and the relationship of creative use of leisure to personality is evident.

Psychologists see self-confidence and self-respect as indispensable to a healthy personality. The youngster who has trouble keeping up with his class in history may find the prestige and confidence he needs in camping or playing basketball. At the same time, he might learn something about getting along democratically. Recreation often gives people a sense of accomplishment. To be able to say, "I made it!" "I did it!" or "I mastered it!" is to take the first step toward enlarging the personality—particularly during the impressionable years of childhood and adolescence. Individuality, which is basic to emotional stability and sound personality, is enhanced by one's capacity to accomplish! Recreation is also a fertile "laboratory for living"; it affords the chance to explore the world beyond. People must have experiences in fields outside of those in which they make a living if they are to relate themselves realistically to life. Most of us have only limited ideas of what life can hold for us. Countless young people who were considered to be slow or retarded in school have blossomed into attractive personalities because recreation became the mainspring of their lives and in some instances their vocation. Recreation is a way of avoiding mistaken identity.

PRINCIPLES OF RECREATION

A principle is the essence of a matter, a governing law or tenet. It is a guideline which points direction rather than a standard which represents a level to be achieved. A principle grows out of experience and emerges as a kind of fundamental truth.

The principles for *community* recreation have been stated in many ways. Nevertheless, it appears that there is wide professional agreement on the following ideas:

1. Wholesome recreation is a basic need of *all* human beings and is essential to their well being. *All* people means both sexes, all ages—all humans without regard to their creed or race, their social or economic status, or where they may reside and work.
2. Everyone should have the opportunity for satisfying and enriching use of his leisure.
3. A democratic society has a responsibility for helping to provide wholesome recreation opportunities.
4. These opportunities must go beyond those available for amusement and entertainment and provide the opportunity for the intellectual, physical, and social involvement of the individual, for his growth, development, and self-fulfillment.
5. Recreation is primarily the responsibility of the individual, but it is also the

responsibility of the family, the community and its social institutions, and the government at all levels. When the need for recreation is greater than that which the individual and family can provide for themselves, the *primary* responsibility for providing recreation lies in the *community*. All other assistance should *supplement* that of the community.

6. Recreation has a claim on and a justification for both the *tax* dollar and the *philanthropic* dollar, in competition with other vital community services.
7. Opportunities for recreation should be available throughout the year.
8. Where opportunities for recreation are provided on a community basis, they should be planned with respect to:
   a. The needs, interests, and competencies of the people.
   b. A knowledge of the type of community (e.g., population composition, distribution, and trends; housing; zoning; economic conditions; and the like).
   c. The cooperative process among agencies, organizations, and institutions. The governmental and non-governmental agencies (e.g., social, civic, and religious groups) are interested in recreation and have resources—in the way of leadership, facilities, and funds—and responsibilities to provide recreation opportunities. These resources should be used, and the efforts of all coordinated.
   d. The full use of existing resources (those of the public agencies, such as schools, [which should be designed and available for community use] as well as the natural resources and the talents of the people).
   e. Intelligent use of widely accepted standards. This refers to standards of leadership and program, as well as the number, size, location, and function of space and facilities.
   f. Involving the public in the planning (both in making the plans and carrying them out) and making the planning a *continuous* process.
   g. The development of a long range, master plan for recreation, with provision for facilities on a neighborhood, district, and area basis, and in relation to comprehensive community and regional planning.
9. Adequate provision should be made in the home, school, church, and community to help educate for the worthy use of leisure.
10. The importance of highly qualified, professionally prepared, personable and interested recreation personnel, in adequate numbers, as well as the intelligent use of volunteers, properly recruited, oriented, and supervised is undeniable.
11. Sound local, state, and federal legislation, broad enough to cover the increasingly wide range of recreation interests and needs, and liberal enough to provide adequate financial support on the basis of *need,* is necessary.

RECREATION AS A SOCIAL FORCE

Leisure has always had a great influence upon culture. Historically, the amounts of leisure which various cultures and societies have had have paralleled their levels of economic production and their standards of living. Because recreation is, by far, the largest consumer of leisure, it is bound to become an increasingly large social force as culture becomes more leisure-centered. Today in the United States, Canada, and many other countries recreation is a major social force and influence. Because leisure can be used in *positive* or *negative* ways, its potential, as an asset or liability, to society is tremendous. Opportunities in a community for wholesome and rewarding recreation are, therefore, as essential as opportunities for health, education, and religion.

Recreation has long been a factor in social control and development. Its role along this line is increasing. It is viewed as a method of attaining and retaining physical fitness, as a device for learning, and as a means of building morale, *esprit de corps*, and unity among persons and groups. It is sought as an attractive way to develop personality and achieve balance.

In addition, recreation is used today to help the ill and the injured on their road to recovery, to help curb the extremes of delinquency and other forms of anti-social behavior, to help erase the problems of community disorganization and to help soften the blows which fall upon the unfortunate. It is encouraging to observe that as citizens become more and more aware of the positive possibilities of recreation in their daily lives, they see it more as an opportunity for growth and development, more as a chance to build better social relations, and less as a potential for decreasing certain aspects of social pathology.

As a social force, the challenges and impact of recreation in the future will increase rather than diminish. This is so for a number of reasons:

The population is expanding. Scientists refer to the rapid increase in the number of inhabitants as the problem of the exploding population. The volume of opportunities for recreation will need to be increased just on the basis of having to serve more people.

Urbanization is increasing. Dr. Marion Clawson has estimated that by the year 2000, urban areas in the United States will increase 141 per cent over what they were in the middle of the twentieth century. Large numbers of people concentrated in certain areas in a highly structured society need facilities and resources for recreation. Congestion of localities, as is the case in centers of high population density, involves many social programs.

There are large advances in economic production. Thanks to technology's gains in automation and other labor-saving, product-increasing devices, together with improved methods of transportation and communication, more people have more time off-the-job. This is especially true for non-professional workers. More goods can be produced with fewer people working fewer hours. For many, making a living becomes a part-time job. The 60-hour work week of the 1890's has been reduced to 40 hours per week or less. Not only do people work fewer hours per week than they once did, but thousands are getting more and longer vacations. And although the advances in technology have made the physical burdens of work lighter, they have not made the jobs of many less routine or monotonous. Opportunities to develop manual skills and outlets for creative expression must be found away from the job. Satisfactions heretofore found in work must henceforth be found in leisure and through recreation. This is not to say, however, that recreation is or can be a substitute for work.

Again, because the goods, products, and services which the public needs can be provided with a reduced labor force, more people are retiring from work at an earlier age. The period of gainful employment is considerably reduced. This imposes a block of *enforced* leisure upon many which, in turn, harbors social implications.

People live longer. Because of advances in medicine, people are not only living healthier lives, they are also living longer. Medical science has increased the span of life. Even though gains in longevity have been made largely through the reduction of the infant mortality rate, there are and will be more older, healthier people confronted with the problem of making their added years happy and satisfying.

Purchasing power is increased. There has been a consistent gain in real income in the United States of almost two per cent annually. More people have more money and more free time in which to spend it. Spare time is *consumption* time. Recreation is big business, a multi-billion dollar business each year in the United States alone. The economic aspects of recreation are ceilingless.

Environmental conditions are complex. We live in a highly structured, fast-moving, complex society. Economic, social, and political forces are pressing and involved. Everything seems to be accelerated. The whole world is in motion. Each year one-fifth of the population of the United States moves. Lightning-like transportation and instant communication indicate the fast pace of our daily living. It is difficult to find privacy, the opportunity to relax and escape the fears, frustrations, anxieties, and problems of the modern world. It is not only the speed, but also the physical characteristics of our environment which sharpen the factors of distress. Noxious agents, including polluted air and water, noises and vibrations, and certainly radiation hazards magnify the problem. Opportunities to divert attention from these strains through recreation must be available.

People are better educated. One must prepare for leisure just as one must prepare for work. Appreciations, interests, values, skills, and opportunities are a prologue to the story of the wise and satisfying use of leisure. Increasingly, people are developing the skills they need to enjoy their leisure. Schools and other institutions, as well as homes in many instances, are contributing to this knowledge. Increasingly, people are beginning to look upon leisure as an *opportunity*.

Social attitudes toward leisure and recreation are changing. The old idea that play and recreation are wasteful and sinful is fading rapidly. Although there are still many people who are ashamed of being caught doing nothing, who feel guilty about relaxing, or engaging in recreation, and while there are those who when playing, play compulsively, such feelings are not nearly as widespread as they have been for centuries in the past. Indeed, if there is any danger in the present attitude of many people, it is not in the belief that it is not good to have leisure, but rather in the erroneous and equally disastrous idea that anything we do as leisure is good!

Nowhere has recreation as a social force been so forcefully brought to the attention of the public as it was by President John F. Kennedy, when in a National Recreation Month message he said:

How we Americans spend leisure time might seem to have little bearing on the strength of our nation or the worth and prestige of our free society. Yet we certainly cannot continue to thrive as a strong and vigorous free people unless we understand and use creatively one of our greatest resources—our leisure. . . . For us today, opportunity for recreation is bounteous and ever-increasing. Perhaps no other nation in the world is more consciously oriented toward recreation, and in no other nation is such a favorable combination of leisure time, income, and mobility coupled with such enormous recreation resources, both existing and potential.

We accept as one of our basic freedoms the right to enjoy our leisure time as we please. We must also accept the responsibility inherent in that freedom: the challenge which free time offers a free people. It is my sincere belief that the moral fibre, mental health, and physical strength of each of us, contributing to the sum total of American greatness, [are] now and will be derived in large measure from the creative use of our leisure. We have enormous capacity, enormous power in recreation. Let us engage in it wisely, not wastefully.[2]

THE WORKSHOP

1. Interview a physiologist and a physical educator and compare their interpretations on the theories of play and recreation.
2. Arrange a debate within the class on the topic, "Resolved, that recreation in its purest sense cannot be 'applied' to treatment of the ill or to other purposes, but must be pursued for its own sake."
3. Ask ten persons for their interpretation of recreation and compare the observations.
4. Examine the philosophies of Plato and Socrates with a view to determining their thinking about enjoyment and pleasure.
5. Intentionally interrupt persons who are engaged in a favorite hobby or recreation and observe their reaction.

2 "President Kennedy's Message for National Recreation Month," *Bulletin* (New York: National Recreation Association, n.d.).

6. Prepare a statement on your own philosophy of recreation.
7. Prepare objective analyses of the recreation philosophies of Joseph Lee, Howard Braucher, G. Ott Romney, Jay Nash, and Edward Lindeman.
8. Give a short talk on how certain forms of recreation have negative influences upon character.
9. Write a short statement on the importance of recreation which would be understood and convincing to junior high school students.
10. Explain in detail the relation of recreation to the social processes.

REFERENCES

Brightbill, Charles K., *Man and Leisure—A Philosophy of Recreation*. Englewood Cliffs, New Jersey: Prentice-Hall, Inc., 1961.

Cutten, George B., *The Threat of Leisure*. New Haven: Yale University Press, 1926.

de Grazia, Sebastian, *Of Time, Work and Leisure*. New York: Twentieth Century Fund, 1962.

Gulick, Luther, *A Philosophy of Play*. New York: Charles Scribner's Sons, 1920.

Huizinga, Johan, *Homo Ludens—A Study of the Play Element in Culture*. Boston: Beacon Press, Inc., 1955.

Kleemeier, Robert W., ed. *Aging and Leisure*. New York: Oxford University Press, 1961.

Lindeman, Edward C., *Leisure, A National Issue*. New York: Association Press, 1939.

Madow, Pauline, ed., *Recreation in America*. New York: H. W. Wilson & Co., 1965.

Nash, Jay B., *Philosophy of Recreation and Leisure*. St. Louis: The C. V. Mosby Company, 1953.

Neumeyer, Martin H., and Esther S. Neumeyer, *Leisure and Recreation*. New York: The Ronald Press Company, 1958.

Pack, Arthur N., *The Challenge of Leisure*. New York: The Macmillan Company, 1936.

Patrick, G. T. W., *Psychology of Relaxation*. Boston: Houghton Mifflin Company, 1916.

Robbins, Florence G., *The Sociology of Play, Recreation, and Leisure*. Dubuque, Iowa: William C. Brown Company, Publishers, 1955.

Romney, G. Ott, *Off-the-Job Living*. New York: A. S. Barnes & Co., 1945.

Veblen, Thorstein, *Theory of the Leisure Class*. New York: Modern Library, 1934.

Comments

The theories and philosophies of leisure and recreation are closely related to the theories and philosophies of living and education. Readers are encouraged to examine comparable literature in these areas and also in economics, physiology, psychology, and sociology.

It will be interesting to relate the philosophies and theories of former years to those of today. Also, it will be challenging to note the significant likenesses and differences as they affect man's recreation interests and practices.

Current works attempt to translate philosophies and theories into practical application of the needs, benefits, conditions, and uses of one's leisure through recreation.

Be alert to note trends, study and discuss current interpretations, and analyze motivation patterns.

Note the influence the theories of recreation of leadership has on individuals, groups, and their practices.

Important Note—Glossary

Because they were essential to explaining and understanding the preceding material, such basic terms as leisure, play, recreation and work have been defined already. There are other terms, however, with which the reader should be familiar. See GLOSSARY—Appendix C.

3

The Economic Significance
of Recreation

The United States is a nation of working people who, with the highest standard of living in the world, see nothing wrong in living comfortably and enjoying themselves. This is not to say that the old Puritanical concept of work as a virtue and play as "being of Satan" does not still prevail in some quarters. However, even though the importance of wholesome recreation, organized or unorganized, for profit or otherwise, is gaining the prestige it deserves, its justification has been based largely, and rightly, upon what it contributes to the social, physical, and mental growth of the individual and the well-being and progress of society.

THE ECONOMICS OF LEISURE

One does not have to be an economist to understand that there is little need to *produce* goods unless they are *consumed*. Indeed, the final purpose of all economic processes is the use or consumption of goods and services. Unless there is production, there is no supply. If there is no consumption, there is no demand. The economy of a society depends upon *production* and *consumption, supply* and *demand*.

If goods and services are to be consumed, people must *want* them and have the money to purchase them. They must also have the *time* to use them—hours available beyond the time needed to *produce* the goods. This is the *leisure* time, the *consumption* time, the time which becomes increasingly significant, economically, in a leisure-centered society.

The editors of *Life* Magazine in a special issue devoted to the "Good Life," wrote:

> Americans have a low threshold of boredom, and they have fought it with every device from anagrams to parachute jumping. In so doing, they have created a vast *new* economic force, the Leisure Business, which could not exist if everyone worked at "useful things" and which, by the buying power it releases and by the dreams it satisfies, has filled the whole economy with energy and ambition . . . The most important thing about this market, however, is not its size in dollars but its size in people, for the leisure market is supported mainly by people who make from $4,000 up a year after taxes. There are 34 million families in that category now, a majority of all the U.S. families, and among them they control most of the $84 billion "discretionary income" (money left after necessary expenditures) in the country.
>
> These new "leisure masses" have acquired not only the money and the time to spend it in, but also—and most significantly—an appetite for the good life.[1]

Charged with preparing a public outdoor recreation plan, the California Public Outdoor Recreation Plan Committee had to look not at the economics of leisure, but at the economics of recreation. In this connection, it saw recreation as having three types of financial benefits:

> (1) the value to the area, derived from the introduction of "new" money spent by visitors and the circulation of the money in the area due to the stimulation of the money spent by them; (2) the appreciation of the property values due to stimulated business and increased interest in the area; (3) the value, appraised in dollars, that could be considered a minimum worth for that recreation to the user, whether or not he has to pay for it.[2]

In other words, a community or an area can receive "fringe benefits" through recreation travel. Visitors spend money in the places they visit, and this can be a real economic advantage. Also, recreation resources have a positive influence on land and property values. The advantages here accrue to those who own property in the area and to the public generally, because property values increase, thus raising assessment revenues. Finally, although measurement is difficult because of the intangibles involved, multiple use projects can add recreation as another function and make it count economically. A reservoir, for example, has its primary economic potential in its usefulness for irrigation, power, and flood

[1] "The Good Life," *Life*, December 28, 1959, 69–70.
[2] California Public Outdoor Recreation Plan Committee, *California Public Outdoor Recreation Plan*, Part II (Sacramento: California State Printing Office, 1960), p. 200.

control. But, if the reservoir is also developed and used for recreation, part of its cost can be allocated to recreation.

The economics of leisure and recreation are closely related to our values. George Soule tells us that the economic developments which have brought more leisure to more people in the United States have been the increases in production and in the size of the labor force in relation to the population. He says that whatever gains have been made in leisure under the market system have resulted from the workers' deliberate choice of *free time* (i.e., attaining the shorter work week) over real income (i.e., working longer hours for more money).[3] This choice, of course, is not evident among all of the labor force. Today, "moonlighting," the practice of holding more than one job, is heavily engaged in, especially in the big cities. Sebastian de Grazia estimates that one out of twelve working Americans, 8 per cent of our labor force, hold two or more jobs.[4] Whatever choice is made then—working longer hours for more income, or having more leisure, more free time, and perhaps more time in which to consume more goods and services—will influence the economy. The matters of *which* choice it shall be and which is the *right* choice are something else.

RECREATION AN ECONOMIC FACTOR

Recreation also contributes immeasurably to the economy of the nation and the economic stability of countless communities. Aside from the billions of dollars spent on commercial recreation of all kinds, community recreation is recognized as a strong economic factor in our national life. It makes communities more desirable places for home-owners, business investors, and industrialists and creates wider markets for capital and consumer goods, for services, and for jobs. The United States Department of Commerce has said that "towns are held together more frequently by religious, social, and *recreational* attractions than by plain business transactions." People want to do business and establish their homes where they can live comfortably and where they most enjoy themselves. Family satisfaction cannot be purchased through the pay check alone. An atmosphere of friendliness and neighborliness is essential. When a family moves out of town, it takes its taxes with it. The town loses both the people and their financial support. That is definitely bad business.

Industries try to locate their plants near raw materials and markets,

[3] George Soule, "The Economics of Leisure," *The Annals of the American Academy of Political and Social Science,* September, 1957, pp. 16–24.

[4] Sebastian de Grazia, *Of Time, Work and Leisure* (New York: Doubleday & Company, Inc., 1964), p. 67.

thus lowering costs of transportation. They are interested in locations where their taxes and overhead will be at a minimum. They are also concerned with the availability and cost of skilled labor and finding places where labor-management problems will be few.

Adequate recreation facilities and opportunities, nevertheless, are among the first considerations of industrial management in determining plant locations. Something more than high pay, good working conditions, and fringe benefits is needed to attract and keep workers on the job. Recruiting and training workers is expensive. Consequently, anything which can be done to help reduce labor turnover—such as making available recreation opportunities for employees and their families—is desirable.

Under certain conditions recreation helps increase land and property values, especially if recreation areas are properly beautified, maintained, and operated. Many are convinced that recreation also reduces accident and health expenses by helping to keep people alert and healthy. Law enforcement authorities have for many years believed that if more were spent for wholesome recreation from childhood through adulthood there would be less need to spend public money on juvenile delinquency and crime. Recreation not only saves tax money, over a period of years, but through commercial recreation pursuits brings billions of dollars into the treasuries of municipalities, counties, states, and the federal government.

Hundreds of thousands of men and women earn their living working for scores of industries which produce materials, equipment, and services designed to meet the leisure needs of the people. Recreation in the United States constitutes an important factor in the nation's economy and accounts for the circulation of billions of dollars. As the recreation movement progresses, it will provide work for more people, from laborers and clerks to skilled technicians and professional workers. It will create new economic wealth, which will have a beneficial effect on our standard of living.

Americans now and in the future will have more "time off" than any people have ever had since the advent of the Industrial Revolution. Labor-saving devices, the shorter work week, the increased harnessing of productive energy, automation, better and faster transportation, increased family purchasing power, more liberal working conditions, longer vacations, and a higher standard of living among more people make the opportunity to recreate a reality for most of us. One has only to remember that leisure time is "consumption time." It is during man's free time that he goes to shows, takes part in sports, reads books, travels, and spends money. Material things are important to a nation's economy—if people have time for them. In the United States they have, and this is why recreation is one of the nation's most valuable economic assets.

RECREATION EXPENDITURES

There is no way of accurately estimating how much is spent each year by the people of the United States for recreation of all kinds. However, it has been estimated that at least $60 billion is spent annually by Americans in the pursuit of happiness during leisure. This amount almost equals the budget for national defense and exceeds the total value of farm output in the United States in a given year. In a year we spend $1.2 billion in motion picture theaters, $70 million in legitimate theaters, and $50 million at concerts. Television is a $900 million a year business and radio, $700 million. In 365 days, people in the United States spend $2.5 billion on boating (boat owners buy 10 million gallons of paint and varnish a year for their crafts), $1.3 billion on swimming (the number of swimming pools increased from 12,000 in 1950 to 250,000 in the 10 years that followed), $1 billion on bowling (there are some bowling alleys with more than 100 lanes) and $850 million on golf. What about fishing? Is there a partial answer in the fact that one dealer alone sells 500,000 worms a week —by mail! From 10–12 million persons take dancing lessons and millions of gardeners spend billions on seeds, tools, and sprays. Most American families spend more on the first three days of their vacations than the annual per capita personal income in India and Pakistan.[5]

Some idea of "how" the money is spent can be ascertained from expenditures on two favorites of United States sportsmen.[6]

	Fishing (Annual expenditure, $3 billion)	Hunting (Annual expenditure, $1 billion)
Auxiliary equipment (1)	26%	11%
Privilege fees and other expenses	33%	20%
Equipment (2)	11%	36%
Transportation Expense	13%	15%
Food and Lodging	14%	12%
Licenses	3%	6%

(1) Such as boats, motors, tents, sleeping gear, cooking and eating utensils, special clothing, lanterns, trailers, cabins, etc.
(2) Such as rods, reels, lines, nets, guns, rifles, shells and cartridges, bows and arrows, decoys, etc.

The expenditures listed above are not complete by any means. The amount of money spent annually in the United States in which recreation is translated into a business transaction is almost endless. Think of the

5 James E. Kenney, "The Business of Pleasure," *America*, January 28, 1961, 562–564.
6 U. S. Department of Commerce, Bureau of Census. *Statistical Abstracts of the United States*. Washington: U. S. Government Printing Office, 1967, 212.

"odds and ends" of expenses for recreation which people seldom ponder but which have their place in the economy. There is, for example, the $400 million spent annually for hobbycrafts (e.g. model airplanes, do-it-yourself craft kits, etc.) and the $55 million which hunters lay out each year just for licenses to track and shoot game. And it is not surprising to realize that during a twelve month period Americans spend as much as $2.5 billion travelling abroad, and ten times that amount at home. Pleasure travel expenditures for 1966 were in excess of $30 billion.[7] The race among cities, states, regions, and nations to attract the tourist and vacation dollar is becoming more and more competitive. For awhile recreation and park planners were worried about golf courses being cut up for real estate development. But in one recent year, 323 new golf courses were opened, 400 more were under construction and the nation's total was more than 6600 golf courses.[8]

It is estimated that each dollar invested in new recreation and tourist facilities results in 20 dollars or more in direct expenditures annually within that community. In other words, the attracting of a couple of dozen tourists a day throughout the year is economically comparable to the acquisition of a new manufacturing industry with an annual payroll of $100,000.[9] Recreation is good business!!

The unbelievably large impact which leisure, and the recreative use of it, has on the economy can be illustrated in many ways and in connection with many different kinds of goods and services. For this purpose, let us choose *one* kind of recreation, baseball, in this instance a *physical* activity, a sport played only in *certain* seasons, by *males* alone, and which does not, by any stretch of the imagination, involve either the largest number of *participants* or *spectators*. Let us also choose only *one* piece of equipment in the game of baseball: a baseball bat.

First, the timber must be felled. This requires lumbermen, properly equipped, and conservationists, tree farmers, and foresters to replace the trees. The lumber must be transported to the saw mill and processed there, with all that implies in the way of manpower and machinery. The lumber is then sent to the factory, where it is manufactured into a baseball bat. Whoever works in that mill—lathe operator, polisher, janitor, bookkeeper, or typist—depends on the product for his living. The product is then advertised, distributed from wholesaler to retailer, and perhaps sold to a major league baseball team. Not only the players' salaries, but also the incomes of the groundskeepers, concession operators, club owners, the television cameraman, and the advertisers of shaving cream are

[7] "Investments Market Balloons in Tourism and Recreation," *Industrial Development.* September-October, 1967, 20.

[8] *Sportscope* (Chicago: The Athletic Institute), VII, No. 3, 1962, 2.

[9] U. S. Department of Commerce, Office of Area Development, *How Your Community Can Profit from the Tourist Business,* 1957.

economically affected by the bat. Apply this observation to all of the goods and services which are used, recreationally, in leisure, and light is shed on recreation's economic aspects and potentials.

It is not only the economic influence of a single form of recreation which is pertinent. Paul Douglass uses gardening for this purpose, but also to show how the common interest of the economic thrust merges with the skills of consumption to provide enjoyment as well as support the economy:

> *Better Homes and Gardens* has 4½ million readers. Garden Editor Fleeta Brownell Woodroff's book, *Better Homes and Gardens,* has moved beyond the 1,000,000th copy. Forty million families are engaged in gardening. The leisure performance of backyard growing of flowers and vegetables becomes a $3 billion dollar sector of the economy. The development and improvement of lawns becomes a $4 billion unit in consumption. The building of a million homes a year calls for 15 million pounds of grass seed, 150 million pounds of plant food; and in addition mowers, sweepers, sprinklers, hose, and weed killers. These items in the annual home garden supply business exceed $2 billion annually. Gardening is an enormous business; a gigantic sector in our economy.
>
> The existence of this gigantic industrial base, however, is essential to provide felt satisfactions. Gardening is an activity which people enjoy. Its combination of physical work with the production of fragrant beauty is a therapy for body, mind, and spirit. It produces health, contributes to peace of mind, pride in the home, and outreach for the mind.[10]

As indicated before, there is no way of accurately estimating how much is spent each year by the people of the United States for recreation. There is no accounting here of beverages and refreshments consumed in moments of leisure. There is no record of the many leisure uses to which people put goods and materials ordinarily thought to be purchased in connection with existing comfortably. There are other unanswered problems—how do leisure and recreation reflect themselves financially in the kinds of clothes people purchase—sport clothes, casual clothes, and the like? To what extent do leisure and recreation influence expenditures for housing and shelter conveniences—summer cottages, cabins, trailers, refrigerators? Is the money which young parents spend for baby sitters when they go out for an "evening of fun" a recreation expenditure? How much money is spent on illegal forms of recreation? One of the biggest deficiencies, however, is the lack of information on how much people spend for all kinds of travel (not just travel abroad), holidays, and vacations.

In addition to these and other items involving leisure and recreation spending, the sums spent by government at the municipal, county, state,

[10] Paul Douglass, "The Administration of Leisure for Living," *The American Recreation Society Bulletin,* April, 1960, 5–16.

and federal levels, by the hundreds of voluntary agencies, institutions, private clubs and organizations, and by real estate developers would also have to be added. Even if the estimated $60 billion annual expenditure for recreation is only partially correct, it adds up to a large share of the national economy, one which cannot be looked upon lightly when it comes to the ringing of the cash register.

Aside from the financial aspects of the rapid expansion of leisure and the growth of recreation, there is much reason for encouragement in the fact that the tremendous increase of recreation expenditures also reflects ever-increasing *participation* in recreation in contrast with *spectator* interest.

INDIVIDUAL PARTICIPATION

When assessing leisure and recreation and their relation to the economy, there is a tendency to condemn commercial aspects of recreation because so many dollars are spent for watching rather than doing. Actually, large amounts of money are spent on forms of recreation which involve individual participation. That this is true is evidenced by the facts that within a year in the U.S.A.:

—There were 8½ million pleasure boats with 6½ million outboard motors in the nation.
—No less than 5 million males and 2,700,000 females belonged to national bowling organizations.
—More than 14 million people went camping; there were 40 million camper visitor days to the national forest camp areas alone.
—Better than 20 million went sports fishing, while 15 million chose hunting. (600,000 of these hunted with bows and arrows.)
—Travel abroad was popular with 6.5 million Americans.
—Gardening claimed 80 million hobbyists.
—Golfing attracted 8½ million players.
—No fewer than 3½ million Americans went in for skiing.
—Pitching horseshoes brought forth 7 million participants.[11, 12]

To be sure, millions of people prefer spending their recreation dollars to watch others perform. Nevertheless, an increasingly large percentage of the population is getting into the middle of the fun, and that is the way it should be. How about the number of people who play bridge regularly? They must purchase their cards. How many homes have their own work benches, movable barbecues, and ping pong tables? Millions of people

11 *The 1961 Compton Yearbook*, Supplement to *Compton's Picture Encyclopedia*. (Chicago: F. E. Compton and Company, 1961), pp. 188–205.
12 U. S. Department of Commerce, *Statistical Abstracts*, p. 207.

play golf, purchasing their clubs, balls, and accessories. Amateur sailors, musicians, and photographers are multiplying everywhere. Paper-back books sell quickly at newstands throughout the land, and publishers are declaring increasingly large dividends.

GOVERNMENT EXPENDITURES

According to available information (many communities do not report their expenditures), almost half a billion dollars is spent annually for the operation and maintenance of slightly less than 2500 municipal and county recreation agencies. Authorities spend another $250 million a year on capital improvements. In 1965, for example, the Federal Government reported that city expenditures for parks and recreation were $611 million, of which $290 million was for land, buildings, and permanent improvement. Parks and recreation expenditures, as used here, include funds spent for cultural-scientific activities, such as museums and art galleries; organized recreation, including playgrounds and playfields, swimming pools and bathing beaches; municipal parks; and special facilities for recreation, such as auditoriums, stadiums, auto camps, recreation piers, and yacht harbors.[13]

Of even more significance is the growth of local expenditures for recreation and parks within recent years. Per capita expenditures for these functions during the decade 1950–1960 increased 29 per cent in centers with less than 5000 population, 6 per cent for 5000–10,000 population, 17 per cent for 10,000–25,000 population, 47 per cent for 25,000–50,000 population, 62 per cent for 50,000–100,000 population, 71 per cent for 100,000–250,000 population, and 76 per cent for 250,000 population and over.[14]

Add to these figures the millions of dollars which are spent for recreation by state departments of public instruction, conservation, forests, parks, highways, welfare, health, and agriculture, as well as what is spent by state colleges and universities, state recreation commissions, tourist bureaus, and youth commissions, and the results are impressive.

To illustrate, in the 1960 Census the states reported that they spent more than $144 million for their fish and game programs, almost $188 million in forestry and park operations, and about $24 million on libraries. On parks alone the states spent $87 million in 1960, as compared with $55 million spent in 1955 and $15 million spent in 1946. State park revenues (e.g., from operated facilities, concessions, entrance, and parking

[13] U. S. Department of Commerce, Bureau of the Census. *Compendium of State Government Finances in 1960* (Washington, D. C.: U. S. Government Printing Office), pp. 14, 15.

[14] U. S. Treasury Department, *Internal Revenue Collections of Excise Taxes, Summary, First Quarter, Fiscal Year, 1962; By Sources of Revenue.* (Washington, D. C.: Internal Revenue Service, November, 1961).

fees) were more than $26 million in 1962, as contrasted with $13 million in 1955 and $3 million in 1946.[15]

Agencies of the federal government also spend public funds to serve recreation needs. Such agencies as the United States Office of Education, the Children's Bureau, and the Extension Service of the Department of Agriculture have been engaged in recreation pursuits of a limited type for a long time. The Veterans Administration has a comprehensive recreation program. Both the National Park Service and the United States Forest Service have billions invested in lands and projects and in addition spend large amounts annually for the maintenance and operation of facilities which have recreation value. The Public Housing Administration and the Tennessee Valley Authority have had both appropriated and un-appropriated funds for recreation. Both the Vocational Rehabilitation Administration and the Administration on Aging (divisions of Social Rehabilitative Service, Department of Health, Education, and Welfare) have established long-term training grants for the preparation of rec-reation personnel. The Bureau of Outdoor Recreation has given excellent leadership to the growth and development of outdoor recreation services by sponsoring workshops, research and curriculum development con-ferences in addition to administering the Land and Water Conservation Fund.

RECREATION AND TAX REVENUES

Financial connections between recreation and government are not limited to the *expenditure* of funds. Recreation is also a means of *bringing revenue* to the local, state, and federal government. Governmental bodies collect taxes from many sources. Recreation yields property taxes, income taxes, corporation taxes, excise taxes, hunting and fishing taxes, and taxes on coin-operated machines. It has been said that the income tax paid by one celebrated professional entertainer would be enough to pay the salaries of all our congressmen!

In a given year, the *states* in license tax revenues collect more than $1½ million on amusements (includes race tracks, theaters, athletic events, etc., but not licenses based on value or number of admissions, amount of wagers, or gross or net income), a little less than $140 million from hunt-ing and fishing (3 per cent of the $4 billion spent on fishing and hunting in 1960 went into license charges collected at *various* levels of govern-ment),[16] and $7 million, plus, from license taxes on pleasure boats, dogs,

15 National Park Service, U. S. Department of the Interior, *State Park Statistics—1960* (Washington, D. C.: U. S. Government Printing Office, July, 1961), p. 6.

16 United States Department of the Interior, *1960 National Survey of Fishing and Hunting*, Circular 120 (Washington, D. C.: U. S. Government Printing Office), p. 8.

and the like. To these would have to be added state income resulting from sales and gross receipts tax revenues. Of this, more than $265 million springs from pari-mutuels (taxes measured by amounts wagered at race tracks, including "breakage" collected by the government), practically $18 million from amusements.[17]

In 1965 the U.S. Internal Revenue Service collected excise taxes of more than $222 million on radio, phonograph, and television sets, $29 million on sporting goods (including fishing rods and firearms), $35 million on cameras, $96 million on theaters, concerts, cabarets, and clubs, $19 million on coin-operated amusement and gaming devices, and $5 million on bowling alleys and pool tables.[18]

A good way to get an idea of the extent to which taxes enter into the recreation and leisure expenses of the people is to ask yourself the following questions:

How much in the way of tax revenue is involved when a person—

Drives a hundred or a thousand miles to camp in a state or national forest (gasoline tax)?
Returns from a vacation in Europe with luxury goods (customs and duties tax)?
Takes his family to the local theater (admissions tax)?
Purchases a radio, television, or piano (sales tax)?
Buys a dog for a pet (dog license)?
Owns land or property used for commercial recreation (property tax)?
Imports a camera or a sports car (tariff tax)?
Constructs a commercial bowling alley (taxes on materials, building permits, etc.)?
Operates a corporation to provide recreation goods and services (corporation tax)?
Earns a salary as an entertainer (income tax)?

Although the influence of recreation on land and property values is discussed later in the chapter, it is appropriate to mention the subject here in relation to their tax yield.

When the tax records of Dare County, North Carolina, where the Cape Hatteras National Seashore Area is located, were examined, it was found that

the total assessed valuation within the county more than doubled from 1950 to 1958, going from $11 million to $25 million. At the same time, tax rates were reduced from $1 to 80 cents per hundred.[19]

17 U. S. Department of Commerce, Bureau of the Census. *Compendium of State Government Finances in 1960* (Washington, D. C.: U. S. Government Printing Office), pp. 14, 15.
18 U. S. Department of Commerce, *Statistical Abstracts*, p. 396.
19 Division of Recreation Resource Planning, National Park Service, *Economic Effects of Establishing National Parks* (Washington, D. C.: U. S. Government Printing Office, June, 1961).

An economic study during the same period of Teton County, Wyoming, where Grand Teton National Park is located, revealed that

In 1950, the year in which the Grand Teton National Park was enlarged, total assessment values of real and personal property amounted to $4.7 million. By 1958 total assessment values increased to $8.2 million. The sales and use tax in Teton County amounted to $76,457 in 1950. Eight years later revenue from this tax had doubled to amount to $153,704. During the eight years, the population of Teton County increased 27 per cent, retail sales went up by 79 per cent and bank deposits nearly doubled.[20]

Finally, it should be pointed out that the Bureau of Outdoor Recreation expects to gross more than one billion dollars through the Land and Water Conservation Fund during the 1970's. In 1967, the Fund was running about $115 million annually with the bulk of the monies coming from Federal recreation fees, net proceeds from the sale of Federal surplus real property and the Federal motorboat fuels tax.[21]

INSTITUTIONAL, INDUSTRIAL, AND VOLUNTARY AGENCY EXPENDITURES

Of the funds spent for social welfare programs in the United States, a large share is allocated to agencies which serve in the social group work and recreation fields. Depending upon the situation, from 40 to 75 cents of each welfare dollar goes to finance the local work of the health agencies, including hospitals, family and child care services, programs for the handicapped, sheltered workshops, institutions for the aging, maternity home care, and social group work and recreation. Many of these agencies and services, of course, are building-centered. Some of the funds they receive may be spent for maintaining facilities other than those used for recreation, as in the case of a Y.M.C.A. which provides rooms for guests. Nevertheless, the amount of money allocated and spent for recreation is considerable.

Trends of recreation expenditures among health and welfare agencies are witnessed in a report financed by the Rockefeller Foundation. This study indicates that within a five-year period the amount of money spent for recreation in the voluntary agency field increased 82 per cent.[22]

20 *Ibid.*

21 Bureau of Outdoor Recreation, *Recreation Land Price Escalation* (Washington, D. C.: Department of Interior, 1968).

22 Ad Hoc Citizens Committee, Robert H. Hamlin, Study Director, *Voluntary Health and Welfare Agencies in the United States* (New York: The Schoolmaster's Press, 1961), p. 69.

In some instances, these agencies have been providing recreational opportunities in summer camps for children of low-income families, or year-round leisure-time activities in community centers and boys' clubs. A growing number of agencies, however, have been providing recreational opportunities to all, regardless of individual or family income.[23]

Few reputable institutions for the dependents, delinquents, and defectives in the population are without recreation facilities and services of some kind. These include penal institutions, homes for the chronically ill, aged, dependent, and maladjusted. The Veterans Administration alone spends from $8 to $10 million annually for recreation services in veterans hospitals. There is no way of knowing the increasing amounts spent for recreation in state and local institutions of all kinds.

Recreation and Employment

Recreation provides gainful employment directly to several million persons in the United States and indirectly to untold numbers. Included are all the producers and distributors of recreation products and services, planners, designers, builders, and maintenance and custodial workers of all types. Included also are recreation executives, supervisory staffs, specialists, leaders, and seasonal or part-time workers, and even teachers. Recreation increases the need for transportation crews, hotel people, restaurant workers, and gas station attendants. Hundreds of thousands of people are employed in the amusement industry alone. Other tens of thousands are engaged in making recreation projects, operating tourist facilities, and running clubs and organizations. Thousands are employed on a full-time and part-time or seasonal basis in public recreation and park departments and agencies at various levels of government; in voluntary agencies; industrial recreation; and public, voluntary, and privately owned resident and day camps; hospitals; rehabilitation centers; and institutions of all kinds. The Office of Economic Opportunity reported in 1967, that over 40,000 of its workers were performing or had been employed in a recreation-related job. The potential of recreation as a field of work for the so-called "less trained" or those at the aide level is relatively unrealized. With our nation's economy becoming more service-oriented, recreation and parks may be the next major employer.

According to the Recreation-Park Manpower Study completed in 1968 by the National Recreation and Parks Association, over 150,000 people are now employed in the local public park and recreation sector alone. Over 500,000 are working in commercial recreation jobs. The following

[23] *Ibid.*, p. 69.

table provides a quick run-down of the positions and number of workers at each position for the local public recreation-park speciality.

LOCAL PUBLIC PARK AND RECREATION PERSONNEL, 1967 *

Work Functions or Occupations	Estimated Full-time Equivalent Personnel 1967
Executive	3,275
Assistant Director	1,002
Division Heads	2,000
Superintendent of Parks	1,065
Superintendent of Recreation	727
Administrative Support Staff	1,489
Clerical	6,230
Related Park Professionals	1,469
District Supervisors of Parks	728
Park Managers	1,649
Park Rangers	1,893
Foremen	6,539
Skilled Park Personnel	19,080
Semi- and Non-Skilled Personnel	49,191
District Supervisors of Recreation	8,573
Recreation Supervisors	12,882
Community Center Directors	4,376
Recreation Facility Supervisors	2,766
Activity Specialists	3,306
Recreation Program Leaders	11,708
Attendants and Aides	13,529
TOTAL	153,477

* National Recreation and Park Association. *Supply/Demand Study.* Unpublished Preliminary Report, NRPA, Washington, D. C., 1968, p. 62.

Nowhere is the influence of recreation on land values more pronounced than along shorelines where plenty of water is accessible for swimming, bathing, boating, and fishing. The value of shoreline lands skyrockets every year. A 30-mile tract of land on the east coast, offered to the government in 1935 for $9000 a mile, was appraised 23 years later at $110,000 a mile, an increase of 1100 per cent in value.[24]

In Southern California, when the state bought back seashore property from private owners it paid $100 per front inch! [25]

That recreation as a positive influence on property and land values is increasing as leisure and people's interest in recreation increase, is indicated in the following:

[24] Hearings, Subcommittee on Public Lands, Committee on Interior and Insular Affairs, 87th Congress, United States Senate, *Shoreline Recreation Areas* (Washington, D. C.: U. S. Government Printing Office, 1961), p. 8.

[25] *Ibid.,* p. 36.

RESULTS OF REMAINDER VALUE STUDIES—
PERCENTAGE OF CHANGE IN VALUES OF PROPERTY
ADJOINING CORPS OF ENGINEERS RESERVOIRS

Norfolk Project, Ark. and Mo.	100%	1940	404%	1965
Beaver Project, Ark.	100%	1960	134%	1965
Bull Shoals Project, Ark. and Mo.	100%	1945	300%	1965
Table Rock Project, Ark. and Mo.	100%	1958	535%	1965
Dardanelle Project, Ark.	100%	1960	800%	1965
Greers Ferry Project, Ark.	100%	1960	800%	1965

Source: Financial and Statistical Reports on Recreational Facilities for Norfolk, Beaver, Bull Shoals, Table Rock, Dardanelle, and Greers Ferry Reservoir Areas, dated 1965, U.S. Army Engineers.

According to the Bureau of Outdoor Recreation one of the best documented case studies of land escalation is that of a non-federal recreation area—the Pearl River Reservoir, near Jackson, Mississippi.

It illustrates a well documented price increase following the announcement of a public recreation project. It also shows how a public project —in this case a local reservoir—can greatly affect land values outside but adjacent to the project. Detailed analysis was made of 304 sales involving some 25,310 acres of land adjacent to or with good accessibility to the reservoir project between 1950 and May 1964. Analysis was also made for the same period of 101 sale transactions covering 11,141 acres in a comparable area not influenced by the project and which served as a "control" area. The average price paid per acre of lands adjacent to the project showed an average annual increase of slightly less than 9 per cent prior to announcement of the project in March 1959. After the project was announced, prices increased 165 per cent the first year, 191 per cent the second year, 216 per cent the third year, 236 per cent the fourth year, and 258 per cent for the first half of the fifth year (through May 15, 1964) when the study was concluded. The sales prices per acre for the control area from 1950 through 1964 continued to follow a normal price trend line. The speculative influence of the project upon prices paid per acre within the immediate area is clearly indicated.[26]

LAND AND PROPERTY VALUES

There is much evidence to support the contention that recreation frequently has a favorable influence on land and property values. This is true in urban centers and in less populated areas as well. The increase in property values, of course, is not automatic. Indeed, unless care is exercised, in urban areas particularly, exactly the opposite—*decreased* property values—can result.

[26] Bureau of Outdoor Recreation, *Recreation Land Price Escalation*, pp. 10 and 11.

Real-estate operators know that when certain public improvements are made in a residential area, property values increase. These increases are reflected clearly in the records of the tax assessor. As the assessment increases, so does the amount of tax which the owner must pay. But the market value of the property also goes upward. Thus, if streets are paved, if sewers are installed, or if a school is built nearby, the value of the property in the area is likely to increase. The same is true if a park or some similar, attractive, recreation center is established. But the recreation center must be well-planned, attractive, and well maintained and operated. If it is improperly located, unattractive, causes traffic and parking problems, is noisy, or is a nuisance in any way, then chances are that it will *decrease* rather than increase property and land values.

In some instances the value of property which is not immediately adjacent to an outdoor recreation center, but which is within approximately a quarter mile radius of it, increases more than that which borders or faces the area. At the same time as surrounding property value increases, so does that of the parks. In one metropolitan county, the land value of some of its major parks increased ten to fifteen fold within a decade, and the increase was not attributed to money inflation.

Real-estate dealers draw the attention of prospective customers to parks and playgrounds in the neighborhood. The real-estate sections of the Sunday papers are full of advertisements which try to sell real estate on the basis of "country club living," urging people to move where there are playgrounds, tennis courts, swimming pools, and golf courses. One real-estate salesman, in trying to sell sites for homes, said, "This is not just a lot of tract homes. In fact, we're not building homes at all. This is a recreational development. We're going to put in a small boat harbor, and later a golf course. There will be a beach club to which all lot holders may belong."

The favorable influence of recreation resources on property and land values is even more pronounced in outlying areas. Unprofitable land areas have been turned to profit through recreation use in countless instances. This was well shown during the depression of the 1930's when the Civilian Conservation Corps, in co-operation with National Park Service, took submarginal land—land which was not useful for agriculture or other utilitarian purposes—and transformed it into state parks.

Often communities in the vicinity of proposed national park and recreation areas fear the loss of tax revenues through the lands being taken off the tax rolls. But experience shows that new enterprises develop adjacent to the parks, and that property values increase. Sometimes, the land remaining on the tax rolls increases in value 50 to 100 times.[27]

[27] Division of Recreation Resource Planning, National Park Service, *Economic Effects of Establishing National Parks* (Washington, D. C.: U. S. Government Printing Office, June, 1961).

RECREATION IN THE FUTURE ECONOMY

A nation's economy depends as much upon the money which is spent as it does upon the money which is earned. Wholesome recreation does not, of course, cure all civic ills, but there is good reason to believe that recreation contributes to improving health standards, decreasing accidents, and curbing crime and delinquency. If the investment of funds in recreation can help young people find meaningful and wholesome ways of self fulfillment and less need to strike out at society, thereby saving the taxpayer some of the money he might otherwise spend on law enforcement and reformatories; if it can save a few of the lives of the thousands who are slaughtered on our highways; and if it can help make our citizenry more physically fit and thus assist in lowering medical and hospital bills, it is wise from the economic as well as the humanitarian point of view to support it fully.

Assuming that nations will find the way to "live in peace," it is likely that the scientific progress of man will result in increased production and a higher standard of living in many countries. Moreover, it will be possible to produce more of the world's goods with fewer man-hours of production. In other words, more people will enjoy more leisure. This does not necessarily mean that the work week will dwindle to an absolute minimum. The number of hours manual workers spend on the job each week may not be reduced considerably, but they may enjoy longer vacations. Surely more people will receive vacation periods.

As leisure increases, we can expect purchasing power and the national net income to increase. Organized labor has made it plain that it welcomes more time off the job—but not at the expense of the size of the pay check. Almost every study undertaken shows that the number of a person's recreation pursuits is related to his income. Usually, the higher his income, the more numerous and varied are the kinds of recreation in which he engages. That leisure will loom larger on the economic horizon of the future is certain, barring, of course, wars and depressions. This is so because the leisure market, from the standpoint of what the market can absorb, is practically open ended.

Full employment, in a space age, cannot be achieved through the manufacturing, agricultural, transportation, communication, and mining industries alone. The unprecedented increase of productivity in industry and agriculture means that a larger proportion of the working force can profitably be devoted to service functions, among which recreation is increasingly important. Yet to date, there is no field of human activity where our actual accomplishments have lagged so far behind our knowledge and our needs. Let the fields of health, recreation, welfare, and education flourish, and America will have its foundation for sound, lasting, economic development.

While the percentage of the population working in agriculture and industry in the United States is declining steadily, recreation and education are taking up the slack. We are spending as much on recreation as on food, and expenditures for recreation will increase in the future. While 25 years ago few Americans owned boats, now 12 to 15 per cent own them, and the two (plus) million Americans who travel abroad each year may well reach 50 million in another generation. Clearly, recreation and education seem capable of indefinite expansion because they are not subject to the same limitations of demand as food and housing.[28]

The values of recreation are most frequently expressed in social terms, as they should be. However, the line between social and economic values is not very sharp. Recreation has almost unbelievable economic advantages. Its role in helping stabilize and improve the national economy is large and significant.

THE WORKSHOP

1. Study the effects of parks and playgrounds in your community on the values of properties adjacent to these facilities.
2. Interview management representatives of a large industrial plant and determine what economic value, if any, they place on recreation opportunities for their employees.
3. Compare the costs of crime and delinquency in your county with the amount of public funds available for recreation, for education, for mental health.
4. Estimate the investment your community has made in park and recreation areas and properties.
5. Interview a member of your local Chamber of Commerce for promoting the travel and tourist business.
6. List the number and types of jobs and positions which would be created if the community and commercial recreation facilities of your town were doubled.
7. Prepare a questionnaire which could be used in finding out how much families spend for recreation.
8. Prepare a statement on recreation's contribution to making communities attractive to homeowners and business investors.
9. Set forth the economic implications of developing the international aspects of recreation.
10. Discuss recreation as a major employer of people—both those with and without formal preparation for park and recreation work. Do you see recreation as one of the fields of work which may provide the answer for the employment of the "poor"? Justify your answer.

[28] Harold F. Clark, "Education, Recreation and the Consumer Forecast," *Overview*, December, 1960, 14–15.

REFERENCES

Anderson, Jackson, M., *Industrial Recreation—A Guide To Its Organization and Administration*. New York: McGraw-Hill Book Company, 1955.

Anderson, Nels, *Work and Leisure*. New York: The Free Press, 1961.

Brockman, C. Frank, *Recreation Use of Wild Lands*. New York: McGraw-Hill Book Company, 1959.

Buckingham, Walter, *Automation*. New York: Mentor Executive Library Book, 1963.

California Public Outdoor Recreation Committee, *California Public Outdoor Recreation Plan*. Parts I and II. Sacramento: California State Printing Office, 1960.

Clawson, Marian, *Methods of Measuring the Demand for and Value of Outdoor Recreation Resources for the Future*. Washington, D. C.: 1959.

Denny, Revel, *The Astonished Muse*. Chicago: The University of Chicago Press, 1957.

Galbraith, John K., *The Industrial Society*. New York: Doubleday & Company, Inc., 1967.

Larrabee, Eric, and Rolf Meyersohn, eds. *Mass Leisure*. New York: The Free Press, 1958.

Lindeman, E. C., *Wealth and Culture*. New York: Harcourt, Brace & World, Inc., 1936.

Phelps, Edmund S., *Private Wants and Public Needs*. New York: W. W. Norton & Company, Inc., 1962.

Securities Research Division, *Leisure: Investment Opportunities in a $150–Billion Market,* New York: Merrill, Lynch, Pierce, Fenner & Smith, Inc., 1968.

Comments

Pertinent information on the economics of recreation can be found in literature related to land economics, travel, and the amusement and entertainment industries, as well as in financial publications such as the *Wall Street Journal*. Especially valuable are U.S. government releases issued periodically: *Statistical Abstracts of the United States, Compendium of City Government Finances, Compendium of State Government Finances and Large City Finances* (U.S. Bureau of the Census), and information published by the Accounts and Collection Unit of the Internal Revenue Service.

Magazines such as *The Nation, Business Week, Harvard Business Review,* and the *Investor News,* often contain articles on the "new" leisure and its economy significance. Also, the reports and publications of various state travel and economic development agencies are value resources. They provide an up-to-date analysis of one of recreation's biggest markets—tourism and pleasure travel.

4

Recreation Potentials and
Unequal Situations

Reaping the full benefits of the potentials of the Recreation Movement is one of the most challenging, stimulating and creative opportunities of this decade. Balancing some of the unequal places in the general program becomes society's definite responsibility. The past sixty years has witnessed the achievement of bringing to reality many potentials and creating significant steps forward in health, education, welfare and work along with recreation. Recreators are aware of these opportunities and are busy at work to harvest many additional accomplishments, and ameliorate and prevent negative forces in order to bring to the total population more abundant and wholesome recreation practices and pursuits.

Because humans are not perfect, and because there is always a wide margin between situations as they are and as we would like them to be, inequalities exist in community recreation as they do in any other vital area of society. But where there are deficiencies and inequalities, there are also potentials—and this is encouraging. Despite the significant advances which recreation has made since the beginning of the twentieth century, there is much room for improvement. Before discussing what needs to be done, it may be helpful to reflect upon recent developments.

The Social Work Yearbook for 1960 presents a list signifying some of the major advances of the recreation movement in the past decade.[1]

[1] National Association of Social Workers, *Social Work Year Book* (New York: The Association, 1960).

69

DEVELOPMENTS AND TRENDS

Among the more significant recent trends and developments are these:

Striking increase in number of local tax-supported recreation systems, especially in small towns and cities, and in budget increases for operations and capital expenditures.

Establishment of county recreation systems and park and recreation districts, making possible extension of recreation services to small communities and rapidly expanding fringe areas.

Development of watersheds, forests, large parks, and reservations for recreation uses, especially group and family camping, boating, picnicking, fishing, and related activities. Utilization of resources of public and private agencies, local and national, to serve recreation needs of armed forces personnel and their families.

Widespread recognition of the potentials of recreation among members of the medical and health professions and resulting increase in recreation services for the ill and handicapped.

Gradual development of a body of scientific knowledge on recreation based upon controlled study and research and of marked increase in available literature on all phases of recreation.

Cooperative planning and action by city and school authorities in acquisition, financing, development, management, and use of properties designed for both school and community recreation use.

Marked interest in preparation and use of long-range area and facility plans, related to comprehensive city and regional planning, as prerequisites to the acquisition of properties designed to provide recreation for city residents and rapidly growing fringe areas.

Widespread acceptance of the public recreation department as the central recreation agency providing basic recreation services to all the people.

Tendency to combine the administration of parks and organized recreation service under a single department.

Appreciable rise in the quality of recreation personnel and salary scales; also growing interest in registration and state certification.

Sharp reversal of the downward trend in college graduates with a recreation major and the need for an even greater recruitment effort to provide trained personnel for the ever increasing number of new positions.

Establishment of recreation internships by public recreation departments and state hospitals.

The provision of broad recreation programs for Air Force personnel and their families administered by trained civilian recreation directors.

The greater acceptance of recreation responsibility by the federal government as expressed by the establishment of the Bureau of Outdoor Recreation and plans for the National Cultural Center.

Mounting concern accompanied by an increasing public opposition to threatened encroachments on already inadequate recreation areas, as sites for fire and police stations, highways, schools, and other nonconforming purposes.

Modification of state recreation enabling legislation to meet changing conditions and needs; also marked expansion in state recreation services, administered by widely diversified agencies.

Appraisal and modification of policies relating to public recreation services in southern cities, resulting from the 1955 decisions of the United States Supreme Court. Several cities now make available to all citizens golf and other facilities previously operated on a segregated basis. Others have closed certain areas and facilities. State and local reaction to decisions on parks and recreation generally follows reaction to school decisions.

Unusual equipment and facility developments, construction methods and materials, such as creative playground apparatus, plexiglas and aluminum swimming pools, plastic pipe artificial ice skating rinks, and indoor-outdoor swimming pools.

So much for the immediate past. This chapter presents the areas where action is needed in the immediate years ahead. It offers suggestions for procedures, policies, and practices, so that community recreation will steadily and surely serve *all* the people.

Opportunities for All

The coordinated programs of public, private, and commercial recreation organizations comprise the total program of recreation services to the community. Services of government on all levels, municipal, county, state, and federal; services of private agencies such as the church, industry, youth serving agencies and clubs of many types; and commercial opportunities along all lines of recreation interests, for the most part determine the extent to which the people are served.

The opportunity for the more than two hundred million people living in this country to share in recreation is the supreme challenge to the field. The democratic way of life is based on the principle of equal opportunities. Every objective of recreation aims at providing a broad variety of activities to enhance the freedom of individual and group choices in the arts of leisure.

A vigorous campaign is needed to: (1) create more adequate federal recreation services to help the states and communities in reaching all individuals; (2) establish permanent recreation services in every state, with broad powers and opportunities to help advance community recreation for all the people; (3) establish county, district, and regional organization to provide recreation opportunities in rural areas and unincorporated villages and towns; (4) have every incorporated city in the United States establish recreation, with legal responsibilities designed to provide community recreation opportunity for all the people; (5) increase the recreation resources and services of private interests; and to (6) promote more commercial recreation of a wholesome nature.

The goal is to bring recreation opportunities to the total population, with adequate activities for participation individually and in groups. Following is a discussion of areas where inequalities still exist.

Natural Resources

Natural resources for recreation in the United States are widespread and vast. Unequal situations do exist, however, among regions and states, counties and cities, and also within neighborhoods of one community. We have some fine outdoor recreation resources, but as the population expands, as transportation improves, and with the ever-present pressures of industry, a "land grab" for all uses is evident, and our existing and potential resources for outdoor recreation may be threatened. The stimulating federal and state plans of the Bureau of Outdoor Recreation are most challenging and encouraging.

Ribbons of highways, larger and ever-expanding shopping centers, thousands of housing developments, growing industrial plants, and public demands assert the need for land resources. Lack of water supply dictates the harnessing of water resources to insure a proper supply for human and technological needs. These demands compete with the recreation potential—the use of waters, shore lines, and land resources for numerous recreation opportunities. Here, again, the appeal rises from the people for a democratic society to conserve and preserve a proportionate share of these natural resources for recreation purposes.

Small county forests, private forests, farm ponds and lakes, all form potentials for recreation services.

Areas suffering from floods, droughts, dust storms, hurricanes, and tornadoes are victims of unequal opportunities. Poor health conditions, poor economic return from the land, culture barriers, and folkway taboos, characteristic of certain localities, hinder progress.

While communities can do much for themselves, there is a need for government service to assist in equalizing recreation opportunities. Government subsidies, grants-in-aid, consultation services, and pooling of assistance from outside as well as from local sources are essential to adequate recreation opportunities. Just as the federal and state governments have accepted responsibility in flood control, checking of land erosion, and conserving forests, so must they accept responsibility in matters relating to the equalization of opportunities for good health, proper education, and adequate recreation through the assured preservation and conservation of natural resources.

Races and Nationalities

Throughout the history of the United States, races and nationalities have periodically played a major role in our cultural drama. The problems of race and minority groups are constantly challenging the nation to provide more abundant opportunities for all of its people, as the continuous development of the different ethnic groups moulds our national culture.

Today, the situation which provides the most critical problems is that of the Negro. This problem of race relations is of national significance, and its adjustments and adaptations must produce an equilibrium which takes into consideration what is best for all human beings.

Recreation provides a powerful influence in the assimilation of nationalities and races for social well-being. Programs of Americanization, the integration of immigrant groups, the promotion of wholesome race relations, and the constant processes of infiltration and blending, find in recreation a strong ally. By its very nature, recreation, with its spirit of togetherness, tends to promote the socialization, unity, and loyalty which are so desirable in all human relationships.

There are flagrant inequalities in organized recreation as applied to Negroes, especially in the South and in many large metropolises. Much could be written revealing lack of opportunity, inadequacy of provision, poor leadership, neglect, and prejudice. The story is not one worthy of our democracy.

While progress is slow, there are many indications that action is being taken and adjustments constantly being made. The situation is full of promise, with the trend toward richer and fuller advantages for all in community recreation. The decision of the United States Supreme Court prohibiting segregation in schools, parks, and other public centers, requires the soundest kind of handling on the part of recreation leadership.

The outstanding need is opportunity. Effective opportunity depends largely on practical types of interracial relationships being worked out between the white and Negro races. With two races living side by side, the problem is one of mutual adaptation for the best interests of each.

A few essential principles may be presented: (1) the welfare of all the people depends on the cooperative effort of both races with joint responsibilities, joint obligations, and joint opportunities for serving and working; (2) well informed, competent, and understanding leadership—men and women of goodwill—among the majority and minority is essential; (3) a clear recognition that problems of race relations are both real and difficult is necessary. The problem cannot be solved by sentiment, nor by superficial ideas and makeshift efforts. Neither will it work itself out by being avoided or ignored. Frank and honest recognition by both races of the difficulties involved is essential.

There is urgent need for solutions that are fair, sound, complete, and permanent. Problems must be clearly analyzed and then approached through effective organized effort.

Certain practices can be followed with constructive results: (a) Involve the Negro in *all* plans and procedures in the community recreation program—administration and organization, leadership, areas and facilities, finances, and other factors. (b) Include Negroes on all boards, commissions, and committees dealing with community recreation. (c) Provide adequate programs and services for *all* of the population of the community. (d) Make no discriminatory regulations, legal or traditional, which might hinder free and full participation of *anyone* in the community recreation program. These recreation principles apply to any and all races.

Age Groups

For years there were far more opportunities in community recreation for children and youth of school age than there were for the remainder of the population. In many places, this is still true. Encouragingly, however, the range of community recreation service, as far as groups are concerned, is broadening. The most pronounced deficiencies at present, in most communities, appear to be with adults, particularly young, married adults with families, and, of course, with older persons.

With adults, the feeling has always prevailed that the grown-up can satisfy his or her own leisure needs. As forces of socialization advance, they affect the recreation life of the adult, and community recreation programs assume a more prominent place in satisfying recreation desires and needs. Moreover, shorter working hours have given the average adult opportunity for more leisure.

Adults need skill in leisure activities. Opportunity must be provided to develop and foster these skills. Lack of skill appears to be a common recreation deficiency. Any use of leisure, whether it be reading, "big muscle" activity, or the pursuit of a hobby, depends upon activity, and satisfying activity, in turn, depends upon the use of fundamental skills.

The improvement and expansion of adult activity in community recreation will come about as a process of growth and development rather than through the sudden superimposing of an adult program on a community. The form it takes will be determined by conditions in each local community.

The number of people over 65 is steadily increasing, and community recreation is rapidly recognizing their needs and interests. Special activities under specially trained leaders who understand old age are necessary. Physical limitations, emotional patterns, mental status, and environmental conditions must be weighed. Recreation can help bring to the aging a new, refreshing, and constructive outlook and enrich their contributions to society.

Community recreation should provide opportunities for *all* ages as a part of a well-balanced program, recognizing age differences and serving them accordingly. The program should also include opportunities for participation of families of all ages.

Rural Life

The recreation movement in rural life is gradually becoming a bright picture of opportunities, programs, and actions. The 4-H Clubs, the Future Farmers of America, the consolidated rural school, a few church groups, and the Home and Farm Demonstration groups, along with such groups as the Grange and the Ruritans, include recreation in their programs. In none of these groups, however, is recreation recognized as a *primary* force, and hence it receives only secondary consideration.

The problem of providing a well-organized program of recreation for rural dwellers is a difficult one. It is essentially one of finance, facilities, and leadership, which the various units of government interested in recreation could help alleviate. A federal recreation service, in cooperation with the United States Agricultural Extension Service, could render many practical aids. State recreation services should place special emphasis on recreation for rural life.

The key to the problem could be county or district organization. A county or district recreation staff, with volunteer leaders, sufficient funds, and areas and facilities, could bring to the rural population adequate opportunities for recreation.

The consolidated rural school could also help immeasurably. At present, in many areas it is the leading institution for recreation in rural life. The school should, to the best of its ability and time, recognize and promote recreation.

As is indicated in Chapter 5, the rural dweller often finds recreation in urban centers. As communication and transportation expand, this trend will increase. The rural population is distinct from the urban only by reason of location and economic function. Otherwise, it was never as interdependent as it is today. Municipal life has become the criterion of rural America, and community recreation—public, private, and commercial—the pattern. The goal is to bring to rural life a full share of wholesome recreation without destroying the bases of ruralization.

Communities and Neighborhoods

The community is the focal point of organized recreation and this makes necessary the recognition of the neighborhood as a basic location of recreation service.

There are still many inequalities among and within neighborhoods in urban areas and unincorporated villages and towns. Economic conditions, social strata, political prestige, and group initiative provide for opportunities in one place and cause neglect in another. A policy of universal coverage regardless of location and status is the one way to prevent discrimination.

A survey of almost any locality will show parks, playgrounds, recreation centers, and other facilities in one section, and no provisions in another; adequate facilities for the upper and lower classes, and poor opportunities for the middle classes; the white neighborhood with ample areas, and the Negro quarters with few or none; the central area neglected, and the suburbs served. The old section of town "just grew up," while expanding developments are planned. One progressive rural area is alert to its recreation responsibilities, while another is oblivious. In one neighborhood the citizenry moves courageously ahead; in another it allows politics to block the way.

The goal is to establish a chain between and among neighborhoods within communities and among federal, state, county, and local governments to provide adequate recreation for *all* the people.

The Sexes

In few major aspects of modern society have inventions and technology wrought greater social change than in woman's role. Women are rapidly achieving equal status with men in all phases of life. Old barriers are torn down, old taboos and limitations abolished, and old beliefs and ideas changed. New worlds are opened, new opportunities are presented, and new interpretations are accepted.

Possibly one of the slowest fields to recognize this has been recreation. Separate programs, areas, and regulations for women are illustrative. While there are localities throughout the country where equal opportunity for both sexes in community recreation has prevailed, they are relatively few, and equality is still a thing of the future. There are "little leagues" for boys. Where are their counterparts for girls? To be sure, co-recreation is increasing in popularity both with youths and adults. The expansion of youth centers and teen-age groups can be explained by a desire for co-recreation. The expansion of community centers with co-recreation programs for adults is also apparent.

The youth-serving agencies also need to balance opportunities for girls and boys. Boys' clubs of all types had an early start and gained ground and stability before widespread interest in clubs for girls existed. Today, youth-serving agencies for girls are making rapid strides.

Until comparatively recently, women did not participate in athletics to any great extent. This was, and still is, mainly a man's field, but women are entering it in ever-increasing numbers and participating in a wider range of activities. Women have entered the fields of golf, skiing, tennis, swimming, basketball, softball, and other sports in local, regional, and national competition. In some sports, mixed tournaments are conducted.

The need for more recreation opportunities for girls does not necessarily call for the abolishment of separate activities for men and women. Also, the expansion of activities for boys need not be retarded until there is equality for girls. But we should recognize the needs of girls and women and try to equalize opportunities for them. Co-recreation should be encouraged whenever possible.

Economic and Social Strata

One test of the democratic process is the extent to which people of all economic levels and social strata can enjoy equal recreation opportunities. While it is true that the organized play movement had its origin in slum areas and was sponsored by philanthropy and charity, it no longer follows this pattern, but seeks to establish the principle of social responsibility and opportunity. In considering recreation in families of low income and among people less socially advanced, responsibility and opportunity are the keynotes.

The nation as a whole is just beginning to meet the situation. The federal government has assumed leadership. Through social security, old age assistance, rehabilitation programs, urban renewal programs, slum clearance and other projects, the organic needs of humans are being served. There is equally large need to serve their social and recreation needs. Obviously, families should not be deprived of opportunities for recreation because of their economic or social status. The question has been settled in public education and can be similarly settled in recreation—a social responsibility to be met by public concern and action.

The answer is in the growing, popular recognition that recreation is essential to the well-being of individuals and groups and hence must find adequate expression in every neighborhood and community. Combined public, private, and commercial resources must face the challenge of this responsibility and work vigorously to meet it.

The problem need not involve competition between public and private forces. There is ample room for both, and both are necessary to meet existing and growing needs. The present weakness is public apathy and the lack of public recognition, responsibility, and financial investment.

Recreation Illiteracy

Education has established tests and measurements of educational illiteracy, and statistics to fractions of degrees are available. There are abundant facts on national health, agricultural production, and bank assets. But no figures exist showing the extent of recreation illiteracy. Recreators and students, however, believe that the percentage is high.

The challenge is to teach the individual and the group the arts of living along with the arts of making a living. Recreation illiteracy is dangerous. The misuse, misinterpretation, and unwise use of recreation can cause increased individual and social pathology. Campaigns against recreation illiteracy should be waged as vigorously as those against educational illiteracy.

The recreation department, the school, the church, and the family can join forces in banishing recreation illiteracy. Teaching every person some recreation skills, providing adequate areas and facilities, recognizing abilities and capacities, and encouraging participation will produce a generation of recreation literates who in turn will pass on to future generations the richness of abundant living.

Knowledge About Recreation—Research

Two facts are most evident in the field of recreation: (1) The best in program quality is found in too few places; and (2) Research in recreation has been too long neglected. We need to know much more about recreation and how it can be used to benefit mankind.

The leisure habits and interests of people need to be determined. The techniques and methods of research in recreation need to be developed, tested, and applied. We need to learn more about programming, leadership skills, staff development, the design and maintenance of areas and facilities, equipment, operational costs and finance, and other problems.

Recreation research is an open field. In theory and philosophy, in practices and procedures, for evaluation and measurement, in individual and group desires and needs, for studies and surveys, in planning and in all aspects of organization and administration, more factual knowledge based upon sound research is needed.

The data and findings of research should be widely shared and disseminated. Efforts should be made to interest universities and colleges, foundations, organizations, and individuals in supporting recreation research on national, regional, state, and local levels.

The recreation forces need sound guidance based upon *sound* research in organization, administration, program, personnel, areas and facilities, interpretation, finance, and planning.

Legislative Enactments

Proper legislation to assure soundness of structure, permanency of program, and abundant opportunities has often been too slow in enactment. All government agencies are beginning to show a general alertness and liberality in recreation legislation. A review of recent bills introduced in

Congress, in state legislatures, and by city and county law-makers reveals a trend toward strengthening existing laws, passing new legislation, and encouraging the repeal of laws that hinder the progress of recreation.

In a number of states no court action has been taken to determine the legality of recreation laws or practices. Too often recreation is not recognized by the judicial branch of government as a necessity and hence a constitutional right. Effort must be forthcoming to have state constitutions and local charters recognize recreation as a public need.

Local laws are frequently inadequate, with emphasis on specific limitations rather than on what might be accomplished. Recreation leadership too often neglects the legal aspects of administration.

The goal is to broaden the horizon of community recreation by providing a solid legislative base in the communities, the states, and the nation. Laws should advance, not impede the progress of recreation.

Adequate Funds

A major hindrance to the expansion of organized recreation is lack of funds. Sometimes community willingness is handicapped by insufficient means. There is no money; the tax limits have been reached; all funds have been appropriated; only a meager sum is left; the people do not wish to increase taxes; too many drives and campaigns are already functioning. These factors impede progress.

Under such conditions, the recreation program merely exists, fighting for a pittance, operating on a "shoestring" budget, living from day to day, or balancing the budget by paying inadequate salaries and functioning with few areas and little equipment. A wholesome program, on any level, must be adequately financed. A well-organized community recreation program giving abundant services to the people should be supported to the limit.

Where funds have been budgeted to long-existing agencies, a rearrangement of the budget may be necessary or the tax rate raised. The stronger and richer the program in services, the more popular should be the support.

Community recreation leadership should not request funds out of proportion to a community's financial resources. Unwise and unnecessary expenditures should be checked.

Seasonal Approach

While the emphasis of organized public recreation in many places has been on a summer program, trends show increased recreation services throughout the entire year. There is certainly nothing against a summer program, but the other seasons need attention, too. Shorter working hours, staggered vacations, popularity of seasonal activities, recognition of the need for all-year-round recreation, and other factors require programs on a yearly basis.

Festival celebrations throughout the year, indoor and outdoor activities related to seasonal interests, a continuous schedule of events, special emphasis on other seasons as well as summer, opportunities for tourist interest at all times, and a year-round program of leagues, tournaments, and contests are indicative of ways to meet the program needs.

Community recreation programs should be provided on a full-time, year-round basis.

Types of Activities

Even a cursory study of the activity program, no matter where it functions, indicates that athletics, sports, and games predominate. This is natural and will undoubtedly continue. Too often, however, this is the extent of what is offered to the community.

An effective community recreation program serves the interests and needs of all of the people. The balanced recreation program provides opportunity for enjoyment in each major area of recreation—athletics, games and sports, music, drama, arts and crafts, social recreation, nature recreation and camping, and others. In such a program, no single phase receives the greatest attention or absorbs the bulk of the leadership, facilities, and funds. Variety of choice leads to freedom of choice and opportunity. A well-balanced recreation program is an equitable one for both sexes, all ages, all groups, and all interests.

Areas and Facilities

Community recreation needs adequate areas and facilities for effective operation—indoor and outdoor facilities and equipment together with recreation buildings of all types and specific outdoor areas. Without play spaces, fields, and parks, without centers, aquatics facilities, gymnasiums, theaters, and other structures, the program cannot function properly.

Although it is true that much can be done without any type of facility and with little equipment, it is also true that given proper facilities, the program can be enriched. Location of areas and costs of facilities, maintenance and operation must all be considered, and expenditures apportioned on the basis of numbers served. It is always best to provide areas and facilities within reach of the people and of a type serving the largest number at minimum cost.

The community can well afford to possess both an immediate and long-range plan for acquiring areas and facilities.

Leadership and Preparation

The success of organized recreation depends primarily upon the quality and availability of the professional personnel associated with it. Leadership, perhaps more than anything else, is a resource which must be strengthened greatly in recreation. More people must be brought into the profession who have natural talents and interests in recreation. The resources for preparing persons for the professional field of recreation must be geared to meet the constantly increasing demand for qualified personnel. Undergraduate and graduate recreation curricula in the colleges and universities need to be refined, improved, and expanded. Efforts must be made to strengthen all forms of recreation education and training, including that which takes place on-the-job.

There is also a need to establish professional standards. Job analyses, merit systems, security on the job, promotion opportunity, satisfactory wage schedules, and retirement plans are likewise necessary.

Consideration should be given to the preparation of recreation specialists. Too few opportunities now exist for preparing specialists in recreation for the ill and disabled, as well as in such functional specialties as nature and outing, arts and crafts, athletics, sports, and games, music and drama.

Greater cooperation should exist between the recreation agencies and the institutions of higher learning. The closer their relations, the more efficient will be the results. The teacher must know what is going on in the field and what the field needs in leadership, thereby cementing the ties between preparation and actual practice.

A PROGRAM OF ACTION

Adjusting the inequalities within the recreation framework of our democracy is a social responsibility that recreation leadership should accept. Time and action will overcome most of them and give the population equal opportunities to make of recreation a more potent force for better living.

To assure progress for the future a program of action is presented offering ten specific projects:

1. *Interpreting recreation:* stressing its significance; proclaiming its importance; giving it the dignity it deserves; recognizing the dangers of its misuse and abuse; initiating a program to ameliorate recreation illiteracy; utilizing recreation's preventive values; stating its vigorous role in the national economy; defining its potentials; and correlating its services.

2. *Planning for recreation:* making equal the currently unequal opportunities of recreation in the democracy; getting maximum results from all efforts; eliminating waste, duplication and misuse; looking ahead and planning on a long range basis; applying expert knowledge and "know-how"; providing practical plans for acquiring, building, and maintaining; using natural and technological resources wisely.

3. *Stressing research:* providing more knowledge about what recreation can do for people and about the profession itself through surveys, appraisals, inventories, tests; applying research methods; utilizing and developing university and college opportunities.

4. *Preparing leaders* (there is no substitute for a well-prepared leader, professional or volunteer): formulating development techniques; building curricula, instituting workshops, conferences, and clinics; promoting staff development programs on a continuing basis; establishing personnel standards; developing professional codes; improving salaries, tenure, and retirement provisions.

5. *Enriching program opportunities:* promoting a balanced and continuing program for all ages and races, both sexes, and all social and economic strata; encouraging unique and stimulating practices; stressing opportunities for self-fulfillment.

6. *Building areas and facilities resources:* preserving and increasing areas; building better outdoor and indoor facilities; adding to equipment; utilizing gains of technology; employing qualified planners and engineers; making maximum use of natural resources; providing functional, but also beautiful, physical resources.

7. *Advancing specialties:* serving areas of specialization such as recreation for the aging, the ill, and the handicapped; developing a large corps of technically prepared personnel for these purposes.

8. *Multiplying source materials:* creating, writing and publishing materials of high quality; utilizing the resources of radio, television, motion pictures, and other audio-visual media for enriching programs and adding to the knowledge of the profession.

9. *Coordinating efforts:* coordinating resources for community recreation functions through public, private, and commercial channels.

10. *Taking a stand:* identifying and facing important challenges, controversial issues; being well informed, taking a stand and knowing "why"; being courageous and willing to campaign vigorously, articulately, and convincingly for what is best for the people through recreation.

THE WORKSHOP

1. List all of the inequalities that can be found in the local community recreation program. Arrange these in order of importance.
2. Set forth, briefly, a plan to eliminate these inequalities.
3. Examine the recreation opportunities which exist for minorities in your community.
4. Try to identify six recreation trends in your locality.

5. Determine what age groups are included in your community recreation program. List each group according to recreation opportunities. Where are the inequalities?
6. Present a brief plan to eliminate inequalities among neighborhoods in your community.
7. Examine the causes of inequalities in the local community recreation program and suggest ways to eliminate them.
8. Suggest ways to decrease or eliminate recreation illiteracy.
9. Compare the recreation inequalities between urban and rural living today and several decades ago.
10. Note any developments that might indicate the coming of new inequalities and suggest ways of checking them.

REFERENCES

Current

Anderson, Nels, *Work and Leisure.* New York: The Free Press, 1962.

Brightbill, Charles K., *Man and Leisure.* Englewood Cliffs, New Jersey: Prentice-Hall, Inc., 1961.

Brightbill, Charles K., and Harold D. Meyer, *Recreation—Texts and Readings.* Englewood Cliffs, New Jersey: Prentice-Hall, Inc., 1953.

Burns, C. Delisle, *Leisure in the Modern World.* New York: The Century Company, 1932.

Butler, George D., *Introduction to Community Recreation,* 3rd Edition. New York: McGraw-Hill Book Company, 1959.

Carlson, Reynold E., Theodore R. Deppe, and Janet R. MacLean, *Recreation in American Life.* Belmont, California: Wadsworth Publishing Company, 1963.

Chapman, Frederick M., *Recreation Activities for the Handicapped.* New York: The Ronald Press Company, 1960.

Cutten, George B., *The Threat of Leisure.* New Haven: Yale University Press, 1926.

Douglass, Paul F., John L. Hutchinson, and Willard C. Sutherland, eds., *Recreation in the Age of Automation.* Philadelphia: The Annals of the American Academy of Political and Social Science, 1957.

Larrabee, Eric, and Rolf Meyersohn, eds., *Mass Leisure.* New York: Free Press of Glencoe, Inc., 1958.

Pack, Arthur N., *The Challenge of Leisure.* New York: The Macmillan Company, 1936.

Robbins, Florence G., *The Sociology of Play, Recreation and Leisure.* Dubuque, Iowa: William C. Brown Company, Publishers, 1955.

Slavson, S. R., *Recreation and the Total Personality.* New York: Association Press, 1946.

Zelomek, A. Wilbert, *A Changing America at Work and Play.* New York: John Wiley & Sons, Inc., 1959.

Comments

The reports on the White House Conference on Children and Youth and on the White House Conference on the Aging, available from the Department of Health, Education and Welfare, Washington, D. C., include a wealth of information on recreation inequalities and needs. Additional material can be found in current periodicals with articles on the needs of minorities, the rising population, leadership, all aspects of administration and others.

Also note many references made to this concept in Chapters 1 and 2. Also, references in many of the chapters dealing with special subjects.

It will be a stimulating adventure to test each inequality as applied to the local community, city, and county. Where applicable, note the progress and the needs of state and federal action: set up programs of action to eliminate the unequal places and move toward achievement of the potentials involved.

When agencies and organizations have already delved into these potentials and have set up immediate and long-range plans of action, evaluate results from time to time.

Study the numerous books relative to this subject. Practically all of them in some ways are connected to suggestions and practical procedures to conquer specific inequalities.

As you read current magazines in our field note articles on these subjects and utilize and test suggested plans.

At most conferences, workshops, institutes, and conventions the themes, programs, discussion groups and major addresses are woven around these topics.

The National Recreation and Park Association is making interesting and practical plans to eradicate many of these factors.

II

Recreation
and Government

Above: The public domain.
Right: City playgrounds
promote juvenile *decency*.
Below: The park has a proper claim on the public
treasury.

Above: Children's fairyland. Left: The state park is not *all* land. Below: International flavor in recreation planning.

5

Government and Urban Affairs

GOVERNMENT

Government is *a process through which man functions in an orderly fashion.* It has been said that without government, anarchy and chaos would envelop the people. Actually, government is a political institution, created by people, for people, which, if conceived and administered wisely and democratically, makes it possible for people who have common bonds and interests to do *collectively* what they would otherwise be unable to do *individually,* in the absence of a common authority.

There was a time when government was largely concerned with the security of those it served, providing protection from outside threats and maintaining law and order within its political boundaries. All institutions, including government, if they are to survive, must change as conditions and the needs of people change. And government has done so. It has widened its interests and multiplied its services, at all levels, to contribute more effectively to the well-being of the people.

Because democratic government is concerned with the well-being of its citizens and because wholesome recreation contributes to that well-being, recreation, therefore, becomes a responsibility and function of government. This is not an *exclusive* responsibility. The individual, the family, and all institutions and organizations which purport to serve mankind also have a responsibility for providing opportunities for recreation.

But there are other factors which tend to support the validity of the role of government in recreation:

1. Democratic government is democratically *supported* by all. It should serve
   the *entire population,* regardless of age, sex, race, creed, social or economic
   status. Tax funds are the main basis of support in a democratic government.
   These *public* funds should serve *public purposes,* among them the recreational needs of the people.
2. Government alone has the financial resources to acquire, establish, improve,
   and operate recreation facilities in adequate amounts to meet the needs of
   the public.
3. Government alone has the power of eminent domain, that is, the right to
   take, or authorize the taking of, private property for public use, when such
   action is in the best interests of the public and just compensation is given
   the owner.
4. Government is continuous and permanent. Services such as health, education,
   and *recreation,* which are basic to the well-being of people, should not be
   sporadically provided.
5. Public recreation, largely because it serves the public in volume, can be
   provided at a minimum per capita cost.
6. The majority of the courts in the United States have held recreation to be a
   governmental function. They have done this when questions of liability have
   arisen, acting upon the belief that all of the people are benefitting from
   recreation, with the municipality serving as an agent of the state for governmental purposes.
7. Government, because it represents and serves all of the people, is in the best
   position to develop the basic policy upon which effective recreation service
   must depend.
8. Perhaps the most convincing of all the arguments which buttress the contention that recreation is a legitimate function of government in the United
   States is that the people have "so willed it." Recreation, in one way or another, has been a function of government at different levels in the United
   States for decades. It has been started by the people, used and developed by
   the people, and financed by the people through their town, city, district,
   county, state, and national governments.

THE URBAN SETTING

The growth of cities is the outcome of industrialization, of our once
largely agricultural nation becoming mainly industrial. Since the Industrial Revolution, people have migrated increasingly from the rural areas
(agricultural needs could be met with fewer workers) to the cities for
employment. Cities, however, were located and developed more for reasons of economic expediency (e.g., accessibility of raw materials, manpower, and markets for industry) than for proper living conditions.

At first, the cities created as many problems as they solved. For while
they offered more jobs, sometimes at better pay, they were also noisy
and dirty, and bred discrimination and social unrest. These centers, with

their dense populations and congested living quarters, became the substitutes for the isolation and open space so common in rural areas. Gradually, however, after much hardship and disillusionment, some people became aware of the tragedies of city life and took steps to make their brick and mortar habitats more safe and attractive, while others abandoned it for the suburb and a new form of "country-living." Consequently, divisions of philosophy and thinking occurred and today we have many cities in revolution. The ghetto dwellers are seeking expression, the politicians are reassessing the political forces, and community and civic leaders are charting new legislative and organization patterns to assure the future growth of Urban America. Recreation is one of the factors under study, for the opportunity to engage in a wider variety of recreation has always been one of the attractions of the city.

The rise in urbanization in the United States has been phenomenal. Not only have the cities grown far more rapidly than the rural areas, but there has also been a marked tendency for the population to be concentrated in a relatively small number of areas. By the first half of the twentieth century, 56 per cent of the population in the United States was located in 168 standard metropolitan areas (i.e., counties or groups of counties surrounding cities of 50,000, or more).

According to the Census Bureau today, seven out of every ten, or 70 per cent, of the citizens in the United States live in urban areas. (The Bureau defines an urban area as one which has a population density of at least 1500 persons per square mile and is a densely settled city suburb, or a town with more than 2500 persons.) Six out of ten Americans live in or near the 212 cities with more than 50,000 people. This is in contrast with the situation in 1880 when seven out of ten Americans lived *not* in the cities but on the farms and in small towns. Some social scientists predict that by the year 2000, 85 per cent of the people of the United States will be urban dwellers.

With the growth of cities has come a great transformation in the living habits of society. The city has affected all phases of man's life. The customs, moral codes, behavioral patterns, and cultural conditions of a people revolve around it. New communities, new groups, new ethnic relations, and a multitude of classes make of the city an intricate and complex unit of modern society. As society becomes more urbanized, its controls become more impersonal and group-centered. Its members become more dependent on each other and the social organizations it creates to meet its needs. It requires constant evaluation of its efforts and areas of concern, and as its members become more heterogeneous, its forms of service take on new dimensions and structures.

Along with the problems of meeting health, safety, social welfare, and educational needs in the population centers, there is also the need for adequate recreation opportunities. There must be places where people can participate and places where people can watch others perform. There must be management and leadership. The operation and maintenance of these resources must be financed. Some of the recreation which the city dweller or suburbanite wants and needs can be provided by himself for himself and his family and friends. In other instances, commercial recreation enterprises can satisfy his tastes. Many of his needs, however, must be met through *community* recreation provision, and a large share of these needs must be served through *public* recreation.

The complex, tension-arousing patterns which the stress of work and overcrowding develop in population centers call for various recreation opportunities to help offset these threats to the inner stability of the urban dweller. Recreation of the right kind can provide not only the chance for sociability, but also for quiet contemplation, solitude, and relaxation. It can provide diversion from a routine and regimented existence, thereby releasing us, temporarily, from the burdens of frustration and worry. It can be a means of sparking our physical development in an environment which tends to keep our large muscles inactive. It can provide us with self-fulfilling activities, tie us to the past, and give us a true sense of freedom. Parks, historical sites, recreation areas—all are important to our general well-being and emotional health.

It is interesting to note that in recent years a large number of city residents have sought to return to the more spacious, if not less complicated, living of the suburbs. For example, although the population of the United States grew from 151 million in 1950 to 185 million in 1961, during that same period, the population in the great cities, such as Boston, New York, Cleveland, Chicago, and San Francisco, began to decrease. People moved to the suburbs—the twilight zones between city and country—until the concentric circles of residences which ring the cities began to touch one another. Consequently, in some places it is now difficult to tell what is part of one metropolitan area and what is part of another.

In the suburbs are found open space, plant life, and plenty of refreshing air. Here the healthful outdoor advantages of rural living can be found without the accompanying inconveniences. Here new and self-sufficient neighborhoods with their own schools, shopping centers, and community facilities may be intelligently planned and developed. The suburb is a natural setting for recreation. Although the flow of population has been from rural to urban for decades, for a part of the population it is now a flow from rural to urban to suburban, with even a trickle back to the rural. Many suburbs have their own systems of government, their own institutions, and their own resources for community recreation. The advent of the suburb, however, has not erased the problems of the city. In some instances, it has increased them. Often, those who live in the suburbs use the recreation facilities of the city yet contribute no taxes, are unable to exercise voting rights and assume little leadership in the support and direction of the municipality's recreation and park service. These people may be the best educated, affluent and energetic members of the community, but due to their place of residence they are disfranchised, while those who remain within the city's limits are asked to assume support of a service for which they are less prepared but desperately need. The result of this defection by the more affluent to suburbia is obvious and suggests a redefinition of the community and its area of legal jurisdiction.

RECREATION IN URBAN AND SUBURBAN RESIDENCE

Although the increase in off-the-job time, income, and mobility of the people enlarges the distances they will travel for recreation opportunities which attract them, a large number of recreation resources must be available close to the centers of residence. Reference is made to *neighborhood, community,* and *district* areas of urban regions. Using the area served by the elementary school as the neighborhood, the California Public Outdoor Recreation Plan Committee uses the following kinds of *urban* patterns.[1]

RECREATION USE PATTERN	SERVICE AREA	POPULA-TION	SERVICE RADIUS
For ages 5–14 within 3–10 minute walk	Neighborhood	to 3200	to ½ mile
For young people and adults within 10–30 minute walk or near public transportation	Community	to 25,000	to 2 miles
For adults within 30–60 minute walk, near public transportation or within 15 minute drive	District	to 100,000	to 5 miles

Note: According to the same authority, the above patterns are mainly in Zone #1—*within the neighborhood* and within the community. This is in contrast with Zone #2— within approximately 40 miles of the dwelling and accessible on one-day round trips; Zone #3a—within approximately 125 miles of the dwelling, for overnight trips of one to three nights; Zone #3b—within approximately 250 miles of the dwelling, for vacation trips of four to nine nights, and Zone #4—extending beyond Zone #3, for vacation trips of 10 nights or longer.

HOUSING

Public housing developments, like community recreation services, are a product of twentieth-century urbanization. Housing today implies more

[1] California Public Outdoor Recreation Plan Committee, *California Public Outdoor Recreation Plan,* Part II (Sacramento: California State Printing Office, 1960), pp. 13, 71.

than providing mere shelter. Provisions for family living, city planning, and community services, including recreation, are all a part of modern housing developments.

Possibly two out of every three families in the United States can provide and maintain their own homes, and more than 50 per cent own their own dwellings. But for many families of low income this is not possible. When houses cannot be properly maintained, slums result. Slums breed ill health, crime, and other social problems. Noise, dirt, and confusion are compounded in sub-standard housing areas. Inadequate housing, however, is not confined to slums alone.

Community facilities in housing developments include schools, libraries, religious facilities, and police, fire, and health protection. They also include facilities and services for recreation and cultural activities. Play lots, playgrounds, playfields, and parks, as well as community recreation centers with auditoriums, gymnasiums, club and game rooms, shops, and other facilities are essential in housing developments.

The problems and needs of tenants in housing developments are related to the welfare of the total community. All community facilities and services of housing developments, including recreation, must be a part of the community pattern and a shared responsibility of that community. True, housing developments are planned neighborhoods set apart physically from the rest of the community, but planning to meet the recreation needs of the families within the development cannot be unrelated to the rest of the community. The residents of housing developments should be encouraged to use the recreation facilities and services and to seek community-wide recreation opportunities. Likewise, non-residents of the development should be allowed to use the "on-site" facilities. Recreation has much to offer as an integrating force between the housing tenants and the surrounding neighborhood.

Recognizing the value of recreation for the adequate development of both neighborhoods and communities, the Department of Housing and Urban Development has established several programs to assist local units with their recreation services. Among these are the Neighborhood Facilities, Open Space, Urban Beautification, and Urban Planning Assistance programs. When coordinated with other federal programs, such as the Land and Conservation Fund, they provide an excellent resource for the expansion and improvement of urban recreation facilities.

Planning Principles for Facilities in Housing Developments

The basic principles for the planning, designing, and operation of recreation facilities in housing developments are much the same as those set forth for community recreation generally. (See Chapter 23, Administration.)

Other principles of direct application to housing developments are as follows:

1. The recreation facilities of a housing development should complement rather than duplicate existing community facilities. They should be conveniently located and adequate to the needs of the development and surrounding neighborhood.
2. Provision should be made for play lots, playgrounds, and playfields in addition to adequate indoor community recreation center facilities, including auditorium, gymnasium, social facilities, club and game rooms, lounge, sanitary facilities, kitchen, and storage.
3. Conditions being equal, it is less expensive and more satisfactory in the long run to provide one large area rather than several small ones. This, of course, must be tempered with the problem of accessibility and the age group which the area is intended to serve. Control, supervision, leadership, and program are all made easier when facilities are not scattered.
4. Tenant-initiated self-government and self-help activities and services should be encouraged.
5. If charges and rentals are made for the use of community facilities of the development, they should be made only when and where additional costs of operation are incurred by additional hours of operation. Under no circumstances should charges exceed actual additional costs of operation and maintenance.
6. The extent to which the recreation facilities of the development are used by other than its own residents should be determined by the capacity of the facilities and equipment as related to tenant needs.
7. The more isolated the housing development, the more acute is the need for recreation opportunities in the development.
8. The tenants should be encouraged not only to take an active part in the development's recreation program, but also to become actively interested and assume responsibilities in the community-wide recreation system.
9. It is wise for management, tenants, and the municipality to invest financially in the recreation services of the housing development.
10. Municipal recreation authorities should be consulted and invited to join in the planning of the recreation facilities and services of the development.

Real Estate Subdivisions

The preceding information on housing refers largely to public housing. All or much of it, however, applies to housing developments provided by private enterprise as well. Recreation facilities have been provided in literally hundreds of real estate developments in the last 25 years, and more can be expected in the future. In some localities, public planning requires developers to set aside space for park and recreation purposes. Real estate developers are taking seriously, and with good results, the observation of the New York State Association of Real Estate Boards, "A master plan for parks and recreation areas is not a dream; it is absolutely essential to provide sound, stable real estate values."

Aside from the values which recreation has for the health, safety, and contentment of families, there is evidence to support the contention that recreation properties, properly located, planned, beautified, constructed, and operated have a beneficial effect on raising land and real-estate values. Large and small real-estate divisions alike are providing adequate recreation space. Some developers head their real estate advertisements with the caption, "Use our playgrounds, our community swimming pool, our community center." Sometimes the municipality or larger political subdivision takes responsibility for financing the acquisition of the areas. In other cases, the value of the land set aside is pro-rated among the existing or potential property owners or paid for by the developer himself. Not infrequently, sub-marginal space, or land otherwise not suitable for the construction of houses, can be made available for recreation development. The increasing importance of providing adequate recreation space, facilities, and service in real estate developments is apparent.

With these matters in mind then—the places and conditions of residence, ecological aspects, sociological patterns, and individual characteristics in the urban population center—let us turn our attention to making recreation opportunities available to the public and the concomitant problem of managing and administering them.

PUBLIC ADMINISTRATION OF RECREATION

Purpose of Administration

If recreation is a responsibility of government, it is *first* the responsibility of *local* government. Local government is closest to the people; it is in the local community where recreation is most closely wedded to the interests and needs of the people. Local government, then, is faced with the problem of how to administer public recreation services.

Gilbert Y. Steiner's concept of local government is "as an agency which serves, regulates, protects, administers, democratizes, and employs," although there may be differences in opinion as to the relative importance of these roles.² Recreation as a public service fits into a number of these roles.

The process of mobilizing, organizing, and applying the resources directed toward providing recreation opportunities for the people is what constitutes administration. The recreation facilities and areas must be acquired, developed, maintained, and controlled. Recreation centers and services must be planned, promoted, operated, and managed. Personnel must be employed and supervised. Responsibility for establishing policies and regulations, as well as spending public funds and accounting for them, must be fixed. A managing authority, legally constituted, must be established.

Variety in Public Administration of Recreation

Local administration of recreation in one sense is shaped by permissive *state* laws. Reference is made to the state recreation laws, state park codes, state school codes, and the like, which are discussed later in this book. Insofar as the state laws represent the desires of the people, it can be said that the local people themselves decide how recreation and other public services are to be administered.

Unlike local public education in the United States, the administration of local public recreation has not held to a single pattern. Public school systems, with few exceptions, are administered by local boards of education. Not so with local public recreation systems. In some places, local public recreation is administered as a separate function of government, as is the case with recreation commissions, boards, and departments. In other localities, public recreation is administered in conjunction with parks—park and recreation boards, departments, and districts. Some communities administer recreation in conjunction with schools through local boards of education, school districts, and the like. Still other cities and towns administer public recreation services in a variety of ways other than the three most extensively used that are mentioned above.

Of the larger metropolitan cities, Washington, D. C., is a fine example of the "recreation as a separate function" type, Minneapolis the "park" approach, and Milwaukee the "school-sponsored" effort. Some of the larger cities administer public recreation under more than one authority. Examples are Chicago, with its Park District and Board of Education, and Los Angeles, with its Recreation and Park Department and Board of Education.

2 Lois M. Pelekoudas, ed., *Illinois Local Government,* Final Report and Background Papers, Assembly on Illinois Local Government (University of Illinois: Institute of Government and Public Affairs, 1961), p. 21.

Some idea of both the *diversity* and the *trend* among managing authorities for local public recreation can be ascertained from the following:

TYPE OF MANAGING AUTHORITY	1940 [3]	1950 [4]	1961 [5]	1966 [6]
Authorities administering recreation as a single function (recreation commissions, boards, departments, etc.).	324	702	949	818
Authorities administering recreation in conjunction with parks.	293	532		
Parks only.			549	423
Combined parks and recreation.			466	1304
Authorities administering recreation in conjunction with schools.	186	287	274	102
Authorities administering recreation under other jurisdictions such as welfare, public works, etc.	179	303	530	

As indicated earlier, the patterns of administration vary between and
among states and the cities and towns within them. In North Carolina, for
example, there are many local recreation commissions. Wisconsin cities
administer many public recreation services under the jurisdiction of the
public boards of education. In Illinois, where state park laws are most
liberal as far as recreation is concerned, there are 90 recreation boards
or commissions, 173 park districts, plus 90 other local park authorities.
There is but a *single* authority in the state administering public recreation
in conjunction with the schools.

The number of park departments has increased greatly since the end
of World War II, and when scanned from a national point of view, with
no focus on any particular section of the nation, it is apparent that there
has been *a clear trend in the direction of merging local park and recreation
services under a single authority.* This is best typified at the national
level with the recent merger of the five major park and recreation societies
and organizations into the National Recreation and Park Association.

Although there are a variety of methods for administering local public
recreation services, the pattern of administration must be consistent with
the provisions of the state laws. The choice of one type of administrative
vehicle over another should be made in terms of local conditions. Often
the resources of a department of government or the attitudes, interests,
and capabilities of those associated with it are the determining factors
in deciding which type of managing authority is likely to be the most effec-

[3] *Recreation Magazine,* June, 1941.

[4] National Recreation Association, *Recreation and Park Yearbook, Mid-Century
Edition—A Review of Local and County Recreation and Park Developments, 1900–1950*
(New York: The Association), 1951.

[5] Letter, George D. Butler, National Recreation Association, Dec. 5, 1961.

[6] National Recreation and Park Association, *Recreation and Park Yearbook, 1966.*
(Washington, D. C.: The Association), 1967.

tive. To be sure, the best structured administrative pattern can fail if the people responsible for its progress are uninterested, unwilling, or unable to make it work. Conversely, the "right" people can often make an inadequate administrative structure succeed.

The pros and cons of the most extensively used types of managing authority are as follows:

Authorities Which Administer Recreation as a Single Function (Recreation Commissions and Boards)

This type of managing authority has as its *single* function the provision of public recreation services. Usually, emphasis is upon recreation *program* and *leadership,* rather than on the acquisition and maintenance of property. More often than not, the recreation board attempts to secure the use of resources of other local units of government, such as the parks and schools. It is not unusual for school board and park board members to be members, also, of the local recreation board.

Arguments *for* authorities which administer recreation as a single function contend that under such circumstances recreation receives the undivided attention it requires, and that its progress is not likely to be hampered by the time and effort required for other functions. It is believed that its budget is less likely to be threatened and that the chances for its receiving more adequate financial support are improved. It is held that a managing authority which has representation from the several local departments whose resources are needed for recreation is in a more favorable position to coordinate the total effort. Finally, it is argued that because the range of service and number of people served are great, recreation affairs should be managed by an authority easy to identify when it comes to placing responsibility for the success or failure of the service.

Arguments *against* this type of authority point out that it simply adds to the overhead and burden of an already overweighted administrative structure and unnecessarily creates another device whose function can be served by an existing one; that it would seem better to strengthen existing resources rather than adding new ones. Recreation boards must depend upon the parks and the schools for their facilities or run the costly risk of duplicating them. Under no circumstances can the school and park resources be controlled by authorities other than their own. It is said that difficulties of jurisdiction, responsibility, and administration arise, and that inter-functional representation does not necessarily result in unity of action.

An appropriate *balance of facts* would include the observation that the largest single advantage of the recreation board or commission is that it recognizes the importance of recreation as an essential function on a co-relative, if not a co-equal status (in terms of financial support) with such other vital public services as education and health. Recreation does require a wide variety of resources and the kind of administrative machinery which will coordinate, mobilize, and use them effectively. Recreation should *not* be relegated to a niche of secondary consideration. On the other hand, the elements of dependency and cooperation with other groups are always present with this type of authority, and its success is often determined by them.

Board or Single Department Head

If a community decides that it wants to establish a separate recreation service, it is then confronted with the problem of whether to place responsibility in (a) a board or commission or in a department head who, in turn, is responsible either to the mayor and council or (b) to the city manager. City managers favor the single department head as against independent boards, while recreators frequently take the opposite point of view.

Those who are *for* boards say that for a function that serves the entire public, authority is better placed in several persons than in a single individual, that *group* thinking is preferable in policy making, and that policies so made are more acceptable to the public. They say that an unpaid board is in a better position to reflect public opinion, serve as a board of appeal, and negotiate advantages for the system. Continuity can be gained by members serving overlapping terms, and some also believe that a board tends to discourage bureaucratic tendencies.

Those who stand *against* the board and for the single department head say that single administrators can act more quickly, more economically, and more efficiently than boards. They say, too, that the advantages of group thinking without any of the disadvantages of an official board can be secured through using an advisory committee. With one leader, responsibility is more readily placed, political interference is less, and there is more policy flexibility.

Authorities Which Administer Recreation in Conjunction with Schools (Boards of Education, School Districts)

In some states, school laws make it possible for boards of education to administer public recreation services. Large cities such as Newark, New Jersey, and Milwaukee, Wisconsin, and smaller cities such as Flint, Michigan, Pasadena, California, and Great Neck, New York, have provided public recreation opportunities successfully in this way for quite some time.

Arguments *for* encouraging school authorities to administer local public recreation services hold that while *education for leisure* is not the responsibility of education alone, education must take the lead in advancing it. The point is accurately made that it is virtually impossible, even if desirable, to separate education from recreation, because learning opportunities and values are so common to both. If learning is not the work of the educator and teacher, to whom does it belong? The proponents of this approach say that the modern school, unlike its predecessor, serves the *entire* population and not just children, that the educational process is no longer confined just to the classroom during the school day, and that because of extracurricular activities and adult education programs, schools are well equipped with staff and facilities to inculcate leisure interests and skills. Schools are accessible and include many of the facilities needed for recreation (e.g., gymnasiums, swimming pools, facilities for music, drama, the graphic and plastic arts, etc.). Schools have the advantage of being universal, of enjoying the respect of the public, and of having the prestige that is so necessary to the progress of any community service.

Arguments *against* using the board of education and the schools as the center of local public recreation administration say that the school authorities already have more than they can handle properly in meeting the formal educational needs of the school population; that school districts are pressed for money, space, and personnel for regular educational purposes; and that adding the recreation function can only make more irritating the ever-increasing cost of education. Those who oppose the school-centered administrative device say that the very nature of formal education, with its traditional disciplinary approach to learning, is incompatible with the informal and pleasant characteristics of recreation. Recreation leadership has its own techniques; the able teacher is not necessarily the able leader; recreation should not be handicapped by pedagogical methods and control. There is fear that recreation can only play a secondary role to education in the school setting, that the schools have only *some,* by no means *all,* of the resources that are needed. They have the auditoriums and the gymnasiums, for example, but not the golf courses and beaches. It is also said that when the schools administer recreation, the program is often heavily weighted along physical education lines at the sacrifice of the cultural arts and other popular leisure pursuits.

To balance the facts. Local public school systems do have responsibilities in helping to meet the recreation needs of the people. Whether a board of education or school district should assume the task of administering public recreation services depends upon the adequacy of the state school code with respect to their function, the interest and willingness of school authorities to give recreation attention and support equal to that of formal education, and staff competency in matters of recreation. In any event, the role of the school in community recreation includes:

Education for living. Schools can teach individuals how to make creative, expressive, satisfying use of leisure. In the schools tastes for music, drama, literature, and the arts, as well as games and sports, can be nurtured.

Making school facilities available for community recreation purposes after school hours. Schools are publicly owned and supported; they are well located and easily accessible. They include the very kinds of space and facilities, including shops, libraries, classrooms, gymnasiums, and auditoriums, that are required for community recreation. Thus, in planning and designing schools, it is desirable to provide for community needs as well as for those of the school itself. It is equally important to see that school facilities are open to the community.

Providing recreation through extended school services. Boards of education should be willing to undertake recreation activities on school property after school hours and during vacation. These programs should be varied in scope. If provided in a community where a public recreation system is operated, both services should be coordinated. An extended school service cannot be successfully provided with volunteers alone. It requires paid professional leadership.

Cooperating closely with other departments, agencies, and organizations. Community recreation requires the resources and help of many groups. Boards of education should coordinate their efforts—plan and act jointly—with recreation boards, park boards, private youth-serving agencies, councils of social agencies, churches, and other local groups toward the common goal of providing a community-wide, year-round recreation program.

Authorities Which Administer Recreation in Connection with Parks (Park Boards, Park Departments, Park and Recreation Departments and Districts)

This type of managing authority administers recreation in conjunction with parks. It may or may not include the word *recreation* in its title, and it may or may not have special tax levies for park and recreation purposes. Parks have been closely associated with public recreation in the United States for a long time and appear to be moving closer to it as urbanites increasingly seek their recreation in the outdoors.

The argument *for* this type of administration is that so many of the major facilities which are needed for recreation purposes are planned, developed, managed, and operated by park authorities. Reference is made not only to the parks themselves, but also to outing, camping, and picnic facilities, beaches and pools, golf courses, tennis courts, forests, reservations, and often playgrounds. The park environment reflects the very informality, beauty, and flavor of relaxation so characteristic of the role of recreation. It is said, too, that park authorities are experienced in serving *public* needs and large numbers of people. Advocates of this approach say that a park is a *recreational* resource and can be nothing else no matter what its size or facilities. They also believe that the public is long committed to liberal support of parks, and that the greater the increase in population and urban living, the greater public support will be. Park departments generally have large budgets, and enjoy prestige based upon a long record of performance. Finally, it is said that the old "stay off the grass" approach to park management has given way to recreational use.

Arguments *against* this form of administration indicate that under such auspices, recreation runs the risk of receiving consideration secondarily to the problems of land acquisition and development. It is said that while recreation does need many of the facilities which come under the jurisdiction of the park authorities, it also needs facilities such as schools which are not under park control. Moreover, there is always the danger that funds needed for recreation may be diverted for park purposes (leadership funds, for example, may be used to pave a park road or reseed a lawn).

Many park authorities have demonstrated their ability to administer public recreation services effectively. As the current trend indicates, the role of the park system in providing services traditionally identified as *recreation* is likely to become larger. This is so not only because of expanding public interest in outdoor living, but also because the need for the kinds of facilities which park authorities control assumes increasing importance in a mushrooming urban population. Park facilities should always be available for recreation purposes, whether they be of an active or passive nature. This need does not make the floricultural, horticultural, and conservational aspects of parks less essential. For parks to be recreation centers in the finest sense of the word, they must be both functional and aesthetic. The recreational and scenic attractions of parks should complement rather than compete with one another. If recreation, in the sense of *program* or *service,* is a park function, it must not be a second cousin with funds intended for its support diverted for other purposes. Where such funds are allocated through a special tax levy for recreation purposes, some protection is provided.

The assumption that a park authority cannot achieve inter-departmental or inter-public service cooperation has been dispelled in the so called *park-school* concept. This is an increasingly popular device which brings park and school authorities together for the purpose of planning, acquiring, developing, and operating their respective facilities at a common location and in a way which enables the parks to serve the schools and the schools to serve the parks. Perhaps the most important consideration in deciding whether recreation should be administered in connection with park systems is the principle that parks should always be planned and operated in terms of serving human needs and interests. In the final analysis, parks are for people.

THE WORKSHOP

1. Hold a debate which presents the pros and cons of the different types of public recreation authorities.
2. Interview a school superintendent to learn his views on the role of education in meeting the leisure needs of people.
3. Talk to the chairman of a park board to learn the policies and practices of his department regarding (1) recreation leadership and programs and (2) functional use of park areas.
4. Select two communities of comparable size and make-up, with recreation administered by parks, schools, and recreation boards. Compare their recreation appropriation records over a period of years.
5. Examine and criticize the policies of your board of education with respect to making school facilities available for community use.
6. Discuss with a city manager the difficulties of administering municipal services where independent boards and commissions exist.
7. Visit a housing or new real estate development and make a critical analysis of its recreation facilities.
8. Draft a statement on the functions, duties, and responsibilities of public recreation board members.
9. Devise a plan for bringing about close working cooperation among school, park, and recreation departments, and voluntary agencies.
10. List the ways in which recreation appropriations might be safeguarded if the program is administered by an agency having other major functions.

REFERENCES

Arnold, Serena E., *Desirable Practices for the Administration of Consolidated Municipal Park and Recreation Departments.* Wheeling, W. Virginia: American Institute of Park Executives, 1955.

Burns, James M., and Jack W. Peltason, *Government by the People,* 4th ed. Englewood Cliffs, New Jersey: Prentice-Hall, Inc., 1960.

Carlson, Reynold, Theodore R. Deppe, and Janet MacLean, *Recreation in American Life.* Belmont, California: Wadsworth Publishing Company, 1963.

Chapin, Stuart, *Urban Land Use Planning.* Urbana: University of Illinois Press, 1963.

Green, Arnold, *Recreation, Leisure and Politics.* New York: McGraw-Hill Book Company, 1964.

Meyer, Harold D., and Charles K. Brightbill, *Recreation Administration*. Englewood Cliffs, New Jersey: Prentice-Hall, Inc., 1960.

The International City Manager's Association, *Municipal Recreation Administration*. Chicago: 1960.

Shivers, Jay, *Principles and Practices of Recreational Services*. New York: The Macmillan Company, 1967. Chapters 4 and 7.

Weimer, David, *City and County in America*. New York: Appleton-Century-Crofts, 1962.

Wingo, Lowdon, "Urban Growth and the Planning of Outdoor Recreation," *Trends in American Living and Outdoor Recreation*. (ORRRC Report 122). Washington, D. C.: U. S. Government Printing Office, 1962.

Comments

For a modern concept of local government, its services and problems, see *Illinois Local Government,* Final Report and Background Papers, Assembly on Illinois Local Government, Lois M. Pelekoudas, ed., Institute of Government and Public Affairs, University of Illinois, Urbana, Ill., 1961.

Refer to standard volumes in the fields of political science, urban sociology, and city and regional planning for information on the role of government and the problems of modern urban living. Population data and vital statistics are available through publications, particularly the annual *Statistical Abstract* of the Bureau of the Census, U.S. Department of Commerce.

6

County and District Organization
for Town and Country

Today the term "rural" is an ever-expanding concept, including more and more interrelations between city and country and calling for ever-broadening views in rural and urban planning. It is often difficult to differentiate between rural and urban, for the two are constantly blending. This is especially true in the case of village and town life. Yet in many localities there are traits that appear to be distinctively rural. Special forms of community life and social institutions, agricultural occupations, the composition of the rural population, its cultural heritage, and its relation to land, nature, and the out-of-doors create distinctly rural patterns.

Among new conditions producing changes in farm life are: (1) universal schooling, creating a demand for higher standards of living; (2) the automobile and good roads, which lessen the need for small towns and tend to depopulate the less attractive areas in favor of more attractive ones; (3) the shorter working day in industry which draws farm people to what they believe is a better life in the city; (4) the development of commercial farming, which in some cases, as in the wheat belt, virtually substitutes migratory laborers for settled families in the harvest and planting seasons; (5) the spread of electric power into farm areas; (6) the tendency of city interests to dominate the mass media in such a way as to produce a city-minded nation; (7) the continuing program of the federal government in the interest of rural people.

A glance at the forces listed above shows clearly the transition through which rural life is passing. The drift continues to be townward. Isolated farm life is abandoned, and a new age is ahead. Properly regarded, the new possibilities of rural living are bright, and recreation is an essential part of the changing pattern.

The pioneer farm family made its own recreation—the home was the center. The new age seeks most of its recreation elsewhere. Much of the folk resourcefulness and self-sufficiency has gone. The rural population must gain broader vision and perspective to build a new type of recreation to meet its needs.

Wholesome recreation is winning a place in rural life. Organized activities and programs are becoming more universal. The possibilities of leading people to develop and maintain a recreation program that is constructive in social development need to be emphasized. Recreation can be made to yield true compensatory values and thus help to meet some of the rural needs. But although the purposes of urban and rural recreation may be the same, the approaches are different. Hence, if urban recreation were transplanted to rural areas without modification, defeat of the primary aim would probably result.

The rural population is rapidly improving the development of public school recreation facilities. True, the district school has always been something of a local community center. In addition to providing opportunities for children of the neighborhood to play together during the school year, the school building has housed many of the local recreation activities —box suppers, lectures, debates, singing schools, political rallies, spelling bees, and the "exercises" of the pupils to which parents were invited on special occasions. During recent years, this recreation function of the rural school has been greatly increased. Consolidated schools have brought together larger numbers of people and given opportunities for play that were formerly out of reach of rural communities. The larger staff of teachers in such schools has facilitated specialization in recreation supervision in athletics, drama, glee clubs, orchestras, and bands. And yet in spite of this advance, many of the popular urban forms of diversion are still regarded in the country as luxuries for which no considerable expenditures should be made. In small towns and the open country the establishment of parks, playgrounds, athletic fields, golf courses, and tennis courts lags far behind.

At one time the county courthouse and the county fairgrounds were almost the only county properties that served any recreation purpose. The courthouse site in county seat municipalities served as a kind of "in-town" park for the people of the local community and the surrounding country. Now, however, in many communities the county fairground is being used for athletics, civic celebrations, and other forms of community recreation. A few of these areas have been transformed into genuine community parks. Establishment of county recreation and park systems is on the increase.

COUNTY PARKS AND RECREATION

At the outset in county recreation there was an emphasis upon parks rather than program. In some areas, separate boards were established in the same county, one known as the "park" board, the other as the "recreation" commission. The trend today is to combine both functions in one board. County managing authorities in 1966 were: [1]

TYPE	NUMBER	PERCENTAGE
Combined Park & Recreation	173	48.3
Separate Recreation	32	8.9
Separate Park	82	22.9
School	1	0.3
Other Public	70	19.6
Total	358	100.0

In the five years prior to these data, the type of managing authorities for parks and recreation were: Combined Park and Recreation—40 departments or 63.5% and Separate Park—13 departments or 20.6% of the 63 new authorities. Separate Recreation and Other Public accounted for the other 10 departments. Other Public authorities consist of conservation, highway, welfare and youth departments, and forest preserves.

With the many villages, towns, and small cities making up rural and suburban life, the county has been found to be a logical political unit for the promotion of public recreation programs.

To meet these needs, the counties will have to hurry. Rural areas, particularly those within 50 miles of our metropolitan centers, are feeling the impact of the "decentralization of industry," the "urban sprawl," and the "population explosion."

County parks are useful to urbanites and are important links between city-owned parks and parks owned by the states and the national government. They are, nevertheless, most useful to those from the rural districts. The number of communities of under 2500 population which have adequate parks is limited. Many rural people have no parks or playground space. They have open fields and vacant lots, but anyone who knows village life appreciates how inadequate these are for recreation.

In thickly populated counties, the program conducted by a county park

[1] *Recreation and Park Yearbook*, National Recreation and Park Association, Table 22, 1966, p. 46.

or recreation system is not unlike that found in the large metropolitan cities.

SUGGESTED APPROACHES FOR ADVANCING RURAL RECREATION

The problem is essentially one of organizing local resources. Land, structures, and other facilities, and the interests, skills, and enthusiasms of the people need to be used for the enrichment of leisure. Voluntary and private agencies can be of assistance, but there can be no adequate program without public organization and support. Boards of county commissioners, boards of supervisors, district or county boards of education, park districts, county park and forestry departments, or other agencies of this nature must see their responsibilities and act. There should be a permanent county or district recreation establishment.

County government in the United States was established to carry out certain administrative functions of the state. Programs of education, health, and public welfare are illustrations. Most state enabling laws permit counties, or districts, to function for recreation. Permissive legislation in many cases allows for the creation of county parks and county libraries.

The adoption of the "County Park Act of 1895" by the New Jersey Legislature was one of the most significant legislative achievements in the history of the public recreation movement.

Not only did it make possible the establishment of the first county park system in Essex County, N.J., in the same year, but it paved the way for general recreation-enabling legislation for tax supported municipal recreation. This occurred first in 1915, also in New Jersey.

At present there seem to be at least six administrative alternatives for providing recreation areas and programs in rural communities: [2]

1. There is an overwhelming trend toward creating a combined county department of recreation and parks.
2. Separate recreation and park departments continue to be established with a combined total about equal in number to the number of new combined recreation and parks departments.
3. Special districts usually result by default of local governmental units who have not accepted their responsibility.
4. School districts can be found in the Mid Atlantic, Great Lakes, and Pacific

[2] *Recreation and Park Yearbook,* National Recreation and Park Association, 1966, pp. 44–46 and Outdoor Recreation booklets, #3 *Organization* and #5 *Areawide and Multigovernmental Opportunities,* National Association of Counties, Research Foundation, 1968.

Southwest regions; the Southern and Pacific Northwest regions report no school districts.

5. There are conservation boards and forest preserves found in the Midwest region.

6. The multigovernmental concept of regional cooperation, city-county combination, cooperation with schools and cooperation with the private sector offer other administrative alternatives.

County Organization

With the growing interest in recreation, boards of county commissioners are beginning to accept recreation as a responsibility of county government and are organizing county units.

The State Planning Board of Pennsylvania, in stressing the importance of county recreation systems, says: [3]

A legally authorized county park and recreation system is one basic approach toward the development of a sound program to meet the needs and interests of all our people. Concerted effort and good planning in the wise use of our natural resources is not only good business, but serves as a sound investment in the preservation of our American way of life.

A COUNTY RECREATION PLATFORM

A park and recreation program operated on a 12-month basis should be provided for all, regardless of age, race, creed, or economic status.

The county park and recreation program should not compete in any way with community programs, but should supply areas, facilities, and leisure-time opportunities that are not or cannot be offered by any one community.

The park and recreation program should be administered by the highest type of trained park and recreation leadership available. *Trained personnel are the best protection for your investment.*

Public park and recreation services should be supported chiefly by public tax funds.

A county park and recreation plan should result in the fullest use of all resources and should be a part of, and integrated with, long-range planning for all other county, township, and community services.

County park and recreation services should be definitely aimed toward

---

[3] *County Recreation,* bulletin of the Recreation Division, the State Planning Board of Pennsylvania. The material presented above is excerpted from this bulletin, which deals with a plan and guide for recreation in the county. The material should prove of value in organization and administration procedure.

the enrichment of family and community life, and are valuable only to the extent to which they are directed toward this goal.

Urge the County Commissioners to prepare and publish an ordinance creating a Park and/or Recreation Board and to appoint such a board.

Also request the County Commissioners to appoint a Recreation Advisory Council of 25 to 30 members with county-wide representation. *The Country Planning Commission, if one has been created, may serve as the executive committee for such an advisory council.*

Encourage the park and recreation board to hire the best trained park and recreation personnel available to serve as superintendent and staff.

The Recreation Planning Committee should determine through survey:

(a) The possibility of strengthening all existing programs, areas and facilities.

(b) Existing land areas that can be acquired for recreation or park use and that would be accessible to the greatest number of the county population.

(c) The areas, facilities, and programs of all communities in their county; so that the development of the county park and recreation system will not duplicate or overlap adequate services already offered.

Public Recreation Through Contract

Another workable plan is the "contract" system. This method has been used successfully in the field of health, and it could be adapted for recreation. The contract plan is a method whereby municipalities enter into a contract with the legal recreation authority of a larger political subdivision to provide recreation services to the community for an annual fixed sum.

The problems of small communities, especially those adjacent to larger cities, are inescapably bound to one another. Moreover, in attempting to meet local recreation needs, it is not always possible to follow and adhere to corporate lines Hence the need for administration under the larger political subdivision.

The contract system has many advantages. Services and needs can be met on a wider scale. There is uniformity and coordination of administration. Through the pooling of all local resources, the tax dollar can purchase more. The contract system means progress through the sharing of experiences and through joint effort. It tends to encourage and not impede progress, which is often not the case where needs cut across political

boundaries. Moreover, individual local initiative is retained and autonomy preserved through local financial participation and opportunity to
decide annually whether participation is warranted.

Special Districts

In sections of the country where county government does not exist, or
is inadequate, yet where there is a need for some type of regional recreation organization, the park or recreation district has provided this service
in a most satisfactory manner.

The organization of special recreation taxing districts within rural
areas has increased within recent years. The *district* establishment, among
other things, overcomes the objection of providing rural recreation out
of general county funds raised in large part through taxes assessed on
city property. Recreation districts, or combination recreation and park
districts, might well include all incorporated areas in the county, particularly in smaller counties, or two or more districts in larger counties.
This function can be administered by a district board similar to municipal
recreation boards. These districts need to be confined to the boundaries
of a single county.

Special recreation taxing districts make it possible for small communities to provide collectively what they would be unable to give to their
people individually. As many as a dozen communities, sometimes located
in adjacent counties, can pool their facilities, funds, and leadership.

INTERRELATIONS

Rural and Urban

In addition to the county recreation authority, there exists in each of
the larger municipal units managing authorities with tax funds operating
independently of the county recreation agency, but cooperating with it.
Where good leadership prevails there is no conflict, and the county board
assists by conducting training institutes, acting as a coordinating agency,
and supplying facilities for the promotion of local activities as well as
county-wide programs. This is particularly true in terms of the larger
facilities such as: swimming pools, golf courses, playing fields with
stadiums, trailside museums, riding stables, shooting ranges, artificial
skating rinks, boating areas, picnic groves, and day camp sites.

With the constant population increase, nonurban areas assume greater
significance. People desire close-at-hand recreation areas and facilities.
Hence there is an urgent need for county-city cooperation in all matters

relating to the organization, administration, planning, and supervision of recreation areas. While the federal government must accept responsibility for areas of national interest, and the state government for areas of state-wide use, the close-at-hand areas are largely the responsibility of the county, district, and municipality. Parks, parkways, camping sites for weekend and day camping, swimming facilities, golf courses, and hiking trails should be within easy reach of both urban and rural dwellers.

The County Recreation Council

For various reasons, it may not always be immediately practicable to establish county recreation on a governmental basis. In such instances, consideration might be given to creating a recreation council.

A county recreation council is composed of at least two representatives from each community or town in the county. It should be organized with officers and necessary committees. The same community representatives should attend the county programs each month and in turn be responsible for the programs and progress in their community.

This is illustrated by what is happening in the Tri-State New York Metropolitan Region. A report completed under the joint auspices of the Metropolitan Regional Council and the Regional Plan Association, Inc., makes projections indicating the future problems of all rural areas located near metropolitan centers. This report discloses that in 1959 the nine northern counties in New Jersey had in county park acreage 16,625 acres of park land. It is projected that the counties should acquire 93,999 additional acres by 1985 to adequately meet the outdoor recreational needs of the people living in that area by that date. This will be impossible in several of the counties because of the amount of acreage already utilized for industrial sites, homes, shopping centers, and schools.

A NATIONAL RECREATION AND PARKS POLICY FOR COUNTIES

Unanimously adopted at the Feb. 1964 Nat'l Assoc. of Co. Officials, Mid-Winter Meeting

Preamble

A major goal of civilized societies everywhere has historically been *leisure*— the progressive diminishment of the effort required to provide the necessities of human physical and economic survival. In the 20th century, we are approaching the attainment of this goal. It is the purpose of this National County Recreation and Parks Policy to suggest some guidelines by which county governments in the United States may contribute toward effective utilization of leisure by participating in the provision of a balanced program of public parks and recreation.

Such a balanced program will involve every level of government, as well as the private sector, and will serve every segment of society. Our youth will be helped to develop physically, mentally and spiritually, and youth problems may be lessened. Our young and middle aged adults will have an outlet from the tensions of a competitive and industrialized urban environment, and a chance to express their individuality and creativity. Our senior citizens will find meaning and purpose in their retirement years.

The Role of the County

The special role of the county should be to acquire, develop and maintain parks and to administer public recreation programs that will serve the needs of communities broader than the local neighborhood or municipality, but less than state-wide or national in scope.

In addition, the county should plan to coordinate local neighborhood and community facilities with the cooperation of the cities, townships, and other intra-county units, and should itself cooperate in state and federal planning and coordinative activities. Finally, where there is no existing unit of local government except the county to provide needed local neighborhood or municipal facilities and programs, the county should provide such facilities and programs, utilizing county service districts, local assessments, and other methods by which those benefited will pay the cost.

Organization: internal and external.—Counties should create organizational structures for meeting their park and recreation responsibilities.

Internally, such organizational structures should fix responsibility for the county park and recreation program clearly with the elected county governing body.

Counties are urged to employ a parks and recreation director and staff qualified by education and experience to assist in planning, implementing and managing the park and recreation program. In addition, they should fully utilize the wide range of technical services that are available through the state governments and the various national park, recreation, and conservation organizations.

County park and recreation responsibilities involve several facets of county government. Other county departments should be kept fully informed and invited to cooperate in the development of these programs.

Externally, park and recreation facilities and programs serving a community larger than an individual county but of less than state-wide scope should be administered jointly through cooperative arrangements between two or more counties. In the event that creation of a new unit of government is necessary to attain an effective and economically feasible solution of regional park and recreation problems, the final responsibility for its administration should vest in the elected county governing bodies involved.

Finance.—County park and recreation programs should be financed principally through general taxation. This may be supplemented by such sources as general obligation and revenue bonding, donations of money, land and services from private individuals and groups, and user fees.

County government strongly supports the concept that users of certain kinds of public park and recreation facilities and programs should pay fees for such use. Revenue from this source should be applied to the acquisition, development, maintenance, and administration of recreation and parks programs. Fees should not be so high as to prevent those in modest circumstances from enjoying the benefits of public parks and recreation programs.

Planning.—Parks and recreation should be an integral element of all county land use planning and zoning. Such planning and zoning should embrace not only areas to be acquired for the county recreation park system, but full use of zoning and other regulatory powers should be made to preserve open space, protect scenic values, and otherwise enhance recreational opportunities in private developments.

Counties should jealously protect existing park and recreation areas against both public and private encroachment, and should yield such areas for other purposes only upon condition that areas lost are replaced by others of comparable value serving the same population.

The County and Other Local Governments

Counties should encourage, through planning, consultation and other services, the provision of adequate local neighborhood and community facilities and programs by municipalities, townships and other intra-county units of government. Municipal governments should step up their efforts to secure open space and recreation areas, particularly in and around urban centers.

Municipal, township and other intra-county units should be guided in their programs by existing county plans. Their requests for technical and financial assistance should be made first to their county governments. If the county is unable to provide such assistance, it should forward the request to the appropriate state agency, and should support the local unit in its request. All such requests should be restricted to those instances in which the county lacks the resources to provide the requested services on its own behalf.

Counties should also, where appropriate, enter into intergovernmental contracts or agreements with municipalities, townships and other intra-county units for the joint use of personnel and for joint administration of facilities and programs.

The County and State Governments

Every state should acquire, develop, maintain, and administer park and recreation facilities and programs which provide values for the benefit of the entire state. In addition, every state should provide enabling legislation, if necessary, so that counties and other local governments have full authority to provide a balanced program of park and recreation services and to finance it adequately.

The states should also provide technical assistance to local governments in their park and recreation endeavors and, where possible, financial incentives to assist them in accelerating their park and recreation programs.

The states should consult formally with the local governments involved, from the inception of their planning process, before deciding to acquire or withdraw lands from local tax rolls for state park and recreation programs.

Where state or federal recreation areas are being used primarily by residents of a single county, the state and federal governments should give consideration to offering such areas to the county government for operation.

The County and the Federal Government

The excellent Report to the President and to the Congress in January, 1962, entitled "Outdoor Recreation for America," by the Outdoor Recreation Resources Review Commission, is strongly recommended as a source of information of lasting usefulness. County government endorses the basic recommendation of this bi-partisan group that the primary responsibility for adequately meeting the nation's recreation and park demands lies with "private enterprise, the states, and local government" and that the role of the federal government should not be one of domination, but of cooperation and assistance in meeting the recreation and park challenge.

The federal government should acquire, develop, and maintain park and recreation areas which have scenic, scientific, historic, or special recreation values of significance to the entire nation. Federal agencies responsible for multiple use management of other federal lands should integrate recreation land use, wherever feasible, with other federal land uses. In all federal land use planning for management, withdrawal or disposal of federally designated recreation areas and general multiple-use lands, county governments should be consulted and invited to participate from the earliest stages of investigation.

In the disposition of federal surplus land, including military reservations bases, the states and local governments should be given a preference if they are able and willing to accept and manage such lands for public recreation and park purposes. In such cases, the federal government should transfer these lands to the state or local agencies for a nominal consideration. Acquisition of surplus federal land by states and local governments for recreation and park purposes should be in accordance with long range plans and with the ability of the states or local units to finance the maintenance and administration of the facilities and programs.

County government supports a program of federal grants-in-aid to states and local governments for planning, acquiring and developing park and recreation facilities, along the lines recommended by the Outdoor Recreation Resources Review Commission. Federal laws should require that the county governments involved be consulted before federal grant funds are used by states to acquire park and recreation areas.

The County and the Private Sector

Some two-thirds of the nation's land is privately owned; collectively these lands have an enormous potential for recreation development at private expense which has been only partially realized. Counties should seek opportunities to stimulate such development. County cooperation should include the provision of access roads, where feasible, to permit the recreation development of private lands.

Counties should support state legislation exempting private owners of land from tort liability where such lands are opened for general public recreational use without charge to the public.

Counties should encourage their agricultural extension agents to provide advice and demonstrations of the recreational development of private lands for profit.

Public agencies should acquire conservation easements over private lands, where feasible, to preserve open spaces in and around urban areas.

Counties should cooperate with and support in every way possible the efforts of private businesses and of charitable, service and civic organizations to acquire and appropriately manage recreation sites which serve public needs.

Planning

The forms of recreation suitable to county parks are not as highly specialized as in the cities. Fishing, picnicking, hiking, nature lore, camping, outings, boating, swimming, horseback riding, and winter sports are popular. Some county parks near cities have golf, tennis, children's play activities under leadership, athletic leagues, and many other features commonly found in city parks. Facilities may include marinas, band stands, zoos, dance pavilions, and botanical gardens.

An adequate number of such recreation areas with proper capacity is important. The National Resources Planning Board states that:

Experience indicates that an attractive nonurban park which offers a diversi-. fied and efficiently administered outing program including water sports, may be expected to attract close to five per cent of the population living within a 15- or 20-mile radius (the maximum distance for frequency of attendance at nonurban parks) on a normal summer holiday, provided it has adequate accommodations and no competing areas of equal quality. Thus, it appears reasonable to plan for that large a percentage of the total population in a long-range development program for a region or locality. Attendance and use figures for southeastern parks, supplemented by preference surveys conducted on several of these parks, further indicate that the ratio of facility capacities to population should be approximately as follows: swimming, two per cent; picnicking, two per cent; fishing, one per cent; boating, one per cent; informal sports and games, one half of one per cent. Other facilities required in a nonurban park to provide a well-balanced program of activities include nature museums and nature trails, council-fire circles and amphitheaters, hiking, and bridle trails, recreational buildings and shelters to afford protection against unfavorable weather conditions, and organized camps, family cabins, lodges, and meal-serving facilities to make possible overnight and vacation outings.

The kind and quality of available resources will frequently determine the usefulness of nonurban recreation resources . . . The distance people can and will travel for an outing is determined by factors of time, cost, and available means of travel. Numerous studies of attendance and use of parks in the Southeast supplemented by park patron questionnaires and by highway travel surveys indicate that by far a majority of southern people are confined to within 10 to 15 miles of their homes for weekday outings, 15 to 20 miles for holiday outings, a hundred miles for extended week-end outings, and three hundred miles for vacation outings.[4]

To meet these needs, the Park, Recreation, and Open Space Project has set a standard of 12 acres of county parks for every 1000 of the county's 1985 population, or five per cent of the county's total area, whichever is greater. The five per cent is to make allowance for population levels beyond 1985. The project suggests the following activity distribution for the 12 acres per 1000 persons standard: [5]

Swimming and beach use	1 acre per 1000
Picnicking	3 acres per 1000
Golf	2
Organized games and specialized activities	¾
Boating	¼
Natural area activities	5
	12 acres per 1000

RECREATION OPPORTUNITIES FOR RURAL PEOPLE

In the absence of specialized recreation facilities, the function of recreation has been assumed by institutions or organizations established primarily for other purposes.

1. The early system of "trading help," or cooperative labor, had many recreation implications in bringing people together. However, husking bees, barn raisings, and quilting bees, which once flourished, have disappeared.

[4] National Resources Planning Board, *Regional Planning*, Part XI, "The Southeast" (Washington, D. C.: U. S. Government Printing Office, n.d.), pp. 231–232.

[5] *The Race for Open Space,* final report of the Park, Recreation, and Open Space Project conducted under the joint sponsorship of the Metropolitan Regional Council and the Regional Plan Association, Inc., Tri-State New York Metropolitan Region, 1961.

2. Family solidarity has been more apparent in rural areas than in urban centers, and a large proportion of recreation was secured within the family group. At present, as we have pointed out, with improved roads and transportation, this is changing. Consolidated schools have changed considerably the complexion of play groups from brother-sister combinations to groups of the same age and sex.

3. The rural church traditionally has served as a meeting place, has formed clubs and organizations, and has sponsored such group activities as picnics, box suppers, seasonal festivities, and pageants. It should not be forgotten, of course, that the rural church has also censured certain amusements and diversions, particularly dancing, cards, and billiards.

4. The growth of consolidated schools has multiplied opportunities for rural recreation. The consolidated school, more than any other agency, can become the rural community center.

5. Agricultural extension services, especially the 4-H Clubs, promote recreation.

Extension's interest in recreation is twofold: Improvement of rural living itself and improvement of organized extension activities.

Since recreation is an integral part of family and community life, extension service necessarily involves recreation.

Resources should be available in every state extension organization for offering recreation assistance. The role of recreation in youth and young men's and women's programs must be fully appreciated if these programs are to succeed. No extension educational program should be overbalanced with recreation, although it must be realized that recreation can and does occupy a much more important place in the program for some age groups than for others.

Recreation services have also been rendered in rural areas by such youth-serving organizations as the Y.M.C.A., the Y.W.C.A., the Boy Scouts, and the Girl Scouts in their extension programs.

THE WORKSHOP

1. Report on the recreation program in a chosen rural area.
2. List the services of agencies now functioning in recreation within a certain county.
3. Determine the differences, if any, between recreation for rural and nonrural areas. Learn what has caused these differences.
4. Explore prevailing trends in rural life and determine their relation to recreation.
5. Investigate the effect of mobility on recreation for rural dwellers.
6. After studying rural recreation services, present some of the difficulties of administering the program.

7. Suggest ways of coordinating the recreation efforts of private agencies functioning in rural areas.
8. Prepare a brief statement on the interrelation of urban and rural recreation forces.
9. List the ways in which consolidated school systems can contribute to rural recreation.
10. Draft a set of "Policies and Procedures" for a county recreation system.

REFERENCES

Adrian, Charles R., *State and Local Governments*. New York: McGraw-Hill Book Company, 1960.

Brightbill, Charles K., and Harold D. Meyer, *Recreation—Text and Readings*. Englewood Cliffs, N.J.: Prentice-Hall, Inc., 1953, Chapter IV.

Danford, Howard G., *Recreation in the American Community*. New York: Harper & Row, Publishers, 1953, Chapter II.

Lancaster, Lane W., *Government in Rural America*, 2nd ed. Princeton: D. Van Nostrand Co., Inc., 1952.

National Association of Counties Research Foundation, *County Parks and Recreation . . . A Basis For Action*, 1964. 1001 Connecticut Avenue, N.W., Washington, D.C. 20036.

National Association of Counties Research Foundation, in cooperation with the Bureau of Outdoor Recreation, U.S. Department of Interior, *Outdoor Recreation*, a 10 booklet series, 1967–68, 1001 Connecticut Avenue, N.W., Washington, D.C. 20036.

Phillips, Jewel C., *State and Local Government in America*. New York: American Book Company, 1954.

Snider, Clyde F., *Local Government in Rural America*. New York: Appleton-Century-Crofts, 1957.

Vettiner, Charles J., *A New Horizon of Recreation*. Louisville, Kentucky, 450 Armory Place, 1956.

Comments

The U.S. Department of Agriculture established the position of Program Leader, Outdoor Recreation Education, Division of Agricultural Science, Technology and Management, Federal Extension Service, Washington, D.C., 20250 in 1967.

Through the extension divisions at many of the land grant colleges and universities you can obtain field service and publications.

The U.S. Agriculture Extension Service of the Department of Agriculture (Home Demonstration, Farm Demonstration, and 4-H Clubs) offers recreation services. The Bureau of Agricultural Economics of this Department also publishes bulletins.

American Country Life Association, Inc., publishes a monthly magazine, *Rural America,* and also the proceedings of its annual meetings. Much space is given to recreation for rural life.

The National Association of Counties, through a grant from the Bureau of Outdoor Recreation and in cooperation with their various state counterparts and state recreation agencies, held one-day recreation institutes in 40 states during 1967 and 1968.

National agencies such as the Boy Scouts, the Girl Scouts, the Y.W.C.A., Y.M.C.A., and other youth-serving agencies have rural divisions.

Regional and national church organizations have rural divisions which publish aids for recreation.

The U.S. Office of Education and the National Education Association, both located in Washington, D.C., have reference material of practical value to rural leadership.

Planning Recreation for Rural Home and Community by Nederfrank and Musselman, published by the U.S. Department of Agriculture, Information Bulletin 20 (n. d.), offers rich material.

The North Carolina Recreation Commission in Raleigh, North Carolina, has a brochure, *County Recreation In North Carolina,* 1966, that is valuable for organization and administrative guidance.

7

Recreation—A Function of State Government

State government is a foundation stone of the American way of life. It functions as a vital factor in the social well-being of all the people. Stateways along with folkways tell the story of citizenship in social correlations, social control and social services.

The voice of the people through state-delegated authority comprises the federal pattern. Thus, from the local community on the one hand and from the federal government on the other, the state serves in both directions. Granting authority to the local unit and building federal responsibility, the state stands as a bulwark to help balance the rights and responsibilities of individuals and groups. It is true that the federal government is larger with its political sovereignty in the entire people, but in many respects the work of the state comes closer to the individual's family, home and business, including the establishment and control of local government.

DEVELOPMENT

The most significant development of state government in recent years has been the multiplication of public services.

The upsurge of these social services can be attributed to no one cause, but rather to the composite effects of modern civilization. The state is busily engaged in promoting the public well-being. The promotion of education, the protection of health, the acceptance of responsibilities for the socially pathologic through modern social-work techniques, the improvement of living and working conditions, the expansion of communication and transportation are a concern of the modern state.

The states are beginning to accept their responsibility with regard to recreation as a *major* and *basic* service. Under our early philosophy of government, responsibility for education and health was left largely to the individual and to voluntary philanthropic organizations. Today, government at every level recognizes its job in the fields of health, education, and welfare. Recreation is following the same pattern of development as older public services, and many outstanding leaders recognize recreation as a major responsibility of state government.

The states have multiplied their recreation resources and services in many ways and administer them in a variety of methods and jurisdictions. Some state agencies are responsible for parks, forests, wayside picnic areas, winter sports facilities, game preserves, monuments, institutions, museums, and waterways. Some provide consultative recreation assistance to their political subdivisions, and others furnish services ranging from promoting the tourist trade to preparing young men and women for careers in recreation and related fields.

In addition to the existence of recreation services and facilities made available by state agencies, other significant developments in the states show the increasing trend toward state participation in rendering advisory and consultant services to recreation. Among these are the following:

1. Establishment of state recreation, or state recreation and park commissions, boards, and departments.
2. Examination and analysis of recreation resources and needs on a state-wide basis through studies and surveys.
3. Employment of recreation personnel in state departments and agencies whose responsibilities are broader than recreation, such as Youth Commissions, State Park Departments, Departments of Public Instruction.
4. Enactment of laws making available broader permissive legislation to enable communities to mobilize their resources for recreation—commonly referred to as state recreation enabling acts.
5. Appropriation of public funds not only for administering state recreation services and acquiring, developing, and operating state-owned recreation areas and facilities, but also for giving supplementary financial assistance to communities.
6. Advertisement and promotion of recreation resources and attractions by state tourist bureaus and development commissions.
7. Acceptance of responsibility by state universities toward helping communities establish, improve, and develop their recreation services.

8. Provision for personnel on a full-time or part-time basis to assist in recreation in rural areas through agricultural extension services.
9. Acquisition, development, and increasing use of land and water resources for conservation and outdoor recreation purposes.

These state recreation developments can be summed up in four major categories:

1. The states are enacting better and broader permissive legislation to enable the local governments to use and develop resources for recreation.
2. State agencies to provide advisory and consultant recreation services for the political subdivisions are becoming an accomplished fact.
3. The states are surveying their recreation potentials with an eye toward expanding recreation developments.
4. State universities and colleges are assuming more responsibility for helping to improve recreation, especially through the enrichment of activities as the extension services.

STATE RECREATION ADMINISTRATION

Despite the traditional services which the older agencies of state government have been providing, which amount to a valuable contribution to beneficial use of leisure, great deficiencies remain. It cannot be said that the states have fully developed even long existent services, and it cannot be assumed that if all of the traditional services were developd to the limit, the total need would be met. Hundreds of communities are seeking help in appraising their physical and human resources, organizing their recreation systems, developing broad and attractive programs, finding funds, selecting and training leaders, and planning facilities and areas. They want to know how to interpret what they are doing in terms the layman can understand, how to project efficient and productive plans, and how to secure assistance not now provided by any state agency. These communities are looking for standards which they can understand, apply, and use as a basis for demanding action.

THE PROBLEM

The problem is how and by whom state recreation services can be most satisfactorily provided. It is unlikely that a formula will be found which can be applied to all states. There are, however, tests to determine how state recreation services should be administered. The primary consideration is to provide the opportunity for every man, woman, and child to engage in leisure pursuits that are most appealing and satisfying to them.

Underlying this premise is the assumption that recreation is indispensable to the lives of everyone and to the enhancement of community life.

It is probably a mistake to assume that any agency which has a stake in recreation, or which contributes to it, can *ipso facto* adequately and satisfactorily provide technical advisory services on total community recreation problems. Alternatives need to be evaluated in terms of the following considerations:

1. Which possibility gives recreation the independence of action it needs in order to bring extensive recreation opportunities to the people? Under what auspices can recreation best continue to grow as an important public service with the status and prestige its contribution to society demands?

2. Of the several alternatives, which is most likely to bring together all the departmental resources of the state and rally the interest of public and private agencies and commercial, industrial, institutional, religious, and civic groups?

3. What kind of administrative state machinery will allow unhampered flow of services to the communities through the many different types of local managing authorities?

4. How can the continuity of state recreation services best be preserved and strengthened? It is common knowledge that some state departments are subject to major policy changes for a variety of reasons, sometimes political and sometimes functional. Recreation should be ready to face policy changes when they deal directly with recreation, but should not be exposed to arbitrary policy changes more directly concerned with other functions of state government.

5. What instrument will best promote, stimulate, and coordinate recreation without actually entering into the field of operations? The functions of promotion, stimulation, and coordination are not likely to exist side by side under the direct operation of the same administrative authority without arousing competition between major and minor political subdivisions.

6. Which type of administration can best provide the soundest understanding of recreation by the electorate? Under what sponsorship can the nature, place, and function of recreation be most easily comprehended? Where can the recreation issues and claims be best judged on their own merits?

7. Most important, under whose jurisdiction will recreation be assured steady and adequate financial support and sound, stabilized fiscal policy? Where will recreation find full and sustained, rather than piecemeal administrative understanding, support, and encouragement?

8. The significance of recreation in contemporary society has enhanced its political values. No longer are political candidates timid or

frightened about mentioning recreation as a platform of need and progress. This is shown at every level of government and constantly growing in popularity year by year. Recreation becomes a vote-getting device and thus obtains political prestige and dignity.

9. The recent merger of six lay-professional park and recreation organizations into a single fellowship group is a forward step of unparalleled significance and of unlimited potential values. The future is ahead for its influences, powers, and actions. The National Recreation and Park Association must advance with a dynamic program of action, well planned and meaningful. It must become the voice of the recreation and park field in molding unity of interests, understanding, and relationships. Here again the state is important as a force to create state, lay and professional groups to coordinate and cooperate with national fellowships.

10. There is a strong need for the states to have a clearer understanding with the media of communication—the press, the TV, the radio, writers of articles, commentators and others. There is too much evidence indicating the lack of understanding purposes, programs, agency construction and function. Here public relations is of paramount importance and perhaps its best voice for constructive values could come through state advisory-consultant recreation services. This becomes a powerful force for interpreting recreation to the people.

11. There is need for the state recreation and park associations or societies to take an action part in promoting state recreation services— in being heard in the Legislatures—in molding legislation and in dynamically working for passage of needed Legislation. This influence can also reach into the Halls of Congress and the local city and county boards, councils and commissions.

It is not reasonable to suppose that state advisory recreation services can be efficiently divided among half a dozen departments, any more than can health, education, or law enforcement. If they are, the recreation function is likely to become everybody's business and, consequently, nobody's. Any state may make its own choice of whether the service is to be delegated to an existing agency or provided by a new one. If it is assigned to an existing agency, there should be the largest possible amount of independence of action for recreation, and the funds appropriated for recreation services should be protected against diversion to other purposes.

State recreation trends are directed toward service to the total community, toward expediting the unhampered flow of recreation services to the communities, providing for permanency and continuity, and guaranteeing that recreation services will have well-grounded, stable fiscal support.

FUNCTIONS OF A STATE SERVICE FOR RECREATION

If a state creates a state recreation service, it does not mean that the state imposes recreation programs and ideas on the local community, nor that the state employs recreation leaders for the towns or even dictates personnel qualifications. It does not imply state power to determine the length of the recreation season, the activities to be conducted, or the character of recreation structures and equipment. What it means is that the state recreation service aids each community in doing its own job by advice and help rather than by supervision and authoritative control. More specifically, state assistance would perform the following functions:

1. Prepare surveys, studies, and appraisals of state-wide and specific community recreation needs and conditions.
2. Assist in organization for community recreation and in helping establish and improve local recreation systems.
3. Assist in methods of financing and budgeting for local recreation.
4. Provide assistance in securing and improving local and state legislation and related legal recreation problems.
5. Help develop and enrich total recreation opportunities and programs to meet the varied interests of entire communities.
6. Serve as a clearing house for the exchange and dissemination of information regarding recreation programs, plans, and services.
7. Assist in the preparation of long-range local plans for recreation and in the layout and design of recreation areas and facilities.
8. Promote and promulgate standards of recreation leadership, finance, areas and facilities, and program.
9. Assist in recruiting, placing, and training professional and volunteer recreation personnel.
10. Secure wider use of existing local and state recreation areas and facilities.
11. Influence the development of commercial recreation.
12. Promote institutes, conferences, and meetings in the best interests of recreation.
13. Coordinate federal, state, and local recreation efforts for systematic application within the state.
14. Investigate and help meet recreation needs in special settings such as rural areas, industry, institutions, religious groups.
15. Formulate, in cooperation with other state agencies, interested organizations, and citizens, a comprehensive recreation policy for the state.
16. Provide and administer supplementary financial assistance to the political subdivisions as the need arises and as funds are made available for the purpose.

A study of the fifty states was made by the North Carolina Recreation Commission and submitted to the National Recreation and Park Association at its 1967 Congress.

SOME CONCLUSIONS OF THE STUDY

The study clearly portrays specific movements and trends all indicating that state governments are making progress in rendering to the people under their sovereign jurisdictions services in recreation. The following conclusions are expressed judgments from the data gathered and the analyses and interpretations of the material.

1. Most of the states at this time are offering some type of service to Recreation and by agencies with other than Recreation as a primary responsibility. There is marked evidence from many sources indicating a definite trend to establish Recreation Commissions or Boards with full-time and primary advisory and consultant duties and responsibilities to Recreation.
2. There is overwhelming evidence indicating that states should recognize Recreation as a primary service for the duties, responsibilities and powers cannot be effectively rendered by a limited service through an agency with other primary legal authorities. Advisory-Consultant services to local, state and federal government groups, private and commercial Recreation interests for individuals and groups is the essential way to advance Recreation for all the people.
3. The two statements above emanate from the facts and factors that in our contemporary society stress the importance of Recreation, such as the growth of population, centralization of power through concepts of control in the changing patterns of democracy, technology, automation and cybernation multiplying their forces, mobility of the people, urbanization portraying a metropolitan culture in an industrial civilization and social responsibilities indicating new functions in the democratic process. Others can strengthen this listing while case studies, research reports, social and economic surveys fill the pages of current journals, magazines, newspapers and the media of TV and radio—all clearly substantiate these trends.
4. The concentration of population into urban areas portrays a form of living demanding Recreation as an essential for a balanced life along with Health, Education, Welfare, Work and Religion.
5. County government, at its annual national meeting held in Hawaii in 1963, gave its primary attention to Recreation as a function of county government and set forth in a master proclamation ways and means of advancing this field, especially in its relationship with city and state recreation services. Every evidence points to the fact that the problem of City-County Recreation Administration Authority and Action will have to be solved through state advisory-consultant leadership for attainment of maximum results.
6. The study demonstrated the fact of the growing need for leadership, thus

challenging the institutions of higher learning to accept responsibilities in Recreation Education and produce, for the field, a continual flow of Recreators to take charge and produce progress for today and in the tomorrows.

7. The passage of legislation relating to Recreation in the 88th and 89th Congress sessions of the Federal Government has been outstanding in creating new areas, programs and in the tremendous growth of grants-in-aid along many lines to indicate willing cooperation with the states and local government units in advancing Recreation services. There is no doubt but that this development has been a major force in promoting interest in State services.

RECOMMENDATIONS

A Program of Action

I. That The National Recreation and Park Association assume leadership
   A. To establish in every state of the union an agency with legal authority and with its primary concern, on a full-time basis, offering advisory and consultant services to the field of recreation. That where constitutionally possible, this state agency be established as a separate and independent agency within its own right and power.
   B. That where existing agencies are now serving recreation in some special capacity, these practices continue, and that a program of cooperation with the legal recreation advisory and consultant agency be established through a recreation interagency committee designed to correlate and coordinate the various functions.
   C. In forming within the association a strong division to further the many aspects of state government recreation and park developments.
   D. In promoting research and planning in recreation thus giving the field more knowledge about state government needs and practices; making surveys, studies, appraisals, inventories, utilizing university and college opportunities; a system of collecting data, correlating its values, and developing programs to activate research results and findings. Through planning to aid in making equal the unequal places of recreation in the democracy; getting maximum results from all efforts, eliminating waste and misuse; looking ahead immediately and on a long range basis; applying expert knowledge of the "know how"; providing functional and practical plans for building; wisely using natural and technological resources; form the habit of sound planning in all aspects of the program.
   E. In being the voice of recreation throughout the nation to interpret the place of state recreation to all the people; stressing its significance; proclaiming its importance; giving it the dignity it deserves; a sentinel to recognize the dangers of its misuse and abuse; a program to ameliorate recreation illiteracy; utilizing its preventive values; stating its vigorous place in the national economy; defining its potentials; and correlating its services.
   F. As the liaison organization throughout the Halls of Legislation—Federal,

state and local—introducing needed Legislation, promoting it, and working closely with the leadership of government to obtain effective results.

II. That state recreation and park associations or societies assume leadership

    A. In bringing together the various state agencies serving the Park and
Recreation movement in coordinated and cooperative action for maximum results.

    B. In advancing the concept of a state recreation and park commission or
board rendering full-time advisory and consultant services to public,
local, state, and federal, private and commercial interests, individuals
and groups.

    C. In organizing into one professional fellowship the recreation and park
leadership of the state representing all types of recreation interests and
programs.

    D. In enriching program opportunities, advancing specialisms, building,
resources—areas and facilities and the stimulation of source materials.

Promoting a balanced program for all ages, both sexes, all social and
economic strata; developing a program including a wide variety of
activities insures a democracy of choice; a year-round program; progressive activities, unique and stimulating practices and an everlasting stress
of interesting things to do for individuals and groups.

Gearing the programs of recreation into service for highpowered specialization, such as recreation for the aging, programs in our institutions
for the pathologic, patterns of effective value for rural folk, enhancing
family life, church interests, and the values of recreation in the hospital
setting—developing a strong army of technically trained people to administer the program.

Constantly increasing areas; building better outdoor and indoor facilities, adding to equipment, utilizing values of technology; employing
planners and engineers; maximum use of natural resources; demanding
functional tools and, at the same time, stressing beauty and attractive-
ness, creating, writing, publishing books, bulletins, magazines and the
like. Utilizing the genius of radio, television, and motion pictures in
the audio-visual opportunities for program enrichment and adding
knowledge for professional status.

III. That individual recreators and interested lay leaders assume leadership

    A. By taking a stand, in furthering the concept of a state recreation com-
mission or board as the finest means by which state government can
service the recreation needs and interests of the total population of the
state in bringing to them through advisory and consultant recreation
services more abundant and wholesome recreation.

The recreation movement is on the march and in its rapid expansion,
dynamic procedures, effective policies, vigorous actions, and intelligent
guidance become musts for established patterns. Thinking in terms of
our total human and natural resources to achieve these goals, may we
ever be found in the forefront of progressive action for advancement
and achievement.

Using the North Carolina Recreation Commission as an illustration, the beliefs, policies, and functions of a state recreation service are presented here. The North Carolina Commission believes:

GENERAL POLICIES

1. The Recreation Commission firmly believes that its tasks are stated in the powers and duties of the Commission Act and every effort is made to function within the sphere of these powers and duties.

2. The Commission is *not* an operating agency and, at this time, believes that it should not enter the operating field. Its primary interests are in consultation and in general services for the advancement of recreation.

3. The approach of the Commission is on invitation and by request. No efforts are made by the Commission to force the issues of recreation in the local situation nor to interfere with established and accepted procedures.

4. The Commission strongly believes in the principles of economic free enterprise and hence avoids participating in activities which would, in any way, interfere with free enterprise. Its general principle would be to assist such agencies and to interest them in furthering recreation.

5. Since organized recreation is a comparatively new endeavor of state government, the Commission's responsibilities in interpreting the field, establishing its values, promoting its benefits, achieving its needs, and, in any and every way, bringing more abundant recreation opportunities to all the people of North Carolina, are fully accepted and will continue to be conscientiously assumed by the Commission.

6. The Commission stands ready to cooperate in services, to correlate its efforts with other departments and agencies and to coordinate recreation activities for the earliest attainment of maximum desirable results and quality performance in all phases of recreation.

7. In the light of the newness of the Recreation Commission as a State Agency, the accepted policy of recreation adventure, aggressive initiative, practical planning, professional research and enterprise in furthering recreation in all of its aspects, is herein expressed.

8. While the Commission is a public agency and functions with all public recreation departments, it also serves private and commercial interests. Industries sponsoring recreation programs, church recreation groups, rural life agencies and organizations which, increasingly, recognize recreation as a basic rural need, hospital and institutional interests in recreation, the many youth-serving agencies, and all forms of commercial recreation enterprises receive the attention, concern, and action of the Commission whenever it is requested.

9. The Commission accepts the interpretation of the field of recreation which generally falls into an eightfold division—arts and crafts, dancing, dramatics, music, nature and outing, literary activities, social events, sports and games. It believes that, in the field of recreation program activities and administrative

units, these are the areas of interest into which planned efforts for promotion
and development of recreation services must be directed.

10. It is fully realized that staff and budget limitations constrict the capacity
for action. The Commission is aware of the many potentialities in the field and
will make every effort to move forward with additional staff and increased
budgetary provisions as they can be made available, to achieve satisfactory goals
and render maximum recreation services.

11. There can be no retreat from the sociologically established fact that it is the
duty of the local government to provide and operate its own recreation program
and services in terms of local needs, interests, and conditions. This is equally
true in the towns and in the neighborhoods where recreation is firmly wedded
to and deeply rooted in the lives of the people as well as in neighborhoods where
inertia, lack of knowledge of ways and means, or other factors have caused
large groups to be deprived of the benefits of planned opportunity. It is a rule
of state government as in welfare, education, law enforcement, and health to
assist political subdivisions, at their request, in satisfying local recreation needs.

12. That previous thinking of the North Carolina Recreation Commission is
confirmed to the end that the effectiveness and the continued sensitiveness to
the recreation needs of North Carolina will be promoted at a greater rate of
speed and with better adaptation, to the North Carolina situation, through the
North Carolina Recreation Commission in its capacity as an independent recreation agency within the state government.

SERVICES

FIGURE 1.   THE NORTH CAROLINA RECREATION
COMMISSION'S SERVICE TRIANGLE IN
NORTH CAROLINA

Duties of the Commission:

(1) To study and appraise recreation needs of the state and to assemble and
    disseminate information relative to recreation.
(2) To cooperate in the promotion and organization of local recreation systems
    for counties, municipalities, and other political subdivisions of the state, and
    to advise them in the planning and financing of recreation programs.
(3) To aid in recruiting, training, and referring recreators, and to promote
    recreation institutes and conferences.

(4) To aid in establishing and promoting approved recreation standards.

(5) To cooperate with: (a) state and federal agencies, (b) Recreation Advisory Committee, (c) private membership groups, (d) commercial recreation interests, and with individuals in their recreation interests.

These duties are assumed by the Commission, without charge, through:

* Consultation
* Correspondence
* Telephone Aid
* Publications
* Planning
* Research
* Surveys
* Organization Help
* Film Referrals
* Legislative Assistance
* Resources Files
* Bibliographical Services

* Local Talks
* Personnel Services and Records
* Advice on Finances
* News Media
* Institutes and Workshops
* Conferences
* Training (and Aids)
* Local Data Records
* Coordination (Local, State, National)
* Interpretation
* Promotion
* Referrals

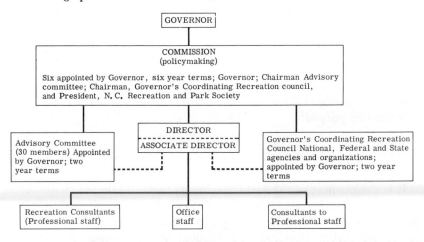

FIGURE 2.   ORGANIZATION CHART OF THE NORTH CAROLINA RECREATION COMMISSION

SERVICES DESIGNED TO ASSIST
PUBLIC—PRIVATE—COMMERCIAL RECREATION

Municipalities
Industries
Hospitals
Business Groups
Universities and Colleges
Youth Serving Agencies

Churches
Private Groups
Schools
Individuals
Civic and Service Groups
Commercial Recreation

Vacation and Tourist Travel
Rural, Town, and County Units
Institutional Homes for Children and Adults
Penal and Correctional Institutions

SERVICES THROUGH INSTITUTIONS OF
HIGHER LEARNING

This public service function might be illustrated with a description of the Recreation and Parks Field Service which is a part of the Department of Recreation and Municipal Park Administration at the University of Illinois.

Consistent with the long established and recognized functions of The University of Illinois, namely, *teaching, research,* and *service,* the Department of Recreation and Municipal Park Administration includes a program of park and recreation field service.

The need for Field Service grew out of the increasing impact of leisure upon the lives of the people which resulted in more widespread public interest and a heavy increase in requests for help in multiplying and strengthening recreation and park resources.

Administration

The Field Service is administered through the Department of Recreation and Municipal Park Administration which has limited staff available for this purpose.

Purpose and Method

It is the purpose of the Field Service (1) to assist selected communities and their organizations by helping them to develop their park resources and opportunities for recreation, (2) to strengthen the University's teaching efforts in recreation and parks through staff participation in research and practical field work problems, (3) to share the findings and results with all who may have an interest in them.

The purposes mentioned above are fulfilled through (1) providing professional assistance and counsel, (2) preparing and disseminating information on various phases of recreation and park management and promoting acceptable standards.

Policies:

1. Field Service is rendered only upon request.
2. Any community is entitled to one visit without charge (subject to availability of staff).

3. All other services, and particularly those involving extensive research and printed publications, are provided on a cost basis.

4. Cost estimates are available upon request.

Availability:

As resources permit, the Field Service is available to:

Local tax-supported governmental units.
Voluntary social agencies.
Institutions for the ill, handicapped and aged.
Religious organizations.
Industrial, civic, fraternal, and professional organizations.

Types of Service:

Examples of services are:

Assistance in establishing local authorities for recreation and parks.
Counseling on administrative problems concerned with organization, personnel, and finances.
Analysis and recommendations for program development.
Preparation of surveys, appraisals and research studies.
Conducting educational workshops for professionals and laymen in all aspects of Recreation and Park Management.

There is now proposed a merger between the Field Service of the University and Rural Recreation; Cooperative Extension Service. This concept of the services of the United States Department of Agriculture with Extension Services in the states of the Union will add greatly to the state recreation services for all of the people. It is an additional service to the State Recreation Departments, Commissions, and Boards. This merger plan is explained in Chapter 8.

THE INTERAGENCY COMMITTEE

In recent years, considerable attention has been given to the interagency recreation committee as a device for coordinating the recreation efforts of state departments and agencies. The purpose of such a committee is to exchange information, discover gaps in state recreation activities, bring about coordination and cooperative planning, and stimulate greater understanding of responsibilities in relation to state recreation facilities and services. Such state departments as parks, conservation, education, health, welfare, highways, agriculture, and planning are represented on the committee.

The principle of cooperative effort through formal interagency affiliation is as sound for recreation as it would be for education, health, welfare, and other public services. Michigan is an example of a state in which the interagency recreation committee has played a prominent role.

It is erroneously assumed that an interagency recreation committee, once created and operating, effectively bridges the gaps in providing total state recreation services. Actually, the interagency recreation committee has well-defined limitations, as well as potentialities. The major problem is to secure assistance from the states in helping the towns and cities to meet total—not piecemeal or fragmentary—community recreation needs. Therefore, the limitations of the state interagency recreation committee for meeting *total* community recreation needs should be kept in mind.

Because of the organic representation of the committee, there exists a constant risk of confusing the issue and overlooking the paramount need (i.e., so many of the agencies have responsibilities other than community recreation).

The total of split parts does not always add up to the whole.

An interdepartmental or interagency committee cannot substitute for an agency or department charged with the major responsibility of developing total recreation.

Although the interagency committee may decrease the chances of one department transcending the jurisdictional areas of its neighbor, it is no guarantee for eliminating (and can also be the means of sustaining) existing gaps and deficiencies in recreation services.

WORKSHOP

1. Study the scope, functions, and activities of several state departments involved in recreation to learn whether their services conflict, duplicate, or supplement one another.
2. Interview legislative leaders of your state for their opinions on recreation as a responsibility and function of state government.
3. Report on present state practices in providing recreation services to political subdivisions of your state.
4. Interview community leaders to determine what kinds of state recreation services would be most helpful to their towns.
5. Explore the ways in which state universities and colleges are contributing or might contribute to the development of community recreation.
6. Enumerate the functions and responsibilities of (1) a state recreation commission, and (2) a state recreation advisory committee.

7. Plan and conduct a forum on the question, "How to administer state recreation services."
8. Compare the state's recreation services with its services in education.
9. Explore the ways in which your state gives financial assistance to its political subdivisions.
10. List precautions to be taken in preventing competition in recreation planning among state departments and between states and communities.

REFERENCES

1. *The Bureau of Outdoor Recreation,* Department of the Interior, Washington, D.C., 1968, has a collection of "Comprehensive Outdoor Recreation Plans" for practically every state in the nation. This is perhaps the finest collection of state recreation programs, activities, organization and plans ever assembled.
2. *The North Carolina Recreation Commission,* Raleigh, North Carolina has the following information for distribution; 1968:
    American Recreation Society Policy on a State Recreation Service, 1952.
    "Policy Statement, Role of State Government in Organized Recreation," National Advisory Committee on State Services, National Recreation Association, August, 1958.
    "Recreation—A Function of State Government," made by North Carolina Recreation Commission, February, 1963.
    North Carolina Recreation Commission Act, revised by the 1963 General Assembly, May 23, 1963.
    "State and Provisional Recreation Services—Trends and Patterns," North Carolina Recreation Commission, revised February, 1965.
    "Outdoor Recreation for America—Its Implications at the Federal, State and Local Levels," North Carolina Recreation Commission, revised, March, 1965.
    "The Twenty First Anniversary Celebration of the North Carolina Recreation Commission and the North Carolina Recreation Society," published by the North Carolina Recreation Society, February 21, 1966.
    "The Twenty Point Recreation Program for North Carolina," North Carolina Recreation Commission, Publication No. 37, July, 1966.
    "A Study of Recreation and State Government, Its Advisory-Consultant Services to Local Government, County, City, to Public, Private and Commercial Recreation Interests in the Community," North Carolina Recreation Commission, Harold Meyer, July, 1967.
3. Meyer, Harold D., and Charles K. Brightbill, *State Recreation.* New York: A. S. Barnes & Co., 1950.
4. Outdoor Recreation Resources Review Commission, ORRRC, *Study Reports, Directory of State Outdoor Recreation Administration,* Washington, D.C., U. S. Government Printing Office, 1962.

Comments

Excellent resource materials on the activities and trends of state recreation are found in the studies, committee and conference reports, planning board reports and planning council studies, special legislative committee reports, college research studies and theses, and fact finding groups of recreation societies in the various states.

Frequent reports are available from the Bureau of Outdoor Recreation, Department of the Interior, Washington, D.C.

The various professional societies in the states offer source material. Obtain a list of these from the National Recreation and Park Association. State universities and colleges often have pertinent materials available.

Write to the State Recreation Commission in Raleigh, North Carolina, and the Board of Recreation in Montpelier, Vermont, the Georgia Recreation Commission, Atlanta, Georgia, the South Carolina Recreation Commission, Columbia, South Carolina for aids.

Write to the State Societies for activities and reports of their work.

8

The Federal Government
and Recreation

Recreation is not new to the federal government. Many of its departments have been engaged in recreation and related functions on both a permanent and emergency basis for a long time. No agencies, however, have all aspects of recreation as their major responsibility on a permanent basis. Nevertheless, as George D. Butler says, "Although these programs in many instances are incidental to the primary function of the agencies conducting them, taken together they represent a significant contribution to the field of recreation." The federal government has always shown a concern in recreation for both the public and its own employees. Today, that concern, stimulated by more leisure and more public demand, is deeper than ever. To understand the existing and potential place of the federal government in the recreation movement, it is essential to survey its present recreation functions. The following list illustrates the organizational structure of the executive branch and will be helpful in understanding the role of the various departments, agencies, boards and commissions in recreation:

Executive Office of the President:

The White House Office
Bureau of the Budget
Council of Economic Advisers

National Aeronautics and Space Council
National Council on Marine Resources and Engineering Development
National Security Council
Office of Economic Opportunity
Office of Emergency Planning
Office of Science and Technology
Special Representative for Trade Negotiations

Departments: (Each Headed by a Secretary)

Department of State
Department of the Treasury
Department of Defense
Department of Justice
Post Office Department
Department of the Interior
Department of Agriculture
Department of Commerce
Department of Labor
Department of Health, Education, and Welfare
Department of Housing and Urban Development
Department of Transportation

Agencies, Boards and Commissions

Administrative Conference of the United States
Advisory Commission on Intergovernmental Relations
American Battle Monuments Commission
Appalachian Regional Commission
Atomic Energy Commission
Canal Zone Government
Central Intelligence Agency
Civil Aeronautics Board
Commission of Fine Arts
Commission on Civil Rights
District of Columbia
Equal Employment Opportunity Commission
Export Import Bank of Washington
Farm Credit Administration
Federal Coal Mine Safety Board of Review
Federal Communications Commission
Federal Deposit Insurance Corporation
Federal Home Loan Bank Board
Federal Maritime Commission
Federal Mediation and Conciliation Service
Federal Power Commission

Board of Governors of the Federal Reserve System
Federal Trade Commission
Foreign Claims Settlement Commission
General Services Administration
Indian Claims Commission
Interstate Commerce Commission
National Aeronautics and Space Administration
National Capital Housing Authority
National Capital Transportation Agency
National Foundation on the Arts and Humanities
National Labor Relations Board
National Mediation Board
National Science Foundation
Panama Canal Company
Railroad Retirement Board
Renegotiation Board
St. Lawrence Seaway Development Corporation
Securities and Exchange Commission
Selective Service System
Small Business Administration
Smithsonian Institution
Subversive Activities Control Board
Tax Court of the United States
Tennessee Valley Authority
U. S. Arms Control and Disarmament Agency
U. S. Civil Service Commission
United States Information Agency
United States Tariff Commission
Veterans Administration
Virgin Islands Corporation
Water Resources Council

FUNCTIONS OF FEDERAL AGENCIES

A complete description of recreation and recreation-related functions of the above organizations would require a volume in itself. The following are illustrative examples only, and are not intended as a complete description.

The U. S. Department of Agriculture

Farmers Home Administration—This agency is authorized to make loans for recreation purposes to individual family farmers and to local public bodies or non-profit groups associated with communities of not over 5,500 in population. These loans may not exceed 5 per cent interest or

40 years repayment. Under this loan program funds may be authorized to local government agencies and non-profit agencies and organizations up to 100% wherever eligible to purchase lands for certain recreation purposes and to develop specified types of recreation facilities.

Federal Extension Service—The Federal Extension Service and Cooperative Extension Services provide technical and educational assistance to state government agencies, local government agencies, non-profit agencies and organizations and private organizations. Technical information and feasibility studies are available in the areas of design, development and landscaping. A sampling of services available are: assisting landowners in converting cropland to recreation uses; farm vacation businesses; recreation leadership training; and development and operation of tourist attractions. This program cooperates with and functions through Land Grant Colleges and Universities.

The work of the Extension Service is on an advisory and consultative basis and operates through rural organizations. A large part of the Service's recreation efforts are through the 4-H Clubs. The goal of this program is the development of youth through practical training and experience in agriculture, home economics, and good citizenship; recreation is a regular inclusion.

Recreation materials and publications are provided and rural recreation specialists at the land grant colleges and universities organize and conduct recreation training institutes and provide other helpful recreation services. State, district, and county 4-H camps play a large part in the recreation of rural young folks.

Some states have full-time recreation specialists and others have professional personnel who give part of their attention to recreation. Thousands of volunteers provide additional recreation leadership. Broad interpretation and public demand for service have provided recreation services through the Smith-Lever Act of 1914 (Section 2) and subsequent acts of Congress.

Forest Service—General Forestry Assistance is technical and given to individuals, industries, organizations, and agencies when the State Foresters cannot do so, by providing special technicians from the Regional, Area, and Chief's offices of the Forest Service. Aid may be furnished on all types of forestry work, particularly highly specialized technical activities generally not handled by the separate State Forestry organizations. Assistance with management problems on state and community forests—including recreation as one of the multiple uses of the forests—is given high priority. General Forestry Assistance also contributes to the USDA Rural Areas Development Program by serving on state and county Technical Action Panels and helping to evaluate forest resources and new market potentials and job opportunities. Forest Service publications include Agricultural Information Bulletin No. 265—"Forest Recreation for Profit."

The Forest Service, through the National Forestry Research Program, gives a limited number of grants to universities and other non-profit research institutions and organizations for basic and applied research related to forestry, including recreation. In general, a principal investigator, prominent in the field to be studied, is designated to carry out a project.

The primary purpose of the Forest Service is to preserve the forests as an important national resource, but through such efforts public recreation needs are served extensively. These forest lands are available for recreation consistent with the protection of the areas, the over-all public needs, and the health and safety of the public.

The national forests have facilities for picnicking and camping. Hiking and riding trails, facilities for swimming, boating, water sports, and mountain climbing are included in some areas. Particular attention is given to nature lore, wildlife, and other aspects of life outdoors. Wilderness areas in themselves are great recreation resources for sports such as fishing and hunting (where allowed) and for enjoyment of scenic beauty in its primitive form. Millions of persons visit the national forests each year. Facilities include camp and picnic grounds, swimming areas, organization camps, and hotels and resorts. Hunting and fishing in the national forests, except in a few areas, are controlled by state laws.

Permits to construct recreation facilities in the national forests are given to public and semipublic organizations. The Forest Service Organic Act of 1897, and laws passed subsequently, authorize the recreation functions.

Plant Industry Bureau—The Plant Industry Bureau provides information and an advisory service on the selection of trees, shrubbery, grasses, and the like for parks, playgrounds, golf courses, and other recreation facilities.

Soil Conservation Service—In connection with its major purpose, conserving the land, the Soil Conservation Service encourages camping, picnicking, hunting, fishing, and other forms of recreation. Some of its projects include recreation as a project purpose. These recreation areas are on the shores of water impoundments and can be administered as units separate from the soil conservation lands. Local groups are sometimes authorized to make recreation improvements. Most of the service's facilities are for public day use, such as picnicking, swimming, boating, and fishing, but there are also often overnight cabins available.

Under the provisions of the Watershed Protection and Flood Prevention Act (P.L. 566, 83rd Congress, as amended) authority is granted for cost sharing assistance for land, easements, and rights-of-way acquired by sponsoring local organizations for approved public recreation or fish and wildlife purposes. The Federal share of the cost of the land rights may not exceed 50 per cent of the cost allocated to these purposes which is borne by the sponsors in acquiring the land rights in fee simple title. Land eligible for cost sharing assistance includes the dam site, spillway area, area within the reservoir dedicated to recreation or fish and wildlife use plus contiguous land needed to provide public access and public use of the planned facilities.

Cost sharing assistance may be made available to qualified local sponsoring organizations under the Small Watersheds Authority for the installation of measures for public recreation or public fish and wildlife developments which are an integral part of approved watershed work plans. Single-purpose recreation or fish and wildlife projects, or single-purpose developments for these purposes within a project, are not eligible for assistance.

Department of Commerce

Bureau of the Census—The United States Census Bureau is responsible for the population count. It provides information on the size, nature, and characteristics of the population. Such data are helpful in answering the recreation needs of the people. The bureau also provides information on the amounts of money which states, counties, and municipalities spend for recreation, the revenues which accrue from recreation, and other pertinent facts. From the Census Bureau and other programs in the Department of Commerce also comes information on industries related to the leisure and recreation fields.

Department of Defense

Army Corps of Engineers—The main purpose of the Corps of Engineers is to develop and maintain rivers and waterways in the interest of navigation and flood control. This work is related to the field of recreation through forestry and wildlife conservation.

Picnic facilities, hiking trails, observation points, public boat launching and docking facilities, facilities for swimming and fishing, public camp grounds, and organized camps of nonprofit agencies can be found in areas under the jurisdiction of the Corps of Engineers. The recreation possibilities of all reservoir projects are closely examined and developed.

There is close cooperation between the Corps of Engineers and other federal, state, and local agencies.

The Flood Control Act of 1944, as amended by the Flood Control Act of 1962, authorizes the Chief of Engineers, under supervision of the Secretary of the Army, to construct, operate, and maintain public park and recreation facilities at water resource development projects under jurisdiction of the Department of the Army, and to permit such construction, operation, and maintenance by local interests. Water resource projects may include not only reservoirs but other types of projects, providing a potential exists for recreation use related to the project. Federal facilities, however, shall not be a substitute for municipal park facilities. The Secretary of the Army is also authorized to grant leases of lands, including structures of facilities thereon, for such periods and upon such terms and for such purposes as he deems reasonable in the public interest. Leases to non-profit organizations for recreation purposes may be granted at reduced or nominal consideration, and preference shall be given to federal, state or local government agencies. In some appropriate cases, licenses or leases may be granted without monetary considerations.

The Federal Water Project Recreation Act of 1965 (P.L. 89–72) states that the federal government can assume up to 50 per cent of the separable costs of recreation development at a water resource project and all of the joint costs allocated to recreation, and that recreation and fish and wildlife enhancement can be considered a project purpose if local interests agree to participate to the extent of 50 per cent of the separable recreation costs, all costs of operation, maintenance, and replacement thereof, and administer project land and water areas for recreation and fish and wildlife enhancement. This act applies to all water resources development agencies.

The Department of Health, Education, and Welfare

Administration on Aging—Under the Older Americans Act funds may be allotted for minor alterations and repair or to purchase or construct various recreation facilities. These are authorized to state government agencies on a ratio of 75 per cent for the first year, 60 per cent for the second year and 50 per cent for the third year. Up to 100 per cent funding for local government agencies and non-profit agencies and organizations is available. Federal funds may be authorized under Title III and IV of this Act to pay all or part of the salaries of personnel employed in planning, supervising or conducting such recreation activities as active games and sports, arts and crafts, collecting, drama, literary activities, music, nature and outing, service and social.

Welfare Administration—The Children's Bureau of the Welfare Administration makes grants to institutions of higher learning to train personnel for work in the field of child welfare and to help institutions of higher learning train a greater number of persons for work in the field of child welfare. Child welfare training grants can be made to schools of social work and other institutions of higher learning for student traineeships and for short-term training projects such as institutes, seminars, workshops.

It is easy to understand how a bureau that is concerned with all matters pertaining to the welfare of children includes recreation as one of its interests. The Bureau does not have recreation personnel, per se, on its staff but seldom are steps taken by the Bureau which do not reflect the recreation needs of children.

Established in 1912, the Children's Bureau, from time to time, has encouraged adequate play space for children and promoted recreation as essential for children in both urban and rural areas. The Bureau investigates and compiles reports which include recreation. It makes studies and has published materials on games and other aspects of play and recreation for children. The Bureau works cooperatively with the states and other federal and national agencies and organizations on recreation and related matters. Its decennial White House Conference on Children and Youth focuses much attention on recreation needs.

Office of Education—It is the purpose of the United States Office of Education to promote the cause of education throughout the nation. It discharges this responsibility in different ways, including the collection and dissemination of facts, promulgation of standards, and provision of consultative assistance. In cases where the federal government gives financial assistance to the schools, such service funnels through the Office of Education.

The Office stresses the importance of teaching the wise use of free time, and many of its studies and publications include material on recreation and its relation to school responsibilities. Staff members participate in conferences, institutes, and workshops on recreation. The Office recognizes recreation and play as significant parts of education. Much of its work is with state departments of public instruction. Specifically, the U.S. Office of Education helps in school-community-recreation planning. It also advises on conditions, trends, and needs, and includes recreation in many of its publications. It is concerned with the leisure and recreation needs of the community, particularly the school population, and the resources of the school in providing adequate recreation opportunities. The Organization Act of 1867 is its basic legislation.

Public Health Service—The United States Public Health Service serves recreation where matters of health are involved. It provides information and assistance, for example, concerning sanitation and health in relation to park and recreation facilities, including pools, beaches, camps, water reservoirs and other facilities. Studies are made of recreation resources which may include water supplies, food handling procedures, refuse collection and disposal systems, and the like. The Public Health Service also provides recreation in its own hospitals.

The National Institutes of Health, which come under the jurisdiction of the Public Health Service, provide federal funds for research and training. Some of these efforts are related, at least indirectly, to advancing recreation in relation to health, particularly mental health and the aging.

Any federal or state agency may call upon the Public Health Service in the planning, development, operation, and maintenance of recreation facilities which bear upon the transmission of communicable diseases and in the installation and operation of sanitation works and services.

The Rehabilitation Services Administration—This agency provides trainee grants for graduate study in the field of therapeutic recreation. It encourages state, public and other non-profit rehabilitation organizations and agencies as follows:

1. Rehabilitation centers, sheltered workshops, and other special facilities to furnish adequate recreation services for handicapped persons participating in the programs.
2. State and local institutions providing extended hospitalization and chronic disease care to incorporate adequate recreation activities into the treatment and rehabilitation programs within such institutions.
3. State vocational rehabilitation agencies to arrange for such recreation services, where needed and possible, for persons served by the state rehabilitation programs.

Grants are made to state and other public and non-profit agencies to pay part of the cost of research and demonstration projects. The federal percentage of the project cost varies. To date, the Rehabilitation Services Administration has supported four projects involving recreation for ill and handicapped persons, development of a university information center on recreation for the handicapped, and analyses of methods by which community recreation programs can be changed to include recreation for the handicapped. This agency makes grants to schools, universities, and non-profit organizations and agencies to cover part of the cost of professional education of personnel in field, including recreation, which can contribute to vocational rehabilitation of the disabled.

Department of Housing and Urban Development

Housing Assistance Administration—The Housing Assistance Administration has responsibility for low-rent and emergency-housing. Effort is made to include in the housing developments adequate space and facilities for the play of children and the recreation of all of the tenants. Toward this end the Administration has published information and standards for recreation, provided technical assistance in the development of adequate recreation facilities, and generally assisted in encouraging the increase and improvement of housing resources for recreation. Housing Assistance Administration policy holds that community facilities, programs and effective community planning are services essential to the successful development and management of public and private agencies. HAA works constantly to secure and channel needed social services to help improve the family and community living standards of tenant families. HAA also urges each Local Housing Authority to realize its potential as a major community resource, and to work as a partner with other local agencies concerned with the provision of recreation along with other services. The Administration does *not* allocate funds for recreation leadership, but small expenditures for recreation equipment and supplies are permitted. Public Laws 11, 67, and 412 provide the legal authorization for this work.

The Renewal Assistance Administration—administers Title VII of the Housing Act of 1961, which authorized Federal grants to the states and local bodies to assist in the acquisition of permanent open-space land.

The purpose of the authorization is to help curb urban sprawl and prevent the spread of urban deterioration, to encourage more desirable urban development, and to help provide necessary recreation, conservation, and scenic areas by assisting public bodies in acting promptly to preserve open-space land essential to long-range development. This encourages the acquisition and development of recreation facilities and emphasizes the importance of sound planning.

Department of the Interior

Bureau of Indian Affairs—Contributions of the Bureau of Indian Affairs to recreation include recreation for the Indians on the reservations, tourist attractions, Indian lore, and hunting and fishing preserves for sportsmen.

Each year tens of thousands of tourists seeking recreation visit the Indian reservations to enjoy the scenery and ceremonials, and to examine and understand the Indian crafts. With permission of the Indian tribes, hunting and fishing are allowed on parts of the reservations.

In some cases, camping grounds are available, although only the Eastern Cherokee Reservation in North Carolina includes cabins and lodges. Some reservations have museums which house Indian arts and crafts. The recreation of more than 400,000 Indians is served to some degree through a few community centers and a concern for the play opportunities of Indian children.

Bureau of Land Management—The Bureau of Land Management leases and sells unreserved nonmineral public lands to the political subdivisions for recreation and park purposes. It also leases or sells small tracts of land of five acres or less to individuals for camp, cabin, or recreation use. Lands in the public domain of the United States and Alaska total over

400,000,000 acres and are used for recreation in many ways, including travel, hunting, fishing, camping, hiking, and picnicking. Much of the planning of the Bureau of Land Management is aimed at securing the recreational use of the public lands. The Recreation Act of 1926, the Small Tracts Act of 1938, and the Taylor Grazing Act of 1934 include recreation provisions.

The Recreation and Public Purposes Act of 1954 provides that state and local governments and qualified nonprofit organizations can acquire certain Federal lands for recreation use and for other purposes. The Secretary of the Interior has established the purchase price to states and other governmental agencies at $2.50 an acre, and the lease rental at 25 cents an acre per year for recreation purposes.

Prices to nonprofit organizations are based on appraisal of the land, after taking into consideration the purposes for which the land is to be used. Public agencies may lease land without regard to acreage limitations for public recreation purposes, and for other purposes to which the reduced sale price applies, for 25 cents an acre payable in advance for 5-year periods, with a minimum rental of $10.

The term "recreation" is interpreted in a broad sense for the purposes of this act. Included are expansion of existing parks and establishment of new parks and recreation areas, campgrounds, picnic areas, sites for boating, swimming, skiing and other water and winter sports, county and municipal playgrounds, hunting and fishing camps, and a wide range of outdoor activities. The definition also provides for group recreation such as youth and institutional camps, sites for civic organization recreation and outdoor activities. Also included are wildlife improvements such as the installation of structures and improvement of habitat. Less intensive recreation uses of land, such as hunting, fishing, sightseeing, hiking or rock collecting ordinarily are not the basis for a lease or patent unless substantial financial investments in facilities are proposed, or unless the tract is needed to complement a program on adjoining lands.

Outdoor Recreation Resources Review Commission

The Outdoor Recreation Resources Review Commission was authorized by Congress in 1958 under Public Law 85–470 and was terminated in 1962. The Commission consisted of two majority and two minority members from each of the Senate and House Committees on Interior and Insular Affairs, and seven citizens at large. It had an advisory council of 25 private citizens and liaison officers from interested federal agencies.

The establishment of the ORRRC grew from increasing public interest in and use of outdoor recreation resources. The act's preamble explains the purpose of the Commission: "In order to preserve, develop, and

assure accessibility to all American people of present and future generations such quality and quantity of outdoor recreation resources as will
be necessary and desirable for individual enjoyment, and to assure the
spiritual and cultural and physical benefits that such outdoor recreation
provides."

The Commission made a nationwide inventory and evaluation of outdoor recreation directed toward providing answers to the following
questions:

What are the recreation wants and needs of the American people now, and
what will they be in the years 1976 to 2000?

What are and will be the recreation resources of the nation available to fill
what will they be in the years 1976 and 2000?

What policies and programs should be recommended to insure that the needs
of the present and future are adequately and efficiently met? [2]

Bureau of Outdoor Recreation—Growing out of the recommendations
made by the Outdoor Recreation Resources Review Commission, this
Bureau of Outdoor Recreation was established in the Department of the
Interior in 1962 as an agency to spearhead the over-all development of
outdoor recreation resources. It serves as a focal point for coordination
of recreation policy, planning, programs, or management, as they relate
to the more than 20 federal agencies with services involving some aspect
of outdoor recreation. The Bureau assists the Secretary of the Interior in
carrying out his federal outdoor recreation coordination responsibilities,
sponsors and conducts recreation research, conducts recreation resource
surveys, develops a nationwide recreation plan, disseminates outdoor
recreation information, and implements federal outdoor recreation
policies. There is an Outdoor Recreation Advisory Council made up of
the heads of federal departments and agencies principally concerned with
outdoor recreation.

The Bureau of Outdoor Recreation administers the Land and Water
Conservation Fund which provides for 50 per cent grants to states, and
through them to political subdivisions and other units of states, for
planning, acquisition, and development of public outdoor recreation
areas and facilities. This program is financed by (1) proceeds from entrance, admission, or user fees and charges at federal recreation areas;
(2) receipts from the sale of surplus federal real property through the
General Services Administration; (3) taxes from the sale of motor boat
fuels.

Bureau of Reclamation—The great dams of the United States, such as
Hoover Dam, Grand Coulee Dam, and Bonneville Dam, are outstanding

[2] Outdoor Recreation Resources Review Commission, *Progress Report* (Washington,
D. C., January 1961), p. vii.

resources for many kinds of recreation. They are of particular interest to the tourist, sportsman, and camper. Bureau of Reclamation dams and canal systems bring irrigation water to over eight million acres in 17 western states. The Bureau encourages fishing, boating, camping, picnicking, swimming, hiking, riding, travel, and other activities. In dam areas are found miles of scenic attractions. The Bureau works jointly with the National Park Service and state bodies in planning and developing outdoor recreation facilities. State or local governmental organizations may administer and develop recreation resources at the Bureau's reservoir areas, which are receiving increased attention. Extensive studies for recreation land and water use are undertaken.

The Reclamation Act was passed in 1902. Annual appropriation acts for the Bureau of Reclamation provide for the exploration of reclamation projects for recreation.

The Federal Water Projects Recreation Act (P. L. 89–72), enacted in 1965, provides new guidelines for analysis and development of the recreation and fish and wildlife enhancement potentials of water resources projects within the program of the Bureau of Reclamation. It includes provisions applicable to project development proposals considered for future authorization as well as to existing and previously authorized projects. This law provides that non-Federal recreation and fish and wildlife management agencies which participate in the program shall share pertinent development costs on both old and new projects and meet reimbursement requirements through cash payments, crediting values of lands and facilities, repayment with interest over a period of time (not exceeding 50 years), or a combination of these.

Fish and Wildlife Service—The purpose of the Fish and Wildlife Service is to protect and increase fish and wildlife resources, to educate the public with respect to these resources, and to enforce the federal game laws.

The Bureau of Sports Fisheries and Wildlife, a part of the Fish and Wildlife Service, administers National Wildlife Refuges and National Fish Hatcheries in most of the 50 states. The refuges protect a variety of wild life, including migratory waterfowl, migratory birds, and big game. The fish hatcheries are devoted almost entirely to the preservation and development of freshwater game fish and salmon.

The refuges make their greatest contribution to the nation's recreation in the production and protection of wildlife. Migratory fowl supply the game for millions of hunters, just as fishermen benefit from the hatcheries. The refuges are also used for observing and photographing wildlife, fishing, boating, and picnicking. They are visited by millions of people each year. Some recreation facilities are provided by the Bureau, while others are accomplished through concessionaires or agreements with local governmental or civic groups.

Through this service, the federal government finances up to 75 per cent of the total cost of state wildlife and fish projects. Authority for the recreation efforts of the service is in the various Congressional acts for the protection of migratory birds and game mammals and the wildlife conservation and restoration laws.

The Federal Aid in Fish and Wildlife Restoration programs give financial assistance to state fish and game departments for projects to restore, conserve, and manage fish and wildlife resources. The programs are supported by excise taxes on sporting arms, ammunition, and fishing tackle. Funds are distributed to states by prescribed formulae; approvable activities include research, development, management, maintenance, and coordination.

National Park Service—By administering the National Park System, the National Park Service plays a prominent role in serving the outdoor recreation interests of the nation. This system includes national parks, historical parks, one national memorial park, national battlefields, parks, and sites, national monuments, national military parks, national historic sites, national memorials, national cemeteries, national parkways, national recreation areas, national seashore recreation areas, and the national capital parks consisting of many units.

The operations of the National Park Service are administered through the central office, four regional offices, and the staffs of the various parks, including a superintendent of each area.

Recreation facilities of the national parks are quite extensive. They include hiking trails, bridle paths and stables, museums, facilities for picnicking, camping, and outings. In these parks are also found tourist facilities, restaurants, hotels, information stations, cottages, and cabins. In certain areas there are opportunities for mountain climbing and other adventuresome outdoor sports. Opportunities for swimming, boating, and nature study are plentiful. During the summer season, naturalists conduct tours and automobile caravans, take visitors on nature hikes, and present illustrated lectures and demonstrations.

Other functions of the National Park Service include:

1. Interpreting the national resources and historical implications to the public.
2. Cooperating with other federal agencies, such as the Fish and Wildlife Service and Forest Service, in developing outdoor recreation facilities.
3. Managing reservoir recreation areas.
4. Surveying historic and archeological sites.
5. Studying public park, parkway, and recreation area programs, park problems, charges, and fees.
6. Preparing plans and working drawings for the Bureau of Reclamation.
7. Consulting with the states in the development of state parks.

   The National Park Service has a State Assistance Program under which technical and advisory assistance may be furnished to state and local governments. This technical and advisory assistance is generally on a programmed and reimbursable basis on such matters as park agency organization, administration, planning, and the operation and maintenance of park systems or units, personnel training, historical and archeological programs and general development planning. Other specific areas of assistance are design, facilities, land acquisition, standards and zoning.

8. Investigating federal surplus properties requested for park use.

The National Park Service was also instrumental in developing recreation demonstration areas for state use during the days of the Depression. It supervised park projects carried out by the Civilian Conservation Corps. Considered as a whole, the work of the National Park Service contributes greatly to recreation in the United States as it relates to parks and the public domain.

Under a joint program, the National Park Service, the National Conference on State Parks and the National Recreation and Park Association offer technical, planning and operational information through the Park Practice Program. The privately financed publications under this program include *Design,* which offers planning concepts; *Guidelines,* which offers administrative and policy information; *Grist* (with supplements), which provides information helpful at the field maintenance and operational levels; and *Trends in Parks and Recreation,* a quarterly stressing new concepts and philosophies. This program is available on a subscription basis to interested agencies, organizations and individuals.

The Service's two major legislative authorizations are in the 1916 Act establishing the National Park Service, and the 1936 Park, Parkway, and Recreation-Area Study Act.

The Historic Preservation Act authorizes the Secretary of the Interior to expand and maintain a national registry of districts, sites, buildings, structures and objects significant in American history, architecture, archaeology and culture; to grant 50 per cent matching funds to states (based on need) for preparing comprehensive statewide historic surveys and plans, and for the acquisition, preservation (i.e., protection, rehabilitation, restoration and reconstruction) and development of such properties by state and local governments. Each statewide historic plan must be coordinated with the state's outdoor recreation plan (prepared in accordance with the Land and Water Conservation Fund program). The respective state, local or private agency must bear 100 per cent of the cost of continued maintenance, repair and administration of approved projects.

National Park Trust Fund Board—This Board is authorized to accept and administer gifts of personal property for the benefit of the National Park Service, its activities, or service. Gifts which entail expenditures not met from the gift may not be accepted without the consent of Congress.

Department of Transportation

Bureau of Public Roads—The Public Roads Administration comes into the recreation picture because much of the travel on the public roads is for recreation purposes. This Bureau not only works with the Forest Service and the National Park Service in constructing roads into forests and parks, but also work with state highway departments in developing major and secondary roads which serve recreationally motivated traffic. Travel to hunting and fishing grounds, to picnic areas and camps, to winter sports areas and to golf courses as well as other recreation centers, depends upon an adequate, safe, network of highways. Roadside parks, off-road parking facilities, turnouts for scenic, historic and rest points, footpaths from roadways, and roadside erosion planting are all a part of such service. The several Federal-Aid Highway Acts are the authority for the Bureau's program.

Under Title III of P. L. 89–285, The Highway Beautification Act of 1965, the Secretary may approve as a part of the construction of Federal-aid highways the cost of landscape and roadside development, including acquisition and development of publicly owned and controlled rest and recreation areas and sanitary and other facilities reasonably necessary to accommodate the traveling public. These are funded up to 100 per cent. The selection of individual sites acquired for the restoration, preservation and enhancement of scenic beauty adjacent to the highways continues to be the prerogative of the state highway departments.

OTHER FEDERAL AGENCIES

The President's Council on Recreation and Natural Beauty, established in 1966, is concerned with the problems of restoring and maintaining the quality of the environment. Recreation has a recognized role in this concern. The work of this Council includes the study of ways in which federal property can be used to increase outdoor recreation services, regional recreation planning to help meet the increasing visitor pressures at recreation attractions, and scenic roads and parkways.

President's Council on Physical Fitness—Following the recommendation of the Conference on Fitness of American Youth, the President's Council on Physical Fitness was established by Executive Order 10673, June 18, 1956, to stimulate the advance of fitness. The Council consists of the Secretaries of the departments of the Interior, Defense, Agriculture, Commerce, Labor, and Health, Education and Welfare, and the administrator of the Housing and Home Finance Agency. The Secretary of the Interior serves as chairman. The President's Citizens Advisory Committee on the Fitness of American Youth advises the Council.

The Council attempts to work with existing agencies and organizations—official, voluntary, and private—to encourage and assist them in strengthening recreation programs, especially with regard to physical fitness implications. The Council's staff of four full-time professionals provides consultative assistance in the areas of programming, public relations and research, prepares publications and visual aids, conducts advertising campaigns, and carries out other services.

Tennessee Valley Authority—As a by-product of its major purpose—producing electrical power—the Tennessee Valley Authority exerts a strong influence on the development of recreation resources in that region.

TVA develops recreation facilities on its shorelands and reservoirs. These facilities are operated as concessions at 12 of the major dams. Among the facilities are more than 50 boat docks, fishing camps, and small resort sites, better than 23 group camps, and over 1100 lots for cottages, which are either leased or sold. In these areas, the Fish and Wildlife Service maintains more than 100,000 acres of game refuges.

TVA through its recreation resource development program encourages recreation development by making land available to other Federal agencies, state and local agencies, private organizations, and individuals through transfers, conveyances, leases, licenses, or sales. Reservoir lands with identified recreation potential are made available through transfer or lease to state and local agencies for park, recreation and other purposes. TVA has also made lands surplus to its needs available to private organizations for related purposes such as club sites or group camps, through sale at public auction.

As a part of early demonstrations in recreation resource development, recreation facilities were constructed by TVA and subsequently conveyed to the state in which they were located. Additional facilities constructed during this early demonstration period included boat harbors and marinas which were leased or sold to private organizations and individuals.

The services and assistance provided by TVA are primarily oriented to the Tennessee Valley region. As a part of its total program for economic development in the Tennessee Valley, TVA actively encourages utilization of surrounding shorelines. It conducts studies and demonstrations in the use of land and waters in the region for recreation purposes and provides technical assistance toward achieving optimum use and development of these resources.

TVA is currently developing the Land Between the Lakes Demonstration in Western Kentucky and Tennessee. This project is being done as a demonstration to show how an area drained of many of its natural resources by previous generations can be restored to serve the recreation needs of our rapidly urbanizing society and at the same time give impetus to the economic growth of the surrounding region.

Veterans Administration—The Veterans Administration, through its

Recreation Section in the Physical Medicine and Rehabilitation Service, operates a program at each V. A. hospital and home. Its program includes sports, music, entertainment, radio, motion pictures, social recreation, arts, crafts, special events, hospitality services, and hobbies.

The purpose of the recreation program in Veterans Administration hospitals is to provide, as an integral phase of the total medical program, a comprehensive, well-balanced, and professionally executed range of recreation activities to meet the needs, interests, and capabilities of all patients. All activities offered by the recreation program require medical approval.

The recreation program is planned to assist the doctor in getting his patients well and to make life as satisfying and meaningful as possible for those patients who must remain in the hospital for long periods of time. The diversified activities which constitute the program are designed to accomplish the following objectives:

a. Assist in facilitating patients' adjustment to hospital life and medical treatment.
b. Provide doctors with opportunities to observe patient behavior and response to activity.
c. Assist in orienting patients in their physical limitations and potentialities.
d. Contribute to the development and maintenance of normal physical condition during the patients' stay in the hospital.
e. Develop interests and skills in so-called "carry-over" activities; that is, activities in which patients may participate safely and beneficially during their stay in the hospital as well as after their discharge from the hospital.
f. Contribute to the total social and psychological readjustment of patients.[3]

In order to develop and maintain a recreation program at each hospital and center, the positions of recreation director, assistant recreation director, recreation technician, sports technician, music technician, radio technician, projectionist, and similar positions have been authorized.

RECREATION FOR FEDERAL EMPLOYEES AND THE ARMED FORCES

The federal government and its agencies employ hundreds of thousands of people. Consequently, a number of federal agencies and departments conduct recreation programs for their own employees as part of their personnel services. In many ways, these recreation programs are not unlike the programs conducted in private industry for employees and their families.

[3] Special Services Pamphlet 6-3, Recreation Services, Veterans Administration (Washington, D. C.: U. S. Government Printing Office, n.d.).

The scope of these federal employee recreation services vary with the degree of recreation opportunities available in the community, the location of the federal work, and the amount of funds available. The Atomic Energy Commission, for example, with its plants in isolated spots of the nation, has had to help build entirely new communities and include recreation along with schools, hospitals, sanitary facilities, and the like. Practically all of the major departments of government provide recreation opportunities of some kind for their employees.

The armed forces have also provided recreation services for their many civilian employees located in various parts of the country. Recreation first went to war on a large scale in World War I when a number of national voluntary agencies, such as the Young Men's Christian Association, Salvation Army, Knights of Columbus, Jewish Welfare Board, and American Library Association, undertook major responsibility for catering to the recreation and social needs of uniformed personnel on the posts and overseas. The American National Red Cross joined these groups in serving the needs of the armed forces.

In order to understand the place and function of recreation within the armed forces, it is important to know the services provided by these divisions within the several components of the military establishment.

Army

"Special Services" includes a variety of programs, facilities, activities, and services provided on-post, in maneuver areas, and overseas theaters, primarily for the off-duty use of enlisted personnel in the interests of their moral, mental, physical, and social well-being. The Army Special Services program consists of voluntary recreative sports, library service, arts and crafts activities, and musical and theatrical programs, and a variety of recreation services and activities in which the service club is the focal point. Post theaters and motion-picture theaters are operated by a Special Service officer under the guidance, technically, of the Army and Air Force Motion Picture Service. Dependent Youth Activities were established in 1968 as the sixth core program as a result of a growing realization that the welfare and morale of the soldier include his family, particularly his children.

The Special Services program was established in the Army to provide for the American soldier, wherever stationed, a well-rounded, wholesome, entertaining, and constructive program for his off-duty hours. A good Special Services program is an inducement for enlistment in that it offers to prospective soldiers a recreation program comparable to that offered by the average civilian community. The program further compensates in some degree for separation from family, duty at isolated posts, and other hardships of the military service.

In sports, high level competition has been encouraged, including inter-service competition. In athletics major emphasis is placed on the conduct of intramural sports; however, support is also continued to national and international competitions such as the Pan American and Olympic Games. In arts and crafts the relatively simple hand skills have been augmented by progressive programs in well-equipped shops.

During World War II the Special Services Division operated directly under the Commanding General, Army Service Forces. Immediately fol-lowing the cessation of hostilities. Special Services was established as a separate branch of the Army and the recreation program was the re-sponsibility of the Office, Chief of Special Services. As of March 1, 1950, the Office, Chief of Special Services, was abolished and the Adjutant General's Office assumed the responsibility. Special Services is now a division of the Adjutant General's Office.

The function of the Special Services Division is to advise the Adjutant General and other interested staff agencies on all matters pertaining to the recreation program of the Army and its effect on the welfare of the soldier. This division is responsible for the planning of the over-all recre-ation program of the Army and for liaison with civilian agencies in-terested in this program.

Civilian personnel performing Special Services duties are used to a considerable extent and are paid from two sources: funds appropriated by Congress and local nonappropriated funds derived principally from dividends from the the Army and Air Force Exchange Service and the Army and Air Force Motion Picture Service. Civilian positions are described and their qualifications and salary ranges defined in the GS-188 (Recreation Specialist) and GS-410 (Librarian) series of the United States Civil Service Commission.

Air Force

"Special Services" is defined as the agency established by the Depart-ment of the Air Force to provide those programs, facilities, activities, and services deemed necessary for the maintenance of a high state of morale. The U.S.A.F. Special Services program consists of voluntary sports, library service, arts and crafts activities, musical and theatrical programs, motion pictures, entertainment, and a variety of recreational services and activities. The service club is the focal point for many Special Services activities. Special Services also makes its services available to officers' and noncommissioned officers' messes, providing assistance to mess personnel in the conduct of the entertainment and sports program.

The actual operation of the Special Services program is performed at installation or base level.

In addition to the utilization of civilian personnel, civilian specialists in various entertainment and recreation fields may be employed by higher command staffs or headquarters.

The Air Force does very well in coordinating its program with communities near its bases and in using volunteers from those communities.

Marine Corps

"Special Services" are those services or activities, generally nonmilitary, provided each Marine and his dependents, where appropriate, which have a bearing on his general welfare. Special Services includes the following programs: recreation, athletics, education and information, personal affairs, and Marine Corps exchanges.

The Special Services program was established to provide for the maintenance of mental and physical stamina and high morale of Marine Corps personnel. An organized program of sports, recreation, education and information, and personal affairs, largely financed by exchange profits, accomplishes this purpose.

The Special Services Branch at the Headquarters, U. S. Marine Corps, in 1945, was activated as an organization of the personnel department. Similar staff agencies were established in Fleet Marine Force units down to the battalion level and at all posts and stations.

The scope of the program has increased since the branch was established.

The Special Services Branch at the Headquarters level, U. S. Marine Corps, administers and supervises the Marine Corps Special Services program. The responsibility for the conduct of a Special Services program unit remains with each local commander.

Navy

The recreation program in the Navy is under the control and direction of the Special Services Division.

In general the program includes a wide variety of activities, services, and facilities aboard ships and stations. Included are entertainment, motion pictures, voluntary athletics, enlisted men's clubs, chief petty officers' clubs, commissioned officers' messes, libraries, live entertainment (participants and spectators), hobby craft, musical activities, and miscellaneous activities centered around the clubs.

The function of the Special Services Division is to develop and execute programs intended to increase and sustain higher level personnel efficiency and morale throughout the Naval Establishment. This is accomplished through planned programs and facilities for leisure-time occupation, mental stimulation, self-education, and physical development of the individual.

The Special Services Division is responsible for technical control; that is, specialized or professional guidance and direction of the welfare and recreation program throughout the Navy, including the physical fitness programs, recreation programs, motion-picture program, library services, regulation and administration of messes and clubs, liaison with Associated Services for the Armed Forces and similar organizations concerned with welfare and recreation of military personnel control and administration of appropriated and nonappropriated funds. Broad outlines of plans and policies for these programs are determined at bureau level and promulgated. The various commands of the Naval Establishment administer and operate these programs at the activity level.

Basic to the on-post recreation needs of service personnel are the day rooms (for writing letters, playing games, reading, and relaxation); post exchanges with their snack bars; motion-picture theaters; indoor and outdoor athletic and sports facilities; libraries, hobby shops, officer and non-commissioned officer clubs and, of course, the service club. The modern service club is considered not only a facility to "house" certain functions, but also a "hub" from which many activities are generated.

THE WORKSHOP

1. Interview a county agent for the purpose of learning what assistance the federal government is giving in helping provide recreation opportunities for the residents of the county.
2. Trace the development of federal recreation services since the turn of the century.
3. Compare the recreation programs provided by the government in so-called normal times with those made available during emergencies.
4. Ask local public and private recreation leaders what kinds of recreation service the federal government should provide.
5. Discuss the relationship of local and state recreation services to federal recreation services.
6. List the kinds of problems which could be acted upon by an interdepartmental federal recreation committee.
7. Criticize or defend the contention that the federal government should establish recreation standards.
8. State the case for and against federal grants-in-aid for recreation.
9. Argue the point that federal recreation services should flow through the states to the communities, rather than be given directly to the political subdivisions of the state.
10. Analyze the thesis that "recreation is a function of government at all levels."

REFERENCES

Brightbill, Charles K., and Harold D. Meyer, *Recreation: Text and Readings.* Englewood Cliffs, N.J.: Prentice-Hall, Inc., 1953.

Brightbill, Charles K., and Theresa Brungardt, "The Establishment of an Office for a Federal Recreation Service," *The American Recreation Society Bulletin,* XII, No. 3, April 1960, 36–38.

Ernst, Morris, *Utopia, 1976.* New York: Holt, Rinehart & Winston, Inc., 1955.

Hearings by the Committee on Education and Labor on S. 2070 and Senate Report No. 1648 (Calendar No. 1678), 79th Congress, Washington, D.C.

Hutchinson, John L., *Principles of Recreation.* New York: A. S. Barnes & Co., 1951.

Kaplan, Max, *Leisure in America: A Social Inquiry.* New York: John Wiley & Sons, Inc., 1960, Ch. 9.

Lindeman, Edward C., *Leisure—A National Issue.* New York: Association Press, 1939.

Outdoor Recreation Resources Review Commission, *Outdoor Recreation for America.* Washington, D.C.: U. S. Government Printing Office, 1962.

Romney, G. Ott, "What Place Should the Federal Government Assume on the Total Recreation Program?" *The Journal of Educational Psychology,* January, 1949.

Smithee, Kenneth J., *Federal Assistance for Recreation and Parks.* Washington, D.C.: National Recreation and Park Association, 1967.

The Role of the Federal Government in the Field of Recreation. No. 3. Revised. Washington, D.C.: Federal Interagency Committee on Recreation, 1961.

Comment

The most satisfactory information on the recreation functions of the federal agencies can be obtained directly from the information offices of the departments and agencies discussed in this chapter. *The Congressional Record* is another fruitful source of information on the subject, including the controversial issues. Write to the Bureau of Outdoor Recreation for its many publications and reports.

A basic philosophical view of the federal government, its roles and challenges, can be found in: *Goals for Americans: The Report of the President's Commission on National Goals,* Ch. 12; *The Federal System* by Morton Grodzius; and *The Public Service* by Wallace S. Sayre, Englewood Cliffs, N.J.: Prentice-Hall, Inc., 1960.

Current information on recreation in the armed forces can be obtained by communicating with:

Army—Chief, Special Services Division, Adjutant General's Office, Department of the Army, Washington, D.C.

Air Force—Chief, Special Services Branch, Personnel Services Division, Directorate of Military Personnel, Deputy Chief of the Staff Personnel, Department of the Air Force, Washington, D.C.

Marines—Chief, Special Services Branch, Personnel Department, United States Marine Corps, Washington, D.C.

Navy—Chief, Special Services Division, Office, Assistant Chief of Naval Personnel, Department of the Navy, Washington, D.C.

For information on the community aspects of recreation as it concerns military personnel, communicate with:

American National Red Cross, 17th and D Streets, Washington, D.C. 20006

National Recreation and Park Association, 1700 Pennsylvania Ave., N.W., Washington, D.C. 20006.

United Service Organizations, 237 East 52nd Street, New York, N.Y. 10022

The publications and other material of the above organizations and agencies provide pertinent material on this subject.

Specific publications of value on recreation in the armed forces are *Free Time in the Armed Forces*, President's Committee on Religion and Welfare in the Armed Forces, Superintendent of Documents, Washington, D.C.; *Off-Post Recreation for Servicemen and Women*, California State Recreation Commission, Sacramento, California; *Recreation for Community Living*, Athletic Institute, Room 805, Merchandise Mart, Chicago, Illinois; *Jobs in Faraway Places*, Overseas Branch, Civilian Personnel Division, Department of the Army, Washington, D.C.

9

Recreation
Among Nations

Enduring, universal peace still remains the great hope of mankind. It can be achieved only through tolerance and good will, and there can be neither tolerance nor good will in the absence of international understanding and individual opportunity. Recreation and facilities for leisure pursuits can make a genuine contribution to the development of satisfactory international relations and lasting peace.

Recreation's contribution to international good will lies in the opportunities it offers for: (1) understanding and sharing those things which are fine and generous in a nation's heritage and culture; (2) communicating at the most basic and common level of participation which makes life richer for every man regardless of language, government, religion, or economic status and aids in overcoming personal and group prejudices; (3) encouraging national pride to express itself in socially contributive rather than selfishly acquisitive outlets, thereby reducing national rivalries.

Many pages of this book have been devoted to the philosophy and role of recreation in the United States. A case as convincing and more far-reaching could be made for its place in every country, regardless of living standards or economic and social progress. Man weighs issues in terms of values, and it is not amiss to repeat here that (1) recreation is a basic, universal desire and necessity of human life; (2) it contributes to man's physical, intellectual, spiritual, emotional, and moral needs; (3) it is no less important than welfare, health, and education to the social well-being of a people; and (4) wherever it flourishes it is a responsibility of government. The intelligent and wholesome use of leisure molds the social and cultural aspects of nations as it does the character of individuals, families, and communities. It is in leisure that those skills and habits, those attitudes, emotions, and desires of indivduals and the groups which contribute so vitally to the enhancement of the total social welfare are developed. The very essence of culture is transmitted in the play of the young. It is a major force in socialization and, according to Huizinga and Roger Caillois, an index of civilization.[1]

The social-welfare problems of a people, or of all peoples, cannot be approached intelligently and adequately without great concern for their leisure needs and interests.

Increased leisure and a higher standard of living in industrialized countries, longer life, and earlier retirement are forcing profound consideration of needs and expanded opportunities.

SOME HISTORIC MOVEMENTS

Although at present there is unusual interest in international recreation a number of events during the first half of the twentieth century indicated concern in this field and are presented here as background material.

The National Recreation and Park Association has a long history of international service. In 1912 Dr. and Mrs. C. A. Goethe, pioneers in park service in the United States, went around the world representing the then National Recreation Association. Through their efforts playgrounds were opened in many cities in the Orient.

In 1931 and 1932 Laurence Pearsall Jacks, former president of Manchester College in England, made a tour of the United States, lecturing on recreation as having fundamental values in education. This was one of the first approaches dealing with international relationships on a worldwide basis.

In 1932 at Los Angeles, California, the National Recreation Association organized and was host to the First International Recreation Congress—a tremendously inspiring experience shared by 101 delegates from 26 foreign countries in addition to those from the United States. This meeting did much to create common understanding of recreation as a means of life enrichment for all the peoples of the world.

[1] Roger Caillois, *Man, Play and Games*. New York: Free Press, 1961.

During World War I and World War II countless millions of people, members of the armed forces and civilians as well, from different nations were brought in contact with each other during the conflict and period of occupation. They brought their favorite kinds of recreation from their homelands and displayed them for all to witness. Often people of different nationalities joined in forms of recreation which were new to them. People learned the recreation habits, customs, and desires of persons from across the sea. Long-established recreation activities of one nation spread to another, with certain forms of recreation, heretofore popular in one or two countries, taking hold in many new places. It would be impossible to measure the extent to which such cross-fertilization of interests in recreation has influenced the cultures and relations of nations, but there is valid reason to believe that such influences have been significant in the building of good-will among nations.

The Olympic Games, Pan American Games, International Sports Tournaments, and other athletic events for years have brought together peoples of different lands in relationships which have a potential for producing good will. Add to these world travel, music and drama festivals, art and craft exhibits, dance festivals, and other rich contributions, and the result is an effective force for understanding and appreciating the cultural resources of the community of nations.

Many organizations, national and international, make large contributions to improving international relations through recreation. Just a few of them include the World Federation of Churches, the International Red Cross and its constituent national counterparts, the Boy Scouts and Girl Scouts, the International Service Clubs, and the Y.M.C.A.'s and Y.W.C.A.'s. Of inestimable value in this respect have been the efforts of the United States Department of State and the activities of private interests in making available the exchange of students, teachers, recreators, and youth work personnel on an international basis.

For several years, the American Recreation Society, now a part of the National Recreation and Park Association, had an International Recreation Committee. It was charged with the responsibility of fostering international recreation goodwill and developing cooperative exchange programs, as recreation is an excellent way for the less technically developed nations to contribute to the world's body of knowledge and goods. The European Recreation Society resulted from the work of this committee.

INTERNATIONAL RECREATION ASSOCIATION

Outstanding in the world of international recreation cooperative efforts is the work of the International Recreation Association and its director, Thomas E. Rivers. For the past two decades, it has been the only agency solely concerned with the problems and potentials of a truly world-wide recreation service. Patterned after the National Recreation Association and adopting some of the philosophy and techniques of the United Nations, it has sought to provide direction to this emerging field of work.

The legal basis for the International Recreation Association was established when the Board of Directors of the National Recreation Association (USA) approved the incorporation of the international group under the laws of the State of New York. A charter was granted in May, 1952, on the basis of a petition outlining the aims of the International Recreation Association and specifying the relationship to the National Recreation Association (USA).

When the International Recreation Congress assembled in Philadelphia in 1956, the groundwork had been laid, and the International Recreation Association was formally launched with the approval of the National Recreation Association, distinguished leaders from foreign countries, and the National Advisory Committee of the International Recreation Service, a group representing the professional recreators of the United States.

The stated objectives of the Association are to:

Serve as a central clearing house for the exchange of information and experience among recreation agencies of the world.

Aid countries in establishing central recreation service agencies upon request.

Forward the development of a world recreation movement designed to enrich the human spirit through wholesome use of leisure.

Encourage the provision of land and facilities, training of leaders, development of varied programs, and public interpretation of the values of play for children, recreation for youth, and creative use of leisure for all ages.

Provide a medium through which the recreation authorities of the world may work in unity on one of the common problems of man.

The International Recreation Association sought and secured appointment as a nongovernmental organization affiliated with the United Nations. Among its services to specialized agencies has been the provision of recreation supplies to United Nations Emergency Forces in the Gaza Strip and in the Congo, and to the government of South Vietnam.

The Association has carried out community cooperative recreation exchange projects under the U.S. State Department. Recreation agencies and organizations of all kinds have provided training and hospitality to the foreign guests. In October, 1967, it convened an international recreation symposium in Geneva, Switzerland, to coincide with the opening of the Geneva Center of the IRA. The following resolution was passed:

RESOLUTIONS OF SYMPOSIUM PLAN FOR UNITED ACTION

We, representatives of organizations concerned with all aspects of recreation, gathered in Geneva at a Symposium under the auspices of the International Recreation Association to consider ways and means of meeting cooperatively the global needs of recreation, recognize

The vital and ever-increasing importance of recreation today and in the future.

To achieve its true potential for the benefit of all people, recreation must maintain the highest standards of facilities and of leadership, both professional and voluntary.

To secure the widest possible recognition from all organizations, governmental and non-governmental, national and international, particularly the United Nations and its specialized agencies.

It is essential to secure cooperation and coordination among all organizations and all agencies concerned with recreation, and to establish a centralized instrument to achieve these purposes.

We therefore agree to work together and initially to take the following steps:

1. To ask IRA to serve as the instrument for effective coordination of efforts directed toward meeting world recreation needs.

2. To prepare a directory of the organizations working internationally and concerned with some aspects of recreation, kept up to date, with the basic information of each organization, its purpose, structure, and programme.

3. To accelerate the systematic collection, classification, and dissemination of information and materials about recreation to all concerned.

4. To ask IRA to explore the feasibility of establishing joint working groups and committees on specific issues and questions of significance to the world recreation movement, in particular to undertake the study of a 'Recreation Charter' for possible adoption as an annex to the Declaration of Human Rights.

This Symposium, recognizing the vital importance of finance to world recreation efforts, notes with satisfaction the decision of IRA to establish a world fund for recreation.

Recognizing the ever-increasing need for extending international service to accomplish these objectives, the delegates note with satisfaction the establishment of the Geneva Center of IRA and hope that additional centers may be established elsewhere.

In conclusion, the participants in the Symposium extend an earnest invitation to all organizations concerned with recreation, particularly those invited to the Symposium but unable to be present, to endorse all these goals and objectives and to join with them in this effort to further the world recreation movement in a spirit of cooperation and coordination.

The International Recreation Association is assisted by distinguished and dedicated volunteers—veterans of the recreation movement who give lectures, demonstrations, and advice in all quarters of the world.

THE UNITED NATIONS

The United Nations has within its organization two divisions concerned with international recreation:

1. United Nations Educational, Scientific, and Cultural Organization
2. International Labor Organization

The first stresses the cultural aspects of recreation in art, music, and drama. The second functions through the Correspondence Committee on Recreation. The special emphasis of the committee is on recreation for the laboring classes and planned vacations and holidays.

THE MACHINERY OF INTERNATIONAL RECREATION

Since government has a primary responsibility for the promotion of organized recreation, any adequate scheme of international recreation organization must assume international cooperation of world governments. Organization might center in an international recreation council, composed of representatives of member governments, which would collect, analyze, and disseminate specialized information, and reports; initiate and conduct research investigations; formulate programs of international cooperation in recreation activities; develop and disseminate recreation principles, policies, and standards; draft conventions and agreements involving matters within the scope of the council for submission to governments; prepare for and convene conferences; promote international cooperation in the training, utilization, and exchange of technical recreation personnel; cooperate with voluntary national and international organizations engaged in the promotion of recreation activities and services; and perform such other related functions as may be appropriate for the enhancement of recreation programs, facilities, and opportunities throughout the world.

With such an organization and the cooperation of member nations, implemented by world-wide distribution of recreation representatives of each government (partially accomplished, perhaps, through recreation specialists at all consulates), the promotion of good will, fellowship, understanding, and good-neighbor relations would be greatly accelerated and intensified. The recreation council here described might well find its place in the United Nations Organization in accordance with the plan suggested below.

GENERAL ASSEMBLY—Composed of delegates from all member nations. Discusses questions relating to peace and other matters under Charter. Makes recommendations to Security Council.

ECONOMIC AND SOCIAL COUNCIL—Eighteen members elected by Assembly. Coordinates affiliated organizations to remove economic and social roots of war.

EDUCATIONAL, SCIENTIFIC, AND CULTURAL ORGANIZATION—Organized to foster world intellectual cooperation through education, science, and culture.

RECREATION COUNCIL—To promote and develop international recreational opportunities.

The Need for a Careful and Proper Approach

There is little if any precedent for the projection of recreation on such an extensive and significant scale. For this reason the whole plan for establishing adequate international machinery should be approached with care and understanding.

The first and major consideration would seem to be a mutually acceptable international definition and understanding of recreation. Recreation in its highest sense is an integral part of the general welfare and well-being of a people.

Moreover, it is essential that the organizers and promoters of an international recreation program avoid presumption and any intimation that their own national culture, tastes, and habits as reflected in leisure activities are the most desirable.

One nation's ideas of recreation might prove incompatible with those of another whose good will is being cultivated. No nation can assume the final adequacy of its own culture and expect it to be widely acceptable. Every country has its own set of precious cultural traditions which are sacred and full of meaning—its art, music, folkways, and all the other things which it reveres and which speak the language of its inner spirit. If nations are to venture into the realm of international recreation, they must be sensitive to the significance of those modes of living expressive of the things a people cherishes in daily life at home, in daily work, and in neighborhood relations with one another. Music, painting, and poetry are not the only expressions of a people's individuality which must be considered in order for one nation to be accepted as another's friend. A penetrating insight into those things which govern daily life is needed. These are guide-posts to remember in opening the way to international recreation.

Possible Emphases and Activities of an International Recreation Program

Although the list of activities and services which might be promoted in an international recreation program is almost limitless, early consideration could be given to:

1. *Wider promotion of international games and sports, with greater emphasis on the mastery of skills and techniques and less on the combative spirit and defeat of adversaries.* Recreation in its broadest sense has been little attempted on the international level. Competitive sports, largely through the Olympic Games and international tennis and golf matches, have been promoted for many years, but with the primary emphasis on competition. While these sports undoubtedly present a civilized form of combat, it is combat nonetheless because of this emphasis. As a result, national pride finds its outlet in defensive battle against alien attack. This is not to say that there is no place for competitive sports on the international level. It would be unfortunate, however, if international good will were to depend entirely upon mutual acquaintance gained solely through that medium. Only seldom, and far less dramatically, has that same national pride been challenged to display its warmer and more generous side through socially contributive rather than selfishly acquisitive outlets.

Competitive sports, moreover, need not be based solely on individual or international competition. It would be far better if the competition were to become a joint undertaking against the inherent difficulties of the sport itself. The game and the numerous difficulties of its mastery thus become the competitor and not the individual or the national team. A combined attack of united skills can then be enlisted for a greater mastery of the sport rather than for combative competition between individuals.

Doubtless there will always be athletic rivalries in recreation. They develop spontaneously. However, those recreation activities which can avoid them will receive the attention of recreation leaders in developing an international program. One more suggestion in connection with games and sports involves the exchange of eminent athletes so that they may demonstrate their skill and share it with interested youngsters by advice, coaching, and friendly criticism of their beginning efforts. Such a system would enhance international good will by constructively enlisting the visiting athlete's love of his sport.

2. *International promotion of youth travel and exchange through movements similar to the youth hostel group.* The youth hostel movement has done much to promote international friendships. Although in the past precariously financed in the United States, abroad it is an example of a government-aided development which still retains its autonomy in operation. It is a useful and pioneering demonstration of recreation possibilities in international relations. It sends youth from many countries abroad with only such bare necessities as they can carry in light knapsacks on their bicycles. They travel, dance, sing, and prepare their simple meals together. They share labor and laughter, thrilling to the discovery that whatever their lands of origin, they all share the same basic human desires, observe the same decencies, and want the same sat-

isfactory returns from their investment in living. They help patch each other's tires and face each other's difficulties together. They exchange songs, food recipes, crafts, games, stunts, and dances, with never a thought of combat or championships. International relations of this type deserve the attention of all governments at this time. However, the hostel movement is explorable and exploitable for major usefulness only in the hands of wisely sympathetic reciprocal agencies of government—agencies sensitive to the possibilities of intercultural contacts among the common folk of nations no longer permitted isolation from each other.

3. *Promotion and exchange of international camping experiences among people.* The possibility of going abroad to camp with the people of other nations, and the contribution this could make to international relations need to be studied. The organized camp provides unusual opportunities for humans to grow, live, work, and learn together. Emotional differences can be leveled in a primitive environment in which men, women, and children of many nations make their temporary but common home independent of national ties and influences. Enlightened social participation will develop. Deep and mutually continuing interests will have an opportunity to flourish. The intimacy of camp life insures the growth of mutual tolerance, understanding, and appreciation.

4. *Promotion of international travel through the organization and exchange of travel groups.* With modern rapid and comfortable transportation, higher incomes, and a society interested in mobility, travel has become an important factor in international relations. The ordinary citizen on his two weeks' annual vacation is a potential visitor of the remote corners of the earth. Contact among the common folk of nations thus becomes a factor in international understanding or misunderstanding on a scale hitherto unknown. There is obvious need for more organized group travel under leadership which will keep the traveler sensitive to their responsibility to avoid offense. The currently expanding exchange programs in education should be duplicated in recreation. In this manner, a whole new range of international contacts could be established.

5. *Exchange of folk art and native crafts methods and materials through the international organization of hobby clubs and interest groups.* One would search far to find a closer fraternity than hobbyists, and no better means exists for utilizing this lasting influence for good will, tolerance, and understanding than the development of their interests. The gardener loves his gentle art, and any fellow gardener, whatever his language, is a brother enthusiast and therefore readily accepted. The same is true of the musician, the photographer, the painter, the potter, or the wood carver.

Exchanges might be negotiated in wide variety, from postage stamps to works of art. Correspondence friendships might develop individual contacts on the basis of common tastes or interests. Experiences involving anything from tool uses to food recipes, lace designs, or pottery patterns might be shared across international boundaries. Available native materials such as wools, woods, or mineral specimens might be exchanged for tools, patterns, or materials more readily obtainable in another land. Current events clubs might exchange collected press clippings of mutual interest, seldom quoted overseas because they are neither sensational nor provocative. New developments in such hobbies as photography might be described. By federating enthusiasts in each country, still or motion photographs could be exchanged, with expense as little burdensome to individuals as the exchange of seeds and bulbs by the gardening fraternity. The sharing of toys, games, holiday decorations and costumes alone, offer an endless list of possibilities.

These speculations are based on familiar patterns but presenting them in connection with exploring international recreation serves to direct thought along lines other than the mere intensification of the old patterns of sports competition. They provide a broader understanding of the inclusive features of recreation and, it is hoped, open the way to further and more imaginative suggestions which will doubtless be made as others interest themselves in expanding the idea in infinite variety.

6. *International sharing of recreation skills and interests through the exchange of persons possessing specific talents and skills.* Recreation skills, pursuits, and needs are basically the same for all mankind, and yet environment, culture, climate, and geographical features have resulted in increased specific skills among certain peoples. Witness the dancing of the Balinese, baseball in the United States, rugby in England, the sculpture of Greece, the music of Italy, the pottery of China, and the crafts of the Scandinavian countries. What better means can be found for increasing the world's appreciation of its own skills and talents, and thus promoting good will, than the international exchange of skilled artists and artisans?

The possibilities of international recreation are infinitely varied. Consular office forces, commercial representatives, service clubs, educational leaders, youths and social workers, travelers, religious workers, youth organizations, sportsmen, hobby devotees, and internationally minded citizens or groups—all are potential contributors to the program as they come to realize the hopeful possibilities of closer and more understanding fellowship in a cooperative rather than a competitive spirit. No better means exist for utilizing the native good will and neighborliness of man than that offered by recreation. Its need is inherent in all peoples, and it provides them with an outlet for self-expression, creativeness, service, and personal development. It is a lively springboard to international good will.

THE RECREATION OF OTHER NATIONS

Interest in and opportunities for recreation are not limited to the United States, even though the organized public recreation movement is somewhat unique to this country and Canada. There follows a brief description of recreation in a few other countries. This presents just some of the characteristics and highlights and is not exhaustive.

England

The English people have always been great sports enthusiasts and respecters of the "holiday." Cricket, rugby football, soccer, boxing, tennis, and horse and boat racing are among their traditional favorites. Hunting, particularly fox hunting, and fishing are also popular. Holidays, with long weekends, permit families to go away for several days.

The world's first settlement house was established in London. The English, of course, have had enriched opportunities to pursue the arts—drama, music, literature, and the like. England's great art centers, historical edifices, and museums are an unending source of recreation. Libraries can be found in the communities. Even the English "pub" could be called a neighborhood center where sociability prevails.

Increasing interest in recreation, however, resulted in the appointment by Parliament of the Albemarle Committee on Youth Service. It recommended a National Youth Council with grant-aiding powers charged with the provision of an adequate supply of qualified youth leaders, coordination and development of youth service, and supervision of research to explore new ways of reaching hard-to-get young people. Proposals also included increased grants for the performing arts and support of national galleries and museums. Grants have been made to local groups for leaders and facilities. Active effort is made to reach employed youth between the ages of 15 and 20. The breadth of the program is impressive—mountain climbing, boat-building, or whatever gains active participation.

A similar report made after a three-year study by a committee under Sir John Wolfenden for the Central Council of Physical Recreation has had important results in furthering cooperation among bodies responsible for outdoor recreation. In 1967, a grant was given to the Center for Urban and Regional Studies, Birmingham University, to develop techniques for assessing and projecting the supply and demand for outdoor sports and recreation facilities. The findings should complement those of the Government Social Survey and provide British recreation planners with data similar to that developed in the United States by the Outdoor Recreation Resources Review Commission.

The Amateur Athletic Association, Football Association, Swimming Association, Youth Hostel Association, National Association of Mixed Clubs and Girls' Clubs, National Playing Fields Association, and the Physical Recreation Association have assisted in the promotion of recreation. The latter two organizations have been especially active in promoting the acquisition of land areas for general public recreation use and in the stimulation of activities.

Canada

The recreation habits and customs of the people of Canada are similar to those of the United States, England, and France. Nevertheless, as a pioneering nation in a vast land with great economic, political, and social promise, Canada has developed many recreation pursuits that are peculiarly its own. Indeed, in a number of ways, recreation developments in Canada have moved far ahead of the United States.

The most pronounced similarities between Canada and the United States—perhaps best explained by the fact that they are both English-speaking neighbors with interrelated cultures—is in the organized public recreation movement. Both are establishing a broad network of parks, playgrounds, community centers, and other recreation facilities. Both are appropriating public funds for the purpose. Both are striving to raise standards of program and leadership.

Many Canadians and their fellow professional recreators south of the Canadian border belong to the same professional organizations. Common problems and experiences are shared. Canada, however, also has its own professional groups, interests, and plans.

Public and voluntary recreation in Canada is assisted and encouraged by the government of the Dominion of Canada, by the provincial governments, and by local governments. The Dominion and some of the provincial governments provide financial assistance to communities developing their recreation systems and services. Official certification of professional recreation personnel has been inaugurated in some sections of Canada.

In the Province of Ontario the Ministry of Education, through its Community Programmes Branch, provides financial as well as consultative assistance on community recreation problems. Public recreation commissions and park departments can be found throughout this province. Attention is given to developing sports, camping, arts and crafts, theater, music, citizenship training, social recreation, group discussion and forums, use of the radio and television, and the like. Much emphasis is placed upon leadership training. Several Canadian universities and colleges offer a recreation major, while others provide courses in parks and recreation.

Germany

The German people, especially the young, are active in all forms of sports—indoors and outdoors. They like to hike into the hills with their knapsacks on their shoulders, swim in the lakes, cook on an open fire, and generally enjoy the outdoors for which they have great respect. Germany has traditionally been a leader in conservation and the development of forests. Camps, inns, and hostels serving the outdoor tastes of the Germans can be found almost everywhere. The Germans are proud of their famous mountain health resorts.

Indoor sports have placed much emphasis upon drill, calisthenics, and the *Turnverein* type of physical recreation in which precision, skill, and agility have been respected. Many sports and games are of a "team" nature. Association football, swimming, fencing, and all kinds of winter sports, including tobogganing, skating, and skiing are widespread. Much of the organized play in Germany has revolved around the schools, although playgrounds were established as early as the latter part of the nineteenth century. Germany has fine parks, but many of the sports and play areas have been controlled by amateur sports organizations and clubs.

The Germans are also great lovers of music and dancing. Their open-air gardens and restaurants have long been centers of merry-making, singing, and dancing. These opportunities for neighborliness and fun are multiplied through festivals and fairs.

During the Nazi regime, recreation, like everything else, was regimented and directed toward the glorification of the state. The Hitler Jugend (youth organization) had much sport, song, marching, and outdoor living, but its recreation ends were perverted toward militaristic ends. The *Kraft durch Freude* (strength through joy) movement of the laboring groups also had an extensive recreation program, including vacation "trips into the blue."

After World War II the Germans reverted to many of the forms of recreation they had experienced traditionally, and, with the influence of the allied democracies, patterns of public recreation as practiced in the United States, for example, began to take shape. These included the inauguration of recreation centers, especially for children and youth, interest in which was first stimulated by the United States Army and later by the U.S. State Department. Through the exchange programs of Germany and the United States, recreation and youth leaders of both nations have visited across the Atlantic to help develop recreation on a broader base. Its interest in tourism ranks second to none on the European continent.

Scandinavian Countries

The people of Sweden, Norway, and Finland are enthusiasts for gymnastics and vigorous outdoor sports. Both the climate and the geography of these nations are such as to make interest in the outdoors perfectly natural. The sun and the snow are great attractions which supplement the enjoyment these people find through calisthenics and physical education indoors. Practically everyone participates in exercise. These people also like to swim and use boats for pleasure and are famous for their accomplishments in track and field. The steam bath, or *sauna,* which takes the bather from hot steam to cold water within a short time and is supposed to be good for one's circulation and relaxation, is a Finnish institution.

The Scandinavians are also participants in feasts, festivals, and celebrations of all kinds, many of them related to the folklore of the countries. They are richly steeped in arts and crafts, as well as music and literature, and are known throughout the world for their work in therapeutic recreation. Their park systems are often imitated but seldom duplicated in their imagination and design.

Japan

Japan is a nation whose natural surroundings are a fine attraction to those who love nature and find pleasure in its beauty. The country is surrounded by water, and seven-eighths of its surface is covered with mountains. The Japanese get much satisfaction from their gardens—where space permits. Tours to witness trees, plants, and flowers, and visits to shrines and resorts, are not uncommon in Japan.

Being lovers of beauty, the Japanese have splendid arts and crafts. Painting, sculpture, drama, lacquer ware, porcelain, ivory carving, and metal work are among cultural interests. Music in Japan in these times is a combination of oriental and western organization.

The Japanese have long been active in combative sports, including different kinds of wrestling, boxing, and the wielding of weapons. In recent years, interest has increased in track, swimming, lawn tennis, soccer, and rugby. Baseball is extremely popular. The Physical Education Bureau, which is a part of the Japanese Government, has promoted physical activities, and not long ago the National Recreation Association of Japan was organized.

In 1959 a successful Asian Recreation Congress was held in Yokohama, Japan. Twenty-five delegates from 13 countries faced the recreation problems of Asia and called for the setting up of national recreation bodies in each country.

A research group at the University in Yokohama has specialized in creative playground equipment. Examples can be seen on Yokohama playgrounds.

Tokyo has developed youth houses on the outskirts, tempting young people to hiking, camping, and enjoyment of the out-of-doors.

India

India has made outstanding strides toward meeting the recreation needs of her people. Following the Philadelphia International Recreation Congress, Dr. G. D. Sondhi returned to his country and put in five years of hard work as a volunteer building understanding and support of a national recreation movement. In 1961 the Indian National Recreation Association was launched at the first Indian National Recreation Congress at Chandigarh. Pilot projects for centers in cities and villages were presented to the government. The movement recognizes the broad program that must be included and the basic place of training of leaders. It has given the world such innovations as the Chacha Nehru Toy Library where children borrow toys, rather than books, and has made the Eastern music art form popular in Western societies.

Union of Soviet Socialist Republics

With the little information which comes out of the U.S.S.R. data on opportunities for recreation there cannot be said to be entirely accurate. For centuries, leisure was the privilege of only a small group. With the national effort since the Revolution geared to an economic and political struggle, there is little reason to believe that leisure exists in large quantities today. But to the extent that leisure does exist, it is more widely shared than ever before.

The Soviet Union has its schools and universities, its museums, operas, theaters, parks, playgrounds, resorts, and sports centers. Much emphasis is placed upon mass participation in sports, drill, and calisthenics. Russians are developing skills in various athletics and sports. Outdoor sports are popular, including hiking and mountain climbing. There has been extensive development of children's playgrounds, and pleasure parks can be found in the cities. The forests, hills, and seacoasts are sprinkled with vacation centers and tourist resorts, most of which are government owned and operated.

International recreation is a field where there are unlimited opportunities for growth. Recreation, a real potential for the development of international good will, must be strengthened and expanded on the international scene.

THE WORKSHOP

1. Discuss the role of play as a bearer and shaper of culture. Give specific illustrations.

2. Present the essential differences in organizing recreation internationally as compared with establishing a national program.
3. Suggest ways in which our national youth-serving agencies might cooperate in advancing international recreation.
4. Prepare a prospectus on the need for developing recreation as a means of securing better understanding and good will among nations.
5. Analyze the effects of the Olympic Games upon international relations.
6. Discover what plans are being made by the United Nations, the Department of State, and the National Social Welfare Assembly for promoting international welfare programs.
7. Secure full information and data on the purposes, functions, and plans of the United Nations Educational, Scientific, and Cultural Organization in regard to recreation.
8. Write a paper on the services and activities of the International Recreation Association.
9. What can professional fellowship groups such as the American Park and Recreation Society do to promote international recreation?
10. Suggest types of recreation in the United States which might lend themselves to international promotion.

REFERENCES

Annual of Architecture, Structure, and Town Planning, India: Publishing Corporation of India, 11 Dalhousie Square East, Calcutta-1, 1961.

Burton, Thomas A., *Outdoor Recreation Enterprises in Problem Rural Areas.* Kent, England: Wye College, 1967.

Caillois, Roger, *Man, Play and Games.* New York: Free Press, 1961.

Deutsche Olympische Gesellschaft, *Der Goldene Plan in Den Gemeinden.* Germany: Frankfurt-am-Main, 1960.

Harper, Paul, *Spare Time Education in Communist China.* Washington, D.C.: Department of Health, Education and Welfare, 1964.

Hunt, Sara, *Games and Sports the World Around.* New York: The Ronald Press Company, 1964.

Medeiros, Ethel Bauzer, *Jogos para Recreacao.* Brazil: Centro Brasileiro de Pesquisas, Educacionais, INEP, Ministerio da Educacao E Cultura, Rua Voluntarios da Patria No. 107, Rio de Janeiro, 1960.

Mederic, Paul, *Loisir et Loisirs.* Montreal: Ministere de la Jeunesse, Service des Cours pan Correspondance, 1961.

Nakhooda, Zulie, and Kitab Mahal, *Leisure and Recreation in Society.* India: 56A Zero Road, Allahabad, 1959.

Neighbor, H., *Recreation in Brazil, Ghana, Israel, Japan, Turkey,* Books 1, 2, 3. New York: UNICEF, United Nations, 1961.

Rivers, Thomas E., *Mountains Cannot Meet, But People Can.* New York: International Recreation Association, 1960.

Vendien, Lynn, and John Nixon, *The World Today in Health, Physical Education, and Recreation.* Englewood Cliffs: Prentice-Hall, Inc., 1968.

Weir, L. H., *Europe at Play.* New York: A. S. Barnes & Co., 1937.

Comments

Refer to the published material of the International Recreation Association, 345 E. 46th Street, New York, New York.

Write to the State Departments of various governments or the ambassadors and ministers of each of these governments for general information. The National Association of Social Workers (Group Work Division, New York) also provides information on this subject. Travel bureaus here and abroad furnish data on recreation in foreign countries, and youth-serving agencies functioning on an international basis can assist—Junior Red Cross, Boy Scouts, Girl Scouts, and others. Helpful bulletins include *Youth Service*, Ministry of Education, Curzon Street, London, W. 1, England; *IRA Bulletin*, International Recreation Association; *Parks and Sports Grounds*, 66 Hill Street, Richmond, Surrey, England.

III

Recreation and the
Social Institutions

Above: Little people in big places. Right: Rose gardens in a city park. Below: Family fun.

Left: Portal to leisure and learning. Below: Children's Chapel of Peace—Oakland, California.

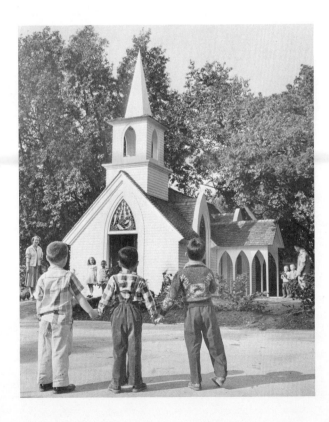

10

Recreation and the Community

THE COMMUNITY

When we use the term *community,* there comes to mind a group of people living in the same area under the same local government and laws. These people are bound together by a common environment and are held together by psychological as well as economic, social, and cultural bonds. Because of their common interests, needs, and concerns, they create for their own use institutions of a governmental, educational, economic, recreation, and religious nature. The population identifies itself with the community, which may take the form of a town, city, or some other political subdivision of the state.

Although public services, including recreation, are a responsibility of the state and federal governments, they are not a substitute for those which can be provided in and through local government and the *community's* non-governmental resources. As mentioned earlier, beyond the efforts of the individual to provide recreation opportunities for himself, the primary responsibility for community recreation belongs to the community itself. It is in the community where people live that their individual recreation interests and needs are best determined and served.

There is a feeling among some political scientists and planners, however, that, particularly in large metropolitan areas, the cities may have to look to the larger political subdivisions to provide, for example, open space for recreation. Apparently, the people of the city and suburbs often cannot or will not act to meet the need. Such factors as class distinction and discrimination, entangled jurisdictional tax problems, and the inability to act "in time" push the responsibility on the larger unit of government—state or federal.

Yet when the community can and will act, the community recreation services it establishes often express themselves in patterns unlike those of other communities. This is as it should be if recreation is to serve the varied interests, needs, and conditions of those residing in a given locale. Indeed, the specific organizational pattern to which community recreation is shaped is less important than the assurance that the system is sound and appropriate. This means an orderly approach which will mobilize all available resources, on a continuing basis, to serve the recreation needs of the people in the community. It means the acceptance and identification of a recreation system which is inter-locked with other social systems and affected by them. Also, it means the acceptance that recreation has impact on all other systems and is a factor in community organization.

COMMUNITY ORGANIZATION

The process of mobilizing, organizing, and using the various resources of a community toward reaching predetermined objectives is known as *community organization*. It involves a variety of efforts and devices, coordinated and focused at a single functional purpose. Community organization does not occur in a vacuum. It is organization for *something*— for better education, for better health and sanitation, for improving the lot of dependents, or for strengthening recreation services. It is *not* an end in itself and is only effective when it has a functional purpose. Through a variety of organized efforts to improve local life, community organization has gained wide use in the United States. More recently these efforts have involved national direction and legislation. For example, the Office of Economic Opportunity has been assigned a major role in community organization; its personnel are often charged with the responsibility of coordinating community planning as it relates to poverty groups. Also, the Model Cities Act, passed by the Congress in 1967, requires comprehensive planning at the local level prior to the awarding of Federal grants. Here we are interested in community organization as a helpful instrument for community recreation.

Community organization brings people together, as individual citizens or as representatives of groups, not only to determine needs and plan ways of meeting them, but also to mobilize and use the resources to accomplish their objectives.

Nowhere, perhaps, has the community organization process been developed to a finer degree than in the field of social welfare. It has been used particularly to coordinate and integrate the social services of local communities by devices such as United Community Services, Welfare Councils, Councils of Social Agencies, Planning Councils, and United and Community Funds. The process is a technique of democratic leadership and involves scientific method. To achieve the ends of community organization, facts must be obtained, resources and services analyzed, representatives of the various interests involved, agreement and consensus of views obtained, priorities established, consequences of decisions determined, and action taken. The latter step involves both financial and moral support and will result in success only when the prior steps have assured broad support and involvement.

Whether the machinery for community organization is highly refined or not, at the heart of the effort is *coordinating* various resources and actions in a way which will set them in motion in an integrated effort to accomplish desired ends. If there is another key idea in community organization in addition to the term *coordinate,* it is *totality.* This refers to totality of resources, totality of function, and totality of need. It is the consideration of the *totality* which reminds us that communities have organizations quite apart from and more fundamental than the structures that find expression in formal institutions and other organized forces. A deeper and broader concept of community organization would include the folkways and mores of the people, attitudes and interests of individuals and groups, the situations in which they interact, procedures by which their behavior is regulated, the conceptions which people have of themselves and their fellowmen—all vital factors in community living. Often these forces are the determining ones that mold the patterns of institutions, agencies, and organizations; their actions shape the designs of community organization.

COORDINATING ORGANIZATIONS

A brief description of some of the coordinating organizations' functions in the community will indicate community opportunity for cooperation in social services.

United Community Council (Council of Social Agencies). In communities where a number of social agencies function, there is frequently a united community council. It is composed of public and private agencies working together to meet total community needs through coordination of services, consultations on policy and program, and joint planning and study.

Such an organization studies human needs and coordinates services to meet them.

Often, the united community council divides its organization according to functions and clusters of service, such as health, dependency, recreation and social group work.

United Fund (Community Chest). The major agency for cooperative, united, federated financing of social groups is the united fund, which raises and disburses money through one united campaign. Experience has taught that in communities above a certain size, this method is the most economical way of raising funds for social agencies. Although most of the groups that constitute membership in the fund are private agencies, public and quasi-public agencies sometimes participate. Often recreation departments obtain supplementary funds from chest sources. The fund is concerned with community recreation as well as with other social activities and can be of effective service in interpreting the recreation program to the public.

Social service exchange. In many communities welfare agencies form a social service exchange as a clearing house. The exchange is made up of public and private groups interested in social work among individuals and families. A card index is kept of all names of individuals and groups needing and receiving assistance. The exchange refers cases to the proper agencies and sees to it that necessary action is taken. In some communities, the local Community Action Agency (OEO) performs an exchange service for those groups involved in the War on Poverty effort, especially those agencies receiving Federal grants.

Such a service promotes cooperation among the community organizations, in consultation service and coordination of activities. Recreation agencies are usually members of the exchange.

ORGANIZING FOR RECREATION

Included among the resources for community organization in recreation are those of local governing and managing authorities, such as the recreation, park, and school boards discussed in Chapter 5. In addition, there are the voluntary agencies, commercial enterprises, and groups of an educational, religious, political, business, service, fraternal, patriotic, and cultural nature. There are also the resources of individuals, whose efforts can be interwoven through the establishment of committees dedicated to accomplishing a given task or series of objectives.

Organization of community forces for recreation includes the establishment of such groups as the community recreation council, community recreation association, neighborhood recreation council, and recreation federation. Many have national counterparts as all are a part of the recreation system, a system which has both horizontal (local) and vertical (state, regional and national) elements. The names of these organizations vary among communities, but their functions are similar. Brief descriptions follow:

Community Recreation Council (or Committee). This is usually an *advisory* body to an operational unit responsible for providing recreation services. In small communities the community recreation council is responsible for establishing policies and overseeing the actual administration and operation of the recreation program. Its functions usually include helping to discover and use resources for community recreation, relating the needs, services, and developments in recreation to other services and organizations in the community, helping to find and develop recreation leadership, reflecting community interests, attitudes, opinions, and customs, helping to secure better facilities and financial support for recreation, promulgating recreation standards, interpreting the values and need for recreation, and sponsoring recreation projects.

Community Recreation Association. This is a nongovernmental, privately organized and supported group. Often it is incorporated as a nonprofit organization, and it is always community-wide in its representation as well as its interests. The association is established to promote, support, and develop community recreation services. Its efforts may be financial—through contributions, dues, and money-raising projects. Sometimes the association is a member of a united fund, and membership is open to anyone who is interested. In some instances, the association employs professional recreation personnel and offers a recreation program. Very often, the community recreation association is the forerunner to the establishment of a public recreation service financed with governmental funds.

Neighborhood Recreation Council. This group, as its name indicates, is organized on a neighborhood basis and is mainly interested in improving neighborhood recreation conditions. It may or may not be related to an existing public recreation service. It, too, promotes public support of recreation for its area. It also serves as a means of promoting neighborhood identity and socialization. It often sponsors recreation events and raises money to make neighborhood recreation improvements. It may operate as an independent recreation body or it may be a committee of a larger neighborhood council.

Recreation Federation. This organization pools the interests and efforts of a number of groups interested in improving community recreation. The federation encourages interest in *total* community recreation needs. Each participating organization has one or two representatives in the federation, whose functions are similar to those of a community recreation association. The difference between the community recreation association and the recreation federation is mainly in the manner in which they are organized and not in their objectives.

HOW COORDINATION WORKS

Perhaps the coordination of community recreation services can best be understood by seeing how it operates, how it is actually applied in terms of specific needs. Such an illustration can be found in the following: [1]

In its broadest sense, coordination is a community organization proposition, going far beyond what one might ordinarily regard as simply establishing cooperation between existing agencies, although this is one of its primary objectives. The following purposes are the business of the organized coordination of recreation:

1. To encourage and develop cooperation of social, educational, public service, and civic agencies, and to correlate the recreation work in a given area;
2. To increase the efficiency of recreation agencies and recreation work generally;
3. To study recreation problems;
4. To secure publicity of, and to endeavor to educate the public to a better understanding of recreation;
5. To act as an advisory council to recreation agencies;
6. To plan for the meeting of recreation needs;
7. To do such other things or to engage in such other activities as may be determined necessary to the general interests of recreation as an essential community service.

Every large city in the United States and a number of smaller ones have a coordinating agency which includes recreation in the scope of its activity. Many counties have developed such organizations and there are an increasing number which are metropolitan-area-wide, in and around the very large cities. In general terms, though perhaps differently phrased, they operate for the purpose stated in the foregoing paragraph. In . . . the larger cities, these councils have staff specialists responsible for recreation, working under various designations, for example, recreation division, informal education division, group work section, youth agencies' council, or combination of these and other titles. . . .

It should be emphasized that these organizations are voluntary associations of many different kinds of social and civil agencies as well as individual citizens who are interested in fostering such unified efforts. The usual pattern is the creation of a delegate body of professional leaders and laymen to constitute the final authority for actions of the coordinating organization. The delegates usually elect a board of directors which is empowered to establish whatever "machinery" is necessary to carry out

[1] Department of Justice, *Recreation for Youth—The Coordination of Community Recreation,* Section VI, Washington, D. C.

the purposes of the organization. There may be divisions or sections, as referred to above, for handling functional fields of service, such as recreation, health, and others, or there may be less highly organized committees to deal with the community's needs. Much research and discussion are required in connection with the discovery and development of feasible coordination plans and mechanisms for smaller cities and towns.

Emphasis is placed upon the voluntary nature of these associations of agencies and interested citizens. As in recreation itself, where the individual's opportunity to choose his leisure-time activity is the element which makes it truly recreational, so in the coordination of recreation services—what is done because agencies and individuals choose to do it of their own free will is the worthwhile thing. It isn't always the quickest way, but in the long run it is the best.

But to get down to cases, what do we do? How do we get these high purposes translated into action? What are the limitations?

The first and most obvious place to start is with the exchange of information about the recreation services that exist in any given community. As simple a thing as two people having lunch together to tell each other about the programs of their respective agencies is a good beginning. Extended to a highly organized plane, the luncheon meeting, arranged periodically for interested representatives of all existing agencies, gives an opportunity for more widespread knowledge of services available.

In this connection, experience has shown that personal acquaintance with the other fellow is one of the most important single factors in successful and effective coordination. No matter how important an organizational structure itself is, it always depends upon execution. The soundest organization can fail miserably if the individuals acting within its framework are selfish and uncooperative. This is a truism, and not peculiar to the subject at hand, but nevertheless should be borne in mind. . . .

Exchanging information has other aspects. The press, television, and radio are very important media. Newsworthy material, of course, is eagerly sought by both, but editorial columns, educational pages, and picture sections are frequently available. It is especially important to make sure that the broad scope of recreation activities is interpreted properly, overcoming a popular notion that recreation consists of sports only.

The publication of periodical pamphlets, magazines, and directories is another medium for the exchange of information. All agencies conducting recreation programs issue materials advertising their current services, monthly organs of interest to their participants, or annual reports, but the coordinating organization is the one place where information about the work of all agencies may be assembled. The pages of its own pamphlets, magazines, and directories are available to the public as well as the agencies. In one city, for example, almost 1000 inquiries are answered every year about summer camps for children. A directory listing some 75 camps is distributed so that parents may make direct contacts with those of their choice. In another city, copies of a quarterly magazine are circulated. In most instances the editorial work connected with such publications is done by a combination of staff assistance and committee direction, the latter determining policy.

Coordination is like a fine cut diamond. Each facet contributes to the sparkle of every other one. Countless reflections cross and crisscross to make it into the jewel it is. One surface alone cannot be viewed without seeing the effect of all the others. So it is with coordination. It is difficult to analyze each component part separately. Unlike the diamond, there are no mathematical or geometrical formulae to use in analyzing it. So we go from exchanging information about existing services to securing and using facts about unmet needs, even though the two are interlocked very closely and involve complicated factors.

Reference has been made to the broad scope of recreation activities. This is soundly based upon the wide interests of people, individually and collectively. It is the function of recreation to serve the interests of all—children, youth, and adults—in wholesome, constructive activities in their leisure time. It is the function of coordination to discover the community's needs for program and facilities and to initiate community action to secure them.

Generally speaking, we know through experience what people like to do. Standards for minimum requirements have been developed to serve as guides for the acquisition and development of recreation areas. Legislation has been enacted to insure the preservation of open space and the designation of community land for park purposes. The provision of adequate facilities is a highly technical job involving engineering and architectural knowledge, understanding of the functional use of facilities, legal complications in the acquisition of land, and many other factors. In large measure, the provision of facilities on a community-wide basis is accepted as a public responsibility, although in practice most communities have facilities created through voluntary contributions. It is not the purpose here to discuss the principles of voluntary and tax funds, but the two should work together, if both are to be used.

Because tax funds are widely used to develop recreation facilities, it is usual to find some public agency responsible for planning them. This may or may not be a planning commission, but in any case it becomes necessary to establish a relationship between the coordinating organization and the planning agency. One successful device has been a coordinating committee on recreation plans. It is purely a technician's committee, with representatives of a planning commission, municipal architect's office, municipal repair shop, recreation department, park department, public schools, and the recreation division of the council of social agencies.

Meeting monthly, it processes all plans for location, type of facility, its component parts, size, and all other technical factors.

The coordinating committee on recreation plans is only a recommending body. Each representative carries back the findings to his own agency for action. It is a classic example of cooperation. Its recommendations carry their weight because they are the result of considered expert experience.

The presence of the representative of the recreation division of the United Community Council (Council of Social Agencies) on this coordinating committee affords a full opportunity to bring together the interests of the voluntary and the public agencies. If and when one of the voluntary agencies projects its own plans to create a new facility, it is possible to determine the best location with respect to existing and projected public facilities. Complementary and supplementary relationships between the two may thus be established.

Of course, the voluntary agency cannot be compelled to consult on its plans for the future, but the logic of doing so is a strong impelling influence. Public support can be mobilized much more quickly and easily for any proposals which come out of such planning.

Two facets have now been outlined briefly. A third is coordination of recreation activity programs. It is less tangible than exchanging information and planning facilities, though obviously depends upon them. Perhaps a few examples will illustrate the possibilities. In music, a committee, knowing what each of its member's agencies can and is doing and what facilities are available, arranges a city-wide, or county-wide, Christmas carol sing, or perhaps a music-week program. Through the committee, agencies not having music as part of their program but having interested individuals or groups, might learn about skilled leaders who would be available. In a community lacking facilities, such a committee might spearhead the work of securing them. Similarly, committees set up by the coordinating organization might stimulate drama, sports, or any other activity in which there is interest.

The training of volunteer leadership is another reflection of program coordination in recreation. Considerable follow-up is necessary to assure satisfactory placement after training. The coordinating organization must do a skilled job through committee planning of all the arrangements. This will not only make sure that the contents of the training course will meet the needs of the agencies and community, and secure the best leaders, but it will also guarantee that the volunteers are given challenging assignments that will hold their interest. Most of the responsibility for this last will rest, of course, with the agencies benefiting from the placement, but it will help materially if the committee work affords an exchange of experience in handling volunteers.

In connection with leadership, two other coordinating functions are feasible and desirable. Files of available positions and applicants seeking employment can be maintained for use by all agencies. Standards of personnel qualifications can be developed, too, through committee study and agreement.

The diamond has still another facet, especially in the larger cities, but not by any means confined to them. Recreation is a very personal business for the individual. Community-wide, it becomes a neighborhood business. Mobilizing all the forces of the neighborhood to promote recreation is an approach in coordination that is getting considerable momentum. There are at least two ways of going about it. One is through the neighborhood council, which usually is interested in many community services such as health, welfare, recreation, and others. Within it, there might be a recreation committee. Its part would be to serve as a magnifying glass for its particular interest. It creates opportunity for expression under circumstances most conducive to discussion. The people are among those whom they know best, and before whom they can speak most easily and freely.

In many cities, leadership is being made available to neighborhood councils through the coordinating organization. It has been found that while they are usually self-starting, they are not often self-propelling. There is a lot of leg work involved and someone, volunteer or professional, who will do it is absolutely essential.

The other neighborhood approach is through neighborhood recreation councils, organized directly around this one interest. The principles are the same as just described. So are the problems, particularly financial ones. While it is not the purpose of coordination to raise funds, the coordinating organization is usually the one place in a community where there is the over-all, community-wide knowledge of needs. Within the sum total of funds available, the coordinating organization can be the best adviser on their distribution. United funds over the country raise large amounts of money for voluntary agencies. It is the practice to consult the coordinating organization about equitable distribution. Much progress has been made in raising our sights to meet the needs, but there is still much to be done in this direction.

With respect to the appropriation of tax funds, there are complicating economic factors and limitations. The coordinating organization can and should support the need for adequate funds for recreation. Some interesting comparisons can be made between amounts spent for other public services such as fire and police protection, garbage collection, institutional care, education, and others.

The basic recreation service in community recreation for all of the people is the public department. The coordinating organization can and should work toward the establishment of such a department wherever it

does not exist. . . . In one city, the coordinating organization successfully carried out a long-range objective over a 15-year period, working
with all other organizations in that community for the unification of
three public agencies into one department.

This position regarding public recreation as the basic service in no way
minimizes the place or importance of the voluntary agencies. In fact, the
need for service is so great that there is room for all. Working together
will help each to do a better job. The maintenance of a high standard
of service should be one of the guiding principles, with plenty of precautions taken to avoid selfish, vested interests, and at the same time
guard carefully against quackery seizing opportunities to fill the gaps.
Good working relationships with other community-wide groups, such as
the board of trade or the parent-teacher association, are fundamental to
the success of public recreation.

Finally, where the coordination of recreation is being considered, it is
wise to look for the existing organization created for the purpose and
more than likely already doing a job for the community. If it isn't the best
job that could be done, the reason can be, and often is, because the very
people who want to see things done are not making use of what the community has in its midst. As does the planning of a city itself, with all its
physical components, so recreation in all of its manifestations needs
sound planning and coordination.

A POINT OF DEPARTURE

As emphasized earlier, recreation is an essential part of daily living
and, since most people live in a community, it becomes the legitimate,
continuing concern and responsibility of that community. To meet the
need to recreate, organizations develop and opportunities are provided.
As the community is comprised of many groups, so is the recreating public. Consequently, many recreationally oriented groups and organizations
are formed, each molded to meet the needs of its members. The sum
total of these organizations and groups comprises the recreation system.

In order to insure the full development and integration of the many
resources and opportunities which comprise the recreation system, the
concept of community recreation is an absolute necessity. It is suggested
that every community should have its citizen's recreation council representing all of the interested groups, in addition to its official board or
commission which is responsible for directing the tax supported public
recreation program. Furthermore, it is recommended that:

1. Opportunities and programs for organized recreation should be available
   for all the citizens of the community throughout the entire year.

2. The recreation programs should be planned to meet the interest and needs of the many groups and individuals which comprise the "community."

3. Community planning for leisure requires cooperative action on the part of the public and volunteer agencies which have recreation interests and resources.

4. Whenever possible, federal, state and local agencies should correlate their plans for the planning, acquisition, development and use of recreation facilities.

5. A community recreation plan should be coordinated with the long-range planning of the other services of the community so all its resources may be fully utilized.

6. Each agency, organization or group which has recreation functions and facilities should employ an adequate staff of qualified personnel to meet its share of the community's needs.

7. Adequate financial support for recreation services, in the form of either public or private contributions must be assured if quality opportunities are to be provided.

8. Each member of the recreation system has the responsibility and obligation to assist in developing the public's awareness of the social significance of recreation by interpreting its needs, services and opportunities.

9. Recreation services, actual and potential, should be evaluated continuously in terms of their contribution towards enriching individual and community life.

The above principles are given a chance to succeed when coupled with the following reliable procedures for initiating a community recreation program:

1. Community recreation initiated by the efforts of a single institution or agency—generally within local government, either as a recreation department or commission, recreation and park department, or under an existing agency such as a school board, park board, or welfare department.

2. Community recreation initiated by the collective efforts of all agencies interested—schools, health agencies, youth-serving groups, churches, civic groups, and other units. Not all of the agencies may exist in the same community, but a number of them are operating in most communities. When possible, these agencies should combine their efforts in initiating and providing the community recreation program. This prevents the program from becoming institutionalized and unites community leadership.

3. A combination of a well-coordinated program of public, private, and commercial interests. The governmental agency, private agencies, and commercial enterprises set up a community recreation committee through which the activities of all are correlated to assure the community of adequate recreation opportunities.

The recreation program, of course, will be made more efficient in proportion to its coordination with total community planning. Among the essentials for developing a local public recreation system are:

Know your community. The character and distribution of population, the traditions, needs, problems, resources and social climate of the community.

Pool your resources. Work together for full use of all potential assets—from public and private agencies, neighborhood groups, organizations, individual leaders, state and regional representatives and interests.

Check your legislation. Determine what legislation you need and what you have; and then, if necessary, work to get laws that provide an adequate legal base. Authority to develop public recreation depends upon state and local laws.

Establish a legal managing authority. A responsible lay board with legal authority to administer the program, assuring recreation the community status it warrants.

Get good leadership. Insist on a trained, full-time executive, responsible to the board and on-the-job the year-around. Choose subordinate leaders with equal care on a basis of qualifications and training. Select and use competent volunteers within this framework of professional leadership. Utilize recreation aids and allied professionals.

Make the most of existing facilities. Municipally-owned schools, buildings, parks, playfields, playgrounds, and water areas. They may be supplemented by use of privately-owned property and fuller use of state and federal resources.

Secure a separate budget. Obtain a definite, adequate amount of public funds through special tax levy or other public appropriations, earmarked for the sole purpose of community recreation.

See that your program is community-wide, year-round, has broad appeal. With interests for young and old, indoor and outdoor activities, athletics, music, arts, crafts, drama, lectures, forums, social recreation, and community events.

Maintain public partnership. Keep popular opinion abreast of your program. Use all media available to interpret community recreation and win public support for it. Involve the public in program planning and determination.

Plan for the future. Make a place for recreation in long-range town planning. Good planning should include not only physical facilities but also program leadership and finance and should be coordinated with the development of other community systems and regional recreation plans.

THE WORKSHOP

1. Consult representatives of opposing political parties for their views on the roles of the community, the state, and the national government in recreation.
2. Make a brief plan for organizing the groups in a small community or neighborhood for recreation.
3. Visit the offices of a united fund or some similar coordinating body and discuss its organization with the executive.
4. Attend the meeting of a united community council (a meeting of a recreation and social group work committee, if feasible) and report to your class.

5. List the agencies in your community which you think may be engaged in providing recreation services. Use the following headings: *governmental, private membership, commercial,* and *other*.
6. Compare the kinds of problems faced by the modern community in comparison with the community of 25, 50 years ago.

REFERENCES

Buell, Bradley, *et al., Community Planning for Human Resources.* New York: Columbia University Press, 1952.

Butler, George D., "The Structure of Public Leisure Agencies," *The Annals of the American Academy of Political and Social Science,* CCCXIII, September, 1957, 119–125.

Carlson, Reynold E., Theodore R. Deppe, and Janet R. MacLean, *Recreation in American Life.* Belmont, California: Wadsworth Publishing Company, Inc., 1963.

Harper, Ernest B., ed., *Community Organization in Action.* New York: Association Press, 1959.

Hunter, Floyd, *Community Power Structure,* New York: Anchor, 1963.

Nelson, Lowry, C. E. Ramsey, and Codie Verner, *Community Structure and Change.* New York: The Macmillan Company, 1965.

Russ, Murray G., *Community Organization: Theory and Principles.* New York: Harper & Row, Publishers, 1955.

Sanders, Irvin, *The Community. An Introduction to a Social System.* New York: The Ronald Press Company, 1966.

Warren, Roland L., *Studying Your Community.* New York: The Free Press, 1965.

Wurster, Catherine B., "Framework For An Urban Society," in *Goals for Americans.* Englewood Cliffs, New Jersey: Prentice-Hall, Inc., 1960.

11

The Family and
Its Recreation

It would be reckless to assume that most of the things people do outside the home are not as good for them as the things they do inside the home. Yet nothing can really take the place of a happy home life. There is no substitute for family affection and mutual respect in cementing the family circle. An important help in making family living attractive is to make recreation a part of family living.

To the individual and the family, the home as a facility and the family as a group represent basic recreation resources. Many of the foundations of a good recreation pattern are laid early in life, and the child in his early years uses the home as his major play locale.

As a facility, the home can provide opportunities for individuals within the family to participate in recreation peculiar to their individual interests, age, and sex characteristics, and it can also provide opportunities for all members of the family to participate jointly in common recreation interests . . .[1]

Numerous attempts are being made to stimulate family recreation. A number of leaders have, with some success, organized backyard playground campaigns for small children. Homemade equipment plans have been furnished by recreation departments. There are books and pamphlets

[1] *Recreation for Community Living* (Chicago: Athletic Institute, 1954), pp. 30, 31.

describing games for home use. Hobbies are becoming increasingly popular, and the recreation needs of individuals are receiving the attention of many agencies and groups.

There is renewed interest in family parties, picnics, camping, and travel. Family-planned automobile trips continue to grow in popularity.

Every effort should be made to revitalize the family as a functional unit of recreation and to encourage new families to establish definite patterns of recreation as an essential part of family solidarity.

The importance of budgeting for family recreation, making an early start, and following certain guide lines is stressed in the following: [2]

BUDGET FOR RECREATION

Nobody knows exactly how much money Americans spend for recreation each year, but we do know that these expenditures are great. Few families keep account of what they spend for recreation, but they should, because it can amount to more than they realize. Funds for family recreation should be budgeted just as mortgage payments and other recurring expenditures are. The family should discuss what to do recreationally and should make lists of activities and their approximate costs. Included in each list should be such items as vacations, holiday celebrations, week-end trips, admissions to movies and other spectator events, membership dues in recreation agencies, expenditures for toys, reading material, and all the things which families buy for their recreational pleasure. This may include the purchase of swimming suits, camera films, gardening tools, and bridge prizes.

There are literally hundreds of activities a family can do together which cost little or nothing. Interestingly enough, we often enjoy most of the things which cost the least. A hike into the hills, exploration of an old mill, or group singing of familiar tunes may be remembered longer than expensive activities.

START EARLY AND BE AN EXAMPLE

Family recreation is no problem if the members develop interests and skills in the right kind of recreation at an early age. The right kind of recreation is socially acceptable. It strengthens rather than weakens children's personalities and makes them healthier persons. Because the home then is the first playground and the place where play habits and interests are formed, responsibility for development in the desired direction belongs to the parents.

In the family, as elsewhere, the most effective method of leading and teaching is by example. If you want your children to become interested in good literature, you should read good books in the home. If you want the youngsters to appre-

---

[2] Brightbill, Charles K., *How To Make Recreation a Family Affair* (Chicago: F. E. Compton and Company, 1958), pp. 6, 13.

ciate classical music, you should be sure the children hear such music. Recreation, like other skills, requires participation. Children will follow their parents' example in the way they spend leisure time. Recreation is not a passive thing. It is active, creative, and takes thought and skill.

GUIDES FOR FAMILY RECREATION

Parents should realize the important role which recreation plays in developing well-adjusted people and in sustaining the family as the basic institution of our society. The continued interest of children in their family, and their desire to be a part of it, depends to a large extent upon how attractive family living is made. Recreation is one way of making family existence worth while.

1. Although it is important for parents to guide the recreational development of their children, the kind and amount of guidance must be adapted to the development of the child. The things that interest a youngster when he is 12 will not interest him when he is 16.

2. If parents are careful to expose their children to proper kinds of recreation during the early years, they will be able to share the recreational interests of their children for a long time.

3. It is not enough for parents to be concerned with the family's recreation within the home. They should also be interested in the experiences their children have outside the home. Many parents meet their children's school teachers and Sunday School instructors. They should also know their children's playground leaders, scout masters, and club directors.

4. Families should support public and voluntary agencies in the community which are dedicated to developing wholesome recreation opportunities. Such agencies are most valuable when they serve the entire family.

Planning

Family recreation cannot be successful unless it is planned. The idea is not to have a rigid structure, but to understand family membership and formulate workable plans to be informally carried out. Suggestions must be applied to individual family conditions and modified accordingly. They are presented here only as ideas.

Since any family recreation program depends upon participation by the entire family, everyone should have a voice in the planning. Mother, father, and the children all have valuable contributions to offer. A ready-made schedule is less palatable and may fail to arouse and sustain interest. Every member of the family should be encouraged to use his imagination in suggesting activities the entire family might enjoy. Family planning might take place with the group gathered around a table with a list of suggested activities read by father or mother. Activities might be planned for a period of several months or on a seasonal basis. A recreation calendar might be used for blocking out the activities.

While an activity may be suited to only one season, preparation for it may be necessary in another. An example is the preparation for the opening of the fishing season. Fly-tying and the making of other artificial fish lures have strong appeal during the winter months. Fishing rods need repair; fishing reels, nets, lines, and other equipment require attention. Preparation during the off season for future recreation activity should not be overlooked in the planning.

The actual planning begins, then, with the selection of suitable activities from a wide range of possibilities. In addition to the suggested list, anyone should feel free to add other activities. As the activities are selected and the dates noted, the information is recorded on the recreation calendar. When the selection is complete for a given period or season, detailed planning for the various activities takes place. This planning includes such considerations as time, place, method, facilities, and equipment required.

The construction of recreation facilities and equipment can in itself be recreation. Having decided upon a cook-out, the family discovers it needs a fireplace. Suggestions for the type may come from mother, who finds several plans in magazines. Working plans may be required. One member of the family mixes the cement while another sets up the forms; others may carry the bricks, stones, and other materials. The outdoor fireplace will be a source of much pleasure, especially when all members of the family have had a part in building it. The younger members of the family may want an outdoor gymnasium. The materials required for building a horizontal bar, flying rings, and swing are inexpensive, and they are easily constructed. There is sufficient diversification in recreation to offer any family more leisure activities than it can possibly find time to pursue.

Most satisfying activities are sufficiently inexpensive to be within the means of most families. The following group of activities, while far from complete, will permit a selection to meet the interests of families regardless of economic status. There are hobbies and activities that can be afforded only by those in the higher-income bracket, but there are also hobbies and activities within the reach of the low-income group. In addition to being classified for indoor and outdoor participation, the material is further divided into seven groups as follows: active games and sports, social events, musical activities, arts and crafts, dramatics, nature, and collecting.

Active games and sports. Games requiring little organization, such as club snatch, prisoner's base, poison, and hide-and-seek are suitable for participation by parents and young children. The children find this type of game a source of merriment, and the parents derive considerable pleasure from the antics of the children.

For older children and parents, net games including tennis, badminton, ring tennis, and paddle tennis lend themselves well to mixed doubles. Badminton requires a space 25′ x 60′, and complete sets can be purchased at a modest cost. Here again the courts should be laid out and maintained by the family. The same space required for badminton will also suffice for ring tennis. Slight modifications in the dimensions of sports' facilities will not materially affect the play for the family group; in fact, it may be advisable to modify the dimensions for younger members of the family.

Other games which may be adapted for family participation are horse-shoes and quoits, which call for approximately the same space requirements, croquet, and tether ball. For the family addicted to fresh-water fishing, fly casting and bait casting are interesting. To make these two activities safe, the hooks are removed, and a substitute weight, such as a fly or plug, is used. The activity can be organized into a game by setting up targets for the casters—an old tire or an area marked off on the ground. Kite-flying can be made into a fascinating contest, especially if the kites are homemade.

Archery is an interesting sport and lends itself to participation by parents and older children. Certain safety precautions must, of course, be taken to prevent injury to person and damage to property, but safety is far from being an insurmountable problem.

While lack of space in most homes may curtail it, there are some games and sports that may be conducted indoors. Low-organization games for small children may be used occasionally. Hide-and-seek and ring games are representative types. Billiards, pool, table tennis, and indoor quoits or horseshoes will afford the family many pleasant hours together.

Special activities. One of the sources of greatest pleasure for the family is the activity centered around the outdoor fireplace which the members have themselves constructed. The fireplace will be the locale for cook-outs, storytelling, and social gatherings. Cook-outs may range from toasting marshmallows to preparing an entire meal. Children and oldsters alike want to try their hand at outdoor cooking. The fireplace should be so designed and constructed that it has removable grates and grill and an oven that will burn charcoal, wood, or coal.

Another activity which provides fun for all is the treasure hunt. There are many ways of organizing it. One of the most popular is that of placing at various "stations" written directions which give a clue to the location of the next direction, each direction leading toward the hidden treasure. Age levels must be considered, so that although the contest is challenging, it is not so difficult as to cause loss of interest. Marked differences in age might be neutralized by using different colored paper for the directions for various members. Directions for younger children should be easily understandable.

Drama. One of the most keenly enjoyed activities of children is the marionette or puppet show. With little material and effort a small outdoor stage can be constructed for this purpose. Children are delighted to participate in this form of dramatics.

Nature. Nature activities can capture the attention of all members of the family. Here is a phase of recreation which may begin in childhood and continue throughout life. Raising poultry and livestock and keeping bees are challenging hobbies. Pets are almost a basic need for children. Insects may be collected on the home grounds and mounted in cases built by the family. The mounting can be as elaborate as financial circumstances will permit. The collection and mounting of insects lead to the labeling of various specimens and a study of their habits. Bird study may also take place in the backyard. Colored pictures of birds indigenous to the locality can be obtained in advance so that all members of the family may know which ones to expect at certain times and thus have a basis for identification. This naturally leads to a study of the habits of birds.

Gardening. Gardening will find a place in the interests of the family. Children should be permitted to help with the preparation of the soil, the planting of seeds, and the harvesting of the crop.

Parents and older children will find much pleasure in the construction and maintenance of a weather station. A comparison of weather reports published in the newspapers and announced over the radio with recordings made at home increases the interest. These data might be used when planning fishing trips, picnics, and other outdoor events.

Astronomy. This can be developed into a most interesting study for leisure. The exploration of space has brought new interest in natural, as well as man-made satellites. This activity requires preparation of charts of the sky for the various months, watching newspapers and periodicals for notice of the appearance of interesting phenomena, and perhaps the construction of a small telescope.

Collecting. Perhaps no form of collecting holds such universal appeal as that of stamp collecting. Its cultivation is desirable because it opens up so many areas of related study—history, art, science, civics, geography, printing, design, and social relationships. Here is a hobby which makes history a live subject; it becomes something more than a list of places, dates, and events. Using a projector to illustrate the stamps and the geography of the country which the stamps represent provides a constant stimulus to learn more about the other peoples of the world, their habits, customs, and background.

Social activities. There is an endless list of activities of a social nature which can be conducted in the home. Of universal appeal to all ages are card games. They should be selected in accordance with the age level of the children and range from simple matching of cards to rummy, pinochle, and bridge. Checkers, chess, dominoes, and parchesi are always popular. To provide enjoyment and continuity, contests can be organized on the basis of points or games over a period of several weeks or a month. Teams can be organized with various combinations—parents versus children, or father and one child versus mother and another child.

Holiday and birthday parties can be significant events in family life.

Music. The family that does not include music in the recreation program is overlooking one of the most effective opportunities for unifying the family. There is something seriously lacking in the home that does not have music in one form or another. Music in the home may consist of periodic gatherings around the piano for a song fest, playing together in string ensembles, or listening to phonograph records or a radio or TV broadcast. Whatever form it takes, no recreation calendar will be complete without the inclusion of music. Harmonica solos, duets, or other combinations are popular with children and inexpensive to arrange.

Arts and crafts. Arts and crafts appeal to all ages and may be combined with other family activities. Repairing a boat or constructing a new gadget to gain an advantage in the next season's races, designing and constructing instruments such as a weather vane for the weather station, making outdoor furniture for use around the outdoor fireplace, constructing aquariums, bird houses and bird baths, metalware, sports equipment, and game boards, are a few of the applications of arts and crafts to the family recreation program.

The making of holiday greeting cards by block printing is an absorbing use of leisure. Photography is a hobby that recognizes no age barriers and is limitless in possibilities. One family may be satisfied to make contact prints, while another may go in for elaborate enlargements. One of the most interesting forms of photography is the filming of the year-round activities of the family. The results may be shown as moving pictures or slides, or in albums.

Other phases of arts and crafts are pottery making, weaving, painting, sketching, and metal, wood, or leather craft projects.

METHODS OF GETTING INFORMATION AND INSTRUCTION TO THE FAMILY

The recreation department should lead the way in stimulating family recreation. Any plan that is adopted should be carefully worked out and tested. Two methods suggested for getting this program of recreation to the family are (1) through a community advisory service on recreation and (2) through a variety of publicity media.

The community advisory service of the advisory council should be so organized that it can demonstrate any of the classified phases of recreation at the recreation center or in individual homes, as well as give assistance in planning to those who request it. The community advisory service should have available a supply of printed materials, written for lay persons, and including diagrams and space requirements for the full range of recreation activities.

Effective public relations calls for a certain amount of journalistic ability to supply information in an interesting, readable form. All available media for getting the program to the family should be used, e.g., newspaper, radio, TV, special bulletins, library, and school. "Public relations" also implies personal contact with other agencies of the community, public and private, such as the board of education, the school staff, the police department, civic and social agencies, the Boy Scouts, the Y.M.C.A., and veterans' organizations.

SPECIAL SUGGESTIONS

If at all possible, every family should have play space in the home. The attic, the cellar, and the playroom, for example, can each have a special function in recreation. Where possible a room devoted to recreation should be a part of all home-building plans. The backyard, driveways, and the front lawn can all be used for special activities. Where possible, a definite outdoor play area should be provided.

In addition to individual hobbies the family can have a hobby—furnishing the home, beautifying the grounds, family singing. An orchestra, family arts and crafts, and numerous activities can be promoted with family unity. Too, each member can share in the special hobbies and collections of the others. This is often difficult because of conflicting work hours, school schedules, and extracurricular and community activities. However, attempts should be made to have the entire family together frequently.

Recreation departments might provide families with suggestions for activities best suited for rainy days. Even when it is necessary to stay indoors only a few days, there are problems of entertainment, especially if there are young children in the family. Activities suitable for porches, basement, attic, living room, and halls can provide release for pent-up energies.

Children's toys are important recreation equipment in the home. The National Recreation and Park Association asks the following questions regarding toys:

1. Is the toy suited to the child's development?
2. Is it made to stand good hard wear?

3. Is it hygienic—washable?
4. Is it safe—no sharp parts or pieces that will break off?
5. Has it many play possibilities?
6. Is it attractive and artistic?

Every family is faced with sickness from time to time. There are many activities that are suitable for convalescent patients. Games for the bedside, table games, magic and tricks, quizzes of all types, peg board games, cutout material, simple arts and crafts, reading, and drawing, illustrate the possibilities. The family can collect material of this type for this special service.

Reading aloud, with each member of the group taking part, is a valuable means of bringing the family together as well as a source of lasting pleasure. Storytelling is a constant challenge to the imagination of the teller and a refreshing pastime for every age group.

Many other activities are possible, and the family should be alert to new ideas and practices, thus keeping the program attractive and stimulating.

STRENGTHENING FAMILY TIES

Wholesome recreation activities can strengthen family ties. They can also contribute to the growth of the intellectual, moral, spiritual, social, and informational aspect of family life.

The family should focus on recreation needs for different stages of family development:

1. The young couple often in cramped quarters and with meager income.
2. The restricted couple with small children.
3. Pre-school children and their neighborhood ties.
4. The school-agers of the family and the relationships with school life.
5. The adolescent and all the teen-age activities woven around family and community life.
6. Recreation for the adult members and the oldsters in the family union.

At each stage recreation can assist in attaining individual and family development needs. For example:

To develop solidarity between young couples, to foster community relationships, and to promote internal resources of the family.

To provide relief from the rigors of child-rearing and to project plans for the future.

To develop social capacities in children.

To foster intellectual interest and good adult relationships with the children.

To foster wholesome and maturing patterns of growth.
To recognize and adjust recreation to age differences.
To provide opportunities in sharing common interests for common goals.

The family can function only in relation to the larger social order. Each is inevitably and vitally affected by the stability of the other. The social values and controls centered in other institutions also affect the family. Just as the family is the basic unit in the whole social order, so the characteristics of family life are in part determined by outside influences. The forces of organized recreation in the community, therefore, join hands with the families of the community in bringing about enjoyment of the good life as fundamental to both.

THE WORKSHOP

1. Make a few case studies of family recreation and report on them.
2. List the major social forces of contemporary society which affect family recreation. Classify the changes according to whether they help or hinder family unity.
3. Suggest ways in which family life can be related to community recreation.
4. Present a list of ways in which community recreation programs can aid family life.
5. Discuss family recreation in relation to age differences.
6. Report on ways churches, schools, private agencies, and other community groups are assisting family recreation.
7. Plan a program of recreation activities for a rural family, a suburban family, and the city family living in an apartment.
8. Interview parent-teacher association leaders for their opinions on family recreation.
9. Design a recreation room for a small home.
10. Prepare a list of recreation activities which best lend themselves to indoor recreation for a family with elementary school age children.

REFERENCES

Edgren, Harry D., and E. H. Reginer, *Fun With the Family*. Champaign, Illinois: Stipes Publishing Company, 1959.

Edgren, Harry D., *1000 Games and Stunts, Family Parties for Each Month of the Year*. Nashville, Tennessee: Abingdon Press, 1961.

Eisenberg, Helen and Larry, *The Family Fun Book*. New York: Association Press, 1953 (Fourth Printing, 1963).

Fairchild, Roy W., and John C. Wynn, *Families In The Church*. New York: Association Press, 1963.

Komarousky, Mirra, *Blue Collar Marriage*. New York: Vintage Books, 1967.

Smith, Marie Anne, *Play for Convalescent Children in Hospitals and At Home.* New York: A. S. Barnes & Co., 1961.

Thompson, Wayne E., and Gordon Streib, *Meaningful Activities In a Family Content.* New York: Oxford University Press, Inc., 1961.

Comment

Reports from both the 1960 White House Conference on Children and Youth and the 1961 White House Conference on Aging have many constructive recommendations dealing with family recreation. Proceedings and recommendations may be obtained by writing to the United States Government Printing Office, Washington, D.C.

Home Play in Rural Areas, a bulletin of the National Congress of Parents and Teachers, prepared by William McKinley Robinson, is a program outine for rural parent groups.

Home Recreation, prepared by the Los Angeles Department of Recreation, offers a compilation of recreation activities adapted to family use.

The following organizations are directly concerned with family life, and their programs often relate to recreation: American Home Economics Association, 1600 Twentieth Street, Washington, D.C.; Catholic Conference on Family Life, Washington, D.C.; Child Study Association of America, 132 East 74th Street, New York; Child Welfare League of America, 345 East 46th Street, New York City; Family Service Association of America, 192 Lexington Avenue, New York City; National Council of the Churches of Christ in the United States, Committee on Marriage and the Home, 297 Fourth Avenue, New York City; Jewish Institute on Marriage and the Family, 40 W. 68th Street, New York City; National Council on Family Relations, 5757 South Drexel Avenue, Chicago, Illinois; National Council of Parent Education, Poughkeepsie, New York; National Congress of Parents and Teachers, Chicago, Illinois; Children's Bureau of the Department of Health, Education and Welfare, Washington, D.C.; Agricultural Extension Service of the U.S. Department of Agriculture, Washington, D.C.

12

The School and
Recreation

Education is the guidance of the intellectual, moral, physical, and social development of the individual. And while learning is not confined to formal education, a large part of the responsibility for organized education falls upon the school—the *public* school, which is tax-supported and publicly controlled.

The school, whose role it is to pass on to each generation the fundamentals of man's accumulated knowledge, which sifts the useful from the useless, centers its educative experience upon the individual, usually, during the impressionable years.

Because the school, as an institution, is an instrument and reflection of the culture and the society in which it exists, its role is necessarily shaped by them. If the needs of the culture are multifaceted and complex, the functions of the school are likely to be the same. When affluency results in more leisure for more people, education is confronted with the challenge of helping individuals to learn how to use that leisure in ways which will contribute to their fullest personality expression. This is what brings the recreative use of leisure—recreation—into the sphere of interest and *shared* responsibility of learning's most formidable ally—the school. The educated person is the person who is not only prepared to *work* but also to *live*, to live fully and completely in his *discretionary* as well as his *obligated* time.

Life and culture are in a constant state of change. Consequently, the roles of institutions change with changing conditions. In this respect, the modern public school in the United States is different from its predecessors. Today's school, for instance, has added *planning* and *community service* processes to the *teaching* process (some think far too much). Also, it often serves throughout the lifetime of the individual, not confining its services to the elementary and secondary school years. An examination of the present school will reveal other ways in which it differs from those which preceded it.

EXTENT OF RECREATION IN THE SCHOOLS

Recreation in the schools of the United States is not exactly new. After all, the Latin School in Salem, Massachusetts, opened its outdoor physical educational facilities for recreation use as early as 1821, and New York City opened school buildings as evening recreation centers in 1888.

Not only have educators accepted the "worthy use of leisure time" as one of the objectives of education, many schools have recognized their obligations in recreation and are committed to meeting them. School authorities have supplemented the programs of physical activity in the elementary and secondary schools with activities in the graphic, plastic, and manual arts, and in music, drama, and social recreation. A variety of recreation opportunities, including the use of such school facilities as the gymnasium, swimming pool, library, auditorium, shops, and playing fields, are available to the out-of-school population in a number of public school systems.

School laws and codes in a number of states are liberal in their provision for the recreation services of the public schools. This is especially true in Pennsylvania, New York, Wisconsin, and California.

It cannot be said that the national trend is *toward* administering local public recreation systems under the jurisdiction of boards of education or school districts. Nevertheless, in some states a very large part of the responsibility for public recreation in the communities is assumed by the schools. Professor Frederick Coombs, of Pennsylvania State University, has estimated that 70 per cent of the local public recreation programs in that commonwealth is sponsored by school districts. According to Professor Milton Gabrielson, of New York University, 90 per cent of the public schools on Long Island had full time recreation programs by 1956.

Effective, local, public recreation programs can be found in places of varying sizes and locations. In some large metropolitan cities the boards of education sponsor the same type of community recreation programs as do other municipal and county departments. Typical are New York, Chicago, and Los Angeles. Somewhat smaller cities, such as Milwaukee and Newark, have offered extension public recreation services of high quality for decades. Still smaller cities, such as Flint, Michigan, and Madison, Wisconsin, present unique public school conducted recreation opportunities for the entire population. Monterey, Pasadena, and Long Beach, all California communities of varying sizes and types, are typical of school systems which have pooled resources to gain fine recreation programs.

In most smaller communities, the population depends upon the schools to meet their recreation needs. Often in the small town, the school is the *only* public group which has the facilities needed for recreation. The consolidated school in sparsely settled rural districts is typical.

THE RESOURCES OF THE SCHOOLS

In addition to the fact that the values of recreation are often the same as those of education, the school has resources which are frequently identical to those which are needed for recreation.

Facilities

A physical plant—indoor and outdoor facilities—is needed for recreation programs, and the schools have this. Auditoriums, gymnasiums, swimming pools, shops, libraries, club rooms, and specialized facilities, such as darkrooms for photography, are necessary for indoor recreation. Playing space for games, ball diamonds, tennis courts, gridirons, picnic areas, and facilities for swimming, fishing, and camping are among facilities needed outdoors. There is need for the playground, the playfield, and the athletic field. Many school systems have such facilities within their jurisdiction— facilities acquired or purchased, developed, and maintained with *public* funds.

Moreover, the centers of these facilities are properly located for community use because they are planned to be accessible to the school population. The elementary school is in the neighborhood, and if properly planned and located, it may include space for the neighborhood playground. Similarly, the junior or senior high school, serving a given district of the city or county, can be and often is the location of the playfield with facilities for sports and athletics.

There is little to be gained in including various kinds of recreation facilities in a school building unless the structure is open and available to the community. Community use cannot have a priority claim over school use of school facilities—and this is, admittedly, a clear disadvantage for community recreation—but there are too many school buildings which have recreation facilities which could and should be available for after-school recreation and which are not. Even under the best circumstances, when schools are used for the dual purpose of education and community recreation, there is the problem of *scheduling* and co-ordinating the uses in a way which will best serve both needs.

There are two developments in the modern world of public education which are directly related to the challenges of leisure and, therefore, community recreation. Although they express themselves in the tangible form of *facilities,* they are quite as much *concepts* as combinations of space and structure. Since they are not without their proponents and detractors, it is pertinent here to know what they represent. Reference is made to the *community-school* and the *park-school.*

The *community-school* is one in which the school has obligations beyond erasing illiteracy. Here the school, as a community institution, involves itself in the social structure and the social needs of the community. The community-school and its relation to recreation might be interpreted in this manner:

The school's responsibility for recreation consists of two types—instructional and service activities. Within the framework of the community and in co-operation with other agencies, the concerns of the community-school for recreation may be described as follows:

1. To provide competent leadership to assist in the planning and development of community-wide activities for the instructional and service programs of the school.
2. To teach skills with opportunities for their application; to facilitate the acquisition of knowledges, appreciations, and attitudes necessary for maximum participation in leisure-time pursuits.
3. To provide adequate facilities for the instructional and service programs.
4. To co-operate with other community agencies that have responsibilities for community programs and facilities.
5. To serve as the focal point for planning and initiating service projects in the community.[1]

The *park-school* concept is less ambitious than that of the *community-school* idea in that it does not engage itself with the multiple social needs of the community. Also, its emphasis is mainly upon the location and functions of *facilities.* In the park-school approach, the school is located in a park or comparable outdoor recreation area. In this manner, the indoor recreation facilities of the school and the outdoor recreation facilities of the park complement one another. The building and the area may or may *not* be under a single managing authority. In some instances, both might be the property of the school district. In another, the outdoor area might be under the management of a park system or a public rec-

---

[1] *Leisure and the Schools* (Washington, D. C.: American Association of Health, Physical Education and Recreation, 1961), p. 25.

reation department. In any event, the advantages of the park-school concept are apparent. It can reduce costs of land acquisition and development, secure wider and more effective use of physical resources, conserve public funds, and minimize competition among public services.

Another growing resource for recreation in connection with the schools is in *outdoor education*. The principal purpose of *outdoor education*— enjoyment, appreciation, and use of the natural environment—brings it into the interest of the school. This is understood even more fully when the specific objectives of outdoor recreation are considered:

1. To develop a sense of responsibility for the preservation, care and wise use of the natural environment.
2. To develop an awareness and understanding of the interrelatedness of all nature, including man.
3. To develop an understanding and appreciation of man's heritage of outdoor living, skills, and pursuits.
4. To develop good outdoor citizenship.
5. To make a contribution to physical and mental health.
6. To develop resourcefulness, self-reliance, and adaptability.[2]

Outdoor education (used interchangeably with the term 'outdoor recreation') is looked upon by some school authorities as an opportunity to use the outdoors as a laboratory for learning. Space does not permit a lengthy discussion here of the methods involved in the program, but a listing of some of the settings, beyond leaving the school premises on trips for specific outdoor education purposes, may be enlightening. Among these settings are:

School grounds and properties. These provide opportunities for simple field experiences related to the sciences and uncomplicated opportunities to become acquainted with nature in short periods of time.

Parks, forests, preserves, arboreta, botanical gardens, and even open wild lands are the objects of excursions. These may be town, city, county, regional, or national areas, most of them publicly owned, but some under private ownership.

Estates and clubs. These resources often include natural features of the types mentioned above and may have some special emphasis, such as conservation, beautification, and the like.

Museums, planetaria, aquaria, and zoos. Where these familiar civic attractions can be found, they usually have instructional staff available and provide stimulating and enjoyable learning experiences through their collections, exhibits, and demonstrations.

Gardens (school and community). These resources for bringing together the people and the land are used not only for observation but also for actual growing of vegetables and flowers. Both the agricultural and related scientific aspects

2 *The Recreation Program* (Chicago: The Athletic Institute, 1954), p. 250.

of gardening are interwoven here with the pure enjoyment and recreational satisfactions which come from working with the soil.

School farms. The school farm is to provide learning experiences for students in agriculture, farm life, and rural living. As might be expected, the school farm can be a center for nature field trips, a place to learn conservation of soil, timber, water and game, an area for gardening and animal raising, plus all of the other facets of farm operation.

School forests. The emphasis, of course, in the school forest is upon forest preservation and reforestation. Its concentration is upon conservation not only with respect to timber but also in relation to plants, soil, and water. Nature lore in its varied forms, including the development of crafts made with native materials, together with resources for picnics, camping, and outings are among the attractions of the school forest.

School camps. School camping has developed extensively in some sections of the country. "Upwards of 500 school districts in one-half the states now report programs where learning takes place in a camp setting for periods of a week or more." [3]

National camp authorities tell us that

School camping is an extended school experience which makes use of the school environment. In a sense, it is a form of resident camping, usually taking place during the school year. Children and their teachers from varying age and grade levels go to camp together, usually for a school week. The program aims to make the maximum use of the camp environment to carry forward the accepted purposes and objectives of the curriculum. School camping differs from resident camping in that it is a *continuous living experience* of a group of children and teachers which is a part of the total school situation.[4]

Personnel

Because education and recreation in so many ways strive for common ends, particularly the full development of personality and enrichment of living, it is no surprise to realize that the individuals who shape developments in each field—the educator and the recreator—have comparable interests, purposes, and competencies.

The faculty of a sound secondary public school represents a spread of interests and abilities sought just as much in community recreation as in the school system. There is the physical educator with his skills in sports, games, and athletics, or his interests in the dance. The teacher of the graphic and plastic arts, the speech and drama teacher, the biologist with his interest in nature, the manual arts instructor, the teacher of instrumental and vocal music, and the home economics teacher are there.

[3] American Association of Health, Physical Education and Recreation, *op. cit.,* p. 116.
[4] The Athletic Institute, *op. cit.,* p. 273.

The librarian, the counselor, and others have very special contributions to make to recreation just as they do to education.

To a lesser degree, comparable talent is present in the elementary school and in the self-contained classroom. Here the very qualities which make the teacher a "jack of all trades" are the ones which might serve her well in recreation. She is expected to teach the three R's, but she also performs in the role of physical educator, art teacher, music teacher, health educator, librarian, and counselor.

It does *not* follow, however, that a successful teacher is a proven recreation leader! Unless the teacher knows the philosophy and methods of recreation and can generate the interest of the recreation participant on a *voluntary* basis, she will not succeed in recreation.

The American school teacher, nevertheless, is in an excellent position to make a very real contribution to personality development through the portals of recreation. This role is described in *Recreation For Community Living.*[5]

The modern school teacher has specific responsibilities for recreation. With his background and knowledge of how children grow and develop, and of the importance of play, he is able to organize and direct curricular experiences which will enable children to develop recreation skills, attitudes, and interests appropriate to their needs. Recreation experiences should be a part of the common learnings of every child. The teacher can make good use of his training and background by giving leadership to all age groups. Moreover, his role requires that he know the community and fit into the operation of other agencies involved in recreation and community education.

Many activities for children and youth can provide learning experience and simultaneously develop recreation skills. In nature study, for example, the child may learn how plants and grasses grow and at the same time be shown how to make useful objects of them, thereby developing skills in crafts through the use of native materials. Similarly, the learning skill process can be applied to sports, music, drama, and many other pursuits.

The teacher is in a good position to encourage the use and development of recreation skills of youngsters who may also need help in their social relationships. For example, a boy has an interest in and perhaps talent for singing, but is shy and hesitates to participate with others. Properly motivated and directed by the teacher, the lad might well be encouraged to develop his skill and to join the community choral group, thereby giving expression to both his recreation and social needs.

The recreation role of the teacher need not be confined to the classroom. There are many demands and uses for the recreation skills of the teacher among neighborhood, civic clubs, and organizations, in social groups of all kinds, and in organized community recreation programs.

5 *Recreation For Community Living* (Chicago: The Athletic Institute, 1952), pp. 103–4.

The teacher should organize and direct learning experiences which will use a wide range of recreation skills, attitudes, and interests of children and youth.

The teacher should understand and recognize the recreation interests and needs of children and youth in relationship to their social environment and give proper guidance in the selection of and participation in recreation-learning experiences.

The teacher should, as a professional person, a public servant, and a citizen, make available his particular skills, talents, and interests in recreation to individuals, groups, and organizations in the community.

The teacher should be acquainted with the recreation resources and programs of the community as an aid in counseling and guidance.

THE PROBLEMS OF THE SCHOOLS

The schools have many human and physical resources which can be of large support to recreation. But they also have *problems* which impede the advance of community recreation under the school banner, and interfere with recreation, as an essential action, reaching its fullest potential. Indeed, some of these obstructions often retard the partnership for recreation service between the school system and other arms of local government with a responsibility for public recreation. What, then, are some of these problems?

Inadequate Financial Support

Because of a rapidly increasing school population, higher costs of school construction, maintenance, and operations (including teachers' salaries) and other factors beyond the control of school authorities (including the use of public funds for national defense), the per capita cost of education has risen considerably. Consequently, the schools are encountering difficulties financing their programs. Various methods, including federal aid, are being used to solve these fiscal problems.

Under such circumstances, the prospects of another public service securing a share of the school tax dollar would not appear to be too bright. There are those who question whether appropriations for community recreation should be in the school budget even if it is large enough to accommodate recreation. This is based upon the view that the public is better able to judge results clearly if the financial provisions for each are separated.

Also, unless the appropriations for recreation are earmarked legally for this purpose, there is no assurance that they will be spent for the purposes for which they were intended. It is a fact, too, that the extent of financial support which recreation receives under school auspices is determined to some extent by the attitude, philosophy, and understanding of those who determine the policies of the school system and who are *first* committed to meeting what they and their constituents consider to be basic educational needs. There is always the risk that in school operations, recreation may be the early victim of economy drives.

Limitations of Space

Inadequate space for the school population grows out of inadequate funds for public education and increased enrollment. Each year enrollment increases in elementary and secondary schools, as well as in colleges and universities. In spite of enormous school-construction programs in the United States, there are not enough classrooms to house all who enroll. This means double shifts, an increase in the length of the school day, and a heavier burden upon existing facilities. When these factors are coupled with the demand made upon school facilities for continuing education, adult education, and an endless line of school-sponsored, after-school affairs, the space limitations in many school systems are formidable.

The demand for more square feet for education is not confined to elementary and secondary schools. Recreation space, especially outdoor playing fields, in colleges and universities, is the target for classroom expansion. In fact, the effort to annex campus recreation space for other building purposes is quite as much a threat in the college world as is the encroachment of the highway upon the public park in the community.

Overcrowding and inadequate housing are *not* conducive to the free and essential development of recreation in a leisure centered society.

There is at least one more *facilities* problem holding back the progress of recreation in school systems. While schools *should* be designed carefully for both education and recreation use, too frequently they are *not* so planned. Result: many administrative problems in the operation of the physical plant, and many misunderstandings between school and recreation interests.

Conflicting Methods

The similarities which are so clear in the purposes and ranges of education and recreation are not quite so apparent in their methods. That phase of education which is the bailiwick of the school calls for compulsion, discipline, conformity, and a formal approach. Recreation, on the other hand, cannot flourish in this kind of environment. Freedom of choice, spontaneity, and informality are the elements which characterize recreation at its best. Recreation cannot be brought too close to the formal educational process as far as *method* is concerned.

Differing Views on School Role and Program Content

There are divergent views regarding the appropriate role of the school. Some believe strongly that there should be almost complete emphasis upon the three R's, that only academic subjects and programs are defensible. Those who hold this view want more attention focused upon mathematics, the natural sciences, and modern languages. They see little or no place in the program for the life adjustment—community services approach, and make a case for giving increased attention to the gifted student. The emphasis is upon *excellence,* unswerving dedication—and the trained manpower needed by the nation. The opposing point of view is not without supporters.

The situation is, in one sense, as much a dilemma for recreation as it is for the schools. But if the leisure age is upon us, then we must stress the arts of living as well as the arts of *making* a living.

Difficulty of Co-ordinating School with Community Forces

Strangely, although it is one of the basic institutions of the community, the public school is not renowned as a center for mobilizing, co-ordinating, and integrating the resources of the community, which is so important in community recreation. This does not mean that boards of education have not cooperated over long periods of time with outside institutions, agencies, and organizations. But where this has been done, the school has usually made its facilities available—provided a service—and not essentially taken the lead in affecting a co-ordinated approach to meeting the *total* need. The school might do it, and not a few believe that it should. This, however, calls for a break with tradition, a different philosophy, a broader perspective, and a change in basic policies.

Uncertainty of the Place of Recreation in the Organizational Structure

If recreation is to be an integral part of the school, it must find a place in the administrative structure which will enable it to function well. Without attempting to provide an answer, Ridinger presents the problem:

Where is recreation's place in education? Should it be developed as an integral part of the curriculum—openly referred to as education for leisure? Or should it be offered as an auxiliary service available on a freedom-of-choice basis to the community? From a functional standpoint, where is the best place for recreation in the administrative organization of the public school? Should it be administered by the department of instruction as a curricular or extracurricular program? Or should it be administered by the health and physical education department as a class extended activity? If neither of these, should the administrative responsibilities be vested in a separate department created solely for recreation? Still further possibilities exist with more decisions necessary if the school district enters a jointly sponsored program with a municipality.[6]

EDUCATION FOR LEISURE

What It Is

There is nothing new or mysterious about *education for leisure*. Some of the Greek philosophers felt this should be the major purpose of education, perhaps because they equated education for *leisure* with education for *living*. For our purposes, we can think of education for leisure as the process of helping to prepare people to use their leisure (true or enforced) in ways which are personally satisfying to them, and which, hopefully, may contribute to their full personality development.

Education for leisure assumes that people are going to have leisure and that they must be exposed early and long to experiences which will help them acquire and develop certain kinds of *attitudes* and *values, appreciations, interests,* and *skills*. It is the task of shaping the environment and motivating persons toward the objective of a full, satisfying, and creative use of their leisure. If properly accomplished, it meshes the *desire* and the *ability* of the individual to use his leisure for the flowering of his personality with the *opportunity* to do so. Opportunity need not be confined to the organized resources which society makes available. Education for leisure presupposes not only the growth of all persons in appreciations and skills, but also orientation of the individual on why this approach to full living is vital and, in the end, indispensable in a culture endowed with leisure.

The School Responsibility

No single institution, group, or agency could assume the complete responsibility to educate for leisure. It is a task for parents which involves more than loving their children. It is a duty of clergymen which transcends spiritual enlightenment. It is a challenge to recreators which goes beyond multiplying opportunities for fun. And it is an assignment for

[6] William Ridinger, "School Recreation—Its Problems and Potential," *American Recreation Annual, 1960* (New York: Hoffman Publications, 1960), p. 31.

educators and teachers which oversteps progression in scholarly achievement. If any sector of public interest has a larger role than others in educating for leisure, then surely it is the school which is dedicated to education and which has young minds and bodies under its jurisdiction during their growing, impressionable years. The school should not only prepare people to *make* a living. It should also prepare them *for* living, and this includes living in leisure. In fact, the late L. P. Jacks thought it unpractical, unwise, and perhaps even impossible to train persons in one way for their work and in another way for their leisure.

The school has a *large* role in education for leisure, particularly in motivating persons properly, in imparting appreciations and interests, and in teaching recreation skills.

Skills

The school is almost ideally suited to impart the skills needed to make full and satisfying use of leisure. There are those skills which aid body development, movement, and motor co-ordination. Games, athletics, sports, and the dance are typical leisure activities which can be participated in by individuals (e.g., running, dancing, archery), by two persons (e.g., tennis, fencing, handball), and by groups (e.g., hockey, volleyball, softball).

There are those skills, too, which the schools offer which give pleasure and satisfaction while contributing to the safety and survival of the individual. Examples are driving an automobile and swimming.

Skills which call upon the creative use of the hands—painting, sculpturing, woodworking, and the like—are learning experiences which are clearly a part of the school pattern.

To these skills can be added those which enable the individual to communicate effectively, to write and converse, those which are related to literature and the wonderful world of books; those which help us create vocal and instrumental music or enjoy listening to it; those which encourage expression through drama; those which beckon the learner to serve others; and, finally, those which help bring the student closer to our natural world.

The schools have many of the facilities, much of the equipment, and some of the personnel to expedite the acquisition and sharpening of these skills which have such an increasingly large place in a society with time on its hands. Dr. James C. Charlesworth, political scientist of the University of Pennsylvania, believes that teaching recreation skills is a responsibility of the schools and that they should be compulsorily taught all through the period of school attendance.

In our educational system we do not stop at purely functional objectives. We insist on greater mathematical skill than is required to add up the grocer's bill or to compute our income tax. We compel youth to study literature and history; we are not satisfied when they have learned enough to read street signs and the newspaper. Most people who derive great satisfactions from English literature were compulsorily introduced to it at a tender age, and they did not enjoy the initial exposure.

And so it is with a minority of our citizens who were pushed by understanding parents into the mastery of recreation skills.

THE ROLE OF THE SCHOOL SYSTEM
IN SERVING RECREATION

Because the school is an essential and potent institution and force in a democracy, it is not possible to define its *ultimate* role. The school must change with the changing needs of those it serves. This is evident, if we accept the contention that the school is sound only to the extent that it supports and develops understanding and learning, aids full personality development, and contributes to the well-being and progress of society.

With these reservations in mind then, and in terms of the preceding material in this chapter, the role of the local public school system in serving recreation might be set down as follows:

To educate for leisure. The school is admirably suited to help people, particularly young folks, acquire attitudes and values, develop appreciations, interests and skills, as well as opportunities to use their leisure satisfyingly and positively.

To provide recreation opportunities and services. The school has a responsibility to provide recreation opportunities for the school population and, where needed and feasible, extension recreation services for the entire population.

To develop and use its physical resources for recreation. Education is the primary function of the school, and its physical plant must be so oriented. The school, with its areas, facilities, and equipment, also should be designed and used for recreation (within the school day and after).

To guide, counsel, and advise. Just as the modern school makes available counseling services with respect to study plans, personal problems, and vocational considerations, so should it advise and guide on matters related to the recreative use of leisure and professional careers in recreation and related fields.

To prepare individuals for serving in leadership capacities. The school is the institution to which society must turn for its manpower in any field. A leisure centered society needs both professional and volunteer assistance in large numbers. We depend upon the school to prepare such personnel for challenging tasks.

To orchestrate its responsibilities, interests, and resources for recreation with those of other community institutions. Important and essential as is the school in serving the recreation needs of the people, in no sense does it have an *exclusive* responsibility. Therefore, its efforts can bring the best results when they are interwoven with the efforts of other community institutions, agencies, and groups.

ADULT EDUCATION

The practice of offering special educational privileges to adults is widespread, and many types of instruction are given in continuation schools, night schools, colleges, and by correspondence. Courses include, but are not limited to, citizenship training, parent education, elementary and secondary school courses, vocational courses, and university courses. Offerings may include driver education, art appreciation, or study of great books. Activities such as oil painting, sculpture, instrumental music, bridge, dancing, physical conditioning, photography, and sewing are often in the curriculum. Business courses, education, and current events are just a few of the interest areas found in adult education programs.

There is no clear line between adult education and adult recreation, any more than there is between education and recreation under other conditions. When the program is guided by definite scholastic requirements, and accredited for diplomas and degrees, it can be regarded as adult education. The difference *cannot* be established in terms of *activity* or *experience*. The *motive* or *reason* for participating and the *attitude* toward the activity are more dependable determinants of which is one and which the other.

CONTINUING EDUCATION

Continuing education is aimed not only at the middle-aged but also at the youth who leave school before they should, the older adult, and the senior citizens.

Adult education in the past was provided mainly through the Agricultural Extension Service, college and university extension services, private and voluntary agencies. Religious and business organizations and informal groups have made their contributions. In the future we can expect part of the responsibility to be carried also by public and private agencies whose primary functions are related to the use of leisure. In fact almost every responsible organization, local, state, or national, which expects financial support through either tax or private funds will offer some kind of continuing education. This is quite as true of the hospital and family welfare agency as it is of the library and the community college.

Continuing education will broaden its interests from instruction in traditional academic subjects, simple occupational skills, citizenship training, and light avocational interests to the highest kinds of knowledge which probe and enlarge the human mind. Consequently, we can expect continuing education to be more extensive, more varied, more innovative, and more flexible. It will also be more democratic, with more two-way communication between student and teacher, and, if carefully planned and executed, it will be more meaningful than any form of organized education the world has ever seen. The curriculum will not only last throughout life, life itself will be the core of the curriculum! The United States already has the launching pad in the community service programs provided by Title I of the Higher Education Act of 1965.

Continuing education can concern itself with furthering professional education or life enrichment. It is the latter which has grown so rapidly in the last several decades and which will make up the greater part of continuing education as leisure increases. There is already in the United States an insatiable demand for general adult, or continuing, education. There will be phenomenal increase in all forms of it in the future.

THE INSTITUTIONS OF HIGHER LEARNING

Any discussion of the role of the school in connection with recreation would be incomplete without mention of the colleges and universities, which are increasingly active on the leisure and recreation scene. Efforts of these institutions divide themselves into *campus recreation, professional preparation, research,* and *public service.*

Campus Recreation

Traditionally, college and university students have participated in a large variety of recreation activities. Some have been planned and conducted entirely by the students. Others are the cooperative products of the students, faculty, and administrative officers. Fraternities and sororities, clubs, foundations, religious organizations, intramural enterprises, and student or college unions have been active in these efforts. The programs are of a social, cultural, and physical nature and run the gamut from the spontaneous, informal action to the carefully planned event. While the largest part of the program takes place on campus, it is not unusual for programs and events to be held elsewhere. Indeed, some colleges and universities operate recreation facilities away from the campus. These include outing clubs, camps, and the like.

These college recreation programs will expand as student bodies grow.

They will require, increasingly, sound leadership and direction. The most serious threat to their advance is the matter of losing recreation space and facilities as the demand for classrooms grows.

Professional Preparation

Not long ago only a few colleges and institutions provided curricula for professional preparation in recreation; now there are many. And they cannot graduate persons rapidly enough to meet the need.

Outstanding institutions of higher learning in every part of the United States incorporate recreation in their curricula. These include tax supported and privately supported colleges and universities and junior or community colleges. Programs are designed to serve candidates for bachelor's, master's, and doctoral degrees. Preparation is available for those interested in public or community recreation, or some special phase of it such as park administration, and also in such areas of specialization as therapeutic recreation, employee recreation, and the like. It is also possible for the student to combine his preparation in recreation with such interests as physical education, rehabilitation, city planning, conservation, personnel management, religious education, social group work, and the like. Often the undergraduate preparation requires a minimum number of hours in supervised field experience along with the class work.

Increasingly, scholarships at the undergraduate level and scholarships, fellowships, and assistantships for graduate study are available.

Research

The college and university have a growing responsibility for research, particularly in the graduate colleges. Research in matters pertaining to leisure and recreation are relatively untouched. Until recently, research in recreation has been largely of the *survey* type—adding up inventories, asking people's opinions, making interest studies. Research has not been developed sharply within the recreation profession because the demand, up to now, has been largely for practitioners. Also, research in recreation seems to have been "beneath the dignity" of the scientists. Research in many phases of recreation is just now beginning to emerge in a variety of ways. There is recreation research as it relates to community development, land economics, human behavior, and a host of other interests.

The need for more research, however, to help provide an accurate picture of what *is* happening, to help develop and confirm basic principles and concepts, and to help establish the foundation for fruitful policies is colossal. It is also a need which must be met mainly by the institutions of higher learning. Even before advances can be made in recreation research, much investigation will be necessary to establish appropriate methods and techniques, and to *design* research projects.

Public Service

Colleges and universities, particularly state supported institutions, include recreation in their sevices to the off-campus population. These services are as follows:

Community Service. Either through an extension division or through the Department of Recreation, the institution of higher learning frequently assists communities in developing recreation opportunities for the people.

An example of such service is that provided by the Field Service of the Department of Recreation and Municipal Park Administration at the University of Illinois (See Chapter 7).

Publications. Publications about various phases of recreation administration, programs and services, guides and directions are often a part of the college's public service.

Correspondence Courses. Some institutions provide instruction in recreation through correspondence.

Extension Courses. Recreation courses are offered off campus. College credit is earned.

Institutes, Conferences, and Workshops. More and more refresher courses and training sessions are provided by colleges and universities. These enable professional recreators and volunteers to gain new knowledge and skills as well as sharpen old ones.

Lecture Service. In some institutions, speakers are furnished for meetings, conferences, and other events.

THE CHALLENGE

As Arnold Toynbee has said, "The creative use of leisure by a minority in societies in process of civilization has been the mainspring of all human progress beyond the primitive level." In this sense then, leisure is the finest of all human goods.

The school and college of a democracy, while aligning themselves with the needs of *all,* must meet the challenges of a vast new leisure.

Schools and colleges, as cultural institutions, do not stand alone. They stand with the habits, values, and behavior of the society they serve. They stand with what is done in the home and in the community, with what people do to make a living, but also with what and how people live! Their future program must be shaped accordingly.

In a world which places a high premium on science, too often as a means of keeping one nation more powerful than another, it is easy to forget that the most important subject of the human race, and hence of education, is, or should be, *man*. Not powerful, affluent, and possessive man, but resourceful, selfless, and creative man—and with leisure, *re-creative* man!

Our schools and colleges of the future will have to help generate appreciations, develop interests, nurture values, and sharpen skills which go far beyond those needed in the world of work to those called for in living a *full* life. These skills will need to be those which aid body development and motor coordination, as well as those which contribute to our safety and survival. They will have to include the qualities which will help make young people articulate, aid them in the social graces, and encourage them to use their hands creatively. Knowledge which helps us understand our universe, savor *all* life, and come close to nature must also come into the *mainland* of the school and college program. Add to these the need for youth to learn to create and appreciate music, to express themselves through the written, spoken, and acted word, and make fine literature a *living* part of their daily lives, and the immensity of the task is comprehended.

The *real* test of our future schools and institutions of Higher Learning will be their capacity to help persons prepare not for a *work*-centered existence, but rather for a *leisure*-centered life to which they will eventually have to give themselves up, emotionally and intellectually.

THE WORKSHOP

1. What are the legal statutes in (a) your state and (b) your community relative to the participation of schools in organized recreation? What are the legal limitations?
2. In a given community determine how (a) the recreation department, (b) private agencies, and (c) commercial interests serve the school recreation program.
3. Poll the opinions of several educators on the responsibility of the schools in educating for leisure.
4. State the place of the school in an integrated program of community recreation along with other public, private, and commercial units.
5. What are the advantages and limitations of financing community recreation through the schools?
6. Outline a well-balanced extracurricular activity program for a school.

7. Prepare a code of standards which could be used by schools in advancing recreation in line with the cardinal principles of education.

REFERENCES

American Association of Health, Physical Education and Recreation, *Education for Leisure,* 1957; *City and County School Programs in Health, Physical Education, Recreation, Athletics,* 1961; *Leisure and the Schools,* 1961; *Outdoor Education,* 1956; *Recreation Education—A National Conference Report,* 1963—Washington, D.C.—The Association.

Brightbill, Charles K., *Educating for Leisure Centered Living.* Harrisburg, Pennsylvania: The Stackpole Company, 1966.

Carlson, Reynold E. and Theodore R. Deppe, and Janet R. MacLean, *Recreation in American Life,* Belmont, California: Wadsworth Publishing Company, 1963.

Danford, Howard, *Creative Leadership in Recreation,* Boston: Allyn and Bacon, Inc., 1964.

Englehardt, N. L., and N. L. Englehardt, Jr., *Planning The Community School,* New York: American Book Company, 1940.

Everett, Samuel, ed., *The Community School,* New York: Appleton-Century-Crofts, 1938.

Gabrielson, M. Alexander, and Caswell M. Miles, *Sports and Recreation Facilities For School and Community,* Englewood Cliffs, New Jersey: Prentice-Hall, Inc., 1958.

Kraus, Richard, *Recreation and The School,* New York: The Macmillan Company, 1964.

Lies, Eugene T., *The New Leisure Challenges The Schools,* Washington, D.C.: National Recreation and Park Association, 1933.

Olsen, Eden A., ed., *The Modern Community School,* New York: Appleton-Century-Crofts, 1953.

Punke, Harold H., *Community Use of Public School Facilities,* New York: Kings Crown Press, 1951.

Pomeroy, Janet, *Recreation for the Physically Handicapped Child,* New York: The Macmillan Company, 1964.

Sapora, Allen, and Elmer Mitchell, *The Theory of Play,* 3rd ed., New York: The Ronald Press Company, 1961.

Taha, Hilda, *School Culture,* Washington, D.C.: American Council on Education, 1955.

Comment

An examination of the *Journal of Health, Physical Education and Recreation* (American Association of Health, Physical Education and Recreation) and *Parks and Recreation* Magazine (National Recreation & Park Association) will reveal a number of articles on school and recreation.

Colleges and universities, educational periodicals, and the Boards of Education in cities such as Milwaukee, Philadelphia, San Francisco, Los Angeles, Newark, N.J., Flint, Michigan, and Long Beach, Pasadena, and Monterey, California provide appropriate sources of information.

13

Religious Organizations and Recreation

There is evidence that the church
and synagogue are adapting themselves to new conditions and new social
patterns. With over four hundred separate denominational organizations,
with a membership of over one hundred and twenty-five million, and with
a corporate wealth of over fifteen billion dollars, the church is a powerful
and stable social institution.[1] The social emphasis of its program has been
in three directions: (1) attention to a social gospel as well as to dogma;
(2) stress on social and industrial problems in the zone of social justice;
and (3) emphasis upon social service in general. The place of recreation
in the programs of the National Council of Churches of Christ in the
United States of America, the National Catholic Welfare Conference, and
the Jewish Welfare Board indicates constructive and progressive recognition of recreation by the church and synagogue.

Recreation is assuming an increasingly important role in the program of the
church. "Progressive leaders in the church—and by church is meant religious
institutions of all creeds and denominations—see more and more that man's
spiritual life cannot be separated from his physical, mental, and social life.
Since in the realm of physical, mental, and social activities, recreation, play, and

---

[1] *1968 Yearbook of American Churches,* National Council of Churches of Christ in
the United States of America.

wholesome use of leisure are essential to constructive living, it follows that recreation also holds a major part in the development of the spiritual life." [2]

Recreation is a large factor in developing church fellowship. It creates a friendly atmosphere among people and encourages teamwork, both of which are necessary to successful church administration. Those influences are reflected in the community and aid the church in attracting people.

It is fair to say that the organized church has been traditionally in favor of *wholesome* recreation. Certainly today there are many churches which not only give their blessing to broad, wholesome recreation, but which also initiate, sponsor, and finance it. No church should be too severely criticized for not having sanctioned certain forms of recreation until their worth was more clearly established. Today, any church that fails to recognize recreation as a part of its spiritual concern for people is disregarding a valuable asset. Unfortunately, there are still some church leaders who do not understand, or at least have not accepted, the place of recreation in the general scheme of life. This is regrettable, for in the end they may well lose touch with their congregations, especially the young people. Even among the "advance guard," one may find inadequate perception of modern conditions and of needs in respect to recreation. Generally, however, the church has accepted recreation.

RECREATION IN THE CHURCH

If it is to gain from recreation, the church has two definite responsibilities in relation to recreation: (1) to aid the development of community recreation; and (2) to provide a recreation program for its members. We will consider the second of these responsibilities first. As will be seen, the two are interrelated.

SUGGESTIONS FOR PROCEDURE

The major steps of the church in serving recreation may be listed as follows:

COMMITTEES AND LEADERSHIP

1. The church should recognize the importance of recreation in community life and appoint its own church recreation committee.

[2] Opening paragraph of a pamphlet, *Why Church Recreation Programs?* Chicago Recreation Commission.

2. The chairman of this committee should join with chairmen from other church recreation committees to formulate a central church recreation committee.

3. This larger committee should be represented in community recreation affairs. The church need not assume responsibility for the community recreation program. This responsibility should be in the hands of a legally established authority with responsible leadership. The church, where an established recreation authority does not exist, should promote its establishment and support it.

4. The church recreation committee should be responsible for recreation programs and activities within its group.

5. Where practical, the church might employ recreation leadership of its own, or join other churches in doing so.

6. This leadership should develop and use volunteers.

TRAINING INSTITUTES AND CONFERENCES

1. The church should avail itself of opportunities to participate in all types of recreation leadership training opportunities.

2. The church should help sponsor a community-wide leadership training institute.

3. The church should provide training opportunities for its volunteers, including sending representatives to recreation conferences.

4. In employing religious education leaders, recreation skills should be among qualifications for their positions.

PROGRAM

1. The recreation program of the church should be organized to meet its own need. Quite often, church members can participate in the community program, so there is no specific need for an all-out church program.

2. Church recreation should serve *all* age groups.

3. The church recreation program should be well balanced and flexible. Activities should cover a variety of interests.

4. The program should be a year-round one.

AREAS AND FACILITIES

1. Where feasible the church might have its own recreation facility. This might be a church-community center.

2. Where this is not possible, there is always opportunity to use parts of the church auditorium, classrooms, dining room, and social rooms for recreation purposes.

3. Most churches have grounds surrounding them which can be used for outdoor recreation.

4. It is not necessary to have expensive types of equipment. Church members can make equipment.

5. It is good for youth religious organizations, Boy Scouts, Girl Scouts, Camp Fire Girls, YM and YW groups to use the church facilities for recreation.

FINANCES

1. It is the responsibility of a church to set aside funds and plan a budget for recreation. This need not entail large expenditure. The main idea is that the church-governing body recognize recreation in planning its annual budget and in its outlay for capital expenses.

2. Financing might be done through: (a) the church budget; (b) special sponsorship by the men's club or a church society; (c) popular contribution through pledges, drives, and campaigns; (d) donations, collections, and admission for special events; (f) sales to raise money from arts and crafts, drama and musical events.

There is a fine opportunity for municipal recreation departments to offer service to church groups. The recreation executive and his staff should be in touch with church groups and assist them in organizing and planning their work to meet the needs of the particular group.

THE CLERGYMAN

The objectives and purposes of religion and recreation are in many respects similar and complementary. The clergyman is concerned with the spiritual and moral growth of individuals, the recreator with personality development through wholesome and satisfying use of leisure. The compatibility of religion and recreation is perhaps best seen in the dual effort to achieve an abundant, fruitful, and joyous existence for all people.

Frequently, the "best" in people, young and old, develops and flourishes when they are free to do the things they choose, with whom they choose, in time out-of-school and off-the-job. It is often during free time that the teachings of religion and the high standards it represents may be practiced or ignored. Consequently, the clergyman should know what kinds of recreation are available to his congregation, where they can find what they should seek, and what recreation opportunities can be provided to help them give expression to appetites for basically decent recreation and wholesome living.

Church members and their families often look to their clergyman for his opinion and guidance on many community matters which influence their daily lives. Consequently, the clergyman can be both a rallying point and a spokesman for worthwhile civic projects. He can lend his support to securing adequate play space for children in a neighborhood housing development. He can urge his people to support the local music festival and contribute to the Community Chest. He can appear before the city council as an individual, or in cooperation with his colleagues, to plead the case for a youth center. Herein lies the opportunity for the clergyman to substitute positive action for negative admonition.

Competition for time, money, and energy between degrading free time outlets and wholesome recreation enterprise is ever present. More often than not, the socially undesirable operation is curbed only by offering something more wholesome and attractive. The clergyman is in a unique position to make his influence felt to help that which is good or to pass by that which is unsavory.

Many recreation and social activities are an appropriate part of the church program. Clergymen can often combine recreation with the education and worship programs. Recreation facilities and activities can and should become integral parts of the clergyman's efforts and the church program.

With the shortage of building space in many communities and the high cost of new construction, clergymen are making more extensive use of their facilities by keeping them open longer and sharing them with others. Many groups such as the Boy Scouts, Girl Scouts, and Camp Fire Girls can use church facilities profitably for recreation. Clubs, teams, organizations, and groups of all kinds which need to be housed might well find the hand of the clergyman extended.

The clergyman should concern himself with the recreation needs, interests, and opportunities of his congregation, individually and collectively.

The clergyman should lend his support, both in the pulpit and out, to helping secure adequate and wholesome recreation facilities and services for the people of his neighborhood and community.

The clergyman should quickly praise those recreation conditions and attractions in the community which strengthen the fibre of family life and the general social fabric, and quickly condemn those situations which contribute to the disintegration of character.

The clergyman should include recreation and social experiences within the church and religious education program.

The clergyman should encourage the principle of making church facilities available for appropriate recreation activities both to members of the church and to neighborhood residents.[3]

SPECIAL ACTIVITIES

Interchurch recreation. The community ministerial association can assume leadership in promoting interchurch recreation activities. It can

[3] *Recreation for Community Living* (The Athletic Institute, 1952), pp. 89–91.

sponsor team games and sports, play sports, play days, tournaments and leagues, music festivals, drama contests, arts and crafts exhibits, and dances. An interchurch recreation committee may well control the programs, organize the teams, appoint needed committees, schedule the events, provide for proper officials, have charge of registrations, control average and finances, and conduct the leagues and contests. Each event might culminate in a social occasion—a dinner, banquet, picnic, or special meeting. At such gatherings awards can be made and recognition given for various forms of achievement.

Church camps. Camping can be a popular part of the church program. There are denominational and individual church camps. These units vary from large assembly grounds covering thousands of acres to day-camping centers on the church grounds. While organized to give the members camping and religious experience, they are also used for conferences, institutes, and workshops.

The question of whether a church will enter the field of camping should be thoroughly considered by the governing body of the denomination or individual church. Organized camping can be expensive and calls for expert leadership in organization, financing, and administration. It should not be undertaken haphazardly.

Full information should be obtained from camp authorities, and a sound plan of building, maintaining, and promoting the enterprise should be established.

Place of recreation in church meetings. Recreation might well be a part of every church social gathering. Group singing, music, games, receptions, dinners, dramatic skits, exhibits, readings and storytelling, parties, and picnics can all find a place in creating fellowship.

Vacation church school. Throughout the nation there is wide interest in Bible schools conducted during school vacation periods. For from two to eight weeks, each weekday, the children and youth of a particular denomination go to the church for religious education. A major feature of every school of this type is recreation. A well-balanced program of activities suitable to the age groups is promoted. Special emphasis is given to drama, music, and arts and crafts. Quite often the group develops a project of building recreation equipment of various kinds. The community recreation department often assists volunteers in providing leadership and material.

The picnic. This is a traditional outing for all church groups. It is always an enjoyable occasion and a real opportunity for socialization.

Church youth organizations. There are today a large number of church youth organizations. They vary from clubs within a specific church to national and international groups. The total membership of these organizations runs well over several million. Some of them exist only for devotional purposes, but the great majority conduct recreation as a part of their programs.

Practically all of the Protestant churches have their own youth groups. The Baptist Training Union, the Youth Fellowships of the Episcopal, Lutheran, Presbyterian and United Methodist Churches serve as illustrations. There is a youth group for most denominations, with special emphasis on recreation as a feature of the general programs.

The Salvation Army has a number of junior organizations, the largest of which is the Young People's Legion. The Army also sponsors Red Shield Clubs for boys and units similar to the Girl Scouts for girls.

The Newman Clubs sponsored by the National Council of Catholic Men, the Catholic Youth Organization, and the Sodality of Our Lady are the three outstanding youth-serving groups in the Catholic Church. All of the groups organized under these forces promote recreation to supplement their religious and educational objectives. Many local and regional groups also conduct recreation programs for Catholic youth through the Catholic Youth Organization (C.Y.O.).

The Jewish Welfare Board sponsors hundreds of community centers under the auspices of Young Men's and Young Women's Hebrew Associations, featuring general programs of recreation. Synagogues in many places provide recreation services for their people.

There are also Hillel and B'nai B'rith groups for young men and women. Zionist organizations also have branches for young people, and some of these have recreation programs.

Special Forms of Recreation

While all phases of recreation can be sponsored by religious groups, the religious environment lends itself to special forms of recreation. We have already indicated some; others are included in the following:

Religious drama. Innumerable Biblical and contemporary situations, whole books or stories of the Bible, and many church school lessons lend themselves admirably to dramatization.

Pageantry. Every Biblical event, every Sunday school lesson, and every sermon is a theme for dramatization. Writing the drama, producing it, building scenery, making costumes, and all the details of its sponsorship can give real satisfaction.

Group singing. Hymn and folk "sings" can bring large numbers together.

Libraries. These range from a few shelves to well-regulated and catalogued libraries of thousands of volumes.

Clubs. Teen clubs and youth centers, young adult and senior citizens clubs are examples.

Music. Choral groups, choir and glee clubs, orchestras, bands, small ensembles, and other instrumental combinations are popular. Concerts of vocal or instrumental solos, duets, and quartets are enthusiastically received.

Arts and crafts. Hobbies, collecting, exhibits, building projects, and art and craft classes.

Religious holiday celebrations. The Christmas season, Easter, Thanksgiving, church calendar days, and special occasions of historical interest can all find expression in plays, pageants, musical events, and social gatherings. The church can also cooperate with families in the celebration of birthdays and wedding anniversaries to revitalize family life and personal interests.

Reading clubs. Small groups come together to hear books reviewed and to discuss them. This affords a fine opportunity for using church literature and religious themes.

Storytelling. This may be used in many ways: for teaching, for presenting the sermon or portions of it, and for allowing members self-expression in religious interpretation.

Motion pictures. Hundreds of films on religious and contemporary topics are available. Many educational and entertaining films can be secured at slight expense. A church should be acquainted with the local theater management and aid members in deciding upon pictures worthy of patronage.

Radio and Television. Every church should own a good radio and a television set, and should have groups gather to hear and discuss good programs. The church can go on the air itself and give the entire community the full value of its recreation offerings.

Visitations. The aged, the sick, and dependents offer a great opportunity for service. A cordial conversation, a group visit for singing and playing, a gift of books or games, can bring untold cheer.

Sports teams and leagues. While very few churches can provide a gymnasium, there are many opportunities to sponsor sports and games like volleyball, handball, badminton, horseshoe pitching, archery, tennis, basketball, or softball.

Outing activities. These offer the church many excellent opportunities. Hikes, field trips, and gardening are only a few possibilities. Nature museums, nature clubs, and discussion groups are closely related.

THE CHURCH AND THE COMMUNITY
RECREATION PROGRAM

What Is the Relationship Between Community Recreation Agencies and Religious Organizations?

1. Municipal recreation serves as a resource to all other community groups, provides professional leadership, works with all groups in city-wide participation, provides demonstration projects and workshops.
2. The religious organization has a responsibility to help local agencies maintain a high standard in all programs.
3. It has a role to play in all community councils and planning groups, neighborhood groups, and so on.
4. Each should include the use and/or employment of qualified and trained personnel.
5. Each might work with individual youths, fraternities, sororities, and neighborhood groups.

6. Religious organizations should offer their cooperation to community agencies in programs that have wide community interest.
7. Religious organizations have the responsibility to endeavor, whenever possible, to work through existing agencies in taking care of community problems. One of their responsibilities is to improve general community life and living, by raising of moral insights and standards.
8. Religious groups have a major function of interpretation to their own membership in regard to community problems.
9. Religious organizations should cooperate in development of resources and leadership for specific community projects. There should be professional recreation leadership to guide, advise, lead, and enable.

The church not only should have its own recreation program; it also has a responsibility to further the community recreation program. Participation in such a program will offer to church members genuine satisfaction and new social and spiritual challenges. Under certain circumstances the church may take the initiative in establishing a local recreation authority, but secular agencies within the community must be willing to assume their full share of responsibility for the success of the program.

The church can well throw the full weight of its influence into creating wholesome attitudes toward community recreation. It can help by conducting and supporting discussion groups, promoting an understanding of objectives and values, and participating in all phases of the community program. The church will want to oppose undesirable and unwholesome influences in recreation. It must, however, offer constructive substitutes. Condemnation is shallow without positive alternatives. The church can join with other groups in revitalizing family recreation, in encouraging school programs of recreation, in assisting social agencies to serve community institutions, and in providing volunteer leaders for community-wide recreation enterprises.

The local ministerial association should be available in an advisory capacity to the community recreation authorities. It should constantly evaluate the community program in terms of sound objectives and offer its resources to help improve conditions. If the community recreation department is promoting leagues, tournaments, and contests, the churches can participate either collectively or as separate units. The church can also be of valuable assistance in sponsoring community-wide recreation conferences, institutes, workshops, and training opportunities. It can render many services in making preliminary plans and in other organizational details.

Church facilities ought often to be used for meeting places, institute sessions, workshops, clinics, exhibits, and demonstrations.

There is a big selling job to be done. Church members raise objections to such wide support of recreation, and there may be differences of opinion among church leaders themselves. Lack of understanding and lack of knowledge of the field often hinder progress. Constant education in recreation is fundamental to success. An informed church, a participating church will, however, prove to be a supporting church. The recreation department of the community should keep the church informed of its activities by sending church leaders all bulletins, reports, and informational material distributed by the recreation department. Community recreation authorities should meet with the ministerial association, participate in church forums and discussion groups, be active in the programs of church societies and clubs, and attend church-sponsored recreation programs.

A link between church and community exists in the many national, regional, and state organizations which have branch units in churches. Boy Scouts, Girl Scouts, and Camp Fire Girls have many local troops and councils within the framework of the church organization. Y.M.C.A. and Y.W.C.A. interests coincide with those of the churches. Quite often the church can supplement the extracurricular activity program of the public school by sponsoring after-school activities of various kinds. These activities can continue their meetings during vacation periods and, in cooperation with the school, develop the objectives and principles upon which they were founded. Church leaders should never lose an opportunity to discover and bring together those who are interested in clubs. It is hardly necessary to say that the church and synagogue should make full use of the recreation areas and facilities of the community.

PROBLEMS

Sunday Observance

The question of what constitutes proper observance of the Sabbath Day is typical of the problems which may arise when the church sponsors recreation. Certainly, if the church accepts a wholesome recreation program as a fundamental adjunct to more abundant living, it can well afford to consider the problem of wholesome activities for Sunday. A liberalized attitude toward Sunday recreation is almost necessary in the light of industrial and technological changes, of improved means and methods of communication and transportation, and of our general urbanization. The church can give its members many rich experiences through a sympathetic understanding and interpretation of the problem. It will get nowhere by constant condemnation and negative do-nothingness.

Disapproval of Certain Types of Recreation

Certain recreation activities are undesirable; others are on the border line. Certain other activities are not so much negative in themselves as pathologic because of environmental influences and individual practices and interpretations. Some churches have consistently opposed pool, card playing, social dancing, and horse racing, along with outright indecency on the stage, in motion pictures, and in radio and television productions. All of these are not, of course, in the same class.

The fact that an activity is not evil in itself is not sufficient reason for approving it. If environment and individual practice are not up to church standards of wholesomeness and decency, the church has an obligation to object. The church lives to promote a high type of thought and conduct and therefore cannot join in nor sanction practices that experience has shown produce opposite effects.

The church, however, cannot afford to condemn and not recommend. Its task is to create a proper environment and to inculcate wholesome practices. It must govern its principles through effective action. A few illustrations will suffice to prove this point.

Pool and billiards. These games can be enjoyable recreation activities. There is not a single valid argument against the games of pool and billiards themselves. Played in a wholesome environment, pool and billiards lose all negative connotations.

Card playing. This can be good or bad depending on the environment of play and on how the game is conducted.

Social dancing. Dancing has been looked upon with disfavor among some religious groups. Social dancing is popular with most people, especially youth. The church must recognize this fact. No substitute with the same appeal has been found. Folk dancing and square dancing are other forms of the dance. But the church cannot hope to eliminate the word "dancing" and then substitute a practice that is dancing. Such a procedure nullifies church influence. The church, however, can influence dancing to insure wholesome participation and environment.

Use of Church Facilities for Recreation

Churches finding themselves under pressure to allow use of their property as the only available place for a community recreation program face a special problem. Objections to using church property are numerous. Members may object to normal breakage and wear on buildings and furnishings. Religious traditions may prevent the use of church property for certain types of recreation. Difficulty may arise in securing the participation of persons belonging to other faiths. There may be difficulty in securing financial support.

A well-planned community recreation program under responsible leadership can quickly overcome all these objections. There is a marked tendency today for churches to participate more liberally in offering their facilities to the community whenever an assurance of service exists.

The Charge of Proselytizing

The problem of proselytizing in any institution or organization is a difficult one to analyze. Every group wants to expand its membership; that is a healthy sign of growth. If, however, the principal motive of sponsoring recreation or participation in the community program is to proselytize, there is a question as to the value of the recreation involved. The average church can hardly hope to be a community center, recreationally speaking. This is especially true if other churches are near by. They may raise objections. It cannot hope to be a real community center in any case if denominationalism is predominant.

Duplication

The church should avoid duplication of activities. It should not compete with recreation departments, public schools, playgrounds, settlements, youth groups, and other organizations functioning in the recreation field. Such competition is costly in money, leadership, and energy. Programs should be coordinated. Cooperation between community recreation departments and churches cannot fail to result in benefit to both. It means support and help from and to the churches in times of emergency when curtailment of budget or program threatens. Church support can strengthen the municipal recreation.

If people are segregated from the church in recreation, they might segregate themselves in worship and service as well. Recreation is worthy in itself, and when the church sponsors recreation, it is in a better position to help guide the religious growth of its people. The church should be concerned with recreation as a vital force in the development of personality and in the well-being of humanity, generally.

SOME TRENDS IN RECREATION
IN CHURCH SETTING

1. *Recognition of fellowship and recreation as making a valuable contribution to total church life.* There is increasing emphasis on fellowship and recreation activities for all ages being promoted by the church.

2. *Acceptance of universal values of folk games and dances.* Many churches are using folk games and dances in children, youth, adult and family gatherings. Summer camps and conferences almost universally use them. Leaders are learning how to bring out the community-building potential of folk games and dances.

3. *Increased interest in good recreation music.* Not only of youth groups, but of young adults, adults, and general church groups.

4. *New patterns of leadership training.* Almost gone is the tradition of having lectures and long periods of point-making. The recreation workshop pattern is helping people to learn to do by doing. It places strong emphasis on the group, group learning, and on group experiences.

5. *Growth of interest in creative recreation.* Arts, crafts, drama and dance are enjoying renewed interest in the church progam.

6. *Nature recreation* and outdoor recreation are more and more popular.

7. *Movement away from thinking of recreation as only for youth.* Although in some quarters there still prevails the idea that fellowship and recreation are largely a concern for youth and youth workers, the increasing use of recreation in adult and family circles is beginning to change this concept.

8. *Growth of concept of recreation as part of total program of religious education.* More and more the church is accepting the idea that recreation has religious values, and makes a large contribution to the development of a total person. The religious philosophy of a recreation leader is as important as that of a church school teacher or other leader of religious education.

9. *Growing recognition of importance of having social groups, such as scouts, under church board of education auspices.* Voluntary groups such as scouts, meeting in the church, with recreation as a strong part of their program, profoundly affect the lives of youth. Increasingly, churches are bringing these groups into the total program of their board of education.

10. *Increased interest in the whole field of camping.* For families, groups of youths, young adults and adults, and day camping for all ages, on a basis of recreation-education.

11. *Acceptance of work camps and work projects as recreation.* The volunteer nature of these projects, plus their recreational features, tend to make the total experience a recreational one. Groups are increasingly recognizing fellowship values in these activities, as well as in overseas service projects and other service ideas.[4]

Recreation is an essential part of the church and synagogue program. The church and synagogue need recreation, and recreation needs them. Religious institutions, by joining with other institutions in the community, can contribute richly to expanding the horizons of recreation for all the people. Religious institutions can experience revitalized social power and influence as they move forward with recreation.

[4] These trends are suggested by R. Harold Hipps, Director, Leisure-Recreation Ministries, Board of Education of the United Methodist Church, Nashville, Tennessee.

THE WORKSHOP

1. Make a study of the attitudes toward recreation of local clergymen. Classify their attitudes according to positive and negative approaches and try to determine the origins of these opinions.
2. Enumerate ways in which the clergy and religious institutions can contribute to community recreation.
3. Present ways in which the community recreation department can assist religious institutions.
4. Survey the recreation activities of one church or synagogue.
5. List present church facilities and areas for recreation in your community.
6. Prepare an adequate recreation program for the local church.
7. Indicate methods of bringing about a closer coordination of church and community for recreation.
8. Suggest a recreation program for a vacation church school or camp.
9. List the functions and responsibilities of the religious institution in community recreation.
10. Suggest ways of evaluating community recreation programs in relation to the needs of the church.

REFERENCES

Brightbill, Charles K., *Educating for Leisure-Centered Living*. Harrisburg, Pa.: Stackpole Books, 1966.

————, *Man and Leisure—A Philosophy of Recreation*. Englewood Cliffs, N.J.: Prentice-Hall, Inc., 1961.

Lee, Robert, *Religion and Leisure in America*. Nashville, Tenn.: Abingdon Press, 1964.

Boyd, Bob M., *Recreation for Churches*. Nashville, Tenn.: Convention Press, 1967.

Recreation and the Church—A Manual for Leaders. New York: National Recreation Association, 1951.

Clemens, Frances, Robert Tulley, and Edward Grill, *Recreation and the Local Church*. Elgin, Ill.: Brethren Publishing House, 1956.

Rippy, Leo, Jr., *Recreation in the Local Church*. Board of Education of The Methodist Church: Nashville, Tenn., 1962.

Harbin, E. O., *The Fun Encyclopedia*. Nashville, Tenn.: Abingdon Press, 1962.

Schlingman, Edward L., *Good Times in the Rural Church*. Philadelphia, Pa.: Christian Education Press, 1947.

Printed Resources for Church recreation are constantly changing in keeping with constantly changing patterns of church and community recreation programs. For current listings check your local church, community or college library, or write the publishers listed below.

Church Recreation Department, Sunday School Board of the Southern Baptist Convention, 127 Ninth Avenue, North, Nashville, Tennessee 37203.

Office of Leisure-Recreation Ministries, Board of Education of The United Methodist Church, P. O. Box 871, Nashville, Tennessee 37202.

Cooperative Recreation Service, Inc., Informal Music, Route 1, Radnor Road, Delaware, Ohio 43015.

National Recreation and Park Association, 1700 Pennsylvania Avenue, N.W., Washington, D.C. 20006.

American Association for Health, Physical Education and Recreation, a Department of the National Education Association, 1201 Sixteenth Street, N.W., Washington, D.C. 20036.

Magazines

The Church Recreation Magazine, Church Literature Department, Sunday School Board of the Southern Baptist Convention, 127 Ninth Avenue, North, Nashville, Tennessee 37203.

Parks & Recreation, Official Publication of the National Recreation and Park Association, 1700 Pennsylvania Avenue, N.W., Washington, D.C. 20006.

JOHPER—Journal of Health, Physical Education, Recreation, published by the American Association for Health, Physical Education and Recreation, 1201 Sixteenth Street, N.W., Washington, D.C. 20036.

IV

Recreation in
Other Settings

Top left: Shaping and being shaped. Above: School for ski skills. Left: Ready for employee recreation.

Above: Volleyball action on the beach. Below: Camping and survival skills.

14

The Voluntary
Youth-Serving Agencies

We have always been interested in our youth. As potential citizens, builders of families, industrial and agrarian workers, educational and religious leaders, they are a rich community asset. As potential defectives, delinquents, and dependents, they challenge the community. As stimulators of social reform and exponents of social change, our youth cause society to reconsider its folk patterns and attitudes. As members of the family, school, church, and club, they are a vital part of the social system. No previous generation has been subjected to such extensive analysis. There exists an array of facts about youth in every aspect of life. The force and influence of youth in action are immeasurable.

Social institutions have indicated genuine concern about youth and have manifested this interest through organized efforts in their behalf. More than 100 national youth agencies are striving to serve youth in numerous ways. Educational organizations of many types, church young people's groups, family life agencies, governmental departments, and character building groups, along with patriotic and fraternal orders, are all engaged in work with young people. Most aim to develop better citizens of tomorrow. A large number of organized groups have movements designed to interest the youth of the country in the use of leisure, often through programs designed to develop better citizens. When one analyzes the various programs of these groups, recreation is one of the most important parts. Boy Scouts, Youth Councils, Camp Fire Girls, Girl Scouts, Hi-Y's, Y-Teens, Red Shield, 4-H Clubs, the many religious youth groups, extra-curricular activity clubs of the schools, and social clubs of different types have recreation as a major program function.

There is also a general youth movement stimulated largely by youth itself in an attempt to gain those things it wants and believes it should have. This effort may be a kind of rebellion against the barriers between generations, or an effort to express in some dynamic way the interest of adolescents in freedom and democracy. This is evidenced through the many youth centers and teen-age organizations springing up here and there under a diversity of leadership and influences and not affiliated in any way with established agencies.

Statistics reveal many real problems related to youth. These are found in the records on juvenile delinquency, broken homes, undesirable environments, and underprivileged children. Here again the youth serving agencies are prominent in attempting to provide adequately for youth and to ameliorate, eliminate, and prevent pathological or antisocial conditions. Several of the Federal government's efforts in the War on Poverty (Upward Bound, NYC, YES) have stressed the importance of positive recreation experiences as a means of elevating the cultural level of the deprived. Also, these programs provide service opportunities for the more fortunate as well as occasions for youth of different social classes and racial background to meet and discover each other as citizens of the same community.

There is a great cry regarding juvenile delinquency. Too much emphasis, however, has been negative. We need a positive view; we need to substitute "youth adequacy" for "juvenile delinquency." Adequate facilities, adequate leadership, adequate opportunities along all lines may help prevent trouble.

There is an enormous amount of goodwill and interest directed toward building adequately for youth. This is true in all fields of community service, recreation, health, education, welfare, religion, and family life. In the total youth program, recreation assumes a prominent place. Many public and private agencies on national, state, and local levels are established for ministering to the recreation needs of youth. Although they may differ in emphasis and structure, their recreation activities are similar. Studies and experience reveal, however, that while statistics indicate marked growth in service to youth throughout the years, the sum total of service in relation to need is inadequate.

A charge of duplication, overlapping, and unnecessary competition among youth services is frequently made. The accusation may be justified to a certain extent, but by and large the facts show that there is room for multiplied resources. Most youth-serving agencies recently have had large increases in membership, greater numbers of paid and volunteer workers, planned programs of larger scope, more geneous donors, expanding treasuries, better areas and facilities. Community interest is also greater now than ever before.

UNITED EFFORT

Recreation for youth calls for the united effort of all who are interested in the welfare of youth and who feel any social responsibility for this segment of the population. Certain general principles form the foundation of a community-wide recreation program for young people which stress the importance of comprehensive planning, wide community support and the involvement of youth in the establishment and directing of its programs of action. Among them are:

Plan for the whole community. Bring together all community groups concerned with recreation for teen-age youth. Learn what the total needs are, what resources can be mobilized to meet them. Determine how the job is to be accomplished. Provide opportunities for all—omit none.

Let youth participate. Give much of the job of organizing their own leisure-time activities to teen-age boys and girls. Given the opportunity, they will demonstrate ingenuity and enthusiasm, develop self-discipline. Success depends on the extent to which youth is allowed to inject its own thinking and planning into the program.

Allocate responsibility for providing services. Fit all public and private youth agencies into a broad community plan and allocate responsibility to each for the various areas in the community. Gaps in existing services can thus be filled and overlapping or duplication of effort avoided.

Develop neighborhood activities. The neighborhood should be the central point in planning recreation activities for teen-agers. Keep boys and girls in their own neighborhood with their own neighborhood groups by developing varied programs that youngsters themselves want.

Strengthen existing services. Secure wider and fuller use of existing recreation facilities, private and public. Adjust hours of service. Broaden and revise programs to answer all present-day needs of the teen-age group.

Use school and church facilities. Make full use of school and church facilities —during afternoons, evenings, and holidays—for clubs, hobby groups, social activities, and athletics. Lighted schoolhouses are symbols of community concern for its adolescents.

Develop new play spaces. Encourage the establishment of youth centers and playgrounds where needed. Attention of many communities is being called to the fact that their services to youth population are sadly inadequate.

Find capable leadership. Adequate leadership is essential to good programs. Getting the right supervision is of vital importance, and only qualified and sympathetic people should be recruited for the task. A great bulk of the work will be done by volunteers—adult and youth—but professional leaders are needed to direct and coordinate activities.

Diversify teen-age activities. To satisfy all interests, a wide range of activities should be planned—social get-togethers, dances, athletic tournaments, hobby groups, camping programs.

Secure community support. Get youth and parents interested through frequent forums and discussions. Give activities wide publicity. Do a community education job, interpreting the purposes and results of your program.

PUBLIC AGENCIES

Although this chapter deals primarily with nongovernmental youth agencies interested in recreation, it is well to note that a number of public agencies sponsor and operate youth services. Local recreation departments operate in this field through youth centers, clubs, leagues, and societies. The school recreation program for youth is extensive, especially through extracurricular programs. The programs sponsored by the Future Farmers of America, the Vocational Education Division of the United States Office of Education, and the 4-H Clubs of the United States Agricultural Extension Service serve hundreds of thousands of rural youth. The scope of governmental interests and support of youth programs is increasing daily.

PRIVATE AGENCIES

In addition to the recreation promoted through public agencies, there are programs of voluntary groups. A hundred or more private agencies cater to youth, with programs giving major emphasis to recreation. Few are organized primarily for this purpose, however. Recreation often shares the limelight with educational, civic, health, social, or religious objectives.

No community is likely to have all of the agencies, and in a vast majority of cases communities have only two, three, or four. Every agency is a potential asset to community life.

Voluntary agencies can be classified as follows: (1) groups organized and sponsored principally by adults, (2) groups that are supplementary to adult organizations, (3) adult groups sponsoring youth projects, and (4) youth-directed groups. These agencies offer opportunities for any community to provide adequate youth recreation programs. There can be no claim in any community that assistance, at least within certain limits, is not available if desired.

ADULT-LED ORGANIZATIONS WORKING WITH YOUTH

A number of community organizations devoted entirely to youth are sponsored and operated by adults. These are the groups best known by the public. Although it is impossible to mention all of them, a few are presented to illustrate the potential values and opportunities to community life. In this group are such organizations as the Boy Scouts of America, Boys' Clubs of America, the Camp Fire Girls, the Girl Scouts of the United States of America, the Junior Red Cross of the American Red Cross, Red Shield Clubs of the Salvation Army, the Y.M.C.A. and the Y.W.C.A. (Addresses will be found in the Appendix.) There are numerous directories of youth-serving agencies which give the essential characteristics of the organizations, with program content.

SUPPLEMENTARY YOUTH GROUPS

A large number of groups for youth are sponsored by adult organizations either to recruit members from the youth groups or to promote specific attitudes and standards held by the parent body. While recreation is not the major basis of the program of any of these organizations, it serves the purposes of the membership by stimulating socialization, interest, and loyalty. Fraternal orders, patriotic societies, labor unions, and religious sects offer the best illustrations of this type of youth group, and it has a significant place in community life.

The Junior Order of Elks, the Order of DeMolay of the Masons, the Children of the American Revolution, branch organizations of labor unions providing recreation for individuals and families, the Catholic Youth Organization, the National Jewish Welfare Board, and the Christian Endeavor Society offer illustrations of this type. (Addresses will be found in the Appendix.)

BRIEF SKETCHES OF SOME OF THE MORE PROMINENT YOUTH SERVICE GROUPS

Some of the more prominent groups with interesting youth programs may be briefly characterized.

American Junior Red Cross

The Junior Red Cross is an international organization of elementary and secondary school students in more than 45 countries. It aims to develop a spirit of service and friendship among young people throughout the world. The program of the American Junior Red Cross fulfills these aims through such activities as service to veterans and local institutions, the National Children's Fund, educational gift boxes, and international and intersectional correspondence. Its program is designed to be developed through the school program.

Boys' and Girls' 4-H Clubs

The 4-H Clubs are composed of young people engaged in farming, home-making, or community activities under the guidance of Farm and Home agents and local volunteer leaders trained by the agents. Each group elects its own officers, plans and conducts programs based on the needs and interests of the young people, holds regular meetings, and takes part in community activities. The name 4-H stands for Head, Heart, Hand, and Health development and progress. Demonstrations conducted by the members center around such activities as food-growing, poultry-raising, sewing, and industrial household arts. State agricultural colleges and the United States Department of Agriculture provide bulletins, leaflets, and other materials.

Boys' Clubs of America

Boys' Clubs of America is a national federation of Boys' Clubs in the United States. The purpose of the organization is the guidance of boys in health, physical, mental, vocational, social, and character development through the improvement and expansion of the Boys' Club movement. The organization furnishes service to Boys' Clubs in all matters of organization, administration, operation, and expansion, and free service to community groups in the establishment of Boys' Clubs. It provides an advisory field service by trained men; studies programs and methods of Boys' Clubs; recruits, trains, and places men in Boys' Club work; conducts training courses, conferences, and institutes; provides consultation service in the alteration, expansion, and construction of buildings, furnishings, and equipment, and in the care and upkeep of buildings; and publishes booklets and bulletins of value to Boys' Clubs and to the promotion of the movement. The organization is supported by contributions, by income from endowment, and by membership fees.

Boy Scouts of America

The purpose of scouting is to promote character building and citizenship training by providing a wide range of activities under trained, volunteer leadership. Its program is adapted to the following age groups: *Cub Scouting,* a home-centered program for boys from eight through ten years of age; *Boy Scouting,* a vigorous outdoor program for boys 11 years and older; *Exploring,* with activities adapted to boys 14 years of age and older. Essential elements in all programs are the ideals of the Scout Oath and Law and service to others. Community assistance is mobilized to provide manpower, facilities, and financial support, so that the boys may have experiences and influences that help them develop into the kind of citizens this country needs. Its magazine is *Boys' Life.*

Camp Fire Girls

Camp Fire Girls, Inc., has as its primary purposes perpetuating the spiritual ideals of the home and stimulating and aiding in the formation of habits making for health and character. Girls rich and poor, of every race, color, or creed, between the ages of seven and 18 enjoy the organization's leisure program. The organization is composed of three groups: Blue Birds for girls seven to ten, Camp Fire Girls for girls ten to 15, and the Horizon Club for girls 15 to 18. The official magazine is *The Camp Fire Girl.*

Girl Scouts of the United States of America

The purpose of the Girl Scouts is to help girls realize the ideals of womanhood as a preparation for their responsibilities in the home and community. The organization aims to give girls, through wholesome pleasures, habits of mind and body which will make them useful, responsible women. Emphasis is placed on training to develop initiative, self-control, self-reliance, and service to others. The organization favors no creed, party, or sect, but cooperates with any organization which shares its views. The governing body of the Girl Scouts is its National Council with local councils in communities. The basic principles of girl scouting are found in the "Promise" and the "Laws." The four classes of Girl Scouts are comparable to the age range of the four grade divisions of the public school. They are:
Brownies—Primary grades
Juniors—Elementary grades
Cadets—Junior High grades
Seniors—Senior High grades

Hi-Y, Jr. Hi-Y, and Gra-Y, Y.M.C.A.

Membership in the Hi-Y is generally open to mature students of high school junior and senior classes who band themselves together in a definite campaign for the development of Christian personality through high scholarship, physical efficiency, moral worth, and unselfish service. Hi-Y is the Y.M.C.A.'s program for boys of senior high school age. Membership is not restricted to any religious creed, but is open to all who subscribe to the purpose and objectives of the club.

The Junior Hi-Y is the Y.M.C.A.'s program for boys from the ages of 12 through 14 years. The Gra-Y is the program for boys nine through 11 years. Jr. Hi-Y and Gra-Y Clubs may be organized in any setting where junior high and grade school boys are found—in homes, schools, churches, Y.M.C.A. buildings, and neighborhoods. Program materials and aids are published. The Y.M.C.A., of course, offers many youth opportunities beyond the work of these clubs. The Young Hebrew Associations provide similar programs for Jewish youth.

Y-Teens of the Y.W.C.A.

The Y-Teens, a cross section of the Y.W.C.A. reaching girls between 12 and 18, is not a program pattern for girls; it is instead an evolving educational process of work with girls. The movement is attempting, through work based on modern educational methods, to help girls to understand better how to make right choices, to raise their level of appreciation, and to develop their powers of discrimination. Furthermore, it is striving to put spiritual meaning into living and to provide an outlet for spiritual aspiration and idealism.

Catholic youth programs and programs sponsored by Protestant denominations and groups of the Jewish Welfare Board were presented in Chapter 13.

ADULT COMMUNITY ORGANIZATIONS INTERESTED IN YOUTH RECREATION

There are many community and national civic organizations which, while interested, are not organized to advance primarily the cause of recreation. The following groups are typical: the American Legion, the American Farm Bureau Federation, the Federation of Women's Clubs, the Federation of Business and Professional Women's Clubs, the Junior Chamber of Commerce, the Junior Service Leagues, Rotary, Kiwanis, Lions, Optimist, the National Congress of Parents and Teachers, Police Athletic Leagues, the New York City Mission Society, and the National Grange. These programs range from sponsorship of youth recognition days to active support of comprehensive youth service centers and organizations.

YOUTH DIRECTED GROUPS

Some youth centers are planned and directed by youth. Although the number and type of programs have varied in recent years, the pattern of activity and organization has remained much the same. The emphasis is still on the self-directed aspects of the program with youth providing its own leadership with a minimum of adult advice.

Adult groups often encourage the establishment of these centers in answer to community youth problems.

No community should believe that by establishing such a center it will solve all the problems of youth. That calls for multiple action and the mobilization of the community's entire resources. The teen-age club movement is but one force on the whole front. It has, however, a definite contribution to make and can fill a need and be most constructive in community well-being.

The following are some of the characteristics of the teen-age club movements:

1. Many have sprung up independently, sometimes because of initiative of a group of parents, a leading citizen, a civic organization, a particular youth club, police officials, or a family group. Where this is the case, youth centers often do not have adequate and permanent financial backing.

2. Youth-serving agencies, such as the Y.W.C.A. and the Y.M.C.A., sponsor youth centers in their local headquarters, giving the youth group particular afternoons and evenings in which to carry out teen-age club activities. In these cases the club is one phase of the regular agency program.

3. One of the most popular developments in the teen-age club movement is the cooperation between school boards and recreation authorities in arranging a schedule in which the school and its facilities are available to community and neighborhood groups for recreation. Certain rooms in a school are turned over to responsible groups for youth activities. These groups share responsibility for use of the building and for their work with the school officials.

4. Some churches have opened up Sunday school rooms for teen-club activities. In this case the church board and the recreation leaders work out administrative and program responsibilities. The church center is usually not strictly denominational, but allows the youth of the community or neighborhood to use the facilities.

5. Public recreation departments sponsor youth centers. Facilities are made available in the community center, playground area, or a specific building rented for the purpose. It is certainly a responsibility of a public recreation agency to provide opportunities for youth.

Common Features

Teen-age centers usually have these features in common:

1. *Co-recreation.* There is no doubt that this meets the desires of youth. Of course, youth *agencies* do not always function on a co-recreational basis.

2. *Dancing.* Young people will dance somewhere. It is up to the community to see that dancing is done in a wholesome environment.

3. *The snack bar.* Nearly every teen-age center has a snack bar where refreshments, including milk and soft drinks, are served. The sale of refreshments at such a snack bar can often be a fine source of revenue. Prices must be low, making its use within reach of everyone.

4. *The game room.* Many clubs have separate rooms for various activities. There is always a game room. Here ping-pong, checkers, chess, monopoly, and other small games are provided. Another room may be for music, another for reading and writing.

5. *Amplified music.* Practically all the centers have some form of amplified music. This, too, can be a source of revenue for the maintenance of the center. Occasionally centers have orchestras, which can be paid from special charges for a particular occasion.

6. *A broad definition of service.* Youth programs are becoming increasingly more varied. The program of service entered into by these self-directed youth groups include operating youth employment exchanges, raising funds for community causes, conducting radio and TV shows, and serving in advisory roles to local civic, legal, and governmental groups.

Naturally any local community can formulate its own program and may not follow all of these practices. It would, in fact, be valuable to introduce unique and interesting features into the set-up.

Experience shows that youth will respond to the challenge of having its own organization. The club should have as much of the teen-age flavor as possible. This should, of course, be tempered with understanding adult guidance. Youth needs and expects such guidance. Parents of teen-age club members should be familiar with the club program. They should be invited to participate and be kept informed.

LEADERSHIP SERVICES FOR YOUTH GROUPS

A panel on citizen participation of the National Conference on Prevention and Control of Juvenile Delinquency reports that:

Volunteer service may require regular and continuous investment of time and interest, or it may require only occasional periods of time, such as taking groups on hikes, helping with special events, or supplying transportation. The duties to be performed by volunteers offer opportunity for a wide range of ability and experience. There is need for persons of expert competence. There is also much to be done by those of modest ability and little experience.

Adult citizens may act as club leaders or advisors for groups of boys or girls, or mixed groups, and work out a program of varied activities. Or they may be instructors in special skills, such as dramatics, crafts, music, dancing, sports and games, nature lore, and playground activities. Or they may be discussion leaders or project advisers of special subjects, such as homemaking, sex education, public affairs, vocations, etc. With experience in the organization in a comparable field of work, they may supervise inexperienced leaders, and help to provide training courses. They may serve on community-wide councils and committees representing a particular agency. They may serve as consultants, volunteering high grade professional services from another field, such as psychiatrists who help on behavior problems, lawyers who give legal advice, doctors who counsel individuals and groups, and others. They may be people who can help in conducting surveys and research. They may provide counsel and guidance for young people.

Both paid and volunteer workers are desirable. In the very small communities, or in communities where funds are limited, some organizations depend entirely upon their volunteer workers for leadership, direction, and administration of the program. However, in communities where funds are available, they recommend the employment of specially trained, full-time professional workers.

The job of these professional workers is to cooperate with volunteers in doing their work effectively; to provide educational courses and regular consultation periods which help the volunteers understand young people, the agency, and the community; to counsel with adults concerning their role in helping young people plan and carry out programs; to see that time invested in volunteer work with young groups results in new learning, personal satisfaction, and a sense of accomplishment for the volunteer; to see that the total program is administered economically, efficiently, and democratically. To secure a qualified professional worker to administer such a program requires a salary commensurate with other executive positions in the community and in other communities which may have positions open to these workers. Citizens who want a good piece of work done need to give strong support to a plan which makes attractive salaries available.

The national organizations have lay and professional workers constantly at work finding more effective ways of meeting the needs of children and youth, interpreting the needs to the larger public, seeking ways to give more practical help to local leaders.

While national youth-serving organizations recommend policies, operating procedures, and program emphasis, local units of the organizations are encouraged to work out their program in whatever way best fits their own needs. As a matter of fact, in several of the organizations the national program is developed in a convention meeting of delegated representatives of local units.

Some of the organizations already have youth representatives on the boards and administration committees of local units, and on national committees or councils. Certain other organizations recognize the importance of making this youth-adult participation carry over into the administrative aspects of the work as well as in group programs. A workable plan of this kind requires adults who respect the opinions and considered judgment of youth, and it requires youth ready to assume such responsibility. Often young people are more ready for this cooperative experience than are the adults.

Adult citizens who have never before worked with youth-serving agencies should seek literature and, if possible, individual counsel about the program and methods of work, the national resources available, as well as information about the help needed in the particular community in which they live.

Adult citizens who invest time, experience, thought, interest, or money (or all of these), in providing constructive leisure-time activities for young people may receive dividends of two kinds: (1) young people who feel confident and secure because adults care what happens to them; (2) adult citizens five, ten, and twenty years from now who learned by way of a youth group what it means to live cooperatively and constructively with other people.

THE 1960 WHITE HOUSE CONFERENCE ON CHILDREN AND YOUTH

The Sixth White House Conference on Children and Youth brought to Washington 7600 delegates from every state of the Union. The conference's recommendations reflect the hopes and aspirations of all who would strive "to promote opportunities for children and youth to realize their full potential for a creative life in freedom and dignity." Every section of the conference presented recommendations, and in all of them, recreation was mentioned many times. One set of recommendations dealt entirely with recreation and leisure. Those recommendations are noted here because they emerged from needs in recreation for children and youth.

LEISURE

FEDERAL, STATE AND LOCAL ACTION

That a federal recreation bureau or service be created to provide information and advisory services to public and private agencies in states and communities.

That all states establish recreation agencies—
to survey needs and furnish information, so that facilities can be expanded; to provide advisory assistance to public and private agencies in local communities and promote cooperation among them in developing recreation programs.

That local communities establish recreation agencies to plan, organize, and administer community recreation programs.

That state and local governments include in their budgets appropriations for employing qualified professional leadership and financing recreation programs.

That advantage be taken of private funds as well as of public funds or matching grants provided for recreation purposes by existing legislation.

That federal and state governments consider the leisure needs of youth in developing programs for conservation of natural resources, for improvement and expansion of our natural park system, and for protecting and acquiring wilderness areas.

That federal, state, and local governments utilize every opportunity to acquire and develop new land, buildings, and water resources; that existing facilities for leisure-time use be preserved and safeguarded from encroachment; and that large natural areas, such as forests, reservoirs and defense areas be developed for multiple purposes.

That facilities such as picnic areas, hostels, camps, marinas, boat-launching sites, playgrounds, golf courses, athletic fields, recreation centers, libraries, museums, and theaters be provided.

YOUTH PARTICIPATION

That the need for a National Youth Council, with majority representation of youth, to evaluate, coordinate, and extend facilities and activities for youth in their free time, be explored.

That youth be given the opportunity for leadership responsibilities at national, state, and local levels as members of boards and committees of recreation and cultural agencies concerned with youth, with full membership privileges within legal restrictions.

COMMUNITY PROGRAMS

That diversified community recreation programs, including both physical and cultural activities and provided with adequate leadership, be an integral part of every community.

That rural areas provide more opportunities for young people to participate in art, drama, literature, music, sports, and social activities.

That as many youth organizations be organized as may be needed to accommodate all young people eligible to participate and to provide activity appealing to varying ages and interests; that citizens be induced to take leadership roles in such youth organizations; and that each organization maintain an active program with high interest appeal.

That all public and private youth-serving agencies supplement their programs by providing guidance in the use of leisure.

That adequate space be provided for recreation readily accessible and available for the use of *all* people.

That all community agencies and organizations, both public and private, including churches, schools, youth organizations, civic clubs, and commercial recreation interests coordinate their efforts and cooperate in leisure-time programs to insure maximum use of staff, services, facilities, buildings and grounds, including year-round and evening use of schools and playgrounds, in the interests of providing suitably supervised recreation for children and youth and their parents.

That schools and all other community agencies, recreational and social, give special consideration to young adults' physical and emotional health needs by making their facilities available to this group.

That all organizations working with children and youth in the leisure field cooperate to assist each other recruiting personnel; that communities avail themselves of the services of competent professional and service organizations to train both professional and volunteer leadership; that in-service training programs be established to provide opportunities for professional growth; and that every community provide more training for volunteers.

That educational institutions place more emphasis on training leaders for recreation, and provide courses in the creative arts; and that state curriculum committees require such courses in the training of leaders for the recreation field.

PROGRAM OBJECTIVES AND PHILOSOPHY

That all leisure-time programs for children and youth include experiences directed toward the goal of heightening their understanding of God, His power as Supreme Being, their relationship to Him and to their fellowmen. And further that, as they seek to achieve this goal, religious groups and leisure-time agencies reexamine and reevaluate the objectives and philosophy of their programs and recognize the need for opportunities for quiet, meditation, reverie, and being alone.

Minority Report: "We believe that the first part of this resolution would be unfair to the children of these parents whose concern for spirituality derives from nontheistic sources."

That agencies conducting leisure programs for children and youth, as well as agencies working on the development of personality, base their plans on the understanding that in all areas of personal decision the real tensions lie between freedom and authority, and that progress toward maturity consists in learning to confront these tensions and to live effectively and creatively within them.

That public and private agencies make greater use of leisure activities to teach intergroup and international understanding.

That adults avoid exploiting youth by pressuring them into highly competitive organized activities for which their bodies and minds are not adapted; that they recognize children and youth as individuals, rather than as projects in leisure-time pursuits, and allow each one to mature at his own rate.

That creative activities and personal participation be encouraged, and commercial and spectator forms of entertainment minimized.

That more emphasis be placed on cultural activities to provide children and youth with creative outlets and increase their appreciation of beauty and their interest in the arts.

That all agencies give more emphasis to family leisure-time activities; and that serious attention be given to programs on the importance of family recreation and pilot or demonstration programs aimed at building better home and family life.

That parents guide their children in selecting balanced leisure pursuits.

That some time be allowed young people for unscheduled and undirected activities.

That schools and communities cooperate in designing out-of-school programs to provide constructive leisure activity consistent with sound principles of child development, and to counteract pressures for competitive athletics promoted by groups with good intentions but limited knowledge of the physical and social needs of children and youth.

That competitive sports for preadolescents be—

supervised by trained and qualified leaders;

emphasize participation and not stress competition out of proportion to its value for this age group;

available to all children, and not to only the few more athletically skilled;

further investigated as to their value for children.

That efforts be made to increase the awareness of commercial interests of their responsibility for establishing and maintaining standards which contribute to the health and well-being of children and youth.

That the home, the school, and the community share responsibility for promoting and encouraging more intensive and extensive participation in physical activity.

That summer camping be increasingly utilized.

LEISURE-TIME READING

That action be taken to extend public library service throughout the nation, with local, state, and national support, and make it available to all.

That support for public, private, and school libraries be increased, and access provided in school and leisure hours, so that all children, particularly the gifted, make reading a lifetime source of learning.

That organizations serving children and youth incorporate the encouragement of reading into their programs, where possible providing materials and cooperating with other agencies in this activity.

That parents, teachers, librarians, and other reading counselors guide children to read increasingly better books; and that trained personnel be available to guide parents as well as young people in the selection of appropriate materials.

ARTS

That the National Cultural Center work closely with all recreation, education, community, and civic groups and organizations in developing its proposed programs and services to local communities; and that all American citizens enthusiastically and wholeheartedly support the center in its endeavors.

That the programs of public and private recreation organizations provide for experimentation with art media to develop high standards of skill and appreciation of their value.

That public and voluntary agencies, schools, colleges, and communications provide all children and youth with opportunities for participation in creative dramatics, creative writing, and dramatic production under qualified leadership, to develop their talents and give them a basic understanding and critical appreciation of the theater arts.

That a study be undertaken to learn what schools, religious groups, recreation groups, and local, regional, and national public agencies are doing to develop sound theatrical techniques and tastes.

RESEARCH AND PUBLIC EDUCATION

That public and voluntary agencies conduct continuing programs of research, interpretation, and action in the creative and constructive use of leisure time, in developing awareness of needs for planned cultural, social, and physical activities under qualified leadership, with emphasis on programs for girls, older adolescents, gifted and handicapped children and youth, young married couples, and other groups whose recreation needs are not being met by present programs.

That the National Council of Arts in Education be requested to undertake a national research, educational, and promotional program to make American citizens aware of the importance of all creative arts in their lives.

No matter how or under what auspices a youth program functions, recreation assumes a prominent place in the picture. In fact, the overwhelming emphasis, whether acknowledged or not, is usually on recreation. This need should be recognized and increased attention given to it. Recreation will always play a dominant role in the interests and needs of youth. These influences and practices call for concerted community action to guide the forces properly, to plan immediate and long range action, and to integrate the total efforts. A united effort is needed.

THE WORKSHOP

1. Explore the recreation services of the public and private youth-serving agencies in your community.
2. Try to determine the relative popularity and reasons for their popularity of specific recreation activities among youth.
3. Evaluate the extent to which the youth of a particular community are participating in the programs of youth-serving agencies.
4. Interview a number of youths to learn their attitudes toward recreation opportunities and needs.

5. Suggest a plan for the establishment of a representative youth council to meet recreation needs.
6. Outline a program of action for improving and evaluating the recreation opportunities for youth in your community.

REFERENCES

Coleman, James S., *The Adolescent Society*. New York: The Free Press, 1961.

Frederick, Robert W., *The Third Curriculum*. New York: Appleton-Century-Crofts, 1959.

Friedenberg, Edgar, *The Vanishing Adolescent*. New York: Dell Publishing Company, 1962.

Mattick, Hans W., and Nathan S. Kaplan, *The Chicago Youth Development Project*. Ann Arbor: University of Michigan Institute for Social Research, February, 1964.

Michael, Donald, *The Next Generation*. New York: Vintage Books, 1965.

Murray, Janet B., and Clyde E. Murray, *Guide Lines for Group Leaders*. New York: Whiteside and William Morrow & Co., Inc., 1954.

Murray, Kathryn, *Tips to Teen Agers*. New York: G. P. Putnam's Sons, 1961.

National Association of Social Workers, Russell H. Kurtz, ed., *Social Work Year Book*. A description of organized activities in social work and in related fields. 14th Issue. New York: 1960.

Olds, Edward B., *The Spare Time Activities and Interests of Young People*. Washington, D.C.: Health and Welfare Council of the National Capital Area, 1962.

Reissman, Frank, *The Culturally Deprived*. New York: Vintage Books, 1965.

Smith, E. A., *The Youth Culture*. New York: The Free Press, 1962.

U.S. Department of Health, Education, and Welfare, Children's Bureau, *Youth Groups in Conflict*. Washington, D.C.: 1958.

Comment

Youth Publications, prepared by the International Council of Religious Education, is a classified bibliography of materials for youth groups and their leaders.

By getting in touch with the nearest representative of various youth agencies or by writing to their national headquarters, leaders can obtain much information regarding each agency's special organization and program.

The reports of the proceedings from the various White House Conferences on Children and Youth in a Democracy are filled with excellent material—U.S. Government Printing Office.

The Recreation and Youth Services Planning Council of Los Angeles has recently completed one of the most comprehensive youth surveys ever undertaken by a recreationally-oriented study group. Several publications, including *Potential Sources of New Revenues for Recreation and Youth Services Programs,* are available.

The March 21, 1966, issue of *Newsweek Magazine* was devoted to the study of Teen Agers. Several major news magazines such as *Life* and *Look* have also carried Youth Specials.

15

Employee Recreation

The growth of industry and business is one of the most significant phenomena in the United States and Canada. Economic policies and procedures, employment, production, distribution, control of goods, and the operating processes of the economic order are assuming gigantic proportions in the national life.

Outstanding in this movement is the growing recognition of the place of recreation in the industrial and business world. Employer and employee are cooperating with the community in providing recreation opportunities for the worker and his family. While employee recreation is not new, its phenomenal advance through recognition by business and industry, management and labor, is significant. The term "employee recreation" does not mean any special brand of recreation. It is rather the application of recreation to a particular environment or sponsorship. It is the provision for and by the workers of wholesome leisure interests linked in one way or another to their place of employment.

The term does not apply only to large industries or manufacturing plants. It applies equally to nonindustrial firms such as banks, insurance companies, department stores, utilities, transportation lines, service firms, and other business organizations. Many of these firms have well organized recreation programs, sponsor camps, have teams in sports leagues, stage dramatic productions, promote bands and choruses, and serve other recreation interests of employees.

Technology has brought with it many problems that call for adjustments in the interests of individual and social well-being—shorter work hours, specialization, monotony in work, health hazards, absenteeism, strikes, and early retirement. Recreation as an adjunct of industrial life plays an increasingly important, if not immediately discernible, part in helping to alleviate some of these problems.

In a brochure entitled *Better Employee Relations Through Employee Recreation*,[1] the National Industrial Recreation Association lists the following benefits:

Recreation—
    breaks down barriers
    relieves job monotony
    builds friendships
    helps to cut absenteeism
    improves the mental attitude of the employee
    reaches the employee's family
    keeps contact with retired employees
    spots leadership ability
    strengthens public relations
    improves community relations and
    gives a company the reputation of being a
      "good place to work"

The NIRA further states that:

If a properly organized employee recreation program reaches:
    the employee
    the employee's family
    the retired employee
    the employee's friends, and
    the entire community—it must be,
as has been proved in thousands of cases, one of the most effective of today's industrial relations tools.

TYPES OF EMPLOYEE RECREATION

There are a number of ways in which the industrial recreation program can be administered: (1) some programs are sponsored entirely by management, which provides all areas and facilities and operates the program with little or no cost to the worker; (2) in some cases management provides the capital outlay for areas and facilities, and there is joint operation by employer and employee; (3) under the membership plan, the

[1] This brochure is now out of print.

employer provides areas and facilities, and the employees maintain and operate the program; (4) some employee recreation programs are planned, financed, and operated entirely by employees; (5) under the association type, public recreation departments and organizations such as the Young Men's Christian Association operate the program for the industries of the community or, as in the case of Y.M.C.A., the program is managed by employers and employees who are members; and there are situations where the company finances the community program, especially in company towns.

In a number of communities there is even joint action for the building of areas and facilities and the operation of the recreation program. Several industries pool resources for community programs, especially in industrial towns and cities. The Milwaukee County Industrial Recreation Council, Incorporated, sponsored by a number of plants in that city, is a good illustration of this type.

Some of the aims of this recreation council are:

To help member firms by disseminating the ideas of each for recreation programs.

To plan a recreation program for both employees and management.

To cooperate with municipal athletic directors to provide better recreation programs.

To stimulate interest of employees in programs provided by their firms.

To work out activities and schedules which will be popular with industrial employees.

To expand intrashop programs into intershop activities, thereby providing added fun and new friendships for participants.

To put athletic activities on a sound basis of competition by drafting rules and regulations with the help of municipal athletic directors.

To develop a well-rounded program of activities in which large numbers can find enjoyment and recreation.

To work together to obtain more municipal recreation facilities for industrial people.

To meet regularly and discuss policies and developments of industrial recreation.

This council provides direct contact between employees and management. It includes representatives of the industrial relations departments of the firms. These men deal directly with management and employees. The Recreation Council holds meetings monthly. At these sessions each firm has one vote. The meetings frequently develop into a problem clinic at which firms just entering the recreation field can obtain answers to their problems.

The community recreation program is sometimes utilized by industry. In this case, the industry neither provides areas and facilities nor operates a program. Instead, it makes liberal contributions to the community program in volunteer leadership and finances and expects its workers to participate in an overall community program. This pattern is most desirable in places where the industry is but a part of the community and where the workers do not live in company houses located in one section of the community.

ADMINISTRATIVE FACTORS

General

If the employees live near the industry or business, an industry-centered program may be appropriate. If they commute and are widely scattered, lunch period programs, on-the-job entertainment, and occasional plant programs may suffice.

Company policy and size often determine action. Some companies accept recreation responsibility while others argue that the workers should seek and provide their own leisure opportunities. The expense involved in purchasing, operating, and staffing programs, areas, and facilities is often prohibitive for small firms.

The small plant, generally located in a community with other industries, may use off-plant property—in public recreation buildings or areas, in schools, churches, Y's, and others. It may also use commercial enterprises such as bowling establishments.

Leadership

If a firm decides to undertake a recreation program, ideally there should be within the industry or business a recreation department directed and staffed by professional recreators.

Until this stage is reached, however, some program direction can be done by interested plant personnel, skilled in leadership. In some small companies, the personnel manager or a member of his staff may be able to sponsor a few recreation activities with volunteer support.

Committees of employees, groups of volunteers, committees of employers and employees, and trade-union committees can be of invaluable assistance. Their combined effort is desirable.

In some cases, where management provides areas and facilities, the program can be operated by employee groups. While employees should be encouraged to help organize their own activities, full-time paid leadership is invaluable for effective operation. Part-time paid leaders are the next best substitute.

Often, the community recreation director and his staff can help the company program. Many tax-supported community recreation programs serve industries. Private agency leadership, too, can and does function effectively with industrial groups. But studies show that companies employing full-time paid leaders have large and generally more effective programs.

Finances

There are many methods of financing industrial recreation. Among these are:

a. Company financing.
b. Employee recreation association dues.
c. Profits from vending machines, snack bars, canteens, and the like.
d. Admissions, charges and fees.
e. Activity dues or assessments.

Most programs are financed through a combination of these fund sources.

It is wise to have a fixed financial policy. All who are interested in the program and benefit by it should share the financial burden. The so-called "free" program is not satisfying. On the other hand, employees should not be taxed for the total costs. Cooperative, joint financing has many values. Activities that are expensive to operate, which involve awards and prizes, or which call for special instruction, should be self-supporting. Funds should be budgeted on an equitable basis and proper accounting and auditing principles followed.

Areas and Facilities

The company may or may not supply some or all of the equipment and facilities. The latter include indoor centers—skating rinks, bowling lanes, tennis courts, and even country clubs; outdoor areas—fields, tracks, swimming pools, and camps. Company facilities are frequently supplemented by public and private facilities in the community and by those operated under the auspices of commercial agencies. This is especially true of such facilities as bowling lanes, dance halls, skating rinks, swimming pools, and theaters. Often a facility or an area is a gift or is built as a memorial, with funds derived from contributions and drives.

In recent years there has been a trend toward the development of tracts of land on the outskirts of towns as centers for company recreation rather than using facilities adjacent to the plant, or community facilities. Typical illustrations are the employee recreation parks of Frigidaire in Dayton,

Ohio, Scoville Manufacturing Company in Waterbury, Connecticut, the State Farm Insurance Companies in Bloomington, Illinois, and International Business Machines in Endicott and Poughkeepsie, New York, 3M Company, St. Paul, Minnesota and Honeywell, Inc., Minneapolis, Minnesota.

Programs

The industrial recreation program is similar to any other type of program. Athletics and sports of all types are most popular. Within-plant, inter- and intra-league events, tournaments, and contests head the list in participation and spectator attendance. Musical activities of all types and social recreation rank high in popularity. Arts and crafts and outing activities, especially camping, are expanding. The company picnic is an outstanding interest of the employee's family. Motion pictures provided by the company are well received, although the employee in general prefers to attend commercial theaters. Dances of all kinds (social, folk, and square) are readily accepted and supported. Reading rooms are gaining in interest, and parties are well patronized.

What an employee does in his leisure has a direct effect on his efficiency and his attitude toward his work. The program should further the growth and development of the individual employee. A wholesome, well-balanced program of recreation means assets in terms of health, efficiency, *esprit de corps*, morale, and a good place in which to work.

LUNCH-HOUR RECREATION

Obtaining recreation during lunch periods is like coming up for air. Merely eating lunch scarcely breaks the monotony of the working day. Everything good claimed of industrial recreation as a whole can be applied to lunch-hour activities, with the accent on such values as relief from boredom, new inspiration, and stimulation. Experience proves there is no better relief from midday fatigue and boredom than a short recreation period. All the benefits of luncheon club meetings, with which management is familiar, apply to lunch-hour recreation for industrial workers.[2]

It is important to remember that:

1. The lunch hour offers opportunity for a maximum number of workers to participate in recreation.

2. It returns the employee to the job refreshed and stimulated.

3. The spectator interest is valuable. "Kibitzing" the game of checkers or chess, the card games, or the paddle tennis match provides good entertainment.

[2] Opening paragraph in a bulletin, *Lunch Hour Recreation,* published by the National Industrial Recreation Association, 20 N. Wacker Dr., Chicago, Ill.

4. Whether the lunch period is thirty minutes, forty-five minutes, or an hour in duration, there is some time for recreation as well as for eating.

5. Often workers live too far from the plant recreation facilities to return after working hours. The lunch period affords a good opportunity for participation.

6. Recreation activities tend to relieve congestion in dining halls and cafeterias as the workers finish their meals and move into recreation areas.

7. Regardless of the shift of workers the period brings effective results. The program should prevail for all shifts regardless of the hours.

8. Success of the program depends on facilities within or near the plant. Certain features may be carried on, and games played while the employees are actually eating lunch. Where the activities call for equipment it should be close at hand since time is limited. Provisions should be made for participation close to the eating area. An area should be set aside for seating large groups to listen to music or witness a short movie. Arrangements can be made to eat lunches out-of-doors if climate and weather permit.

9. A variety of recreation opportunities is necessary. Surveys have shown that popular noon-hour activities include card games, horse-shoes, checkers, softball, singing, ping-pong, bowling, chess, billiards, listening to music, reading, shuffle-board, and volleyball. Most of these can be carried on every day. Movies, folk dancing, crafts, and sports events may be scheduled occasionally.

10. The program should be entirely informal, providing the maximum of rest and relaxation. Music presented over a public address system or portable equipment is more satisfactory than juke-box music in the dining halls. Properly placed speakers give good results. The musical selections should be varied. Community singing can be enjoyed. Movies are very popular and short subjects—cartoons, comedies, and news features—are more in demand than lengthy features. Short dramatic shows or skits and informal vaudeville are appropriate. Crafts form an excellent activity for the lunch hours. Persons with special handicraft interests or hobbies should have some place where such interests may be pursued. Dancing is popular for both participants and spectators. A nearby reading room or library may be used. There should be at least a reading table with current magazines and newspapers.

CAMPING FOR EMPLOYEES

There are four general types of employee camps: (1) for the entire family; (2) for men or women employees; (3) for youth and children of employees; (4) the day camp. The company provides the camp area and equipment, and the employees generally pay a small fee for use of facilities and for maintenance and expansion of the program.

L. Bamberger and Company (Newark, N.J.) has an employee camp located on 466 acres of wooded country, three hours from Newark. Two lodges, joined by an underground passage and a patio, can house 98 people. Two lounges with open fireplaces provide space for movies, cards, and dancing. Meals are prepared by a camp dietitian and served in the main dining room.

Camp Isida is well-equipped for sports, with three full-sized tennis courts, two badminton courts, volleyball, archery, croquet, and horseshoe facilities, and a stream damned to form a 250-foot pool for swimming and diving. Winter sports include skiing, tobogganning, and coasting.

Camp registration is open to all employees' families. They may register for a weekend or for their entire vacation.

The Ecusta Paper Corporation at Pisgah Forest, North Carolina, has purchased what was once a private camp for the benefit of employees and their families. The camp, within walking distance of many of the workers' homes, is fully equipped for a well-balanced recreation program. There are facilities for swimming, boating, nature crafts, picnics, dancing, skating, softball. Since the camp is adjacent to the homes of the employees, there are no provisions for lodging.

The Ford Motor Company operates day camps for the children of its employees.

Industrial recreation increasingly includes camping as an essential factor in a well-rounded program.

ILLUSTRATIONS OF SIGNIFICANT PROGRAMS

The following programs of business firms and industrial plants are presented because they have been chosen as recipients of the Helms Industrial Recreation Achievement Awards. These awards are given in recognition of outstanding programs. Accounts are taken from descriptions in *Recreation Management,* the monthly publication of the National Industrial Recreation Association.

LOCKHEED OF BURBANK, CALIFORNIA

Employing some 48,000 aircraft workers at its mammoth Southern California location, Lockheed has long been a pacesetter in meeting the leisure needs of its employees.

Its amazingly diversified and well-rounded employee program includes 35 different hobby and craft clubs in addition to well-developed programs in sports, women's activities, youth training, music, and travel.

Almost 300 employees belong to 18 Bible study groups, while others ride their hobbies in such specialized activities as the Lockheed Mining and Prospecting Club, the Pipe Club, the Watch and Clock Club, and more usual activities as skin diving, model railroading, stamp collecting, and dancing.

Lockheed's vast program is entirely self-sustaining. All activities are sponsored by the Lockheed Employees Recreation Club, which derives its income from vending machine proceeds and rental of income properties donated to the club by Lockheed.

LERC charges no membership dues, and all employees, their families, and all retired employees are eligible to participate in the program.

Club activities run almost around the clock, with schedules custom-tailored for day and night shift members.

In addition to a full-time staff of eight, Lockheed's program is conducted by 81 elected employee representatives and 283 volunteer commissioners and group leaders.

The club owns and operates a 15,000 sq. ft. recreation building and a five acre park. However, activities overflow into school, city, and county owned gyms, pools, and golf courses.

STATE FARM INSURANCE COMPANIES

An exceptionally high percentage of employee participation in an unusually large number of activities is characteristic of the recreation program at the State Farm Insurance Companies of Bloomington, Ill.

Of the firm's 1850 employees, more than half will turn out for a smorgasbord dinner or a chuck wagon barbeque (State Farm holds about 10 special dinners yearly). More than 1200 can be expected at a dance. Local bowling facilities are booked to capacity.

The program has built up such interest that last year State Farm sponsored 22 different handicraft classes, 31 sports activities, 25 social events, and 19 youth activities.

In addition to supporting these organized activities, crowds are always heavy at the company's 33-acre park, with picnic, sports, and game facilities, plus a lake for swimming and fishing.

Activities are governed by an employee-elected board of directors, while the park is owned and managed by the company. The activities association is sustained by a fixed company contribution per employee, $2 voluntary membership dues, vending machine profits, and activity fees.

The program is supervised by a full-time activities supervisor and park custodian with four full-time assistants. The 41 part-time employees are concerned primarily with park maintenance and operation.

Extensive travel, ticket, and license services are also handled through the activities association.

FAULTLESS RUBBER COMPANY

The national trend away from spectator sports to active participation could well have been started at Faultless Rubber Co., Ashland, Ohio.

With 505 employees, the Faultless Rubber Co. Athletic Assn. schedules 32 different athletic activities during a single year. In addition to regular league play, 14 sports tournaments are also held.

Number of participants is equally outstanding. In bowling, for example, 34.6% of the employees, or better than one out of three, bowl on a company sponsored team.

Other Athletic Association activities include Little League sponsorship, children and adult Christmas parties, ticket service, award banquets, reading rack.

The program and operation of the Faultless Recreation Building is supervised by the full-time recreation director and his assistant.

The recreation building houses four bowling lanes, two billiard tables, table tennis, and other game equipment. Other facilities include a kitchen, banquet hall, dance floor, television lounge, lockers, showers, and an exercise room.

Employees and their families participate in all activities without charge. Funds are obtained by monthly company contributions, vending machine proceeds, bowling fees, and rental of recreation hall facilities to outside organizations. Funds are allocated according to participation.

FLICK-REEDY CORPORATION

Flick-Reedy Corporation, Bensenville, Ill., has spearheaded the "small company breakthrough" in providing employee services and facilities comparable to those offered by the corporate giants.

Creative management policy has made a comprehensive, year-around recreation program a reality for its 325 employees. Ingenious planning has made the inclusion of a 40' × 60' swimming pool, multi-use gymnasium, and other recreation facilities economical and practical features of its 220,000 sq. ft. plant. Outdoor facilities include playground and picnic areas. Basketball, tennis, badminton, and other facilities are under construction. The plant's water storage "lagoons" are stocked for fishing.

All facilities, when not in use by employees and their families, are available to community groups.

Recreation responsibilities are shared by the personnel and public relations managers, and a swimming instructor is employed part-time. Income is obtained through company contributions, activity fees, and vending receipts, as appropriated by the officers of the Flick-Reedy Employees Benefit Assn.

Classes in economics, public affairs, and political action have proved popular in augmenting programs for sports, social, and hobby interests. Youth activities include Little League, Junior Achievement, amateur show, and "Aqua Capades." Family participation is emphasized.

THE WEST POINT MANUFACTURING COMPANY

The West Point Manufacturing Company's Department of Community Recreation provides the recreation facilities and personnel for West Point, Georgia, and five neighboring communities where West Point plants are located just across the state line in Alabama.

Directed to all persons living in the West Point community, the program includes all the basic sports, club, and cultural activities, plus a long list of others including baton twirling, teen centers, soccer, senior citizens, assistance in the elementary school physical education program, and administration of physical fitness tests.

The program has been substantially expanded to include a weekly half-hour radio program called, "Keeping in Touch," Red Cross instruction, retirement counseling, a horse show, ceramics classes, Little League baseball, a stamp club, and a safety exhibit and patrol.

West Point owns and operates three swimming pools, nine playgrounds, a 9-hole golf course, and four recreation centers to handle its wide range of activities.

The program is administered by a full-time staff of 16, with 14 part-time leaders and 2300 active volunteers.

The yearly recreation budget is approved by the company. Expenditures include salaries, supplies, apparatus, repairs, officiating and coaching, transportation, and special groups. Yearly per employee cost has been approximately $15. In addition, participants share the cost for many special activities and projects.

DISTILLATION PRODUCTS INDUSTRIES

Distillation Products Industries, Rochester, N. Y., completely disproves the notion that small companies cannot compare with corporate giants in providing complete, year-round employee programs. D.P.I.'s 350 employees can choose from 25 different athletic, social, and cultural activities and benefit from special services including a lending library, vacation and travel service, and ticket and license service.

Family participation is emphasized with eight special activities including mixed golf and bowling, doll dressing, toy collecting, and junior bowling.

Administered through the joint employee-company sponsored Vita Vac Club, the program is financed through voluntary $1 annual membership dues and matching company contributions. Funds are allocated to the various activities on the basis of interest and participation.

Some of the outstanding industrial recreation programs over the nation would include, in addition to those discussed, the programs of the Aero-jet-General Corporation, Sacramento, California; Armstrong Cork Company, Lancaster, Pennsylvania; Chrysler Corporation, Detroit, Michigan; Cleveland Graphite Bronze Company, Cleveland, Ohio; Eastman Kodak Company, Rochester, New York; Eli Lilly and Company, Indianapolis, Indiana; Falk Corporation, Milwaukee, Wisconsin; Goodyear Tire and Rubber Company, Akron, Ohio; International Business Machines Corporation, Endicott, New York; McDonnell Aircraft Corporation, Saint Louis, Missouri; Minnesota Mining and Manufacturing Company, St. Paul, Minnesota; Nation-wide Life Insurance Company, Columbus, Ohio; Owens-Illinois Glass Company, Bridgeton, New Jersey; Sun-Oil Company, Philadelphia, Pennsylvania; Tennessee Eastman Company, Kingsport, Tennessee; and Theo. Hamm Brewing Company, St. Paul, Minnesota.

THE NATIONAL INDUSTRIAL RECREATION ASSOCIATION

The National Industrial Recreation Association organized in 1941, contributes greatly in promoting and assisting employee recreation programs. The Association objectives are:

1. To acquaint management with the importance of industrial recreation as a part of sound industrial relations.
2. To emphasize industrial recreation in periods of national emergency, to achieve industrial unity, improve morale, skill, and production.
3. To develop industrial recreation as a benefit to the community and improvement of industrial, labor, and government understanding.
4. To study methods of improving industrial recreation programs.
5. To provide a clearing house for ideas and dissemination of information on industrial recreation programs through bulletins and other media.
6. To aid members in the solution of recreation problems.
7. To encourage further study and research on industrial recreation.
8. To function in any manner beneficial to the industrial recreation movement.

Its main services to members include: providing reviews of new developments in industrial recreation; producing manuals of procedure for establishing industrial programs; publishing *RECREATION MANAGEMENT*, the national magazine of recreation in business and industry, and monthly Newsletters and Idea Clinics; conducting careful research on new problems; providing an individual information service; sponsoring conferences in various sections of the country for the exchange of ideas among industrial leaders and recreation directors, running seven national tournaments in bridge, golf, bowling, and rifle, pistol, trap, and skeet shooting, and sponsoring a national conference attended by employee recreation directors from all parts of the U.S. and Canada.

LABOR ORGANIZATIONS

Labor organizations and their many local branches sponsor recreation: (1) as an important part of regular meetings; (2) by conducting for the membership such activities as picnics, play days, excursions, parties, and dances; (3) through cooperation with local recreation authorities; (4) by encouraging the promotion of a well-rounded community program; (5) by serving as representatives on recreation commissions, boards, councils, and advisory committees; (6) by participating in training institutes, conferences, and workshops.

The International Recreation Department of the United Automobile Workers—A.F.L.-C.I.O. was established in 1937. The Department's stated objectives are as follows:

1. To provide recreation for all U.A.W. members and their families without racial discrimination;
2. To unite the union through the common understanding inherent in leisure-time activities;
3. To offset the "spider-to-the-fly" technique of management, which so often catches workers in the web-of-wooing with the offer of enticing recreation programs;
4. To provide leadership training opportunities to union rank-and-file members through recreational organization;
5. To link the union to the community through the use of community facilities, and through cooperation with community recreation leaders;
6. To provide each member and his family with the benefits of professional recreation leadership for a minimum cost to the worker; and
7. To work toward eventual cooperative labor-management recreation programs for all American workers in every industry.

Perhaps the best example of recreation programs sponsored by the U.A.W. is that provided by the Detroit Area Recreation Council. As the need has arisen for city-wide instruction on a broad scale, classes have been organized in dancing, sewing, golf, and swimming. City-wide competition has been carried on through leagues and tournaments in softball, basketball, bowling, baseball, and an annual ice skating meet. More re-

cent activities include archery, camping, golf, horseshoes, leadership training, outings, table tennis, and target shooting.

The Educational Department of the International Ladies Garment
Workers Union has sponsored recreation opportunities for its members
for years. The A.F.L.-C.I.O. has also been concerned with providing adequate recreation programs for union members and their families.

The Workers Education Bureau of America sponsors recreation in its
institute and conference programs and also publishes material of value
to general community organizations. Many university extension divisions
sponsor workers' education institutes, and recreation is a feature of each
day's activity.

In a number of places major labor union groups have joined to promote conferences for all groups of workers in their locality.

THE WORKSHOP

1. Compare the different methods of administering industrial recreation.
2. Determine the advantages and disadvantages of an industrial recreation program and suggest how and to what extent industry should participate in the
   community recreation program.
3. Discuss the responsibilities of (a) management, (b) labor, and (c) community,
   in relation to an industrial recreation program.
4. Observe an employee recreation program and report on it.
5. Survey the program of recreation activities in a selected list of industries.
6. Suggest ways of integrating the industrial recreation program with the community recreation program.
7. Interview labor leaders for their opinions on employee recreation.
8. Argue the "pros" and "cons" of the question: Should recreation for the employee and his family be sponsored by industry or the community?
9. List ways in which new kinds of industrial recreation services might be provided for families.
10. List the kinds of professional preparation and experience a worker should
    have for recreation leadership in industry.

REFERENCES

Anderson, Jackson M., *Industrial Recreation—A Guide to Its Organization and
Administration.* New York: McGraw-Hill Book Company, 1955.

Aspley, J. C., and E. Whitmore, *The Handbook of Industrial Relations,* Third
Edition. Chicago: The Dartnell Corporation, 1952.

Department of Education, Community Programmes Branch, *Recreation in Industry.* Toronto, Canada: 1951.

Clark, H. E., *Financing Industrial Recreation.* Published Abstract of Master's
thesis, Lafayette, Indiana: Purdue University, 1949.

Golden, William, *Hours of Work*. Berkeley, Calif.: Institute of Industrial Relations, University of California, 1952.

Mayo, Elton, *Human Problems of an Industrial Civilization*. New York: The Viking Press, Inc., 1960.

National Industrial Recreation Association, *Employee Picnics; Industrial Bands; Lunch Hour Recreation; Music in Industry;* and other activity bulletins. Chicago: n.d.

Petrill, Jack, *After the Whistle Blows—A Guide to the Field of Recreation in Industry*. New York: The William-Frederick Press, 1949.

Comment

The National Industrial Recreation Association publishes *Recreation Management*, a magazine for industrial recreators, and also has a service to its members, "Idea Clinic"—a kit of timely materials and information sent frequently during the year. Address: 20 North Wacker Drive, Chicago, Illinois 60606.

Refer to the proceedings of the Annual Industrial Recreation Conferences, published and distributed by the National Industrial Recreation Association.

Check printed material from federal and state departments of labor and from industrial and trade associations, chambers of commerce, trade union journals, and official organs of various management and labor organizations.

Note in local communities the programs operating there and also the many ways in which the public recreation set-up and the industrial program cooperate. Study the many contributions the employee programs offer to the financial aid of community programs. Note the chapters and general references to the employee programs located in general volumes on Recreation.

16

Commercial Recreation Interests

The United States is known as a great industrial nation. Its unsurpassed records of production are reflected in its high standard of living. At the core of its economy is *business* based upon the *free enterprise* system, in which an individual risks his time, money, and effort for a *profit*. This is accomplished by the individual alone, under his own initiative, or in cooperation with others, entering into a business in which products or services are fabricated and distributed for a *profit*.

As we have seen in Chapter 3, leisure is *consumption* time, when products and services are purchased and consumed. Because leisure is used mainly for recreation, recreation, in its endless forms, becomes *saleable*, and its products and services become business transactions, directed toward the making of *profit*. Naturally, the more leisure more people have at their disposal, with an interest and enough money to buy, the more widespread becomes *commercial* recreation. Commercial recreation has grown rapidly in recent years and continues to expand.

Commercial recreation, of course, as is true for all other products and services in business, depends upon public demand. If there is no demand, if there is no market, if there are no sales, there will be *no* profit and hence, eventually, no commercial recreation. When the profit disappears, so does the commercial recreation enterprise.

Commercial recreation, properly regulated and of a positive rather than a negative influence, has a legitimate and important place in helping to satisfy the leisure demands and interests of the public.

Commercial recreation can be identified easily by the following factors: (1) It is owned and operated primarily for profit. A distinction is made between it and other public activities for which a fee is charged mainly for the one purpose of defraying costs. (2) It must have a sufficient demand to guarantee economic backing. Otherwise it loses the element of profit and thus its commercial appeal. (3) It must be flexible and adaptable enough to meet the constantly changing whims and fancies of a heterogeneous population.

Commercial recreation is likely to expand in the future, because leisure is growing, and the population is increasing. Capital can always be found to invest in such business.

In the past, amusement parks, pool and billiard halls, vaudeville theaters, dance halls, motion picture houses, and boxing matches in professional sports arenas were typical of the kinds of commercial recreation enterprises attractive to the public. In more recent years, travel, private clubs, radio and television stations, boating, bowling, skiing, reading, and such professional sports as racing, basketball, baseball and football have developed as popular forms of commercial recreation.

There is scarcely a form of recreation imaginable which has not been or could not be made available "at a price." The form which commercial recreation takes, as might be expected, is subject to the whims and interests of the public and may range from the sale of hundreds of thousands of hula hoops to teaching a new dance step. It can mean a child paying 50 cents for a pony ride or a half dozen men paying several hundred dollars to charter a boat for a fishing trip. It can involve an old couple going out for a drive, or thousands of college youths flocking to the vacation resort.

There is a tendency to commercialize many of the forms of recreation currently or once sponsored by public and voluntary social welfare agencies. The professionalizing of such sports as basketball, tennis, baseball and football are examples. We have had public libraries for years, but book-of-the-month clubs and bookstores and newsstands do a brisk business. Bowling alleys can be found in million-dollar commercial establishments. Amusement parks are almost a thing of the past, but Disneyland manages to take in $13.5 million a year. Skiing, once mainly an amateur outing or club affair, is now the hub of commercial operations all over the world, and skiing isn't confined to snow. In California there are many companies which manufacture water skis. Golf, traditionally, has been offered by public park and recreation departments or private, nonprofit clubs, but the Tam O'Shanter Club near Chicago is in business to make money—and does. It has 300 regular golfers who pay $750 annually to play and who also spend money at the club's eight bars.

As public demand for certain kinds of recreation increases, so does the commercialization of the activity, for the people of the United States have demonstrated both their willingness and their ability to pay for their recreation.

Four Illustrations

The field of commercial recreation comprises most of the recreation interests. Let's note a few illustrations. These may be duplicated by the hundreds. They signify trends and offer opportunities for other adventures and achievements.

CULTURAL ACTIVITIES

Book purchases have risen more than any other recreation expenditure —up 65% since 1960. Figures estimate more than 2 billion dollars spent on books and another 2 billion spent on magazines. It is estimated that 500 million comic books are sold annually. Ticket sales for theater and opera have risen 50% in the past ten years. Theater receipts in 1965 were one-third greater than admissions to all spectator sports. Attendance at theaters, operas, concerts, movies, and community theaters, all indicate a rise over previous years.

The general rise of the level of education may be the major cause and influence of these growing trends.

The number of amateur musicians has increased to approximately 35 million. More than 500 million dollars was spent on musical instruments in 1965 and close to 100 million on classical records.

Museum attendance is constantly increasing. It is reported that visitors to New York's Metropolitan Museum of Art on a single Sunday would twice fill Madison Square Garden Arena.

TRAVEL

It is estimated that the largest single item in the recreation and leisure budget is travel. Travel in the United States is twice what it was a decade ago and is still increasing. Foreign travel is triple what it was a decade ago. Tourism and its companion recreation are now well entrenched as active and important industries. They now hold third place in the economy behind manufacturing and agriculture. An educated guesstimate makes this a five billion dollar investment market for 1965. Total consumer expenditures on tourism, travel, and recreation should reach one hundred billion by 1972.

Longer vacations and shorter work weeks mean larger recreation and travel budgets.

Major outdoor recreation activities increased 51 per cent in 1960–66, and are expected to increase much more rapidly in the next six year period—as much as 150 per cent. Today over 80 per cent of adult trip takers participate in some form of sport.

The 150 per cent increase in recreation activities includes time for golf, fishing, skiing, boating and camping, but does not include spectator sports, such as auto racing, baseball, football, air shows, theaters, and amusement parks, all of which have exhibited phenomenal attendance growth in the past decade.

Present leisure trends favor commercial travel interests, and their actual dollar potential is greater than any available statistics indicate. But it's probably safe to forecast that by 1972, we'll be spending close to $53 billion each year on forms of outdoor recreation and another $43 billion on pleasure travel.

RECREATION BOATING

The boating industry announced that recreation boating became a $3-billion business during last year.

Retail spending attained a new high as an estimated million new boat enthusiasts took to the water. This brought the number of persons participating in recreation boating to 41,375,000. They spent $3,000,100,000 on boats, motors, equipment, services and club memberships.

There are judged to be 8,275,000 boats in existence, of which 4,237,371 are actually registered under the federal numbering system in states and by the Coast Guard.

RADIO AND TELEVISION

The world's supply of radio and television receivers continues to grow, and additional millions of the populations of all nations now have an opportunity to hear—and many to see—events as they happen; to be entertained, informed, and enriched by a wide variety of program fare. In the United States, where more than half of all receivers are located, there are approximately 260 million radio receivers and 75 million television receivers in homes, schools, automobiles, clubs and other recreation areas. The portable transistor radio receiver is carried by millions of individuals.

Nearly 6,000 radio broadcasting transmitters and more than 700 television broadcasting stations are located throughout the nation providing audiences with several different program choices. Particularly impressive has been the recent growth in FM stereo broadcasting, now carried on by over 600 stations, and by the growth in color television. Most programs of all three television networks are now transmitted in color and more than one-sixth of the homes in the United States contain one or more color television receivers. In all, 95 per cent of all homes can receive television programs, and even more homes use radio receivers regularly.

Programming is varied and is designed by the broadcasters to appeal to a wide range of tastes and interests. News, sports, and special events are especially important, with music, dramatic programs, religious services, and other broadcast fare providing information, education, and especially entertainment.

Not only are television and radio important commercial recreation attractions in themselves, they also frequently contribute to the noncommercial, organized recreation programs and services of the community. Telecasts and broadcasts of athletic and sports contests; announcements and reports on community recreation activities; coverage of special events, exhibitions, demonstrations, plays, concerts, and the like are among the wide range of community recreation activities which often involve radio and television enterprises.

Many stations are both willing and anxious to provide help for community recreation activities. Each station is required by law to operate "in the public interest, convenience, and necessity," and its operation is regularly reviewed by the Federal Communications Commission to which stations must apply for their licenses. Community service, therefore, is an integral part of a station's programming plan—and recreation can and should play an important part in the station's local service programming philosophy and operations.

The statistics enumerated in these four illustrations were gathered from many sources—books, articles, news clippings, and bulletins. There are quantities of data available.

Commercial interests not only *follow* the market—the purchasers of their goods and services—but also stimulate the market. Commercial recreation uses advertising and merchandising techniques to create demand, to inform the potential purchaser that the commodities and services are available, and to bring about a desire on the part of the purchaser for these things. Old markets are refreshed, and new markets are established. Athletic equipment; supplies for hunting, fishing, boating; and camping, toys and musical instruments are typical of products merchandised in such a manner. The economic implications of these developments were considered in detail in Chapter 3.

COMPARISON AND CONTRAST STUDY OF PUBLIC, PRIVATE (VOLUNTARY AGENCIES), AND COMMERCIAL RECREATION

PHILOSOPHY OF RECREATION

PUBLIC

Enrichment of the life of the total community by providing opportunities for the worthy use of leisure. Nonprofit in nature.

PRIVATE

Enrichment of the life of participating members by offering opportunities for worthy use of leisure, frequently with emphasis on the group and the individual. Nonprofit in nature.

COMMERCIAL

Attempt to satisfy public demands in an effort to produce profit. Dollars from, as well as for, recreation.

OBJECTIVES OF RECREATION

PUBLIC

To provide leisure opportunities which contribute to the social, physical, educational, cultural, and general well-being of the community and its people.

PRIVATE

Similar to public, but limited by membership, race, religion, age, and the like. To provide opportunities for close group association with emphasis on citizenship, behavior, and life philosophy values. To provide activities that appeal to members.

COMMERCIAL

To provide activities or programs which will appeal to customers. To meet competition. To net profit. To serve the public.

ADMINISTRATIVE ORGANIZATION

PUBLIC

Governmental agencies (federal, state, county, and local).

PRIVATE

Boy Scouts, settlements, Girl Scouts, Camp Fire Girls, "Y" organizations, and others.

COMMERCIAL

Corporations, syndicates, partnerships, private ownerships. Examples: motion picture, television, and radio companies, resorts, bowling centers, skating rinks.

FINANCE

PUBLIC

Primarily by taxes. Also by gifts, grants, trust funds, small charges, and fees to defray cost.

PRIVATE

By gifts, grants, endowments, donations, drives, and membership fees.

COMMERCIAL

By the owner or promoters.
By the users: admission and charges.

FACILITIES

PUBLIC

Community buildings, parks (national, state, local), athletic fields, playgrounds, playfields, stadiums, camps, beaches, museums, zoos, golf courses, school facilities, etc.

PRIVATE

Settlement houses, youth centers, churches, play areas, clubs, camps, and others.

COMMERCIAL

Theaters, clubs, taverns, night clubs, lounges, race tracks, bowling lanes, stadiums, and others.

LEADERSHIP

PUBLIC

Professionally prepared to provide extensive recreation programs for large numbers of people.
Frequently subject to Civil Service regulations.
Volunteers as well as professionals.
College training facilities growing.

PRIVATE

Professionally prepared to provide programs on a social group-work basis.
Employed at discretion of managing agency.
Volunteers as well as professionals.

COMMERCIAL

Frequently trained by employing agency.
Employed to secure greatest financial returns.
Employed and retained at the discretion of the employer.
No volunteers.

PROGRAM

PUBLIC

Designed to provide a wide variety of activities, year-round, for all groups, regardless of age, sex, race, creed, social or economic status.

PRIVATE

Designed to provide programs of a specialized nature for groups and in keeping with the aims and objectives of the agency.

COMMERCIAL

Program designed to tap spending power in compliance with state and local laws.

MEMBERSHIP

PUBLIC

Unlimited—open to all.

PRIVATE

Limited by organizational restrictions, such as age, sex, religion, and the like.

COMMERCIAL

Limited by:
Law (local, state, and federal).
Social conception regarding status and strata in some places.
Economics—limited to those who have the price to pay.

COMMERCIAL RECREATION AND COMMUNITY RECREATION

There should be coordination between public, private, and commercial recreation services. In this respect the following suggestions may be helpful:

1. A comprehensive study should be made of commercial recreation resources in the community. This survey should determine the adequacy of existing facilities and unmet needs.

2. Based upon the survey results, plans should be projected to provide commercial recreation services and facilities when and where they are required.

3. The community should adopt a constructive attitude toward commercial recreation. If wholesome and needed, it should be given encouragement and support.

4. Undesirable forms of commercial recreation should be condemned and proper legal and social controls established.

5. Commercial recreation interests should be appropriately represented in community recreation affairs.

6. There may be a need for a commercial recreation council. On it might be a representative from each type of commercial recreation enterprise functioning in the community.

7. In some cases revenue gained from the licensing and taxing of commercial recreation is used to support public recreation activities. Such

measures, however, are not necessarily substitutes for public appropriations from general tax funds.

8. Recreation organizations—public, private, and commercial—need recreation supplies and equipment. Cooperation on matters of purchase could be mutually beneficial.

9. Public and private recreation agencies should keep up with the advances in commercial recreation. The new facilities and equipment, modern styles, and techniques of commercial recreation are often pace setters. The competition of free enterprise stimulates resourcefulness.

10. It must be recognized that commercial recreation caters to all types of people, tastes, and interests. In order to serve these interests, the quality of the programs offered will, of necessity, vary.

11. The place and influence of commercial recreation should be given attention in conferences and workshop programs.

12. Commercial recreation of the right kind presents rich opportunities for families. The family can bowl or attend the theater, movie, ball game, or concert as a unit. Commercial recreation should consider seriously the many possibilities of serving family interests.

13. The organized or informal club can also make the most of commercial recreation opportunities. Visits to historical sites, attendance at professional sports events and at the performing arts are a few possibilities.

COMMERCIAL RECREATION VALUES

There are differences of opinion with respect to the value of commercial recreation. As is true of almost everything else, there are both desirable and undesirable forms of commercial recreation. Some are of the highest type, wholesome and decent, while others are definitely distasteful and degrading. Some reach out to lend opportunity for growth and development to the individual and even economically, to the community. Others contribute almost nothing to the purchaser in the way of personality development. Some kinds of commercial recreation call for vigorous physical action by the participant. Others simply "expose" the individual to something without even suggesting that he "move a muscle."

It may be pertinent, therefore, to examine the arguments frequently made *for* and *against* commercial recreation.

THE CASE FOR COMMERCIAL AMUSEMENT

To be considered on the positive side are (1) stimulation, (2) the provision of recreation facilities, (3) enjoyment, (4) accessibility, and (5) inexpensiveness.

1. *Stimulation.* Commercial recreation can and frequently does stimulate group interest in wholesome recreation. It has had a beneficial influence upon sports of all kinds, including golf, swimming, winter sports, bowling, and baseball. Its favorable influence can also be traced in music, drama, the arts, and travel.

2. *Provision of recreation facilities.* In spite of all the efforts made to provide wholesome recreation by public and private means, there is an ever-increasing demand for commercial recreation. If all three agencies multiplied their efforts, there would still be a shortage of facilities. Further, commercial enterprises can provide facilities that would otherwise be long delayed in cases where the acquisition of a recreation plant depends upon taxation and public approval.

A striking instance of the refinement and advance of commercial recreation facilities is offered by the theater. The average theater now has comfortable seats, padded floors, good ventilation, and freedom from noise and other distracting influences. It uses its lighting system skillfully and generally provides an attractive and refined atmosphere not often equaled in auditoriums outside of the theatrical and motion picture field. The modern bowling center and resort motel are much needed facilities, and they too, are often extremely attractive.

3. *Enjoyment.* Some commercial attractions, catering to a diversity of tastes and providing artistic entertainment of a high order, can lay claim to giving genuine pleasure and satisfaction. No one can question the delight and value that come from a high quality movie, an hour with a fine television program, a string quartet, a well performed play, an outstanding symphony concert, or a well executed play in professional football.

4. *Accessibility.* Amusements provided on a commercial basis are usually conveniently located and available at all times of the year. They supplement in an effective manner other forms of leisure-time activities, many of which are dependent upon the seasons and are often inaccessible to most people. In spite of recent progress in both public and private recreation, many persons are so situated that for their diversion they largely depend upon some form of commercial amusement. Radio and television are a boon to many older folks and to the ill and handicapped. In small, isolated communities, the drive-in theater may be the only community recreation facility available.

5. *Inexpensiveness.* With the ever-increasing demand for recreation and amusement, their price has been consistently brought within reach of the general public. Many forms of recreation and amusement, once enjoyed only by the rich, are now available to everyone.

Large attendance need not be deplored. Baseball, football, and other competitive games have always attracted spectators, and the ability to serve large numbers of people at a single performance has reduced admission prices. Every effort to place the finest recreation facilities within the reach of all people should be encouraged.

THE CASE AGAINST COMMERCIAL AMUSEMENT

Four salient arguments are constantly used to show the negative factors in commercial amusements. The one most commonly used is the argument of "passivity"—the objection that commercial recreation emphasizes the place of the spectator and minimizes the place of the participant.

1. *Passivity.* Certain forms of commercial recreation are, of course, primarily passive in their appeal—the theater, motion pictures, radio, television, and professional athletic events are illustrations. They have a tendency to foster what has been called "spectatoritis."

2. *Substitution.* The second charge is that of "substitution"—the practice of buying something rather than being something. Horse racing, boxing, and wrestling are illustrations. The feeling is expressed that substitution hinders the spontaneous and wholesome use of human capabilities and provides no participation, stimulation, or compensating rewards. Practically every form of commercial recreation was at one time a community activity. Witness the growth of baseball from the sand lots and town centers. Dancing was once an activity reserved largely for feast and festival days. Football and basketball were at one time confined to school grounds and buildings. Each of these has undergone a process of commercialization.

3. *Demoralization.* "Demoralization" is the third accusation—that certain forms of commercial amusement lead to dishonesty, vice, gambling, crime, poverty, and sex delinquency. Dance halls, night clubs, poolrooms, roadhouses, and amusement parks are most often attacked. Too often, it is true, these are associated with individual and social maladjustments.

4. *Exploitation.* The fourth point is "exploitation"—that gate receipts are the only concern of some commercial recreation leaders and that the emotions of children and adults are exploited for financial gain. It is held that there is no limit to what operators will do in playing upon the desires of people so long as box office receipts are high. The result may be sordid and debased forms of attractions, which only serve to accentuate pathological problems and to lower moral standards.

MEETING THE PROBLEM

There are, then, both advantages and disadvantages in commercial recreation. Larger numbers in attendance, wider varieties of entertainment and amusements, increased facilities, and greater sums paid in admissions are all part of the picture. This growth is neither an indictment of the worth of commercial recreation nor an excuse for its weaknesses. When people accept commercial amusement with good judgment, its ills will be minimized. Until this occurs, there is need for control. Commercial amusements cannot be left to themselves for automatic adjustment to community needs and desires. A *laissez-faire* attitude is not enough. Commercial amusements must be regulated in the best interests of the public. There are a number of ways to exercise such control:

1. *By legislation, regulation, police control, license, and supervision.* Perhaps the least desired, but the most effective way of control is the enactment of legislation to regulate commercial recreation by state, county, and municipal governments. This is least desired, because it functions through police power rather than through enlightened public opinion. Laws tend to say "do not" and "cannot" rather than "do." Yet they are most effective where there is immediate need for control. To a certain extent, legal control is essential. Regulation through legislation tends to discourage exploitation, expedite higher standards of operation, and provide by law what otherwise might be accomplished more slowly by public opinion in safeguarding the public. There must be some legal restraint, some standard for licensing, and some plan of general supervision and guidance. Regulation and control are not to be confused with crusading reform and censorship.

There is another phase of legal control—its application to physical conditions such as fire risks, ventilation, sanitation, and general safety. Unsanitary and unsafe places cannot be tolerated. This development has come largely from public demand for a system of licensing and inspection. No commercial amusement should be allowed to operate without a license. Inspections and investigations are necessary, and if management cooperates at every point, its own best interests are served.

2. *By interest of civic groups.* Control may be exercised through public opinion. No amusement or institution which violates the standards of propriety held by the majority of the people can prosper long. The public has the power to decide whether a given picture is to be a "flop" or a box-office success; it is the final arbiter in determining standards of production. More important than the mere expression of approval or disapproval, however influential that may be at the box office, is the need for constructive cooperation. It is much easier to call attention to the evils than to arouse public interest in the worthwhile advantages of the movies; yet the latter must be done and the best pictures supported, in order to raise production standards. Public opinion, to be effective, must be organized, articulate, and positive.

3. *By trade control.* Considerable control may be automatic so far as the community is concerned. That is, it may be a control exercised within the trade. There is a strong conviction that clean, wholesome amusement

is ultimately the best business asset. The trades, therefore, have undertaken to set standards and bring pressure to secure conformity to these standards.

4. *By censorship.* There are two aspects of control. One encourages the production of higher forms of amusements; another seeks to prevent certain activities unless they come within a prescribed standard. The second object may be accomplished through censorship. The whole subject of censorship is admittedly a matter of taste, opinion, and judgment.

5. *By actual elimination.* Every city has its vigilance committees, anti-vice societies, purity leagues, or protective associations promoted by those who serve as a sort of voice for morals and decency. Quite often these organizations demand that certain types of amusements be legislated out of existence. Not infrequently, such groups encounter resistance even from the public, which may regard members as "do-gooders."

THE OVERVIEW

The impact of commercial recreation cannot be denied as an absorber of leisure, a means of shaping our culture, of influencing behavior and moral patterns, and as an economic and social force.

In one sense the role of commercial amusement is perhaps less important today than in the past. The increasing number of municipal parks, playgrounds, athletic fields, golf courses, and tennis courts, the efforts of the more progressive school systems, private agencies, and churches to provide facilities and leadership for recreation, tend to keep commercial interests from dominating the field.

But despite the advance of recreation under the sponsorship of non-profit agencies and organizations, commercial recreation is likely to expand in a society whose members have both the time and money to purchase the endless number of recreation commodities, services, and experiences which ingenious businessmen can offer. Even at the risk of acquiring the "self-indulgence" label, we can expect more, not less, buying in the future, if for no other reason than that there will be more consumers. The real challenge will be to ward off an avalanche of recreation-for-profit services which might too easily set their sights on "how much" rather than "how worthwhile."

Constant vigilance will be required to establish and maintain high standards in commercial recreation. This can be accomplished, in part, by setting in motion a number of the suggestions made in this chapter. But to a large degree, the success of these standards will be decided by the desires and capacities of the consumers. If the public knows the value of full, recreative living, if it has the appreciations, interests, and needs, and if it places a high premium upon commercial recreation of a high quality, the high standards will emerge and remain.

THE WORKSHOP

1. Make an inventory of commercial recreation within the local community.
2. Study the problem of public tastes in special forms of commercial recreation and attempt to discover the reasons for choices.
3. Study the trade practices of a commercial recreation industry of your own choosing to learn what steps are taken to sustain high standards.
4. Review the controls, legislative and otherwise, for the regulation of commercial recreation in your community.
5. Interview several family heads to determine how much they spend on commercial recreation.
6. Suggest ways of coordinating commercial recreation with the local community recreation program.
7. Criticize censorship as a means of regulating commercial recreation.
8. Establish a code of operation for a commercial recreation council.
9. Suggest ways in which a community recreation system might use radio and television for the mutual benefit of each.
10. Interview the proprietor of a commercial recreation establishment and list the kinds of problems he encounters.

REFERENCES

Current

Brightbill, Charles K., and Harold D. Meyer, *Recreation: Text and Readings.* Englewood Cliffs, New Jersey: Prentice-Hall, Inc., 1953.

Charlesworth, J. C., ed., *Leisure in America—Blessing or Curse?* Philadelphia: American Academy of Political and Social Science, 1964.

Danford, H. G., *Creative Leadership in Recreation.* New Jersey: Allyn and Company, 1964.

de Grazia, Sebastian, *Of Time, Work, and Leisure.* New York: Twentieth Century Fund, 1962.

Dulles, Foster Rhea, *A History of Recreation—America Learns to Play.* New York: Meredith Publishing Company, 1965.

Galbraith, John Kenneth, *The Affluent Society.* Boston: Houghton Mifflin Company, 1958.

Kaiser Aluminum News, *The Theory of the Leisure Masses,* No. 5. Oakland, Calif.: Kaiser Aluminum and Chemical Corporation, 1966.

Kaplan, Max, *Leisure in America.* New York: John Wiley & Sons, Inc., 1960.

Kleemier, R. W., ed., *Aging and Leisure.* New York: Oxford University Press, Inc., 1961.

Larrabee, Eric, and Rolf Meyersohn, *Mass Leisure*. Glencoe, Illinois: Free Press, 1958.

Menke, Frank G., *The Encyclopedia of Sports*. New York: A. S. Barnes & Company, 1960.

Michael, Donald N., *Cybernation—The Silent Conquest*. Santa Barbara, California: Center for the Study of Democratic Institutes, 1962.

Neumeyer, M. H., and E. S. Neumeyer. *Leisure and Recreation,* 3rd Edition. New York: A. S. Barnes & Company, 1958.

Securities Research Division, *Leisure: Investment Opportunities in a $150–Billion Market,* New York: Merrill, Lynch, Pierce, Fenner & Smith, Inc., 1968.

Smigel, E. O., ed., *Work and Leisure: A Contemporary Social Problem*. New Haven: College and University Press, 1963.

Comment

Information on Commercial Recreation is available through publications of the United States Department of Commerce and through the magazines and trade papers of the entertainment, amusement, sports, radio, television, and travel industries.

Practically every recreation activity depends on facilities and supplies. To meet the demands there is an enormous range of commercial enterprises at work. It is well to keep-up with manufactories—wholesale and retail dealers through catalogues and sale-promotional practices. Get on the mailing list of the best in the field along all activity lines.

It is stressed that delegates to conferences and conventions give careful study to exhibits, meet the exhibitors, and get to know their products. In this way we stay abreast of the changes taking place, the latest and best in facilities and supplies as they are demonstrated through information, techniques, and practices tested by experience.

17

Organized Camping
and Outdoor Education

Organized camping and outdoor education have a bright future. The more urbanized we become, the more highly prized outdoor living will be. Trends point toward increasing use of natural resources for camping and other outdoor recreation. The reports of the Outdoor Recreation Resources Review Commission stress this. Family camping is growing in popularity, and day camping increases every year. The outdoor education and school camping movement continues to assume larger proportions. Churches, industries, private groups, and clubs are interested in enlarging their camp programs. Youth serving agencies are continually adding more camping and camp facilities. Camping as a factor in the rehabilitation of the ill and handicapped is growing in volume, reception, and results.

Comments in this chapter are confined to organized camping and related outdoor education activities. One national camping expert looks upon organized camping as "the outdoor merging of recreation and education." This definition includes the fundamentals (recreation, education, out-of-doors) that make up camping. But certain secondary characteristics should be added to further identify the activity as organized camping: the presence of qualified leaders, two or more participants forming a group, a primitive or natural site, and an extended period for the experience.

The beliefs forming the core of this view are: (1) Familiarity with, and

297

knowledge of, the natural environment is the birthright of every child. (2) An understanding of social relationships, as developed through close and continuous contact with cabinmates, is essential to growth. (3) Ability to recognize causal relationships, as exemplified in the responsibility assumed for freedom of choice and self-determination, is a part of the maturation process. (4) Skills in caring for one's self and others, learned quickly and thoroughly with friendly counselors, are highly desirable. (5) Proper attitudes concerning authority and responsibility in a democratic society are a "must" for future citizens.[1]

Another authority, Frank L. Irwin, defines organized camping as: "an educational enterprise, located in an out-of-doors environment, which provides children with the opportunity to (a) live, work, and play in a group situation, (b) obtain experience and insight into many of the basic processes of life, and (c) receive guidance from a mature counselor, who observes and influences the camper twenty-four hours per day over an extended period of time." [2]

It is difficult to provide accurate camp statistics, as the scene is constantly changing. Conservatively speaking, there are over 13,000 organized camps in the United States serving some five million children annually. Approximately one-half of these camps are resident camps. When you add the millions who trip, camp, use the national and state park camping facilities and attend informal camps, the number of campers involved becomes gigantic.

Organized camping has a large variety of sponsors: municipalities, counties, states, and the federal government; commercial enterprises; philanthropic and voluntary youth-serving agencies; schools, churches, and other religious organizations; 4-H and kindred agricultural groups; family and children's service organizations; civic, fraternal, and patriotic organizations; management and labor groups; and private corporations, associations, and individuals. Some camps are operated for profit; others are not. Some facilities are used only during the summer; others are used the year round. Certain organized camps serve only boys or men; others, girls or women. The majority of camps are for the healthy, but there are many for the ill and handicapped. Some camps are open to entire families; some are mobile, the campers being on the move almost constantly in caravan fashion. The variety of camps is almost endless.

Camps are classified in various ways. Four classifications are presented, showing camps primarily for children and youth.

1 Gerald P. Burns, *Program of the Modern Camp* (Englewood Cliffs, N.J.: Prentice-Hall, Inc., 1954), p. 23.

2 Frank L. Irwin, *The Theory of Camping* (New York: A. S. Barnes & Co., 1950), p. 1.

Gerald P. Burns lists:

Agency camps—sponsored by such nonprofit organizations as the Boy Scouts, Girl Scouts, YMCA, YWCA, Salvation Army, 4-H, Camp Fire Girls, and Societies for Crippled Children.

Private camps—sponsored by individuals or corporations and operated as a business enterprise.

Church camps—sponsored by religious organizations and usually operated as a nonprofit enterprise.

Public camps—sponsored by local departments of recreation, park departments and districts, boards of education.

County recreation, park, and education departments and districts.

Regional and metropolitan park, conservation, and recreation systems.

State park, conservation, health, and highway departments.

Federal (national) parks and forest services.[3]

Reuel A. Benson and Jacob A. Goldberg use this grouping:

(1) organization camps, (2) private camps, and (3) public camps. Within each one of these categories a still further classification may be made.

Organization camps are those operated by nonprofit private organizations such as churches, Boy Scouts of America, Girl Scouts of America, settlement houses, Boys' Clubs of America, Y.M.C.A., Y.W.C.A., and other social agencies.

Private camps are those owned and operated by individuals or groups who have as one of their major objectives that of making a profit. It is for this reason that they are often referred to as commercial camps. Some persons are prone to criticize private camp owners for making a profit from youth, yet many of the programs conducted by these camps are richer and more challenging than those of organization camps. Fundamentally, there is little difference between the organization camps and private camps, except perhaps in certain plans followed and charges made.

Public camps are those operated by tax-supported agencies. These include the following: (1) school camps, (2) municipal camps, (3) camps operated by state parks, and (4) camps operated by the Department of Agriculture extension division (4-H camps).[4]

These authors offer a breakdown of the type according to organization and administration:

Trip Camping. As the name implies, this type of camping has as its main objective the covering of a certain distance or reaching a specific place. Illustrations of this type of camping are canoe trips, motor camp trips, long hiking trips, and youth hostel trips. Both the Boy Scouts and Girl Scouts have long programmed trip camping as a preferred outdoor education activity.

3 Burns, *op. cit.*
4 R. A. Benson and J. A. Goldberg, *The Camp Counselor* (New York: McGraw-Hill Book Company, 1956).

Day Camping. This is different from the residence camp. In this type of camping the youngsters are taken out daily to a selected site where the program is carried on, and then they are returned to their homes, usually by suppertime. The Girl Scouts are credited with introducing this type of camping in 1922. It is now very popular in public recreation programming, accommodating some 1,000,000 children annually and is no longer considered a summer activity only.

Short-term Residence Camps. These are camps that accept campers for one-, two-, or three-week periods. Most of the organization camps are short-term camps. The primary reason for the plan followed by these camps is to accommodate as many children as possible during the course of the camp season. Such camps usually operate for at least two months.

Long-term Residence Camps. The long-term camps are those in which the campers remain for at least one month. Most private camps accommodate children for an eight-week period.

Coeducational Camps. Most camps segregate the boys from the girls. Educationally, this is wrong, but the problems posed by co-ed camping cause many to shy away from it. Furthermore, there is a reluctance on the part of many parents to permit their daughters to go to co-ed camps. Churches have advanced this type of camping more than any other group.

Family Camps. These camps are largely sponsored by public agencies and some of the nonprofit organizations. This form of camping helps to strengthen family ties. For a long time the Salvation Army has been notable for its family camps.

Finally, camps may be classified by function or program emphasis. For example, many camps have a *special-interest* appeal such as a baseball or music camp. Other camps stress the *varied-program* approach trying to expose the child to a variety of experiences and activities. Then there are the *special-purpose* camps with programs designed to serve youth who have unusual problems or needs. These are growing in number and have much support among medical and social work personnel.

CAMP VALUES

Properly conceived, camping combines the best in education and recreation. Campers have opportunities to build healthier bodies and minds. This implies, of course, the best of conditions in location, equipment, activities, and leadership. The organized camp operated on high standards is conducive to regular habits of personal hygiene and to rest, relaxation, and exercise.

Equally important is what camping can do to stabilize the emotions of those who participate in it. This aspect of camping is well expressed in *The Place of the Organized Camp in the Field of Education,* published by the American Camping Association:

Camp affords admirable conditions for the diagnosis and correction of emotional difficulties. Here the child is temporarily separated from the subjective influence of the home and therefore, among new personalities and under new influences, has an opportunity to develop a greater independence and self-reliance. Here, a child need not and cannot rely upon the indulgence of home. He is stripped for a time of dependence on the wealth of his parents and lives a thoroughly democratic life in an environment where all are on an even social level. His innermost nature functions because he is in the environment in which he is happiest and in which he expresses himself most naturally, without undesirable inhibitions and repressions, or equally undesirable stimulations. The camp observes and influences him throughout the twenty-four hours of the day and faces no requirements except the welfare of the camper. Unlike the church and the schools, it is free from dogmatic traditions and the requirements of both catechism and curriculum. The camp which would most completely fulfill its educational possibilities must carefully avoid duplicating the academic functions of the school or the formal, dogmatic procedures of the church. Here the child can best acquire the fundamental, basic intellectual attitudes and spiritual consciousness upon which the school and church can build.

Perhaps the greatest contribution of camping is the opportunity it gives the camper to grow, learn, and live as close to nature as is possible in modern society. In camp, a youngster comes face to face with the wind, the rain, and the stars. Here he finds adventure. He discovers the value of skillful hands and a stout heart, and comes to know birds, animals, and plants in all their glory. Living outdoors in a semi-primitive environment teaches him resourcefulness and cooperation through self-reliance, for the camper must match wits with nature itself.

The educational values of camping are only beginning to be realized. It is important that people, particularly children and youths, understand and appreciate the fundamental laws of nature.

Organized camping has much to contribute to the well-being of Americans. Better health, emotional stability, skills, sociability, spiritual growth, citizenship, character growth, and democratic living are among its important assets.

CAMP LEADERSHIP

The success of the camp program, as is the case with all forms of organized recreation, depends upon the quality of its leadership. More than two hundred thousand leaders are required to staff the camps in the United States. They range in experience and background from the high school student serving his first term as a junior counselor to seasoned, professional camp administrators. Most frequently they are drawn from the ranks of college students or school teachers, and from persons in public and private recreation agencies who have professional recreation responsibilities during the noncamp seasons. Among positions and jobs found in many camps are the following:

Camp director	Physician	Counselors (senior and junior)
Assistant camp director	Nurse	Cooks and kitchen help
Director (program and unit)	Dietician	Maintenance personnel
Camp secretary	Librarian	Hostess

CAMP FACILITIES

The type of facilities needed for a camp program depends largely upon the mission or function of the camp. Program emphasis and camp philosophy should dictate the number and character of the facilities desired. In general, however, the general principles governing location, design, and operation of recreation areas and facilities apply equally to camp properties.

The selection of a camp site must take into consideration many problems. Among these are:

Adequate and safe water supply
Safe sewage disposal
Topography and vegetative cover
General environmental health conditions
Food supply sources
Accessibility and transportation facilities
Climatic conditions
Natural resources for camp activities
Adequate fire protection

THE PROGRAM

The camp program is the heart of the camping experience and requires careful planning, execution and evaluation. It is an extension of the camp's philosophy and is conditioned by the leadership, facilities, clientele, organizational and administrative structure available. The sponsoring agency usually develops the overall program for the camping season but the actual day-to-day planning of the program should involve the total camp staff and campers. The successful camp is the one in which individual needs are considered and the activities adapted to the dynamics of the camping situation. There should be no set program except to provide opportunities for the campers to lead and be led, plan and participate, receive privileges, and assume responsibilities and duties.

There should be guidance, stimulation, and supervision. There should be a minimum of regulation and no regimentation. There should be opportunity for organized and unorganized recreation, for passive and active recreation. But whatever the recreation, the nature element should be at the core.

The program of the modern, progressive camp is aimed at improving the quality of the campers' experience in addition to providing a healthful and enjoyable camp existence. Above all, programs must be based solidly upon camper interest. Interests, once identified, help integrate and guide activities. Interests must be discovered, modified, and integrated if camping programs are to be rich and productive.

DAY CAMPS

Day camping has expanded rapidly. Communities are turning increasingly to day-camp programs. Perhaps the trend is an outgrowth of the need for more closely supervised play near home in urban areas. Day camps cannot substitute for extended overnight camping opportunities or for community recreation facilities in general, but they offer a welcome change from the usual routine for the child who does not have access to overnight camping. Properly organized and operated, day camps can contribute richly to the health of children, satisfy their appetites for adventure in nature, and enrich their educational experience.

According to the American Camping Association's Committee on Day Camps, day camping offers the following advantages:

It is primarily concerned with outdoor living.

It leads to an understanding and appreciation of the out-of-doors.

It is a happy, free, adventurous experience.

It helps the individual child become a well-adjusted member of the group.

It offers opportunity for camper participation in planning and evaluating the day-camp program.

It develops skills, resourcefulness, and interest that will have a lifetime value to the camper.

It is a safe and healthful experience that contributes to physical and mental well-being.

The Camp Committee

Once it is decided to conduct a day camp, a planning and operating committee should be formed. The committee will be responsible for (1) determining the size of the camp and securing a location; (2) making a budget and securing funds; (3) deciding camp policy, administration, and program; (4) recruiting paid and volunteer leadership; and (5) evaluating results. Most of these tasks may be assigned to one or two members of the committee, who will visit the camp from time to time.

The Camp Site

A wooded area with ample open play space makes the best camp site. It should be easily accessible by public conveyance, and if possible should be within walking distance of residential areas. Safe facilities for swimming are always an asset. Other factors to be considered are good drinking water, shelter in case of bad weather, facilities for cooking, latrines, and good health conditions generally.

Many day camps are located in parks, on private estates and farm lands, and in sections of established camps not otherwise in use. When no better arrangements can be made, day camps can be conducted on playgrounds and vacant lots.

Expenditures and Revenue

The principal expenditures for the operation of a day camp are the salaries of the director and his staff and transportation costs. When public or private youth-serving agencies sponsor the camp, they may bear all or part of the expense. Campers are sometimes charged fees to pay for milk, transportation, and incidentals such as handcraft supplies. When funds are not available from established agencies, communities frequently secure special municipal appropriations or raise money by public subscription and by grants from trust funds.

The Staff

Camp leadership is drawn from the ranks of trained recreation leaders, teachers, and high school and college students. Mothers with special skills and older children are useful as volunteer workers. A good camp director will set the pace and quality of the work of the staff. Camps with an enrollment of more than 75 generally require an assistant director.

Under the leadership of a counselor, campers are grouped into units of 12 to 20, according to age and interests. Specialized activities, such as nature lore, athletics, dramatics, and crafts, are supervised by program counselors. Every camp should have a registered nurse or an experienced first-aid worker. The entire staff, however, is responsible for the health and safety of the campers and should watch for cases of exposure and over-exertion.

Promotion

The camp committee should tell the public about the camp and its program through newspapers, radio, and bulletin boards in schools, churches, and community centers. Flyers may be distributed giving information about the program, facilities, transportation, and food, and about the kind of clothing and equipment campers will need. Information about where to register children should be on the flyer as well as in other announcements.

Registration

Early registration is necessary for proper planning. A final date, in advance of camp opening, should be set for the return of all forms. A health certificate signed by a physician should be requested of each applicant, signifying whether there are limitations on the child's activities.

Camp Season and Program Content

Most day camps operate five or six days a week for an eight-week season. At the end of this period, a week is often set aside for overnight trips, arranged on a rotating basis. To accommodate all children requiring day-camp service, it is often necessary to divide the season into four periods of two weeks each. If registration permits, children attend more than one two-week session.

Camping hours range from six to eight a day. The time is extended occasionally to permit special twilight programs, such as a council ring ceremony, a dramatic performance, or a group sing. The program should seek to involve the campers in nature activities as well as expose them to both individual and group sports, music, craft, and drama. The factors which condition the camp program in general also apply to day camping.

Equipment

Camp equipment should be adequate for health, safety, and program needs. Some camps operate on park sites which afford adequate shelter; others erect canvas tents or improvised shelters of twigs and branches. Occasional overnight trips require sleeping provisions, such as cots, blankets, and ponchos.

Equipment for eating and cooking varies. Some camps provide milk and require campers to bring their own lunches. Others ask campers to bring provisions to be cooked at camp. Other camps supply all food and charge a weekly fee.

Other equipment commonly needed at day camps includes first-aid kits, water-front equipment, games and sports equipment, craft tools, and the like.

Safety

Every precaution should be taken to assure the safety of children while they are at camp. Capable and alert leadership is the best protection. There should be close supervision, especially during swimming periods. Apparatus should be inspected periodically, and the camp site checked for poison ivy and other hazards. Adequate first-aid supplies should be on hand.

OUTDOOR EDUCATION AND SCHOOL CAMPING

Schools are awakening to the multiple educational advantages in outdoor education—the process of teaching by direct contact and experience with native materials and life situations. This process has led to the school camp movement. Under the direction of the Division of Physical Education in the Department of Public Instruction of the State of Michigan, and through grants from the W. K. Kellogg Foundation of that state, much experimentation, direction, and guidance have been accomplished. Over six hundred school systems in the United States had conducted at least a one-week program in a camp setting by 1960. Today, the number approaches one thousand.

The organizational patterns of school programs in the camp setting vary from region to region and state to state. They range from programs operated by single independent school districts to programs where the camp property is owned jointly by two or more districts and the program administered jointly. State laws, educational philosophies and school administrative structures appear to be the major conditioning factors at the present. Even so, a general trend in operational patterns is reported.[5] The four most discernible types are:

1. A year-round operation of one or more school districts that have access to a camp facility for continuous use, choose specific grades or groups for the camping experience and employ a core staff to assist the classroom teachers involved in the program.
2. A part-time operation which has the school district renting the facility as

5 Julian Smith, Reynold Carlson and others, *Outdoor Education.* Englewood Cliffs, N.J.: Prentice-Hall, Inc., 1965, pp. 105–110.

needed, selecting classes or groups for the outdoor education experience, and relying upon the regular classroom teacher and resource personnel to give the program its leadership.

3. The operation which has the school board relying upon another agency, such as a college or public recreation department, to provide the facility, to assist in the selection of campus, and provide for certain managerial service while using the classroom teachers as staff members.

4. The school system which operated the outdoor educational program during the summer months only. The school may or may not own the facilities, administer the camp or furnish the entire staff. It does, however, develop the program and uses members of its staff to provide the basic leadership.

Lloyd B. Sharp, who has been closely associated with the camping and outdoor education movement for many years, offers the following suggestions to school systems contemplating the establishment of a program of camping and outdoor education:

Outdoor Education

1. Beginning just outside the classroom, every effort should be made to use the immediate environment well before moving out in wider circles. Outdoor education should grow out of the actual course of study and teaching materials of the classroom, and should simply take itself out into the world as far as experience dictates and facilities permit.

2. The aims of outdoor and camping education cannot be realized by a piecemeal procedure of conducting incidental trips now and then, depending upon the initiative and the sudden notion of a teacher. Rather, this type of education is basic at all levels, necessitating serious curriculum studies based upon the outdoor education thesis.

3. Much outdoor education can be carried on without any additional cost. For teachers to take classes outside the classroom for direct experience study requires only the adoption of a policy by the board of education and some initiative and resourcefulness on the part of the teachers. It can begin at once in all schools.

4. Assuming sanction by the board of education, the introduction and development of this movement are chiefly the responsibility of the school administrator and the teaching staff.

5. Trips, excursions, and expeditions are an essential part of outdoor education. It is important, however, that thorough preparation be made in advance through reading, discussion, and organization for such trips and that there be adequate follow-up through discussion of what was experienced.

6. All plans for new school buildings and grounds should be considered in the light of the possible requirements of outdoor and camping education. Specifically affected are: the amount of space provided within the building (it may be less than formerly); the size of the "campus" or free land area around the buildings; and provision for ownership of land at some distance from town for school camps.

7. Experience shows that the public in time will support any reasonable

change in school procedure which gives assurance of better education for youth. But it is the duty of those who are engaged in education professionally to provide the vision and the trained leadership.

8. Little will be gained by merely getting youngsters out of doors. Outdoor education, the same as any other kind, depends for success upon skillful and intelligent leadership. In far too many cases this leadership is not adequately prepared in existing courses. Therefore, teachers and prospective teachers should be encouraged to obtain special preparation in order to handle the problems that will arise in this expanding field.

School Camping

1. The school camp should be an integral part of the total school plant—as much a part of it as the library, the shop, the laboratories, the auditorium, the playing field, or the gymnasium. The camp should be in operation on a year-round basis. Attendance in camps should count for school attendance and credit.

2. The camp should be owned by the board of education and operated by the superintendent and the teaching staff.

3. The operation of the camp should be financed by school funds, just as any other phase of education is financed. In many instances, however, the initial steps have been made by civic groups cooperating with boards of education.

4. Those who are to operate school camps should have special preparation to do so.

5. In many situations, the school camp should be planned to serve the community as a whole. This is in line with the use of school buildings as community centers.

6. In selecting a camp site, the following things are important:
   (a) A large enough tract of land to provide a real camping experience for the youngsters and to provide for future expansion
   (b) Location well away from the city limits
   (c) Distinctive features of natural beauty—woods, fields, streams, hills or mountains, and some tillable land

7. In selecting and laying out a camp site, it is essential that advice be secured from experts in the field of school camping.

8. Standardization of camp structures should be avoided. All construction should be dictated by local considerations and should fit into the landscape and topography.

9. In planning the program for the school camp, the active participation of teachers and students alike should be encouraged. The very essence of outdoor learning involves group participation in the arrangements for living—including clothing requirements, the making of menus, marketing, cooking, the sharing of work—activities at the waterfront, meeting weather conditions, building shelters, gardening, and trips and exploration.

10. Experience has shown that individual personality growth and development are attained best in small groups of seven to ten students living with adult counselors in their own "small camp." The "small camp" should be, in so far as possible, a self-sustaining group, following its own program, with every member of the group taking part in the planning.

11. The "small camps" should be located at a distance from the service area or "camp village," where the group can establish and maintain itself.

12. Campers should have as large a part as possible in designing, constructing, and maintaining the "small camp" in which they live.

13. Shelters for summer season camping should be in simple construction, preferably designed and built by campers under capable staff guidance. Wherever possible, native materials should be used, thus giving opportunity to practice conservation of the native growth. However, it is essential that the shelters be of such quality as to meet all requirements of safety, weather, and health. This calls for the use of canvas or similar material for the roof.

14. The temporary nature of the "small camps" makes it possible to move them from time to time as experience and the desires of the youngsters may require.

15. The school camp should be established and maintained on a philosophy which realizes the twofold opportunity that camp alone has of bringing about growth in youth through group living and through putting them into close touch with their natural surroundings.

16. The school camping program must not be stereotyped; it should emerge naturally out of the local school situation and should be adapted to meet the needs of youth at a particular time and place.

With the continued growth of outdoor recreation and the national emphasis now given to conservation and natural resource development and management, outdoor education will become even more popular and important. Public parks and recreation departments, state and federal agencies will be asked by their constituents to join with the school boards to make outdoor education a vital phase in the education of every school child. Likewise, school officials will be reminded by the public of their responsibility to work with the other agencies interested in recreation and conservation so that education for leisure, for outdoor living, is more than a classroom exercise. It should be the mission of all those concerned with the optimum development of youth and the proper use of our great national resources.

THE WORKSHOP

1. Learn what state and federal agencies are available to offer services to your community in the development and implementation of its outdoor education program.
2. Interview both adults and children who have had experience at camp and learn which camping activities most appeal to them.
3. Discover what your state provides in the way of facilities and services for camps.
4. Compare the services and charges of profit and nonprofit camps.

5. Consult medical and sanitary authorities for their opinions on health and sanitation standards for camps.
6. Plan a training program for day camp volunteers.
7. Visit a school camp and report on it.
8. List the factors to be taken into consideration in selecting a site for a day camp.
9. Prepare a prospectus on the need for the establishment of a publicly sponsored family camp.
10. Discuss and debate the goals of school camping.

REFERENCES

American Camping Association, *Camper Guidance.* Indiana: Bradford Woods, Martinsdale, 1961.

American Camping Association, *Resident Camps for Children—Present Status and Future Needs.* Indiana: Bradford Woods, Martinsdale, 1960.

Carlson, Reynold E., Theodore R. Deppe, and Janet R. MacLean, *Recreation in American Life.* Belmont, California: Wadsworth Publishing Company, 1963.

Doty, Richard S., *The Character Dimension of Camping.* New York: Association Press, 1960.

Freeberg, William H., and Loren E. Taylor, *Philosophy of Outdoor Education.* Minneapolis: Burgess Publishing Co., 1961.

Mitchell, A. Viola, and Ida B. Crawford, *Camp Counseling.* Philadelphia: W. B. Saunders Co., 1961.

Reiman, Lewis C., *The Successful Camp.* Ann Arbor: University of Michigan Press, 1958.

Smith, Julian, Reynold Carlson and others. *Outdoor Education.* Englewood Cliffs, N.J.: Prentice-Hall, Inc., 1965.

Soloman, Julian H., *Campsite Development.* New York: Girl Scouts of the United States of America, 1960.

Van der Smissen, Betty, *The Church Camp Program.* Newton, Kansas: Faith and Life Press, 1961.

Webb, Kenneth B., ed., *Light from a Thousand Campfires.* New York: Association Press, 1961.

Comment

Information on all phases of camping can be secured from the American Camping Association. Particularly important among its publications are THE CAMPING MAGAZINE, published monthly, November through June; such pamphlets as "The Place of the Organized Camp in the Field of Education," "Leadership for Camping NOW—and in the Post-War World," "Is Your Camp

Protected Against Accidents?," "Annotated Bibliography on Camping"; and "The Camping Index Plan," a simple, inexpensive type of portable file.

Both the State Department of Natural Resources of California and the Department of Public Instruction of Michigan have developed materials on importance of, and need for, outdoor education. These are available as are materials on conservation education and natural resource development. The Bureau of Outdoor Recreation, Washington, and the U.S. Department of Health, Education, and Welfare are also excellent sources for publications in this area of study.

V

Recreation for
Special Groups

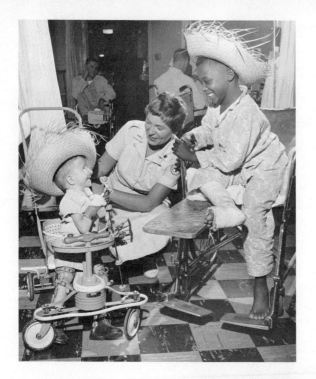

Left: Zest for living. Below: Athletics on wheels.

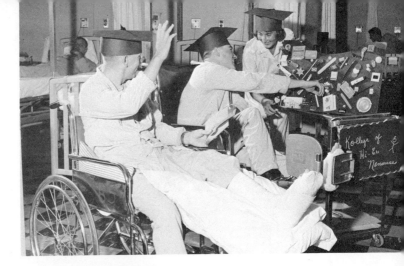

Above: "Light touch" road to recovery. Left: Adding *life* to *years*. Below: Vermont country dance festival.

18

Therapeutic Recreation : The Ill and Disabled

THE SETTING

There will be more ill and disabled people in the future than there are at present. This is so because the total population is increasing and because medical science is increasing the life span. Moreover, those who heretofore would have died because of illness or injury are now sustained with the help of medical science.

It is estimated that there are now about 30 million men, women, and children in the United States suffering from some form of incapacitating or chronic disease and disability, much more than half of these with mental illness. Many of the physically and mentally ill are children and youth. They can be found in the nation's 7000 hospitals, but as many as two million are living in the communities.

Much study and attention are being given to the role and function of recreation in (1) helping to promote sound health and prevent ill health, both physical and mental, (2) helping people regain their health and overcome their disabilities, and (3) helping in the rehabilitation of persons who have experienced illness or disability. These efforts of the medical, recreation, and allied professions are observable in a variety of settings. They can be found in camps established to care for the needs of those with asthma and allergies, cardio-vascular disease, diabetes, emotional disturbances, epilepsy, lowered vitality, orthopedic handicaps, social maladjustment, speech or hearing defects, visual difficulties, and countless other physical problems, in schools for the retarded and nursing homes for the aged and chronically ill. They are in operation in rehabilitation centers and clinics of all kinds, in establishments for alcoholics and drug addicts, in psychiatric, general medical and surgical, tuberculosis, and other kinds of hospitals and clinics with facilities for long term and short term cases. They are reflected in the programs of agencies which provide recreation services for people who, although not in institutions, are "shut in" their homes a greater part of their lives. The counseling which doctors give to their patients includes advice to get more recreation.

Importance of Recreation for the Ill and Disabled

Nowhere is the importance of the role of recreation in the lives of the ill and handicapped more dramatically illustrated than in the environment of the hospital and rehabilitation center. Nowhere have the methods and the work progressed more solidly and more rapidly. The place of recreation in ministering to the ill—both as a social force in daily living and as a scientific factor in therapy—is gaining a solid foundation.

That recreation has a significant role to play in relation to the ill and the handicapped is affirmed by medical authorities:

Dr. Howard A. Rusk, Director, Institute of Physical Medicine and Rehabilitation, New York: "I firmly believe that both individual and group recreation for hospital patients have a direct relationship upon their recovery—these, in my opinion are definitely adjunctive therapy." [1]

Dr. Alexander Reid Martin, Former Chairman, Committee on Leisure Time and its Uses, American Psychiatric Association: "We cannot relegate recreation to a position of secondary importance in the lives of individuals, and in hospitals we cannot relegate recreation to a position of secondary importance." [2]

Dr. Joseph B. Wolfe, Medical Director, Valley Forge Heart and Medical Center: "A survey of 1000 patients has shown that carefully selected recreation to suit the patient's problem and personality resulted in reduction both in drug requirements as well as length of hospital stay, when compared to the control group in the institution without the program." [3]

Dr. Paul Haun, Director of Psychiatric Education, New Jersey State Department of Institutions and Agencies: "Contemporary medicine is coming to think less about the disease and more about people with disease. The strength of the recreation movement is that it thinks about people, and in so doing goes beyond the limitations of medicine." [4]

[1] *Basic Concepts of Hospital Recreation* (Washington, D. C.: American Recreation Society, 1953), p. 7.
[2] *The Doctors and Recreation in the Hospital Setting* (Raleigh: North Carolina Recreation Commission, 1962), p. 7.
[3] Wolfe, *ibid.*, p. 19.
[4] Paul Haun, *Recreation: A Medical Viewpoint* (New York: Teachers College, Columbia University, 1965), p. 54.

The relationship of recreation to medicine and rehabilitation is also stressed in the findings of the late Prof. Charles K. Brightbill of the University of Illinois, who made the following observations after studying recreation in selected hospitals and rehabilitation centers in the United States and Europe.[5]

1. It is primarily the free, informal, nonauthoritative and seemingly aimless nature of recreation which makes it medically useful. In play, adults, as well as children, are more truly their natural selves. Moreover, under carefully planned approaches and conditions, particularly with children lacking motor coordination, there are correlations between recreational experiences and physical and emotional performance. Play is also effective in neutralizing the conflicts of the neurotic child. With mentally ill patients of all ages, recreation is being used effectively during diagnosis as well as in treatment and rehabilitation. Certain forms of recreation, at times, for given kinds of mentally ill persons with ego strength, can help externalize disturbing aggressions and help drain off other undesirable impulses. Recreation is playing an increasingly important role in the controlled environment of the mentally ill. There are medical experts (with research to support *some* of their views) who are of the opinion that recreation, particularly the noncompetitive physical phases, can help reduce medication, nursing requirements, length-of-stay in hospital, hypostatic congestion, morbidity and perhaps even mortality among the older patients.

2. Exchange of scientific information on matters related to recreational therapy is impeded among nations because of (a) the absence of standard terminology (e.g., the word *recreation* has totally different definitions and implications in some languages) and (b) the lack of machinery for the regular exchange of information between professional groups.

3. Increasingly, the role of the recreation *therapist* must be with small groups and individuals, the recreation *technician* working with the large groups and mass activities in the big institutions. Professional preparation of the recreation therapist will also have to place greater emphasis on *human behavior* in relation to illness and handicaps.

4. There may be merit in considering the joint professional preparation of recreational and occupational therapists, on one hand, and physical therapists, corrective therapists, and adapted sports specialists, on the other. In recreational and occupational therapy, the possibilities of an integrated core curriculum, to be followed by specialization, bear careful exploration.

5. In neuropsychiatric institutions it appears that results are better when *work* therapy and *recreational* opportunity are combined with a

[5] Charles K. Brightbill, *A Brief Report on the Study of Recreational Therapy Programs in Selected Institutions of Europe and the United States* (Urbana: University of Illinois, 1960).

required program which aids the patient's physical and cultural expression in such pursuits as movement (dance, exercise, sports and games), the graphic and plastic arts, drama, and music.

6. In the treatment of children with physical handicaps and neurological disorders, interspersing periods of learning with periods of play appears to be highly desirable in helping, among other things, to reduce fatigue and sustain interest.

7. There are medical experts who question whether recreation is of much value in the treatment of the mentally ill patient with a deep psychosis. Their view is based upon the belief that the disease is essentially biological.

8. In recreation therapy it is not the activity which is important, but rather the *attitude* of the patient toward it, how the patient *approaches* it, and what the patient *derives* from it.

9. The *diversional* recreation program in a hospital can be of equal importance to the *prescribed* program. It is *diversional* in the sense of taking the patient's mind off his troubles.

10. The function of recreation in the day hospital is especially significant in expediting the return of the patient to community life.

11. In relation to those who are mentally ill, the freedom of choice and pursuit which are essential in recreational therapy must be governed by the amount of the patient's ego strength.

12. If recreation is of value in therapy and *remedial* medicine, it can be of value in prophylaxis and *preventive* medicine.

RECREATION IN THE HOSPITAL

It is not feasible to give full details here of recreation within all types of hospitals. The orthopedic hospital must stand as an illustration.

Usually, orthopedic hospitals are for operative and clinical care with little or no convalescent home work. Hence, they have a great opportunity to promote a constructive program of recreation suitable from a therapeutic standpoint. The program usually resolves itself into several parts: (1) bedside work; (2) recreation for convalescents, most of whom are in wheel chairs; (3) work with clinical cases who come for further care; (4) work with groups organized for special activities from the clinic cases; and (5) social affairs for either clinic or hospital cases. Particular activities include: (1) adaptation of games; (2) development of dramatics from such simple forms as play reading among ward patients to the presentation of plays, operettas, and circuses; (3) dancing, from which few need be excluded, as rhythm is the object sought, whether it be in social or folk dances; (4) handcrafts, with social rather than craft emphasis; and (5) general social activities—entertaining and being entertained. Recreation is used by the therapist for prevention, furtherance of convalescence, physical and neuromental reconstruction, and for adjustment for social living.

Some of the unique features of this type of work form the basis of understanding of recreation in the hospital setting. They are presented by W. H. Orion, formerly Director, Recreation Services of the Veterans Administration.

FIRST. Patients are in hospitals because they are, in varying degrees and combinations, physically, mentally, or emotionally ill or incapacitated. Consequently, whereas in general recreation one can expect a small percentage of participants to be in impaired health, in hospital recreation one can expect all to be.

SECOND. The patient population is not a homogeneous one—for such contrasting patient types as the paraplegic, tuberculous, blind, and psychotic are to be anticipated, and the program functions in all types of hospitals—military, V.A., state or tax-supported institutions, private hospitals, as well as those catering to particular age groups. Special emphasis must be directed to the so-called "long term" patient—for the hospital is his life and his home.

THIRD. It is immediately apparent that with any population composed exclusively of patients there exists an ever-present possibility of irreparable damage to participants by the use of ill-chosen activities or methods. Because of this fact the choice of activities, methods, and techniques cannot be left solely to the discretion either of the recreation leader or of the patient, except as such choices fall within the limitation of medical dictation.

FOURTH. There is a continuous need for the adaptation of activities, equipment, and procedures to the needs, capabilities, and interests of participating patients.

FIFTH. Because the function of the hospital is to treat patients, physicians determine the specific objectives for patients participating in recreation, individually and in groups. For the most part these same physicians rely heavily upon the specialized knowledge of recreation leaders in the selection of those specific recreation activities, methods, and techniques best suited to help achieve these objectives. No activity is scheduled without medical approval; no patient participates in such activities without medical clearance or prescription.

LASTLY, THE RECREATION LEADER IN HOSPITALS IS A MEMBER OF THE TREATMENT TEAM, A TEAM OF WHICH HE IS AN IMPORTANT MEMBER, BUT NEVER A CAPTAIN.

THE ROLE OF RECREATION IN REHABILITATION

Doctor Howard K. Rusk describes rehabilitation as, "The restoration of the handicapped to the fullest physical, mental, social, and economic usefulness of which they are capable."

Recreation is a necessary part of rehabilitation. All people need recreation and all patients are people. Consequently, no matter what manner of rehabilitation the patient is going through to adjust to his illness or disability, he needs guided or suggested recreation.

For the tuberculosis patient, rehabilitation may be retarded because he is excessively bored and lacks mental stimulation; he is concerned for the future of his loved ones and for their financial security, as anyone who is institutionalized might be; and, he may over-concentrate on his own illness. Also, typically, and for one or more of the above reasons, he may defy the physical limitations of his condition. He may even discharge himself from the hospital without medical approval and jeopardize his chances for an eventual cure.

Therefore, recreation's part in the rehabilitation of the tuberculosis patient is:

1. To keep him occupied within the physical range of his ailment while ill.

2. To help the physician in evaluating the potential of his patient's physical activities during the convalescence or arrested stages.

3. To teach the patient how to provide for his recreation hours without endangering his health on his return to the community, if recreation has aided in his rehabilitation.

For example: Tennis is a poor game for an arrested TB patient, as it is too strenuous, but golf can be taught to him in slow, easy stages, starting with putting and the short game and working up through the years to a strong driving game.

For the chronic patient, particularly the one permanently hospitalized, recreation is his rehabilitation. He is separated, more or less permanently, from his family and community, and only recreation can compensate for these losses. Recreation must make him feel useful and wanted again. The chronic patient must develop new interests and new abilities, not only to make him happier, but to make him less of a problem to the staff.

Now for the neuropsychiatric patient. How can he be rehabilitated if he cannot be brought back into the group society? What better methods are there of getting him to enter into group activities and re-establish contact with his surroundings than his finding self-expression and a possible creative ability in the activities recreation can offer him? Too—before you can successfully rehabilitate a neuropsychiatric patient, recreation must aim to develop an interest which will be satisfactory to him when he is discharged from the hospital.

The neuropsychiatric patient whose condition is chronic, and who cannot be returned to the community, can become active in some form of recreation, and at least keep from deteriorating further. This even if he is merely making feeble attempts at joining in a sports program or perhaps being a member of a percussion band. He is still doing something, not just vegetating!

The long-term patient differs from the chronic patient in that there is a definite, foreseeable limit to the period of his hospitalization. But, while he is in the hospital, he needs a morale builder. His rehabilitation is learning to adjust to his hospital situation and thus to speed up his recovery.

As for the child patient, he has a particular need for happy and healthful play activity when confined by illness or injury. He often suffers an emotional shock when first hospitalized, a feeling of being cut off from his normal world. The problem here is to provide a warmth and understanding to replace loss of the love and security of the child's home environment, and to alleviate his natural fear of the hospital. Games and toys can be as valuable as an added medicine to a child. It is up to recreation to make it good medicine, and thus hasten the child's physical rehabilitation.

Now to the patient undergoing the process of rehabilitation to the community and, more likely than not, to a job, recreation is two-fold. While he is undergoing the strenuous processes of Activities for Daily Living (A.D.L.), he must have something that will relax him when evening comes and help to refresh him from an exhausting day spent with the relearning process. His evenings must also help to counteract the discouragements he will undergo in the rehabilitation processes. Perhaps as important as this is helping him to relearn group living and to overcome the self-consciousness due to his handicapped condition. He must learn not to be afraid of mixing with people once he leaves the security of the hospital. Recreation can help this patient tremendously not only by teaching him interests adapted to his physical limitation, but by helping to overcome his self-consciousness by taking him out as often as possible to recreation events in the community. The recreation department must see that the patient frequently goes to community activities in which he is interested. Each successive time the recreation department takes him to a social event, it must make the traveling conditions less and less protected.

THE PROGRAM

Recreation for the ill and disabled must be planned in terms of the patients' interests, needs, and capabilities. For our purposes, we can think of *therapeutic recreation* as *the medical application of an activity, voluntarily engaged in by the patient during the period of treatment or convalescence, that is enjoyable and personally satisfying to him, even though the activity and the patient's participation in it are structured to achieve a predicted result beyond the patient's own personal satisfaction.* Recreation, in these terms, should be related to the treatment aims. Treatment aims vary with the types of illness and disabilities and the patient. In a hospital recreation setting, there should be *two* motivations at work. These are the motivation of the patient—to engage in what is satisfying and enjoying to him—and the motivation of the recreator—to use recreation in a way which will help the patient get well and remain well.

Perhaps the recreation program can be best understood in relation to criteria for evaluating it:

Evaluation (General)

1. Are the objectives and policies of the hospital recreation service in writing? Are they understood, accepted, and applied by management, the medical staff, and the special service or recreation staff?

2. Does the recreation staff fully understand the policies and objectives of the hospital?

3. Is the recreation program fully coordinated with the medical program? How?

4. Is the recreation program adequately and continuously interpreted to management, the medical staff, the auxiliary services, and the patients? Through what media?

5. Is the recreation program planned, coordinated, and evaluated with the medical staff, nursing staff, attendants, librarians, chaplains, social workers, occupational therapists, etc.?

6. Are work schedules planned and posted?

7. Are regular staff meetings held?

8. How often do recreation staff members attend medical and clinical meetings?

9. How extensive is library material in professional recreation?

10. To what extent is recreation included in case records?

11. How often are patient interests surveyed?

12. In what ways is recreation equipment modified?

13. Is recreation used as a setting for medical research?

14. How well are recreation facilities adapted to needs of the ill and disabled?

15. Are there opportunities for in-service training?

16. Is there participation in professional recreation organizations?

17. Are there educational leaves?

18. Are there student trainee developments?

19. How are relationships with nearby colleges?

20. Is much contribution made to recreation literature?

21. Do staff members attend professional conferences?

Evaluation (Program)

1. Does the program take into consideration the varied interests, needs, and capabilities of the patients?

2. Are the physiological and psychological capacities and characteristics of the patients weighed carefully?

3. Is adequate attention given to the needs of the *individual,* as well as the group?

4. Does the program take into consideration the cultural, economic, social, and educational backgrounds of the patients?

5. Is the program *cooperatively* planned, developed, and conducted with the patient?

6. Does the program provide for the various levels and skills of the patient, with each patient having the opportunity to progress at his own speed?

7. Do the activities have rehabilitation and carry-over values for the patient after he leaves the hospital?

8. Are program segments properly geared to varying leadership capacities and interests?

9. Does the program have adequate financial support? Appropriately modified equipment and facilities?

10. Does the program provide for equality of opportunity in terms of patient interests, medical limitations, and capabilities in skill or knowledge?

11. Does the program make the most of available resources at the hospital and, where applicable, beyond the hospital?

12. Is the program flexible enough to meet changing needs and conditions?

13. Does the program protect the health and safety of the patient at all times?

14. Does the program encourage a high plane of personal behavior and conduct?

15. Does the program consider long range interests—beyond rehabilitation of the patient?

16. Is the cost of the program, or a given activity, in line with the values patients derive from it?

17. Does the program avoid exploiting the patient?

18. Does the program or activity provide release for such basic desires as:
> Enjoyment and fun?
> Sociability?
> Physical and emotional release?
> Security and belonging?
> Recognition?
> Creativity and expression?
> Achievement?
> Mobility?
> Adventure?

19. Is attention given to having the patient come to understand how vital recreational habits are to a happy and productive existence?

20. What is balance of activity
> spectator vs. participation?
> group vs. individual?
> on station vs. off station?
> outdoor vs. indoor?
> ward vs. general facility?
> bed vs. ambulatory patient?
> active vs. passive?

21. Are activities prescribed, approved, or neither—under what conditions?

RECREATION IN FEDERAL HOSPITALS

The American National Red Cross

Planned recreation in federal hospitals has progressed. Because of its unique position as a quasi-governmental agency chartered by Congress, the American National Red Cross has been authorized to maintain recreation activities in certain government hospitals under supervision of the medical officers in charge. To fulfill this obligation, the American Red Cross provides recreators in Army, Navy, and Air Force hospitals. In addition to these specialists, there are the regular hospital social workers and volunteers who devote a portion of their time to recreation.

Red Cross hospital recreators are responsible for conducting a medically approved recreation program and for accepting and coordinating for the hospital commanding officer appropriate recreation services and programs offered by individuals or groups outside the hospital. This recreation program is part of the Red Cross hospital social service program and is provided as an adjunct to medical care.

Use of outdoor areas, picnics, and trips are planned. In the selection of games the recreator considers adaptations which may be necessary in the hospital setting. Music is provided in many forms, as it offers a release from inner tension and anxiety. Parties rank high on the list of special events popular with the patients. In entertainments, emphasis is placed on programs the patients stage, such as amateur night shows, skits, and stunts. Performances by professional and amateurs from groups on the post and in near-by communities are frequently offered. Crafts are part of the Red Cross recreation program in Navy hospitals and in those Army hospitals that have no occupational therapy department. Hobbies and special interest activities have a particular place in hospitals where there are long-time patients.

Emphasis is placed on working with the patient who may need or will benefit from special planning. Such planning is often done jointly with the social worker to increase effectiveness of service. Records of such planning serve as a supervisory tool as well as a means of increasing the worker's understanding of objectives and methods of accomplishment. The program is financed through funds secured in the yearly Red Cross drive. Additional equipment is secured through Red Cross Councils serving hospitals, institutions, and installations, civic groups, and individual donations.

An area recreation consultant and field consultants are assigned to each area to assist with programs and staff development. The consultant staff at national headquarters is available for additional assistance.

The Veterans Administration

The Veterans Administration, through its Recreation Section in the Physical Medicine and Rehabilitation Service, operates a program at each V.A. hospital and home. Its program includes sports, music, entertainment, radio, motion pictures, social recreation, arts, crafts, special events, hospitality services, and hobbies.

The purpose of the recreation program in Veterans Administration hospitals is to provide, as an integral phase of the total medical program, a comprehensive, well-balanced, and professionally executed range of recreation activities to meet the needs, interests, and capabilities of all patients. All activities offered by the recreation program require medical approval.

The recreation program is planned to assist the doctor in getting his patients well and to make life as satisfying and meaningful as possible for those patients who must remain in the hospital for long periods of time. The diversified activities which constitute the program are designed to accomplish the following objectives:

a. Assist in facilitating patients' adjustment to hospital life and medical treatment.

b. Provide doctors with opportunities to observe patient behavior and response to activity.

c. Assist in orienting patients in their physical limitations and potentialities.

d. Contribute to the development and maintenance of normal physical condition during the patients' stay in the hospital.

e. Develop interests and skills in so-called "carry-over" activities; that is, activities in which patients may participate safely and beneficially during their stay in the hospital as well as after their discharge from the hospital.

f. Contribute to the total social and psychological readjustment of patients.

Primary consideration is given to the needs of patients as determined by appropriate medical authority. Following this determination, patient interests and capabilities as well as program resources are ascertained so that appropriate activities may be selected to meet these patient needs. Recreation activities for psychiatric patients, for example, are developed, organized, and designed to encourage maximum active patient participation. Recreation activities for tuberculosis patients are directed toward passive or mildly active participation to the exclusion of programs which tend to excite, disturb, or cause undue exertion. Recreation opportunities for general medical and surgical patients are directed toward the long-term patient. Recreation activities for domiciliary members are especially adapted for older age groups. Frequently these activities are prescribed to insure for the patient the attainment of full value in physical, social, and psychological adjustment.[6]

6 Special Services Pamphlet 6–3, *Recreation Services,* Veterans Administration (Washington, D.C.: U.S. Government Printing Office, n.d.).

RECREATION IN STATE HOSPITALS

The need for recreation has long been recognized in state hospitals, particularly in state mental institutions. Although there have been fine recreation opportunities in some state institutions for many years, it has only been within the last decade or two that these programs have begun to expand. In 1950 state hospitals in 22 states received reasonably adequate amounts from their state budgets for recreation services. And in 1951, the Council of State Governments recommended the training and placement of qualified recreation personnel in all state hospitals.

Many state hospitals now have outstanding recreation programs. Increasingly, they are employing highly qualified recreators not only in the hospitals, but also in state supervisory and administrative assignments. They are conducting in-service, staff development programs, cooperating with colleges and universities in preparing students for hospital recreation work, and offering scholarships and other inducements. Personnel from state hospital recreation rosters are often active members of the National Association.

Sometimes these hospital programs are identified as *Activity Therapies* and *Adjunctive Therapies* which include not only recreation services, but also occupational therapy, library service, industrial therapy, and the like. The Illinois effort is briefly described:

The Activity Therapies Service of the Illinois Department of Mental Health uses activities of work and play to help people who are in state institutions for the mentally ill, mentally retarded, physically handicapped, or the aged. All hospitals and special schools provide activity programs, and the Activity Therapies Service shares with medical, nursing, psychology, education, and social services the following two-fold aim:

(1) To return the individual to the community, if this is feasible.
(2) To help him develop to his fullest capacities and to live as normally as possible in spite of illness or handicap, and regardless of whether the goal for him is to return to the community or continue in the shelter of an institution.

Certain needs common to all of us are particularly acute in those who are ill or handicapped. The activity therapist combines understanding of individuals and groups with leadership skills and knowledge of appropriate activities to help meet the following needs:

(1) To be liked by other people, to have friends, to be a friend, and to feel a part of the community and the family group.
(2) To believe in one's own capacities and feel respected for contributions to the general good, regardless of how small these may be.
(3) To have socially acceptable outlets for emotions and for creative ideas.

(4) To live in an environment providing a balance between work and leisure.

(5) To develop vocational or avocational interests and aptitudes, renew old skills, learn new ones.

The Activity Therapies Service totals more than 500 employees in state hospitals, special schools, and institutions serving more than 48,000 Illinois citizens. Some of these employees have degrees in occupational therapy, recreation, music therapy, counseling, or education. Others are trained on the job. Some of the different classifications of staff who work in the Activity Therapies Service are:

Librarians.

Industrial therapy counselors who are concerned with therapeutic work assignments in mental hospitals and schools for the retarded.

Specialists in using art, crafts, sports, dancing, music, and dramatics as therapeutic or educational media.

Therapists or leaders skilled in applying a variety of activities programs to help adults or children who are mentally ill, aged, mentally retarded, physically handicapped, or dependent.

Many volunteers also assist in the Activity Therapies Service.

RESEARCH

Research in recreation and its relation to health, especially in connection with the ill and the disabled, their treatment and rehabilitation, is just beginning to emerge. A scientific body of knowledge in this regard is very much needed. Knowledge precedes service and theory precedes its application. Some idea of the kinds of questions which need to be answered and hence, the areas in which scientific study is needed are: [7]

—The selection of purposeful recreation as related to the treatment aims.

—The selection of appropriate manipulative materials (in the graphic and plastic arts) in relation to individual treatment aims.

—The evaluation of the therapeutic benefits of outdoor living, particularly gardening and camping.

—The designing of hospitals, clinics, rehabilitation centers, homes for the aging, and similar institutions for functional, therapeutic recreation use.

—The potentials and techniques of avocational counseling as related to total rehabilitation.

—The use of recreation in motivating the patient toward treatment receptivity.

—The use of recreation as a means for improving communication (toward resocialization) among mentally ill patients.

—The effects of recreation upon diet and rest.

—The determination of recreation activities which may be contraindicated for given types of illnesses.

[7] Brightbill, *A Brief Report on the Study of Recreational Therapy Programs.*

COMMUNITY HEALTH SERVICES

Another important aspect of recreation for the ill and handicapped is the *bridge* to the community which Meuli comments upon: [8]

There is a current emphasis on coordinated medical services. For psychiatry, at least, a continuum is suggested including the home, the out-patient department, the day-hospital, the psychiatric specialty hospital, and a variety of follow-up clinics, after-care homes, sheltered workshops, and working settlements. If and as these principles are more generally adopted, it will mean more rapid movement of patients through the hospital, shorter stays and probably more intensive treatment. Also, if these principles are more generally adopted there will be a greater need to clarify where the medical recreator's responsibility stops and where the community recreator's responsibility begins. . . .

. . . The community will play more and more of a role in the development of medical facilities and acceptance of the ill and handicapped as more individuals become recreation volunteers. There is a need for medical recreators to increase the number and quality of trained volunteers to work in recreation programs. Volunteers can assist in the recreation program in many different ways. They most certainly can help with the need for community understanding. Volunteers can help erase erroneous ideas about the mentally ill, physically handicapped, and mentally retarded, becoming interpreters of facts and ambassadors of good will for the medical institution in the community.

As the concept of coordinated medical services is adopted, as the community becomes more receptive to accepting the physically and emotionally handicapped individual, and as the medical recreator more clearly defines his role and objectives, recreation counseling should become an integral part of his function. There has been some experimental work already begun. A notable example of a recreation counseling service is the project carried on between the staff members of the psychiatric unit at the Veteran Administration Hospital in Kansas City, Missouri, and the staff members of the city recreation department. Recreation counseling can help the patient to form new ties with individuals and groups and teach the patient how to make use of available community resources for recreation. Experience from the Kansas City project has shown that the community response to the program has been even better than expected. When made aware of the need, surprisingly large segments of the population are ready to reach out a hand to help the ill or handicapped. With some professional guidance, these human resources can be relied on to assist in furthering rehabilitation processes.

In addition to the concept of coordinated medical services referred to earlier, hospitals are undergoing many changes as a result of the influence of modern methods of rehabilitation. One important element which seems to be influencing change is the theory of progressive patient care wherein patients are separated

[8] Albert Meuli, "Current Trends in Recreation for the Ill and Handicapped," *American Recreation Journal.* American Recreation Society, February, 1962.

into three categories: (1) Intensive Care Unit—requiring constant observation and nursing care. (2) Intermediate Care Unit—requiring full time medical and nursing care, but not requiring continuous observation. (3) Self-Care Unit—the patient is convalescing and does not require continuous observation, but needs to remain under the doctor's and nurse's eyes before going home. The self-care unit is ideally suited to the recreation program, since patients are ambulatory and somewhat self-dependent. Also, with the critically ill patients segregated from this unit, the recreation program will find a welcome reception from nurses and patients alike.

ARCHITECTURAL BARRIERS

Thomas Stein reviews another aspect of community health services: [9]

Many disabled and older persons in our country exist on an island. We seldom see them on the "mainland" in our communities because we have failed to provide them with a bridge, an opportunity to function as first-class citizens. The few who do venture out are often forced, not so much by their physical disability but by barriers of concrete, steel, and wood, to be as dependent upon others as new-born infants in order to overcome the hurdles in their way.

Development of Standards

In 1959, a concerted campaign against architectural barriers was launched with its first objective the development of specific standards. A grant was given to the University of Illinois to conduct research which could result in design recommendations based on tests performed with physically disabled persons. As a result, in October, 1961, the American Standards Association approved and adopted specifications for "Making Buildings and Facilities Accessible to, and Usable by, the Physically Handicapped."

Examples of Progress

Six years have passed since the educational campaign was started. A great deal of progress can be reported.

—Thirty-four states have taken governmental action relating to preventing barriers in future publicly owned buildings at the state, county, and municipal levels.

—The National Park System has taken steps to modify existing facilities so that they can accommodate more of the disabled and aging.

—Over 40 communities have published or are preparing to publish a "Guide

[9] Thomas A. Stein, Ph.D., "A Design for Opportunity," *Parks and Recreation,* Vol. 48, No. 9, September 1965, pp. 586–87.

for the Handicapped" which provides basic information on ingress, egress, and function of community facilities which are intended for public use.

In 1965, the President of the United States appointed a National Commission on Architectural Barriers which has the responsibility to study the effect of national efforts to date and to recommend the need for further activity which can assure the solving of this problem.

We cannot stop people from getting older, nor will we ever completely eliminate accidents. Consequently, the problems of disability and of aging will always be with us. These personal conditions should not be tragedies but, rather, intense living experiences. Let's not underestimate the potential of these handicapped persons—they have a great deal to offer society. In return, they can have the chance to live fully and effectively—something most of us expect as an inherent right. They can be helped to enjoy their changed lives with grace and dignity and to re-acquire mobility and independence.

This problem is truly a design for opportunity. With the continued help of the recreation profession, barriers will be changed to architectural opportunities.

Professional Organizations

As of 1967, the National Therapeutic Recreation Society is the organization devoting full time to the professional development and interests of recreators working with the ill and disabled in hospitals and rehabilitation centers.

The Society represents a merger between two national groups which have been in existence since the late forties—the Hospital Section of the American Recreation Society (now a part of the National Recreation and Park Association) and the National Association of Recreation Therapists.

The combined membership and efforts channeled into one strong society are manifested in more qualitative publications and resource materials and increased effectiveness in areas of training, standards and services. The Society sponsors annual national and regional conferences and workshops for its membership.

The American Association for Health, Physical Education, and Recreation maintains a Recreation Therapy Section in its recreation division and gives a column or more to the subject each month in its JOURNAL. Section meetings on recreation therapy are held during the Association's annual conference, as well as at its district meetings. The AAHPER also sponsors special meetings and issues special reports in this field.

Professional Preparation for
Leadership in Therapeutic Recreation

The demand for professionally trained therapeutic recreators is accelerating at a rapid pace. Colleges and universities throughout the nation are endeavoring to meet this demand through the establishment of undergraduate and graduate degree programs which provide for specialization in this area.

Increasingly, the administrative and advanced supervisory positions in this career specialty require the Master's degree. There are now approximately 25 universities offering programs at this level. Within the past few years, a number of state and national health agencies, both private and public, have established traineeships for graduate study in therapeutic recreation. The Rehabilitation Services Administration of the Department of Health, Education and Welfare and the Joseph P. Kennedy, Jr. Foundation are among those agencies funding these educational grants.

THE WORKSHOP

1. Discuss the similarities and differences between providing recreation in the community and providing it in a hospital.
2. Visit a local hospital to determine what recreation for patients is available. Decide what might be done.
3. Plan a recreation program for one evening and present it in a local nursing home.
4. Interview a physician and a social worker for their views on recreation for the ill and handicapped.
5. Select several pieces of sports equipment and suggest how they might be adapted for the orthopedically handicapped.
6. Report on the recreation program conducted at a camp for children with some form of illness or disability.
7. Investigate and report on recreation opportunities—or the lack of them—for "shut-ins" in your community.
8. Read several articles on the subjects and report on the similarities and differences between occupational therapy and recreational therapy.
9. Discuss the interests, needs, and competencies of patients with varying illnesses and their relation to recreation.
10. Plan a recreation program for visually handicapped children between 9–12 years of age.

REFERENCES

Chapman, Frederick M., *Recreation Activities for the Handicapped*. New York: The Ronald Press Company, 1960.

Davis, John Eisele, *Clinical Applications of Recreational Therapy*. Springfield, Illinois: Charles C Thomas, Publisher, 1952.

Haun, Paul, *Recreation: A Medical Viewpoint*. New York: Columbia University Press, 1965.

Haller, Talbert and Dombro, *The Hospitalized Child and His Family*. Baltimore, Md.: Johns Hopkins Press, 1967.

Hunt, Valerie V., *Recreation for the Handicapped*. New York: Prentice-Hall, Inc., 1955.

Hyde, Robert W., J. Sanbourne Bockhoven, Harold W. Pfautz, and Richard H. York, *Milieu Rehabilitation*. Butler Health Center, Providence, Rhode Island, 1962.

O'Morrow, Gerald S. (Ed.), *Administration of Activity Therapy Service*. Springfield, Illinois: Charles C Thomas, Publisher, 1966.

Owen, Joseph Karlton, *Modern Concepts of Hospital Administration*. Philadelphia-London: W. B. Saunders Co., 1962. (Chapter 36)

Pomeroy, Janet, *Recreation for the Physically Handicapped*. New York: The Macmillan Company, 1964.

Wright, Beatrice A., *Physical Disability—A Psychological Approach*. New York: Harper & Row, Publishers, 1960.

Comments

Such magazines and periodicals as *Park and Recreation,* official publication of the National Recreation and Park Association, *American Association of Health, Physical Education and Recreation Journal, Therapeutic Recreation,* journal of the National Therapeutic Recreation Society, and *Intercom,* published by the American National Red Cross, include articles on the topic.

The proceedings of the Southern Regional Institutes on Recreation with the Ill and Disabled published by the North Carolina Recreation Commission, Raleigh, N.C., contain excellent resource material.

19

Recreation For
Later Maturity

The entire nation is growing aware of the significance of later maturity. The facts prove that we are living longer and that the span of life may be even further lengthened. While this is a thrilling achievement, it is accompanied by a big question: *HOW* will we live these years? If the *privilege* to live is ours—there are these challenges *now:*

1. To change some of the negative concepts about this period of life; revitalize the social and economic status of the senior citizen; and provide opportunities for enriched living during these later years.

2. To have adults prepare for the years of later maturity through the utilization of the knowledge we possess, so that opportunities to enjoy the late years may be better assured, to have these citizens enter the late years with reasonably good health, a fair basis of economic security, individual dignity, and social recognition, to assure for each individual proper housing in a wholesome environment, and to build effective programs of recreation for enriching their hours of leisure.

3. To plan ahead for and with the coming generations so that every factor of contemporary life bearing on the welfare of the individual can be utilized for growth and opportunity; to plan ahead so that when our children reach the years of later maturity, they will be better adjusted, ready and able to live a healthy life, graciously.

There is a real need to establish a definite rhythm between work and recreation throughout all of the life span. At present there are far too many who are not prepared and who especially lack the skills of recreation. Every effort must be made to have a knowledge of many recreation activities enjoyed throughout the years and carried over into the senior years.

To obtain maximum results for the recreation life of older citizens there must be an effective correlation of the basic areas of life—health, education, work, religion, and recreation. As each area is enriched all the others benefit. Where opportunity in any is denied, the risk of individual and social pathology increases. A balance of these elements tends to help produce a better personality and a finer environment.

For a large number of the present over-65 population, family and community status has changed drastically. The majority live in families consisting of husband and wife or as widows heading their own households. All indications, based on cursory observation, show that the majority of persons are faced with extensive blocks of unobligated time. For some, change in economic or vocational status may represent only a minimal alteration in their central life interests, i.e., they are able to transfer their interests from vocational to avocational objectives. For many, retirement represents change to a life with reduced purpose and to a sharp decline in family and community responsibility and status. The post-vocational years have arrived without the individual having made effective preparation, either psychologically or in terms of developing extendable leisure interests, factors which seem to be essential in the maintenance of dignity and feelings of self-acceptance. It appears that too often the later years are accompanied by boredom which, along with physical and mental deterioration, results in unhappiness and self-devaluation. This may be especially true in some institutional settings where the older citizen is often isolated from normal social and community relationships.

Unless there is a long-range plan to offer older persons meaningful opportunities for the development of leisure skills and for social relationships through interaction with a variety of individuals and groups, regardless of age, many persons, because of negative attitudes, dissatisfaction, and inactivity will continue, in increasing numbers, to look to the supposedly "Golden Years" with fear and frustration. The resultant loss to the individual, his family and community will be immeasurable. Therefore, it seems crucial that extensive attention be devoted to the development of programs which are sensitive to the social, as well as the economic, health and spiritual needs of the older people in our society. The responsibility for these efforts must be shared by various institutions and community agencies. One of the key factors is the need for trained personnel to provide effective leadership for such programs.

Needs of the Aging

Many programs have been offered to older people. Some have been accepted; some given tentative approval; some rejected. Some appeal to a few, but do not attract large numbers.

Program planning should not be a random matter. Instead, it should be designed to meet specific needs of real people—people who have the same fundamental drives and desires as human beings of any age. The function of recreation is to enable older people to find the means of satisfying needs formerly satisfied in other ways.

With no attempt to rank them in order of their significance, the following needs are important:

1. *The need to be considered as a real part of the community.* Children, adolescents, and grown-ups have their place in any community. Too often the old people are regarded as "the living dead." "Removed from circulation," their interest or convenience or pleasure is usually not given any consideration in community planning. Neither is their ofttimes rich experience drawn upon, nor is their mature advice sought in matters affecting the welfare of all.

2. *The need to occupy much expanded free time in more satisfactory ways.* Elderly people, who have led full lives, resent "just killing time." Conditions created by their now established way of life often mitigate against doing anything creative.

3. *The need to render some socially useful service.* It warps personality not to have some outreach beyond one's own needs and interests. Aging people need to have the opportunity to make a contribution of time and effort for the betterment of their community, their country, and the world.

4. *Need to enjoy normal companionships.* This is a basic human need at all age levels. Where an aging person lives with a married son or daughter, he sometimes fails to see or have the opportunity to visit with folks of his own generation. Living alone, settled into a rut of comparative inactivity, often means a lack of normal companionship. It becomes difficult for some elderly people to even make the effort to make new friends.

5. *Need for recognition as an individual.* No aging person wants to be known just as "so-and-so's mother," or "old Granddad," or "family problem," but as a real person—a personality—an individual not only with a past with its highlights and interesting experiences, but as a present entity having a place in the present scheme of things and still able to make a contribution to life.

6. *Need to have opportunity for self-expression*—and

7. *Need for a sense of achievement* is tied up with number 5. The earlier years had given plenty of opportunity for self-expression and achievement. To be shut off and shut out may cause creativeness to be blocked up or diminished, but new achievements can be discovered with imagination, courage, and help.

8. *Need to feel free to slow down on work or activities.* A sense of work pressure like a coiled spring at one's back should not be a carryover from the middle years. Aging people should not undertake commitments that are interminable

or exhausting to strength or nervous energy. All work or other activity should be kept within reasonable physical limits.

9. *Need to have health protection and care.* Resistance to the onslaughts of disability lessens with the years. The effects of exposure and overexertion are not thrown off with the speed or casualness of younger years. Prevention is better than cure. Due attention should be given to proper nutrition, reasonable exercise, and posture.

10. *Need for suitable mental stimulation* is a situation observable in the case of many old people. They are out of touch with current affairs. They live in their memories. Many live very drab lives. Aging is a mental as well as a physical process and the down-stream drift of both mind and body can be retarded if there is something more than memories to feed on.

11. *Need for suitable living arrangements.* Most new homes today provide only for two generations. What to do with the old folks when they come to live with a married son or daughter with children is a problem. New York State now requires that five per cent of apartments in large housing developments shall be set aside for and adapted to the special needs of elderly occupants. Insufficient income forces many of the aging to live in substandard quarters. Many others have to accept institutional care. Living arrangements come close to being the number one problem of the aging.

12. *Need for wholesome family relationships.* A mother-in-law or father-in-law brought into a home of a growing family is conducive to domestic strains. This calls for readjustments for all concerned, especially if living facilities are inadequate. Where the adjustments are satisfying, the relationships may be harmonious, and the older person has a sense of self-respect and independence. This need ties in closely with number 11.

13. *Need for spiritual satisfaction.* Whatever an aging person's religious interest, he becomes more aware with each birthday that the sands in his hour glass are running lower and lower. Whatever comfort he draws from his faith should not be disturbed by one with different views, nor should contact with its source or channel be shut off due to poor health or living conditions. Full cooperation by relatives or those responsible for the care of the aging should be given for attendance at religious services or providing devotional material. Also, in the case of those who are housebound, it is important to see that official or lay representatives are available to minister to spiritual needs.

ORGANIZATION AND ADMINISTRATION

Any plan for the organization and administration of recreation for the aging should take into consideration existing facilities and programs in the community, their accessibility to the aging, and their suitability for this segment of the population.

Before initiating the program, a survey should be made to determine what leisure requirements of the group need to be served. In some instances, an agency may be called on only to make available an adequate meeting place for a group already organized. In another community or neighborhood, the total organization resources of an agency may be called on to meet an urgent need that has gone unrecognized for years.

An educational campaign to awaken the community to its responsibility for the agings' recreation may be necessary, as well as studying needs and resources, training leaders, getting budget appropriations or other funds, and procuring and equipping facilities for the program.

The aging who are to participate in the program will derive the greatest satisfaction from it if they have a part in its organization and planning. It is through this kind of participation in which their independence and sense of dignity are preserved, their judgment respected, and their initiative encouraged that the recreation program for the aging serves its ultimate purpose.

The opportunity to participate, alone or in groups, in a creative effort or in competition, whether it be in social activity or language classes, is identified as recreation when participated in and pursued during free-time for one's own enjoyment. Society attaches different attributes, values, benefits, and status to the type of recreation pursued by an individual in his free-time. Agencies attempt to interest and expose voluntary participants to activities in the spirit of recreation pursuits which are seen as valuable to the agency or staff in order to obtain behavior patterns in the participants that are desired by society.

The lists that appear below are statements on how recreation is seen as serving older people.

1. *For the individual:*

Recreation Agencies and Programs:

   a. Can provide the opportunity for learning new skills for personal enrichment in:

(1) Art	(6) Literary Activities
(2) Crafts	(7) Music
(3) Community Services	(8) Nature and Outings
(4) Dance	(9) Sports and Games
(5) Dramatics	(10) Recreation Services

   b. Can provide opportunity for peer group relationships.
   c. Can provide opportunity for creative use of increased amounts of free-time available to the individual.
   d. Can provide the opportunity to be of service to others.
   e. Can assist a person to maintain his physical strength.
   f. Can assist an individual to be creative in the Recreation field of his life.

2. *For the Family:*

Recreation Agencies and Programs:

   a. Can provide new skills and experiences to share with family members.
   b. Can help the older individual be less dependent on family for activity

and interests and not totally dependent on family relationships for emotional support.

c. Can help the individual to continue to contribute to the family's emotional well-being.

3. *For the Community:*

Recreation Agencies and Programs:

a. Can help the individual to remain in the community by assisting him to maintain his emotional well-being.

b. Can help the community be aware of the health and needs of its older members.

c. Can, through membership groups, be a resource of manpower when a community need arises.

Together with these recreation results, certain activities have the further value of providing an integrating vehicle whereby the individual can reach out to the community, to friends and to family; whereby options are opened for service to others and with others; and whereby individual achievement and self-fulfillment needs can be satisfied. Then too, Recreation may provide an avenue for introducing other services to the older citizen with a multitude of problems. He may come to the senior center because of its recreation opportunities but find there other services which he would possibly not seek out except for the proximity and the atmosphere of cordiality which permeates the setting. The role of recreation as an entree for the exposure of the individual to other social services needs to be more fully explored.

A project of this kind may be best set up within the framework of:

1. The public recreation department
2. A private agency
3. Individual operation

Where there is a managing authority for recreation, the organized program for the aging should be an integral part of this department. Responsibility could also be assured by other groups such as Y.W.C.A., church, or private social club. If these, too, are not expedient, then the organization may become an individually operated project within the social welfare or civic sphere of influence.

In starting a program in any community, certain key leaders should be sought: clergymen, public welfare workers, doctors interested in geriatrics, visiting nurses, and many of the older citizens themselves.

Organization: The units should be on the neighborhood basis in larger communities and on the single club basis in smaller areas. As an illustration, Durham, North Carolina, has five Golden Age clubs that meet as separate units, but are under one plan of leadership. At various times the five groups come together for centralized activities. The breakdown into smaller units is desirable.

Every effort should be made to keep the organization as informal as possible. Avoid rigid constitutions and by-laws. Quite often it may be well to operate for a while on an informal basis. Individuals may then know each other better, know what they want to do and how to do it.

Some groups have a board of eight or ten members. The board which assists the director in formulating policies, is composed equally of men and women. A short term of office gives more people a chance to serve.

Leadership: Qualified professional leadership is essential. One person should be responsible for the total project. Part-time and volunteer leaders may assist.

In some groups, the oldsters themselves provide the leadership under the guidance of the professional. Self-directed work is effective, but the oldsters themselves often prefer younger leaders as guides.

There is considerable opportunity for volunteer leadership from youths and young adults. People properly skilled in the various techniques of the program can render many services.

The leaders must believe in recreation for this age and have a sincere desire to serve. The leader should have an interest and a sympathetic understanding of older people, and be familiar with their capacities and limitations. New leaders should be oriented properly.

Finances: It is well to have the project financed through the general budget of the public recreation department or operating agency. If this is not expedient, the supporting agency might finance the project totally, or partially.

Where possible, the facilities should be available without cost to the individuals.

Many organized groups have membership dues. These dues are not high and are paid on a monthly basis. They depend on the ability of the members to pay. This money generally goes to defray the expenses of some of the simple needs, such as refreshments, materials, party favors and the like. Where a member cannot pay, no embarrassment should be felt, and this should not hinder membership. Often the sponsoring agency underwrites these dues.

Where rentals must be paid for buildings or rooms, the sponsoring agency might underwrite this expense.

Charges should be minimal. Members should not feel that every time they come to a meeting, in addition to the regular dues, extra expenses accrue. Volunteers contribute time and money when they wish. Sometimes crafts can be sold.

Facilities: If the community is large, then it is best to think in terms of neighborhood facilities, with possibly a central facility. Where the community is small, the central facility is better. Quite often the group can meet in a recreation center and have special hours arranged for the program.

Where a separate center is not available, the community should be surveyed to find possibilities for meeting places—a church parish house, a schoolroom, an auditorium, private homes, a private agency center, and the like.

The meeting place should be convenient to transportation. Attendance is important, and means of transportation often have to be provided through special sources. Accessibility, numbers participating, possibilities of expansion, and the type of program to be conducted must be considered.

The facility should be on the ground level and perhaps "ramped" so there will be no necessity of climbing steps.

Proper rest-room facilities should be on the same floor as the meeting place. Good lighting, adequate ventilation, and satisfactory heating are essential.

Members: A census of the aged should be taken, a spot map made, and then individual contacts expected. Church membership and family contacts are useful. Departments of public welfare and health can be helpful. County homes and other institutions for the aged offer a source of information. Members can obtain members. Every oldster knows someone else to add to the group. Notices in the newspaper, to community councils, to welfare meetings, and the like, often bring results. Posters may help.

Membership is open to any interested man or women above the age of 60 in most units. In some, 50 is the beginning age; and in a few, membership starts at 65.

The handicapped should belong, even though some may not be able to attend.

Where the membership becomes too large, it is suggested that the club be broken into smaller units. The goal should be to make every member an active participant in the program, with a full share of responsibility.

Meeting: Most clubs meet once a week. Some have organized programs every other week, while others have them once a month. Facilities should be open a maximum number of hours.

Some clubs find it most effective for the oldsters to gather in the morning. Others find it best to operate in the afternoons. Evening programs generally should be avoided, but now and then held to add variety.

Publicity: The organization should be publicized. The oldsters like this. All media should be used.

There should be a publicity committee. This committee might prepare a monthly newsletter, look after absentee members, visit the ill and handicapped, and contact the press and interested agencies.

PROGRAM

The heart of the organized recreation effort is the program.

(1) The program needs effective organization. It cannot be done haphazardly. It needs leadership, direction, and imagination.

(2) A variety of activities is important. Program freshness, relief from regimentation, and the element of surprise are necessary.

(3) Every effort should be made to have a balanced program, suitable to interests, season, group, individuals, situations, and environment.

(4) Attempts should be made to individualize the program.

(5) The program should contain both formal and informal activities with emphasis on the informal. Free time for greetings, chatting, and spontaneous activities is essential. An occasional formal event adds dignity to the program.

(6) Clubs are a form of programming. They can be organized according to interest, neighborhood, and the like.

(7) Hobby shows are popular. These create unusual interest and enthusiasm.

(8) A large portion of the program should be devoted to spectator activities—*attending* musicals, plays, and sports events; *visiting* industrial centers and hospitals; *listening* to radio and *seeing* television.

(9) Variety can be given to the program by having the oldsters share their recreation with the family and neighbors.

(10) The team idea has a place in the program. In St. Petersburg, Florida, there is a Half-Century Club and a Three-Quarter Century Club. These clubs sponsor softball, baseball, shuffleboard, croquet, and bowling.

(11) Members can render many recreation services—assist in making a directory of all the oldsters in the community; write letters to shut-ins and people of foreign lands; visit to interest others in the program; perform office work such as stamping, stapling, and packaging materials; serve on committees; take part in community drives and campaigns; act as hosts and hostesses at events; prepare and serve refreshments; make, mend, and patch costumes; work on the Civil Defense program; make decorations; engage in a toy renovation project; and sew doll clothes.

Sometimes we are so enthusiastic over the planning of activities for the aging we forget that many of the older people cannot take advantage of them. Some are homebound. Some are hospitalized. Some are not interested in this kind of program. Many are in homes for the aged; however, all should have the opportunity to participate.

The following suggestions were not compiled with the above in mind; however, they can be applied to them as well as to oldsters in families and clubs.

A greeting card with a brand new dollar bill (or a new handkerchief or homemade calendar) is a fine individual birthday surprise to be found by the older person at his place at the table, or on his tray if he is bedridden.

A half hour of music in the evening—some group singing of favorite hymns, or records, might please many listeners even though they may not care to join in the singing.

A movie screen and projector to show movies also contribute much.

Reading aloud for a short while directly after dinner (selections to be taken from the library, magazines, the daily newspaper, or other sources) would be of interest.

A book cart carrying books and magazines, as well as *supplies for quiet games* and perhaps for simple craft projects, might be a very serviceable piece of equipment. Perhaps more folks would take advantage of reading supplies and game materials if these were brought to them and they could take their choice.

An exhibit of handwork by the older folks might well be displayed in a convenient place. A china closet, bookcase, or discarded candy showcase would serve the purpose. The contents might be used to demonstrate ways in which people use their leisure time. Such a display might do much to encourage participation.

There are also displays in stores, public libraries, museums, and clubs which could be visited. They would provide "something to see" and "something to talk about."

A Costume Party—or fancy hat party gives everyone a chance to dress up. Party-goers may trim the hats at the party or bring them trimmed.

A few really "big" days can be added to the program. A Thanksgiving dinner, a Fourth of July picnic, a May Day basket morning, and a Mother's Day gift are illustrations.

SPECIAL SITUATIONS

"Special situations" here refers to recreation for people for whom recreation is difficult because of restrictions imposed by institutional care or personal disability. Each person differs significantly from every other one, and ideally recreation should recognize and minister to these differences, but there are three major divisions for special situations: [1]

1. recreation for people who live under congregate care;
2. for those who are homebound or handicapped; and
3. for the "hard cases" from the first two categories.

[1] General ideas from *Recreation for Our Older Citizens,* No. 12, The North Carolina Recreation Commission.

The recreation program of any institution reflects the philosophy of its management by board, director, and staff. Thus, if management regards its mission in terms of perpetuation of a microcosm, isolated from the rest of the world, its recreation program will be shaped to keep the residents or patients inwardly-turned and outwardly-busy, and finally "institutionally-broke" and passive. On the other hand, if management sees the institution as a place where uniquely different people live, who need to be encouraged to retain old human contacts and form new ones in the community, the recreation program will reflect that, also.

The criteria of recreation programs for people who live in group care are individual ones. Because any institutional regimen, even the best one, involves some restriction of individual expression, and tends to generalize human needs, *the aim of recreation should be to particularize and feed the hunger of each individual to be a unique person in his own right.* The appropriate questions to be asked about any recreation activity should begin in terms of purpose: what is the aim of *this* activity for *this* person, at *this* time? It is recognized, of course, that even mere activity for activity's sake can sometimes serve the purpose of a starting point for an extremely dependent or passive person. The question of whether a given activity is worthwhile in its own right is an important one. People in institutions do not differ from people elsewhere in their rejection of pointless activity. *A recreation program and its constituent program elements must have demonstrable purpose, integrating effect, and intrinsic worthwhileness, and give status, challenge, and real satisfactions to the individuals concerned.*

The Homebound and Handicapped

People who are confined to their homes or whose mobility is limited by physical or mental handicap do not differ in kind, but only in degree, in their recreation needs. The differentiating criterion for this group of people is that their individualities are underlined and brought into prominence by the very combination of factors that restrict their creative activities in range and locale.

Loneliness is the scourge-disease, even the great killer of the homebound. Loneliness is not recognized as cause of death in recording our community vital statistics. But any general practitioner, any pastor, any social worker can tell you that this can happen. Therefore, *the primary medium of recreation for homebound people should be other people.* The "friendly visitor" is the practical human instrument within the reach of every community, no matter how poor in other resources. There is no rural neighborhood, no urban community which could not derive dramatic benefit for its homebound people by the organization of such a

RECREATION ACTIVITIES FOR LATER MATURITY

	Arts and Crafts	Dancing	Dramatics	Literary Activities	Music	Nature and Outing	Social Activities	Sports and Games
MEN	bookbinding carving electroplating leathercraft metalcraft models—wooden photography pottery woodcraft	social square tap	imitations movies plays—participation and attending radio readings television	lectures (attend all literary events) reading speaking writing	harmonize listen to music musical instruments sing	fishing gardening hunting identification trips traveling walks	banquets clubs conversations dinners parties	archery billiards bowling checkers chess croquet darts dominoes horseshoes ping pong shuffleboard softball
WOMEN	basketry china painting crocheting knitting quilting rug-making weaving	social square folk	movies plays—attend and participate puppetry radio skits television	book clubs creative writing reading	concert records mixed chorus song fests talent shows	gardening picnics sunning walks	fashion shows (gay nineties) parties picnics	checkers darts shuffleboard simple relays
MIXED	combination of the above picture appreciation visit art galleries	folk social square	attend theaters movies puppetry radio	book reviews games with paper and pencil guessing games lectures letter writing open forums poetry writing visit library write up historical incidents and tell stories	attending concerts community singing musical mixture shows music appreciation playing instruments rhythm bands song fests	car and boat rides day-camping enjoying parks picnics sailing tours visiting museums	anniversary events birthdays bridge canasta cards outdoor cooking picnics pinochle sightseeing by auto, bus, and train Sunday visits suppers trips to industries	attending sports events checkers chess dominoes "party games" simple relays and circle games

corps of visitors. *In matters of local organization, it must be remembered that in any such program, the start must be made where the community itself is. The start must be made where the community has stopped. Flexibility and improvisation must necessarily be the key-words.* For instance, where there are luncheon clubs with humanitarian service programs, it is frequently possible to convince such groups to take motion-picture projectors, "talking Bible" records, or library service, into the homes of lonely and handicapped people.

But mere visiting is not enough. If friendly visiting is to be really recreative, it must have conscious purpose and informed direction. *The aims should be to find and stimulate the inner strengths which exist in even the most hopeless-appearing cases.* These strengths vary from person to person, and are not always readily discernible. Hence there is need for competent supervision and coordination by community agencies. This will both lessen discouragement on the part of beginning visitors and guide and evaluate progress.

It cannot be overemphasized that older people themselves are great resources. The skills and insights that must be sought out, because their possessors are homebound and out of touch with the community, can be especially valuable contributions to the common life.

Even for homebound and handicapped people, who must of necessity spend long hours alone, the primary recreation criterion should be, "Does this activity or program tend to direct this person's attention inward to himself, or outward toward the rest of humanity?"

The Hard Cases

Some people do not appear to respond. Experience tells us that the great majority of these instances of apparent lack of response are not at all what they appear to be. As our own understanding of illness and loneliness develops, it is common experience to note a new range of response which lies below our usual threshold of awareness. Thus, when we use the term, "hopeless case," we recognize that this term may be apt in describing our own attitude toward the sick person, and not necessarily an objective statement of the true situation. But granted that the major cause of lack of recreation success with the "hard cases" lies in our own lack of developed insights and techniques, where do we go from here?

The guiding principle is that a start is made tailored in content and range to the individual's dynamic needs and changing capabilities. This requires sharing of information by the several disciplines concerned with the particular individual under consideration.

The mentally limited, the psychotic, and the deteriorated patients in home or hospital present special problems. In many of these cases, it is possible to utilize the fact that the primitive tactile and kinesthetic coordinations remain functional long after space-time orientation has been lost.

In the hard cases of organic illness and terminal care, recreation is especially valuable. The expedient of providing some growing or living thing in the patient's room, visible to him, has great value.

In virtually every community there is a tremendous reservoir of good will waiting to be tapped for better recreation for older people in special situations. This good will usually expresses itself in "Christmas-basket, Lady Bountiful" fashion, but the point is that *it is there, waiting to be cultivated and transformed into more significant and worthwhile expression.* The start is always made where the community is, and the watchword is that *we do what can be done.* The situation calls for patience, equanimity, and common sense. *We must reconcile the fruitful tensions between idealism and reality, in unreserved commitment to the proposition that the future holds undreamed-of possibilities.*

THE WHITE HOUSE CONFERENCE ON THE AGING

The first White House Conference on the Aging was held in 1961 under the general leadership of Dwight D. Eisenhower, then President of the United States. States sponsored state and county meetings in preparation for this conference, which brought together more than 2500 delegates. The conference discussions and recommendations are provided in *Reports and Guidelines from the White House Conference on Aging.* One of the documents is a "Report on Free Time Activities—Recreation, Voluntary Services and Citizenship Participation—Series Number 6." In this report are the following recommendations relating to recreation:

Recommendations

It is essential that proper provision be made for cooperative planning and coordination of services on all levels of government. It is therefore recommended that:

Well defined legal authorities be initiated to offer recreation services and consultation at the federal, state, and local levels.

Appropriate agencies should be established at federal, state, and local levels to effect cooperative planning, development, and coordination of services of public and private agencies which pertain to recreation for all ages.

Recognizing the urgent need for adequate, trained, professional leaders in the area of recreation and group services,

It is recommended that:

Institutions of higher learning be encouraged to initiate curricula at the undergraduate and the graduate level, to train professionals.

Departments and agencies involved be encouraged to provide institutes and workshops for both professional and volunteer workers.

Federal, state, and local private and public organizations be encouraged to provide scholarships for training recreation professionals.

Volunteers be recruited from the older adults as well as from other age groups.

Older people should be recruited also for volunteer service to other community programs and projects.

A vigorous campaign of recruitment of persons for training in the recreation and group work professions be initiated at local, state, and national levels.

It is recommended that:

Continuing programs of public information be developed, using all available media. Programs should aim to develop attitudes of understanding and appreciation for and by older people, and be directed to stimulating community action, to recruiting professionals and volunteers, to understanding the scope and potentials of recreation, to developing interest in participation by older persons, to making free-time facilities known to older people, and to stimulating older people to take responsibility for organizing and conducting activities.

It is recommended that:

Since it is recognized that the older citizens are as diverse in their interests as are any other age groups, emphasis should be placed on the need for initiating, extending, and implementing a broad range of program offerings through every available public or private agency; such programs to include centers, clubs, social and cultural activities, travel, camping and outdoor recreation, library service, informal education, volunteer service by older people to their contemporaries and to other age groups, and active participation in community affairs as well as central counseling, referral, and information services.

States and communities be encouraged to create and extend library facilities and services, family centered programs, and special programs for the ill and handicapped.

The process of program development and the inclusion of creative participation by individuals should be considered part of a recreation program.

Remembering that a satisfying life at each stage has its roots in the preparation of the earlier years,

It is recommended that:

Emphasis be placed upon the urgent need for education of attitudes at every age toward the importance of active and meaningful use of leisure.

There be preparation in the earlier years for the development of interest, skills, and habits in recreation activities that will carry over into the expanded leisure of the later years.

Pre-retirement counseling give equal emphasis to the triad of concern: time, money, and health.

There is essential need, at all levels of operation, for continuing sound research and special studies to determine needs and interests; to evaluate programs; to formulate proper standards and procedures; and to determine quality of leadership, extent and type of facilities, and needs of older people in special situations.

It is recommended that:

Institutions of higher learning and foundations, both private and governmental, be made aware of research opportunities.

Research be activated and results studied for enrichment of individual and group relations.

Action be taken to implement the collation and dissemination of results of such research data.

It is recommended that:

Existing public and private areas and facilities be made *more* available for the leisure activities of the aged and that, where necessary, and practicable, these facilities be adapted for the special needs of the senior citizen.

Communities be encouraged to provide, whenever necessary and feasible, special facilities for exclusive use of older citizens.

Special needs of the aged be considered in the planning and construction of all future private and public areas and facilities for recreation.

Suitable legislation be enacted to insure that licensing requirements for multiple living arrangements for older people provide indoor and outdoor recreation facilities.

Suitable legislation be enacted at state level to add to licensing requirements mandatory provisions for adequate recreation programs, facilities, and leadership for all institutions, governmental and nongovernmental, which house the aged.

It is recommended that:

The concept of adequate income recognize recreation as a basic human need by the inclusion of a sufficient income to permit older people to participate in recreation.

Private national organizations be encouraged to expand facilities and programs for recreation for senior citizens; and urge their local branches to make facilities available for leisure activities and, wherever possible, to establish programs.

Cooperative planning and coordination be encouraged among national, state, and local organizations and governmental services to provide recreation services for older people.

It is feasible for any agency or organization, public or private, to apply these recommendations to the local situation.

The present population of 16 million persons 65 years and over in the United States is expected to double by the end of the century. Longer life must bring greater fulfillment and richer potentials for all. Here is one of today's most thrilling challenges.

There is a great opportunity ahead for recreation to serve the older citizens.

MULTI-SERVICE SENIOR CENTERS

When an individual receives services from a community agency and cannot, because of physical or emotional limitations, proceed beyond the agency for needed support, then these supportive services continue to be seen as the responsibility of the community and its agencies. Needs of assistance to retain autonomy in the community may in time become much greater for some individuals, depending on his emotional and physical health, than the opportunity for ego-support through interpersonal relationships. Such needs may include assistance with transportation, legal or protective services, education about nutrition and health, meal service, household tasks, home visitors, medical and personal care; all, over and above his continuing need to adapt to his changing environment and opportunity for satisfactory interpersonal relationships.

The incorporating of these additional tasks into the center for older people offering the initial and basic services causes the new concept of the multi-service senior center to emerge. Recreation skills new or old, which can provide the individual with the opportunity for interpersonal relationships, continue his chances at role success as a participant. This permits him to live perhaps more successfully within his given limitations. This concept remains the central or all important function of the multi-service senior center for older persons. This, then, is the emerging concept of the multi-service senior center to provide all services needed by the older person so that he may remain autonomous and self-sustaining in the community and thereby retains his dignity as a human.

Communities have been assisted and encouraged in their provision of such services through the Older American's Act of July 30, 1965. This act provides states, who have a State agency designated by its governor, allotment funds to administer. The allotment funds are allocated in the form of grants to local government agencies and private non-profit community organizations to provide programs and services for older people. It is the community's decision as to how to spend these funds so that they best serve their local needs. Some local governments have used these funds to improve existing program and services while other communities have implemented new programs.

Today there appears to be as many concepts of Multi-Service Senior Centers as there are kinds of sponsors and disciplines involved in their leadership. The types of program vary from a downtown centrally located office that provides information, counseling, and referral services to the type of programs which offers all the aforementioned services as well as food, transportation, adult education, Recreation program and Recreation facilities from the same building located in a high density area of older people. Programs vary according to community needs and the overall plan of services to the total community. However, the area of action in which all disciplines and sponsors of multi-service centers appear to concur is that the older person is in need of a variety of community services which are not easily enough accessible to him through ordinary channels. Also, that it is the community's responsibility to see to it that existing services and other special types of services are accessible and, if possible, used by the older person if he has need of them.

It also appears that the central function is to provide channels through which new roles may be found. The most often accepted tool used to provide this support on a generalized and large scale is through Recreation activity in groups and for individuals under capable good leadship.

THE ADMINISTRATION ON AGING

A unit of the Social and Rehabilitation Service Division, Department of Health, Education and Welfare, this agency has been established "to provide a strong central focus and responsibility within the Federal Government on all matters of concern to older people and those who work with and for them." It is the channel for exchange of information and help between State organizations in aging and the Federal Government.

It works closely with all operation units of the Department of Health, Education, and Welfare wherever aging is involved. When there is a combination or overlapping of services, the Administration on Aging acts as coordinator. It cooperates also with other Federal agencies, with national and local voluntary organizations, and with colleges, universities, and other educational institutions in efforts to develop new knowledge and stimulate new programs.

The Administration on Aging has special competency of its own in the areas of State and community organization, leisure activity, preretirement preparation, and development of education in gerontology. It provides general information on aging, and for the elderly, specifics on services and opportunities available to them. It concerns itself with the role and status of older people as well as with their care.

The Administration serves as a central clearinghouse of information on aging. It issues both single and series publications, covering a wide range of subjects in aging.

Consultative help is available from Washington staff and regional representatives in the nine DHEW regional offices. These offices are located in Boston; New York City; Charlottesville, Va.; Atlanta; Chicago; Kansas City, Mo.; Dallas; Denver; and San Francisco.

Through its grant programs, the Administration works to strengthen and assist State and local agencies, and to see that the services and opportunities it seeks for the elderly reach them in their home communities. These grants will fill gaps where other funds have not been available.

THE WORKSHOP

1. Make a check-list of accomplishments and needs in the local community as related to recreation recommendations of the 1961 White House Conference on the Aging.
2. Plan a recreation program for the aging, designed to fit a local situation.
3. Interview people who have retired for their opinions on recreation for older people.
4. Interview six persons who will retire in ten years and discover what, if anything, they are doing to prepare for their leisure.
5. Discuss the "do's" and "don'ts" necessary to sound program practices in recreation for the aging.
6. Plan and conduct a recreation program in a home for the aging or a nursing home.
7. Present "pros" and "cons" of arguments relating to *special* centers for the aging.
8. Suggest ways and means of correlating an institutional recreation program for the aged with the community recreation program.
9. Debate the topic: "Boredom among the aging is as large a threat to their well-being as not being in good health."
10. Prepare a list of ways in which senior citizens may serve as volunteers in youth programs.

REFERENCES

Administration on Aging (Social and Rehabilitation Services Division), Department of Health, Education, and Welfare, Washington, D.C. Be on mailing list for all material distributed by this agency.

Collins, Thomas, *The Golden Years*. New York: The John Day Company, Inc., 1956.

Gernant, Leonard, *You're Older Than You Think*. Kalamazoo, Michigan: Division of Field Services, Western Michigan University, 1960.

Handbook of National Organizations. With Plans, Programs, and Services in the Field of Aging, United States National Voluntary Services and Service Organization, Washington, D.C., 1960.

Kaighn, Raymond P., *How To Retire and Like It*, rev. ed. New York: Association Press, 1951.

Kaplan, Jerome, *Social Program For Older People*. Minneapolis, Minnesota: University of Minnesota Press, 1953.

Kleemeier, Robert W., ed., *Aging and Leisure*. New York: Oxford University Press, Inc., 1961.

Maves, Paul B., *The Best Is Yet To Be*. Philadelphia: Westminster Press, 1951.

Merrill, Toni, *Activities for the Aged and Infirmed.* Springfield, Ill.: Charles C Thomas, Publisher, 1966.

Mulac, Margaret E., *Leisure-Time For Living and Retirement.* New York: Harper & Row, Publishers, 1961.

North Carolina Recreation Commission, *Manual of Club Organization For Senior Citizens,* Reprint. Raleigh: North Carolina Recreation Commission, 1968.

Ostrow, Albert, *Fun After Fifty.* New York: Woman's Press, 1953.

Resources for the Aging—An Action Handbook. The National Council On The Aging, Inc., 315 Park Avenue, South, New York, New York, 1967.

Stafford, Virginia, and Larry Eisenburg, *Fun For Older Adults.* Nashville, Tennessee: Parthenon Press, 1956.

Tibbitts, Clark, and Donahue, Wilma, editors, *Living In the Older Years.* Ann Arbor: University of Michigan Press, 1951.

U.S. Department of Health, Education, and Welfare, Administration on Aging, *The Modern World.* An Annotated Bibliography.

Williams, Arthur M., *Recreation for the Aging,* rev. ed. New York: Association Press, 1961.

Woods, James H., *Helping Older People Enjoy Life.* New York: Harper & Row, Publishers, 1953.

Comment

The following periodicals from time to time contain articles, on various aspects of recreation for the aging:

Adding Life to Years, monthly publication. (Free from: Institute of Gerontology, State University of Iowa, 30 Byington Road, Iowa City, Iowa.

Adult Education. 1201 16th Street, N.W., Washington, D.C.

Aging. Department of Health, Education, and Welfare, Washington, D.C.

Geriatrics. American Geriatrics Society, 84 South Tenth Street, Minneapolis, Minnesota.

The Group. American Association of Group Workers, 129 E. 52nd Street, New York 22, New York.

Journal of Gerontology. 317 Maynard Street, Ann Arbor, Michigan.

Journal of Living. 1918 Broadway, New York 23, New York.

Modern Maturity. 310 East Grand Avenue, Ojai, California.

Senior Citizens. A quarterly magazine published by Senior Citizens of America, 1129 Vermont Avenue, N.W., Washington 5, D.C.

A leaflet containing the latest facts about Older Americans may be obtained from the Administration On Aging of the Department of Health, Education and Welfare, Washington, D.C. The data are revised frequently thus keeping up-to-date.

20

The Delinquent

THE NATURE OF DELINQUENCY

When a person commits a misdeed or offense against society he is said to be *delinquent*. Delinquency is a form of behavior which is socially unacceptable. It should be made clear that delinquency applies to the undesirable acts of adults as well as to those of children and youth.[1] If delinquency is considered in its broadest sense, that is, as a neglect of duty, a failure, or a shortcoming, there are few people who at some time have not been delinquent in their behavior. The vast majority of undesirable acts committed by persons, however, may not be known to be delinquent behavior because they have gone undetected, have not openly endangered the well-being of society, or have not resulted in a violation of the law.

A child who has broken the law is referred to not as a criminal but as a *juvenile delinquent*. The definition of juvenile delinquent varies among the states depending upon the age set by law up to which the juvenile courts are given jurisdiction over the child. In some states it is age 16; in other states, 18.

[1] The emphasis in this chapter is upon *juvenile delinquency*.

355

THE CAUSES OF DELINQUENCY

In recent years considerable time, thought, and attention have been given to the study of juvenile delinquency, and to its probable causes and solutions. As a result of such investigations, it is widely agreed that delinquency is complicated and has many causes. Therefore, it does not appear that single solutions or one-sided approaches to the problem are wise. In the absence of data indicating otherwise, it may not be wrong to assume that when taken in combination with conditioning factors, the causes of delinquency are extensive.

Among the many causes of delinquency listed by those who have studied the problem seriously are these (not necessarily listed in the order of their importance):

Family breakdown, including low standards of conduct on the part of delinquent
   parents.
Poverty and the lack of job opportunities.
Poor physical and emotional health.
Low income combined with disorganized family life.
Inadequate housing, particularly in areas and districts of changing population
   and cultural conflict.
Lack of ethical and religious training in the home.
Disorganized and confused adult thinking.
Neglect, abuse, and exploitation by adults.
Adult criminal behavior where it serves as a model.
Fears, tensions, anxieties, and uncertainties growing out of world affairs and
   potential national disintegration.
Inadequate and overcrowded school facilities, poorly prepared teachers, and
   lack of resources, including insufficient number of teachers and inadequate
   methods of helping the problem child.
Inadequate laws and undesirable detention and penal facilities.
Undesirable influence of some communication media.
Undesirable influence of some types of commercial recreation.
Stereotyping and cultural prejudices; some children and acts are more likely
   to be labeled delinquent than others.

In general, it is held that delinquecy is a product of the socialization process; the delinquent child was improperly socialized or did not receive the type of support and direction necessary to move him toward the acceptance of social responsibility. To quote the President's Commission on Juvenile Delinquency and Youth Crime:

[Children] are not yet set in their ways; they are still developing, still subject to the influence of the socializing institutions that structure—however skeletally

—their environment: Family, School, Gang, Recreation Program, Job Market. But that influence, to do the most good, must come before the youth has become involved in the formal criminal justice system.

Once a juvenile is apprehended by the police and referred to the Juvenile Court, the community has already failed; subsequent rehabilitation services, no matter how skilled, have far less potential for success than if they had been applied before the youth's overt defiance of the law.[2]

THE EXTENT OF DELINQUENCY

Because juvenile delinquency is a type of behavior it does not lend itself to accurate measurement. Is juvenile delinquency actually increasing or have we just become more adept in apprehending the delinquent? Is the problem more acute, or are we simply giving it more attention? What about the untold number of young people who might be considered delinquent—or potentially delinquent—who are dealt with by parents, teachers, youth leaders, and even law enforcement and court personnel without adjudication by the courts? A wise answer to these questions might be that the rate of increase is of secondary importance. As long as juvenile delinquency exists, it is in the best interests of society to try to stamp it out or at least hold it to a minimum.

J. Edgar Hoover, Director of the Federal Bureau of Investigation, says that crime in the United States increased 98 per cent between 1950 and 1960. The arrests of juveniles more than doubled within that period, while the population of youths aged 10 to 17 increased by less than one-half. In 1965, of the 5 million people arrested in the 4062 agencies that reported statistics for that year, 21 per cent were under the age of 18. Forty-one per cent of the under-18 group were not yet 15 years old. Persons under 25 accounted for 49 per cent of the total arrests. City youths were involved in approximately 69 per cent of auto theft arrests, 62 per cent of the burglaries, 65 per cent of the larcenies, 33 per cent of the robberies, 25 per cent of the forcible rapes, 18 per cent of the aggravated assaults, and 10 per cent of the arrests for murder.[3]

Disturbing as these statistics are, there should be some consolation in the thought that there are hundreds of thousands of youths in the United States who have never been in any kind of trouble with society. It is unfortunate, but nevertheless true, we seem to give more recognition to those who deviate from society's norms than to those who abide by its rules. Delinquency, writes Bredemeier, is not a willingness or willful

2 Report of the President's Commission on Crime in the District of Columbia (1966), p. 733. Quoted in *Task Force on Delinquency, Juvenile Delinquency and Youth Crime* (Washington, D.C., U. S. Government Printing Office, 1967), p. 41.

3 U. S. Department of Justice, *Uniform Crime Reports for the United States, 1965* (Washington, D.C., U. S. Government Printing Office, 1965).

neglect on the part of the individuals involved, but a response to the organization of a socialization structure which determines how rewards, encouragement and support are distributed.[4]

Juvenile delinquency can be found in the suburban and rural areas as well as in the congested cities. It involves girls as well as boys and those both in and out of school. The New York City Youth Board is of the opinion that all but a very small percentage of the youth delinquents in that area come from one and one-half per cent of the families. Although such delinquency is more prevalent among lower income groups, it is also found in families with money and too often in the so-called "respectable" home. Its offenses run the gamut from truancy and petty larceny to murder.

RECREATION AND THE PREVENTION OF DELINQUENCY

It is easy to expect or claim too much for recreation in its relation to crime and delinquency. We saw earlier that the *causes* of delinquency are many. So are the *solutions* to the problem. Such reservations have been mentioned in Congressional deliberations: [5]

The following generalizations are fairly clear, at least in relation to play activities and should be considered realistically when someone enthusiastically calls for a single-sided sports program in the hope that it is expected to correct delinquency: (1) Being a good athlete is no deterrent at all to delinquency; (2) experience in team play through recreation can have no significant amount of carry-over to general character traits or conduct patterns; (3) even highly organized recreational activities do not absorb enough of the energy or time of the child to at least appreciably decrease his opportunities to engage in delinquency; (4) in fact, a play group may itself help to stimulate its members to illegal activities engaged in for fun after the games are over. The probability of this is increased when there are delinquent or near-delinquent members in the group; (5) many of the recreational programs do not in any event reach those children who are presumed to need them most because of their problems of health or delinquency; (6) if a child is disposed toward law violation because of the influences of the family and neighborhood, his early training, his personality distortions or his attitudes toward an authority, it will require much more than games and sports to do anything effective about it; (7) where children have come to enjoy their delinquencies as games, so commonly the case, the thrills thus provided are usually greater than those which organized recreation can provide. The latter can be urged as a substitute not for their intrinsic com-

[4] Harry C. Bredemeier, "Proposal for An Adequate Socialization Structure," *Urban America and the Planning of Mental Services* (New York: Group for the Advancement of Psychiatry, 1964), p. 464.

[5] *Juvenile Delinquency*—A Report of the Committee on the Judiciary, U.S. Senate, 85th Congress, First Session. Report No. 130 (Washington, D.C.: 1957), pp. 99–109.

petitive appeal with their added disadvantage, but only for the social or moral ground; this implies a need for preliminary or supplementary casework or education to establish them as acceptable substitutes.

In order to understand the influence of recreation in helping to mitigate the extremes of delinquency, it is necessary to accept the truth that recreation of the right kind is a *positive* opportunity for growth and development and not basically a measure to correct civic and social ills. Recreation has more in common with opportunities for educational and spiritual advancement than with problems of alleviating maladjustment, dependency, and ill health. The great potential of recreation is in the opportunity it provides for positive, personal development. It is not a time-filler or a way of keeping youth occupied; it is an avenue for self-expression and fulfillment. To provide recreation for any other reason than to offer meaningful experiences for the participants may result in program failure and increased social disorganization.

When attractive play and recreation opportunities for children and youth are provided, positive influences are brought to bear upon their lives—children with wayward tendencies benefit by a wholesome recreation environment and the experiences may prove beneficial to the stable and unstable alike. Often it is a matter of the kind of recreation and play to which the child is first exposed. If the initial contact is in an undesirable environment or if the activities offered are not considered meaningful by the youth or his peers, the program will be rejected and negative attitudes toward recreation services may develop. Likewise, attractive experience will be more readily received and personal fulfillment achieved. The need to be delinquent, to strike out or seek negative means of recognition, should be greatly reduced.

Children and youth constantly seek certain basic satisfactions. They desire to belong, to be accepted, to be wanted, and to be recognized. They must also have the chance to achieve and excel. They seek adventure—life with a kick in it. Wholesome recreation, under able leadership, can be a satisfactory outlet for all of those needs. It often helps the youngster develop in the right way and not infrequently helps to realign the sights and habits of young people who may be headed for trouble.

The recreation program often provides a good opportunity to discover and uncover the problem youngster or the potential delinquent. An alert recreation leader can quickly detect the child who shows signs of animosity, antagonism, and hostility—or of not getting along with other children and youth. Early attention and referral of such cases to appropriate sources can be extremely helpful in the campaign against delinquency. The role of recreation is not to eliminate delinquency, but rather to hold the line against character disintegration by providing the chance for positive personal development.

There is need for a more realistic approach to recreation. Again, the members of Congress speak:

. . . Community recreation programs should not be geared to the so-called delinquent. . . . Recreation should constitute a necessary element in normal community life and should be justified first on this basis rather than as a means of curing some abnormal behavior patterns. Wherever there are children and youth, certainly there must be places other than the street that can be permanently set aside for recreational opportunities. However, the facilities themselves mean nothing unless there are competent, well-trained, and qualified individuals to supervise, to direct some kind of thoughtful or meaningful program. Therefore, we would like to emphasize the positive approach as far as recreation is concerned, and that it is one of the necessary elements of fundamental living in our modern society to help overcome the pressures and the tensions that have become evident.

. . . The results which may be expected from a recreation program should be reviewed with the utmost objectivity. It is only one of the many environmental forces that influences the lives of people. It may make a fractional contribution, but the importance of other factors are many times overwhelming in comparison. As Dr. Henry M. Busch has said:

Don't expect recreation to stem or reverse the antisocial forces of an unplanned society, but look to it to illuminate personal and social life and to make the world a somewhat better place in which to live.

The National Conference on Prevention and Control of Delinquency recognized the true value of recreation and emphasized its positive aspect. The conference adopted the principle that recreation is an important part of a living process and recommended that—

it be presented to youth positively, with emphasis on his choice in free time and on his dignity as an individual, rather than as a cure-all for his delinquencies.

It further recognized that recreation—

is one of the effective instruments for the prevention of delinquency. Recreation serves best as a preventive force when opportunities for wholesome recreation are provided for all youth everywhere.

Looking at recreation from this positive point of view, i.e., that it helps to build character, it is potentially a potent agent in the prevention of crime and delinquency. With this potential, it is not hard to explain why agencies directly concerned with this problem are turning to recreation as an effective ally. Because recreation activities have a strong appeal for youth, delinquency and crime are less likely to flourish in communities where such opportunities are abundant and attractive than in cities or neighborhoods where adequate facilities are lacking. Children or young people engaged in recreation activities on the playground cannot at the same time be robbing a bank, breaking into a home, or perpetrating some other crime. Furthermore, if competent playground leaders are available to help them develop wholesome interests and furnish opportunities for pursuing them, the chance that these children will become criminals is materially reduced. The boy who "makes" the playground baseball team or who excels in the model-aircraft club and the girl who earns a part in the cast for the drama guild play or who is a leader in the nature group are finding outlets for the normal desire for recognition, success, and achievement and do not need to seek such satisfactions in unsocial ways.

Reference is made here not only to the importance of recreation in the community as it often gets its initial impetus in the home and neighborhood. Not all families condemn delinquency; in some neighborhoods and groups, striking out at society is accepted as "normal" behavior. Negative forms of recreation develop and encourage delinquency, even among those not delinquently inclined. Delinquency is a product of our own making and must be recognized as such if it is to be dealt with effectively.

The relationship of recreation to the problem of delinquency becomes apparent. With many of the functions of the home being transferred to other social institutions, it behooves the public to provide an environment in which the child may fully develop. Wholesome recreation should be a part of that environment for play is a natural expression of youth. Organized recreation can supplement the home in the provision of leadership and opportunities testing the social self. The recreation worker joins the teacher, health official, social worker and parent in building the most favorable environment in which children may grow into full adulthood.

RECREATION AND THE CORRECTION OF JUVENILE DELINQUENCY

Despite efforts made to prevent delinquency, a large number of young offenders find themselves committed to institutions—reformatories, training schools, houses of correction, detention homes, and the like.

Training school is a term used for residential institutions, including camps, designed for the treatment, re-education and rehabilitation of delinquent children and youth. The first separate penal institution for young people in the United States was the New York House of Refuge, established in 1825. Training schools are called a variety of names, including agricultural and industrial schools, reformatories, reform schools, and the like. More than 45,000 boys and girls under the age of 21 can be found in the 129 public *state* training schools, 133 private institutions, and 57 *local* public institutions. Detention homes are places where the youth is held in secure custody, usually on a temporary basis, until further disposition is made of the case.

The modern and progressive penal institution for delinquents includes a recreation program. Young offenders are treated differently from adult law breakers. Minimum security in the reformatory is usually the role. Among other things, this widens the range for recreation. There are game rooms, theaters, libraries, shops, auditoriums, gymnasiums, and playing fields. There may be gardens and a swimming pool. Radios and television are permitted. Bands and orchestras, plays and shows, as well as crafts may be included. There is much emphasis on sports and athletics, and social recreation within limitations. All of these opportunities do not mean that the offenders are pampered. They do mean that recreation is an important phase of the institution's efforts at reformation, re-education, and rehabilitation and is vital in the lives of these young people—even more so in this place where they stay not of *their* own choosing—than elsewhere. Recreation in a penal institution may be the offender's main link with normal life.

The recreation program in a training school for delinquent youth does not necessarily differ from its counterpart, *community recreation*, in content. It does differ, however, in some other respects. For example, in the training school:

1. The recreation program is geared to helping sustain morale and expediting the rehabilitation process.

2. The recreation program is restricted to a given area, relatively small in terms of the total community.

3. The recreation program is always *supportive* and is not the main function.

The objectives of recreation programs in training schools for girls can be seen in the Abrahams' study: [6]

OBJECTIVES	NUMBER REPORTING
1. Social adjustment—getting along with others	12
2. Resocialization—developing healthy attitudes, rehabilitating, erasing neurotic tendencies	10
3. Developing skills for carry-over value in the community	9
4. Entertainment, joy, fun	6
5. Developing sportsmanship	5
6. Developing physical fitness	5
7. Releasing excess energy and tension	4
8. Giving status and acceptance, building morale	3
9. A leisure activity	3
	65 *

* Some schools listed several objectives.

[6] Joseph Abrahams, *An Analysis and Projection of Recreation Services for the Illinois State Training Schools for Girls* (Urbana, Illinois: Unpublished Thesis, University of Illinois, 1961).

Principles for Recreation in Penal Institutions

Experience shows that the following principles provide a sound basis for the establishment and conduct of recreation programs in penal institutions:

1. The recreation program must be geared and adapted to the purposes and objectives of the institution, to aid the individual in his adjustment to institutional life and to assist in the rehabilitating process.

2. The recreation service, as with all other institutional services, must function on the assumption that the inmate will eventually take his place in the normal life of the community, that he is capable of being rehabilitated.

3. An effort should be made to establish and maintain a bridge between institution and community life. This includes the integration of certain parts of the institutional recreation program with that of the community, where feasible.

4. Programs, facilities, and approaches should be such as to make institutional restrictions less visible.

5. Opportunities should be provided for the inmate to learn new recreational skills and develop new recreational interests, as well as sharpen and improve old ones.

6. The recreation program should be used neither as a reward for certain kinds of behavior nor as a means of punishment. Recreation is a basic human need and should be programmed as such, not as an extra or reward for good behavior.

The Rehabilitation Mission

Since offenders with few exceptions are eventually released, the reeducation, retraining, and reshaping of their social behavior patterns are of prime importance. Unless the institutions can somehow reshape the motives and attitudes of delinquents and assist them in their readjustment, punishment may actually contribute to further offenses. Penal administration recognizes the supreme importance of reclaiming and rehabilitating the offender.

Leaving aside preventive methods and probation and parole, we are concerned here with the particular part which recreation holds and should hold in institutional treatment. Unless recreation activities are in some way related to the personal situation of the offender there is no relationship between recreation and the rehabilitation process. As long as what is done in the institution is not related to the individual causes of criminal behavior, the recreation therapist operates solely on the theory of diversion or of filling out the day. Recreation is then used for the administrative convenience of the institution. A specialist in crime prevention put it this way:

As long as recreation, in whatever form it may be used, is unrelated to the diagnosis of the individual in the institution and the causative factors of his behavior, then that recreation has absolutely no value in the rehabilitative process. He comes to you with a vast accumulation of resentment, bitterness, discrimination, and repression, and a whole conglomeration of emotional factors which result in his antisocial behavior. Nothing you can do to him can transform him into a socially acceptable human being, as a rehabilitated human being, unless what you do is related to the cause of why he is there. Anything short of that, it seems to me, is a rank extravagance. Anything short of that is a compromise with reality.[7]

An anonymous prisoner, invited to share his views with the prison warden, speaks for himself:

. . . I'm here for rehabilitation. That consists of physical, mental, and moral adjustment in conformation with the standards of society. Unless you gain my sympathy with the effort, you will get exactly nowhere. And when my mind is tortured with a constant struggle to hold back the walls of my cell, when my body is burdened with a futile effort to throw off waste matter and take on new energy, I promise you I will be amenable to one thing only—freedom. Regimentation without feeling, routine without purpose, life without variety—these things convey to me nothing but a sense of punishment.

. . . In society, boredom produces dipsomaniacs, drug addicts, and gamblers; in prison it breeds worse. Either give a man normal interests in life—or he will develop abnormal ones. A man actively interested in a hobby, competitive sport, organized group activity, or any normal form of individual endeavor has very little waste energies to divert into channels of prison intrigue and degeneracy.

. . . In society, when my life became unpleasant through social, political, or economic circumstance over which I could exercise no control, instead of beating back the wall with recreation, I beat my brains out against it. And here I stand. . . .

Garret Heyns, warden of the Michigan Reformatory, considers other aspects of recreation in the rehabilitation process of the penal institutions: [8]

Among the inmates of correctional institutions there are many who have no knowledge or skills which will enable them to make acceptable use of their

[7] From an address by Edwin J. Lukes, Executive Director of the Society for the Prevention of Crime, given at a conference of the Regional Recreation Association of Correctional Institutions.

[8] Garret Heyns, "Penal Institutions," *The Annals of the American Academy of Political Science*, CCCXIII, September 1957, pp. 71–75.

leisure. Most of them lack the avocational interests of the well adjusted. They cannot play, they do not read, they have no hobbies. In many instances improper use of leisure is a factor in their criminality. Others lack the ability to engage in any co-operative activity with their fellows; team work is something foreign to their experience. Still others lack self-control or a sense of fair play; they cannot engage in competitive activity without losing their heads. If these men are to leave the institution as stable, well-adjusted individuals, these needs must be filled; the missing interests, knowledge, and skills must be provided. They must be brought into contact with opportunities which will eventually lead to their seeking out wholesome recreation activities when they return to society. It is the carry-over of such interests which concerns the institution in its effort at effecting rehabilitation.

Special Considerations

In addition to the application of the general principles previously presented, the following special suggestions are applicable to recreation for delinquents institutions:

There is a real need to educate the public to the values of a recreation program in penal institutions. The aim of social readjustment must supplant the aim of revenge and punishment.

It is necessary to understand the problems confronting the inmates, especially those which make them nervous and irritable. They are: problems of aggression, authority, and sex. The least provocation among inmates often leads to assaultive behavior. This must be kept in mind when bringing them in contact with one another in any kind of activity.

The institution should try to help improve human relationships in order to teach the inmates how to live together. There must also be some sort of training to prepare individuals for release. They should be encouraged and interested in self-improvement. Much depends upon stimulation given by the institutional staff.

The inmate's recreation should be relaxing, desired, absorbing, and worthwhile.

Organization

Recreation in a correctional institution must be organized and conducted to fit into the security plan of the specific institution. But here, as in any setting, recreation must be concerned with leadership, areas and facilities, program, and budget.

Leadership: Staff. In order to have a sound recreation program, one person should be given the responsibility to develop and administer the recreation service. Ideally, this qualified recreator should be one with an understanding of the application of the recreation program to the institution and to the preparation of the inmate for release. Preferably, he should be a graduate of a college with a major in recreation and have had supervised internship in a correctional institution that has a sound recreation program. He must be able to interpret and coordinate the recreation program with that of the institution as a whole. His is the task of blending recreation with rehabilitation so both ends are met.

Part-time leaders are sometimes used to supplement the full-time recreation staff. Specialists such as bandleaders or choral directors from the outside are engaged for a few hours each week. These leaders need to be as carefully selected and screened as are the full-time workers. This holds true for volunteers also. A correctional institution is no place for sentimentality, and the attitude of a volunteer should be determined prior to accepting his offer of service, no matter how skilled he may be in his field. He must have understanding of the prison program and be reliable. Part-time leaders and volunteers are a valuable addition to the professional leadership, but they must know and be willing to abide by the rules and regulations of custody and discipline of the institution and the general policies governing all conduct. Both part-time leaders and volunteers are used most successfully in correctional institutions where there is a well-trained staff member responsible for their selection, orientation, and supervision.

Inmates can be used for limited leadership where there is justifiable trust and competent supervision. Those not competent in leading can sometimes be entrusted with care of equipment and materials. Making use of their abilities tends to give the inmates a sense of responsibility and worth which is an important phase in the rehabilitation of some inmates.

Areas, Facilities, Supplies, and Equipment. It is desirable to have field space for sports activities as well as a hard-surfaced area which can serve as an outdoor gymnasium and as a roller-skating rink. Gymnasiums and swimming pools are valuable facilities for any institution.

Play equipment and supplies should be varied and provided in sufficient quantity so that no inmate is deprived of an opportunity to play. They should include arts and crafts equipment, power tools, supplies for music and entertainment (instruments, television sets, motion-picture projector, etc.), games, reading materials and the like.

The Program. At the time of admission, some institutions provide each inmate with a manual which explains the policies and practices of the institution, what the institution has to offer him, and what is expected of him. Included in the manual are lists of recreation opportunities and schedules and regulations governing them.

Also, many institutions do a complete "work-up" or interview of the trainee at the time he is admitted. This profile should include a description of the inmate's recreation experiences and interest. These data should be given to the recreation staff and used in the planning of the program. They are especially valuable for recreation or leisure counseling sessions.

Budget. Recreation program costs should be included in the annual budget of the institution. Some institutions' appropriations include the cost of leadership, but supplies and equipment are often bought from canteen profits. In some institutions, unfortunately, the canteen fund is the only source of money for the entire program, leadership included.

The Plan in Action

The recreation program of the Whittier California State School program is given here as an illustration.

In the way of physical equipment, there is a large gymnasium. . . . This unit is one story in height, with walls of reinforced supports. The floor of the main gymnasium section is of wood. Floors of the foyer, dressing rooms, office, and shower rooms located in the building are of concrete. The gymnasium has a large basketball court running its full length and side courts of sufficient size, but there is a scarcity of indoor athletic equipment. The gymnasium is handicapped by poor acoustic conditions.

There is also a large outdoor swimming pool, which is open most of the year. A well-kept, grass athletic field, with two full football fields and a surrounding 440-yard clay track with sidesloping wooden seats, is adjacent to the gymnasium. Other grassed space surrounding the various cottages is available to the boys for athletic purposes.

The objective of the recreation program is to give the boy exercise and recreation which are physically wholesome, mentally stimulating, and socially sound. Boys are given one period of from fifty to sixty minutes' physical education daily five days per week in six competitive sports, exclusive of build-up and corrective exercises. The fundamentals and skills of each seasonal sport are taught by the instructor. Intramural cottage competition is carried on every Saturday afternoon, and all boys are given an opportunity to participate except boys in the Receiving and Lost Privilege Cottages. As many as eighteen football teams play during ten weeks in the fall and winter. Some twenty intramural basketball teams contest for from eight to ten weeks. Eighteen to twenty track teams and sixteen soccer teams compete for from six to eight weeks seasonally, and there are also indoor baseball and softball teams and swimming teams. Boys are classified into three groups of A, B, and C in all sports and on a three-point coefficient classification of age, weight, and height. Approximately 80 per cent of the available boys participate in daily recreation activities of an organized nature. The remaining 20 per cent consists of those in the hospital, in Receiving Cottage, and Lost Privilege Cottage.

Boys in Receiving and Lost Privilege Cottages are directed in their recreation activities by their respective cottage supervisors. Such activities are limited to exercise on a small volleyball court for a half-hour in the morning, a half-hour in the evening, and on Saturday and Sunday.

The coach finds that the number and variety of teams competing in various sports open many athletic avenues of competition for each boy. As a further means of stimulating interest in sports, schedules of the coming week's events are posted on two bulletin boards in each of the cottages.

Motion pictures are shown in the chapel every Thursday and occasionally on Sundays. The films are loaned to the institutions free of charge and are not selected by the school in advance. Each cottage has its own radio, which is operated under the direction of the cottage group supervisor. Boys are also permitted to have their own radios in their rooms, which many do, as a privilege for good conduct. All radios must be off after 9:00 P.M. The radio is not used as an educational medium.

Although all the principal holidays, including "Admission Day," which is the day on which California was admitted to the Union, are observed, they are marked essentially as quiet days, and boys have no regularly scheduled programs. Up to last year, holidays were celebrated with comprehensive athletic programs.

A magazine known as the *Sentinel,* published for the most part by the boys, is printed at the school every other month. Ten copies are distributed to each cottage, and issues are regularly mailed to similar children's institutions in the United States, to juvenile court judges, and other interested people.

Occasionally, talent entertainments are given by the boys around Christmas, depending upon the leadership of each cottage supervisor.

Outside community activities are represented in the school by the Junior Civitan Club sponsored by the Civitan Club of Pasadena. At one time the school also had a Boy Scout troop which occupied one of the regular cottages, then known as Scout Cottage, but the troop was discontinued in favor of concentrating on the honor club program. The school band frequently plays during the summer months in outside community affairs in neighboring towns within a radius of seventy-five miles. Formerly the school engaged widely in outside athletic competition, but these programs were discontinued when it was found that they restricted athletics to only a few boys.

Outside contacts with service clubs are extensively cultivated. The Elks, Civitans, Kiwanis, and Women's Clubs are interested in the school's work and frequently visit the institution individually and in groups. The Elks, through its Crippled Kiddies Committee, assist boys who are physically handicapped. The Orange County Rotary Club arranges for funds to assist boys on parole through loans. The Veterans of Foreign Wars annually donate a bronze medal to the outstanding boy in the school, who is chosen by the superintendent from a small group of boys selected as competitors by the staff. Judges and prominent persons are also invited to the school at various times and participate as guest speakers at the regular placement breakfast of boys leaving the school. Annually on Decoration Day the boys hold memorial services at the local cemetery over the graves of soldiers who were killed in the war, and who were at one time students at the school.

Boys are permitted to have visits from home on the second and fourth

Sundays of each month. Visitors may remain all day and picnic in a designated visiting area. Those coming from distant points may visit at any time. Permission for visits is granted by the superintendent, the assistant superintendent, or the chief group supervisor.

At the New York State Training School for Boys,[9] there is a full-time recreation staff, headed by a recreation director and three assistants. Under their supervision every boy is given recreation opportunities. There are regularly scheduled play periods, organized sports, individual sports, various types of activities, motion pictures and plays, cottage parties, special events programs, and individual attention whenever requested or desired. The entire recreation program is considered an integral part of a boy's life while he is in the school, and is aimed at giving the boy some standards of sportsmanship, as well as leisure-time recreation.

The Whittier and New York Training School programs are illustrations of what might be done with the delinquent while he is an institution. The rehabilitative process, however, transcends the institution and continues once the parolee returns home. In fact, it begins at the moment of sentence. The social worker assigned a probationer or parolee should be concerned with the leisure moments of the delinquent and should seek out the cooperation of the recreation specialist in the community. Efforts should be made to involve the delinquent in programs with non-delinquents, to move him forward in his acceptance of more socially approved forms of behavior. The task is not a simple one, especially when the community is skeptical of mixing "criminals" with "good" children. In some instances, this is best achieved in a half-way house program. In other cases, it has been effectively handled through special youth agencies such as HARYOU-ACT or through volunteer agencies such as the YMCA. An effective delinquency prevention and rehabilitation program requires the cooperative effort of all involved—the home, the school, the judicial system, the correctional institution, the community. There is no substitute for teamwork and recreation is a member of the team.

THE WORKSHOP

1. Debate the question, "Is there a correlation between an individual's recreation habits and antisocial behavior?"
2. Visit a reformatory or industrial school for delinquents and observe the recreation program and facilities.

[9] New York State Training School for Boys, Department of Social Welfare, Orange County, New York.

3. Interview a judge, policeman, social worker, and parent to obtain their comments on the causes of juvenile delinquency.
4. Discuss ways and means of including recreation in the rehabilitation of a youth who has been incarcerated for an offense against society.
5. Devise a recreation program for a small youth-detention home to which delinquent youths are assigned only for several days or weeks.
6. Discuss the question of how problem children should be handled in community recreation centers.
7. Discuss the role of the home, school, and church in curbing juvenile delinquency.
8. Make a list of danger signs of potential delinquency in children and discuss them.
9. Discuss the gang as a positive social force in the life of a teenager. Offer suggestion to maximize these positive aspects; to prevent the negative ones.

REFERENCES

Goodman, Paul, *Growing Up Absurd.* New York: Random House, 1960.

Heyns, Garret, "Penal Institutions," *The Annals of the American Academy of Political Science.* Philadelphia: The American Academy of Political Science, CCCXIII, September, 1957.

McDonald, Donald, *The Police* (Interviews on American Character). Santa Barbara, Calif.: Center for the Study of Democratic Institutions, 1962.

National Congress of Parents and Teachers, *What PTA Members Should Know About Juvenile Delinquency.* Chicago: National Congress of Parents and Teachers, 1957.

New York State Youth Commission, *Blueprint for Delinquency Prevention.* Albany: New York State Youth Commission.

Shaw, Otto, *Youth in Crisis.* New York: Hart Publishing Company, 1966.

Shireman, Charles H., *The Hyde Park Youth Project.* Chicago.: Welfare Council of Metropolitan Chicago, 1958.

Task Force on Juvenile Delinquency, *Juvenile Delinquency and Youth Crime.* Washington, D.C.: The President's Commission on Law Enforcement, 1967.

Thrasher, Frederick, *The Gang.* Chicago: University of Chicago Press, 1927.

Comment

Youth Board News, a publication of the New York City Youth Board, 79 Madison Ave., New York City, has excellent information on delinquency and bibliographical sources.

The National Recreation and Park Association, National Probation and Parole Association, Children's Bureau and Department of Health, Education and Welfare have materials for distribution on delinquency.

Most worthwhile are the reports from the White House Conference on Children and Youth, Department of Health, Education, and Welfare, and the publications of the President's Commission on Law Enforcement and Administration of Justice.

The reports of the Joint Commission for the study of Power for the Field of Corrections provide some interesting data on recreation and its role in the field of corrections.

Epilogue

Above: Bear dens at Detroit Zoological Park. Left: Modern facilities for modern play. Below: Picnic— standard American pastime.

Above: Exploding recreational use.
Below: Puppet theatre—Oakland,
California.

21

Organizations Serving the Recreation and Park Movement

Need for Professional Groups

The significance of recreation in modern society is partially reflected in the advance of recreation *as a profession*. Recreation, as a profession, is young when compared with education, medicine, law, and religion. But its growth as a profession is shown in many ways. The number of books about the philosophy, methods, techniques, and purposes of recreation is increasing. Job opportunities not only are increasing, but are more attractive in many ways, including better salaries and more liberal employment practices. Inroads are being made in various problems of research. Codes of professional ethics for those who practice recreation have been established and adopted on an everwidening scale. Civil service now lists qualification requirements for advancement and job placement of recreators, and recreation personnel now voluntarily register nationally and in the states. One of the strongest indicators of the new prestige of recreation personnel is the development of organizations dedicated to the advancement and improvement of recreation on a professional basis.

These professional groups give to people in recreation, and to those preparing to enter the field, a chance to pool their common interests for the benefit of the movement and themselves. Through the professional

377

organization, mutual interests, concerns, and experiences can be shared. These organizations also provide a means for establishing and promulgating standards, for exchanging information and ideas, and for interpreting the work as well as making articulate recreation interests.

In 1966 five of these organizations merged into *The National Recreation and Park Association*. A brief historical sketch of these groups follows. They are presented according to their foundation dates.

The American Institute of Park Executives grew from the New England Association of Park Superintendents, which was founded in 1898 and later was known as the American Association of Park Superintendents. American Institute of Park Executives members were drawn from executive positions in public parks throughout the United States and Canada. The Institute had a commissioners section and branch organizations including the Midwest Institute of Park Executives, California Society of the American Institute of Park Executives, and the New England Park Association.

The National Recreation Association was organized in 1906 as the Playground and Recreation Association of America. As the first organization of its kind, The National Recreation Association was a major force in the development of the recreation movement for 60 years. National Recreation Association membership included both professionals and private citizens concerned with providing recreational opportunities for people of all ages. To implement its programs, the Association had district, national and international offices.

The National Conference on State Parks was founded in 1921 as a professional and service organization for state park professionals and laymen. Its purpose was to provide information to the public on the values and functions of state parks, historic sites, monuments and recreation preserves. It encouraged the study of natural history and science, the preservation of wildlife in a natural setting, and the conservation of the natural environment.

The American Association of Zoological Parks and Aquariums was established as an affiliate of The American Institute of Park Executives in 1924. Zoological gardens and aquariums are closely allied to the public park system, but their personnel require substantially different knowledge from the general park administrator. For this reason, The American Association of Zoological Parks and Aquariums was organized to provide a professional association for zoo and aquarium directors, curators and other professionals concerned with the preservation of wildlife and its display for the general public.

The American Recreation Society was established in 1938 as the Society of Recreation Workers of America. Its primary objective was to unite in one organization all recreation professionals in the United States. American Recreation Society branches were instituted to provide special services to practitioners working in the Armed Forces, hospitals, industry, colleges and universities, public agencies at all government levels, rural recreation activities, voluntary organizations and other sectors of the recreation field.

The Merger of 1966—The National Recreation and Park Association

During the first half of the 20th Century, these five organizations were the principal leaders in encouraging the development of parks and recreation throughout the United States. Although their membership included park and recreation professionals, each had a different philosophy, direction and scope which made cooperation difficult.

As World War II drew to a close, however, leaders of these organizations realized that the United States was on the threshold of a new leisure era. The nation had the highest standard of living in the world, and Americans were increasingly seeking new means of expressing themselves in their leisure time.

Professional and lay leaders concerned with resources management and recreation programming realized separate professional organizations were no longer practical and that some means must be found to unify these organizations to better serve both the general public and practitioners.

The first discussion of unification came in 1948 when the Athletic Institute financed a meeting between officials of the American Institute of Park Executives and the American Recreation Society. Although little was accomplished at this gathering, the merger seed was planted, and sporadic talks continued over the next 10 years.

In October 1958, the American Recreation Society and the American Institute of Park Executives each appointed committees to further probe the possibility of unification. Talks continued for the next year, and in September 1959, a joint committee was established. Both organizations took surveys of their membership to determine the will of the rank and file member.

Meanwhile, the American Recreation Society and the National Recreation Association had also been conducting exploratory talks. In January 1962, the boards of both organizations met and appointed a joint sub-committee to study the feasibility of merging the two organizations.

At the American Institute of Park Executives Kansas City conference in September 1962, a panel discussion between representatives of the American Recreation Society, the National Recreation Association and the American Institute of Park Executives was held to acquaint members with the problems that consolidation of the three organizations would bring.

A month later, at the National Recreation Congress in Philadelphia, a joint meeting of the National Recreation Association and American Recreation Society boards was held. The boards agreed to form a joint study committee to map a practical working plan for merger.

As these talks progressed, the executive director of the American Institute of Park Executives was directed by his board in September 1963 to enter negotiations with the National Recreation Association, the American Recreation Society and other organizations to seek unification or federation. A forum was held for representatives of these three organizations at the National Recreation Congress later that month, and the report of the joint National Recreation Association—American Recreation Society study committee was presented at the Congress.

The executive directors of the three organizations continued to work on details of the merger plan for the next few months; and on January 19, 1964, a merger plan was approved in principle at a joint board meeting of the American Recreation Society and American Institute of Park Executives.

Throughout the spring of 1964, further details were hammered out. Then, in April, the National Recreation Association presented a counter proposal that would merge all three organizations. The primary merger obstacle was the makeup of the new organization's governing board. The board members of the American Recreation Society and the American Institute of Park Executives were primarily professionals, while the board of the National Recreation Association was composed of lay leaders. In June, the National Recreation Association stated firmly that it would not enter any agreement unless the corporative board was comprised predominantly of lay representation.

In October 1964, the American Institute of Park Executives Executive Board voted to broaden merger talks to include not only the American Recreation Society, the American Association of Zoological Parks and Aquariums and the National Recreation Association, but also the National Conference on State Parks and the National Industrial Recreation Association. Authorization for this action was based on a previous membership referendum.

In November, a meeting was held in Chicago in which various board members of the proposed merging organizations met to discuss problems and possible solutions. A key proposal suggested that the unified organization should be directed by a board dominated by lay representatives, yet under the basic influence of professionals.

At a meeting at Oglebay Park, Wheeling, West Virginia, on February 28—March 1, 1965, the American Institute of Park Executives, the American Recreation Society and the National Recreation Association formally approved merger. Drafting of the new constitution continued through March; and by April, all recognized national organizations in the park, recreation and conservation field had been invited to join the proposed new National Recreation and Park Association.

On May 23, 1965, the American Institute of Park Executives voted to ratify and endorse the proposed constitution and by-laws; and on August 14, at the end of a two-day meeting at the Americana Hotel in New York City, the merger was consummated under the revised charter of the National Recreation Association.

Essentially, the new organization had two professional branches: (1) the American Park and Recreation Society, which was a combination of the American Institute of Park Executives, the American Recreation Society and the professional members of the National Recreation Association; and (2) the American Association of Zoological Parks and Aquariums, which existed originally as an independent branch of the American Institute of Park Executives and was carried over into the new organization under a revised constitution.

On September 29, 1965, the members of the National Conference on State Parks voted to join the united organization as a branch of the lay division. It retained its name and identity.

The first meeting of the National Recreation and Park Association Board of Trustees was held at the Americana Hotel in New York City on December 2, 1965. Plans were formulated to transfer various properties held by the merging organizations to the National Recreation and Park Association.

The merger became effective on January 1, 1966.

The first Congress for Recreation and Parks was held in Washington, D.C., October 3–9, 1966. This first national meeting of the National Recreation and Park Association was addressed by President Lyndon B. Johnson, Secretary of the Interior Stewart L. Udall, Secretary of Agriculture Orville L. Freeman, Secretary of Housing and Urban Development Robert C. Weaver and the first National Recreation and Park Association President Laurance S. Rockefeller.

The Congress business sessions were also productive. The National Therapeutic Recreation Society and the Society of Park and Recreation Educators were granted charters as professional branches. The National Therapeutic Recreation Society was formed by the merger of the Hospital Section of the American Recreation Society (known as American Park and Recreation Society after the merger) and the independent National Association of Recreation Therapists. The Society of Park and Recreation Educators was organized by professional educators who were formerly members of the American Park and Recreation Society.

On October 19, 1966, the National Conference on State Parks voted to change its branch status from the lay division to the professional division.

This action was ratified by the Board of Trustees at its meeting the following April.

As administrative problems were being overcome, so were the physical problems. On October 21, 1966, the National Recreation and Park Association opened its new national headquarters at 1700 Pennsylvania Avenue, N.W., in Washington, D.C.—just one block from the White House. This move proved to be a major effort, entailing the gathering of personnel, equipment and records from all parts of the United States.

At the 1967 Congress for Recreation and Parks held in Miami Beach, Florida, the Armed Forces Recreation Society and the Commissioners-Board Members Branch were officially affiliated with the Association. The Armed Forces Recreation Society evolved from a special section of the former American Recreation Society, and the Commissioners-Board Members Branch was formed to include members of park and recreation boards and commissions for the first time.

As the merging organizations combined forces, the new Association took on a broad scope. As stated in its literature, "The National Recreation and Park Association is dedicated to the wise use of leisure, conservation of natural and human resources and beautification of the total American environment. It is actively concerned with improvement of park and recreation facilities and programs, and with providing more wholesome and meaningful leisure opportunities for everyone."

The seven professional and lay branches chartered by the Association include the Armed Forces Recreation Society, the American Association of Zoological Parks and Aquariums, the American Park and Recreation Society, the National Conference on State Parks, the National Therapeutic Recreation Society, the Society of Park and Recreation Educators and the Commissioners-Board Members Branch.

The Association is financially supported entirely through public contributions, endowments, grants and membership fees. Much of its income is raised annually through community United Fund efforts. Among the general services the National Recreation and Park Association provides are research and experimentation, information, education, awards, interagency liaison and public relations.

Research and Experimentation—National Recreation and Park Association conducts surveys and studies on the status of parks and recreation in the United States in an effort to predict future trends for planning purposes. It also conducts demonstration projects and experiments to determine if innovations are feasible. Some of these studies have included personnel training; facility design; equipment durability; lifetime sports instruction; recreation programming for the ill and handicapped, mentally retarded, aged, etc.; salary studies; financial resources; federal assistance programs; model legislation; inner city recreation problems; and others. Many projects are conducted in conjunction with research-oriented institutions.

Information—National Recreation and Park Association provides an extensive information program. As new ideas, techniques, procedures and methods are constantly being tried to meet the growing needs of leisure-conscious Americans, the results of these innovations are gathered, evaluated, condensed and filed by the Association.

This information is constantly being disseminated to National Recreation and Park Association members and the general public through correspondence, consultation, publications, a resources library, and a book sales center.

Education and Personnel Services—Throughout the United States the Association sponsors numerous conventions, schools, seminars, workshops, forums, and short courses for professionals in the park and recreation field. In addition to the annual Congress for Recreation and Parks, National Recreation and Park Association has sponsored district conferences, institutes on federal assistance programs, a revenue sources management school, executive development institutes, numerous programming conferences and special schools on various pertinent topics. Many educational programs are conducted by colleges and universities. Additionally, a personnel placement service is provided for professionals and agencies.

Awards—Recognition awards are given annually to individuals and organizations throughout the country for their voluntary efforts to provide better park and recreation facilities and services in their home communities. The purpose of these awards is to foster citizen involvement in community park and recreation programs.

Inter-agency Liaison—As the largest national professional and service organization in the park and recreation field, the National Recreation and Park Association provides a means for public, private, voluntary, commercial, industrial and church park and recreation agencies to reach common understandings in a variety of relationships. By providing this encouragement, the National Recreation and Park Association helps to eliminate overlapping of services and provide greater efficiency throughout the entire park and recreation field. The Association also advises Congress on pending park and recreation bills, develops model enabling legislation for states and encourages merger of community park and recreation agencies wherever feasible.

Public Relations—Through publications, speeches, correspondence, consultation, awards, information and other methods, the National Recreation and Park Association conducts an extensive public relations campaign to acquaint all Americans with the vital importance of parks and recreation to the physical and mental health of all Americans.

The National Recreation and Park Association's information and education programs keep professionals aware of national trends, teach them new methods and new techniques and give them specialized knowledge they might not otherwise obtain in their everyday jobs.

ADDITIONAL PROFESSIONAL ORGANIZATIONS

An exhaustive list of professional organizations actively concerned with recreation would cover many pages. Consequently, just a few of them are briefly described with respect to their purposes and functions.

American Camping Association (Bradford Woods, Martinsville, Indiana). The American Camping Association, incorporated in 1910, is made up of representatives of agencies and institutions interested in the development of organized camping in the United States and Canada. (It is affiliated with the Canadian Camping Association.) Its membership consists of camp directors, members of camp staffs, educators, and others directly associated with the operation of camps or interested in the camping movement. It represents camping of all types: private, organization, church, school, public, and institutional.

The A.C.A. operates to advance camping in all of its branches to reach a constantly growing number of young people and adults. Recently, it added *family camping* to its wide range of promotional interests.

The purpose of the Association, as expressed in its constitution, is: "To further the interests and welfare of children and adults through camping as an educative and recreative experience."

It serves as the voice of camping people, nationally and locally. It assumes leadership in developing camping in new areas. It acts as the channel through which new trends in camping are disseminated to the membership and to the public. It develops standards and operating codes for the improvement of camping practices. It provides fellowship for camping people and those in allied fields.

It interprets camping to related fields and to the general public. It is the organization through which trained and practicing camp directors endeavor to express the views of the profession and strive to lead in shaping policies and techniques of camping in the United States.

The Association consists of sections located in all parts of the country, with a national board representing the sections.

A section is a chartered unit of the Association representing a geographic area, with officers corresponding to the national officers.

The national association sponsors workshops and special conferences where experts from all parts of the country meet to explore new trends, develop standards, and formulate emphases and goals for the attention of the members, and to set the pace for national action.

Camp directors and counselors receive from the Association advisory and consultory service through national and sectional offices, officers, and chairmen of special and standing committees.

The official organ of the Association is the *Camping Magazine,* published eight times a year. In the interest of camping, the Association also issues from time to time pamphlets, studies, reports, and other publications.

American Association for Health, Physical Education, and Recreation (1201 16th Street N.W., Washington 6, D.C.). The AAHPER, founded in 1885 as the Association for the Advancement of Physical Education, is a department of the National Education Association. It is dedicated to the improvement of health education, physical education, and recreation in the United States. The Association has both functional divisions and component health, physical education, and recreation groups in the states as well as in colleges and universities. A number of other allied professional groups, such as the State Directors of Health, Physical Education, and Recreation, are affiliated with the AAHPER.

The Association sponsors district conferences and a national convention. It represents the professional interests of its members in many ways, including the establishment and promulgation of personnel and program standards and the support of legislation of interest to the profession. It sponsors training institutes and workshops, provides technical, consultative, and correspondence services, serves as a center for the exchange of information, and helps recruit and place professional personnel. This Association also does interpretive work among educators, encourages practical research, and publishes bibliographies, conference reports, rosters, bulletins, guides, yearbooks, surveys, and other helpful materials.

Periodicals include the *AAHPER Journal* and the *Research Quarterly.*

Association of College Unions (Willard Straight Hall, Cornell University, Ithaca, New York). The Association of College Unions was organized in 1914 for the purpose of giving unions a chance to share interests, information, and problems and to help in the development and improvement of college unions and their programs and services. College student associations and groups which have as their purpose the promotion of social and recreation opportunities for students, as well as college unions, are eligible for membership.

The Association of College Unions provides a number of services. These include:

Plans and conducts regional meetings and a national conference.
Undertakes research in the union field, including surveys of policies and practices.
Fosters national and regional tournaments in some union activities.
Protects the interests of members in entertainment bookings.
Provides architectural and program planning services.

Conducts photographic exhibition loan services.

Operates an employment service in the student union field.

Among the Association's publications are its quarterly bulletin, conference proceedings, manuals, and handbooks.

National Association of Social Workers—Group Work Section (95 Madison Avenue, New York 16, New York). The purpose of this group is to promote association among education, recreation, and group workers; to raise personnel standards; to encourage continued study of social group work practice knowledge and skills, including professional education; to encourage research; and to provide individual and corporate action on matters affecting group work practice. The Association has local chapters through which its purposes are translated into action. The N.A.S.W. program is also developed through the work of national committees which concern themselves with the function of the professional group worker, personnel practices, professional education, publications, research and study, and social action. The Association also publishes books and pamphlets on various phases and problems of social group work.

Its periodicals include the magazine, *The Group,* and a newsletter.

National Industrial Recreation Association (203 North Wabash Avenue, Chicago 1, Illinois). The National Industrial Recreation Association is dedicated to the purpose of helping to develop and improve recreation for employees. Its membership is made up largely of companies and their branches which have employee recreation programs.

The Association is a clearing house through which information and ideas are exchanged on all kinds of problems related to the planning, organization, and operation of recreation programs serving employees and their families. It provides correspondence and consultation services, issues bulletins, reports, and guides, and aids in placement and training. NIRA's official publications are the monthly magazine, *RECREATION MANAGEMENT,* and NIRA Newsletter, with Idea Clinic.

Professional Service Agencies

Just as there are many professional fellowship organizations, there are also many professional service agencies. Among such agencies are the Athletic Institute, American National Red Cross, American Youth Hostels, Boy Scouts of America, Camp Fire Girls, Girl Scouts of the U.S.A., National Jewish Welfare Board, Young Men's Christian Association, and Young Women's Christian Association and others. In this category, too, would be found the numerous federal and state governmental agencies engaged in some aspect of recreation.

For illustrative purposes, only the services of one such service agency are described here:

The Athletic Institute (Room 805, Merchandise Mart, Chicago 54, Illinois). The Athletic Institute is a nonprofit corporation whose purpose it is to promote, encourage, improve, and help advance the fields of sports and athletics, recreation, physical education, and health education, with a view to securing more widespread participation in these fields. It is supported by the manufacturers and purveyors of sports and recreation equipment who subscribe to the thought that by helping others they help themselves.

The services, efforts, and projects of the Athletic Institute cover a wide range of activities which are extremely beneficial to the advancement of recreation.

The Institute has a board of directors and at least four important working committees which include the Executive-Finance Committee, Membership Committee, Intra-Industry Relations Committee, and the Professional Advisory Committee to the President. The Advisory Committee is composed of outstanding educators and practitioners in recreation, physical education, and athletics.

The Institute translates its objectives into action in a variety of ways. For example, it provides help and financial assistance to such endeavors as the Junior Chamber of Commerce Sports Program, the National and American Baseball Congresses, the Amateur Softball Association, and American Legion Baseball. It makes available low cost, audio-visual instructional slide films on many sports. It produces outstanding films on recreation such as "Careers in Recreation" and "Town and Country Recreation." The Institute publishes pamphlets, guides, and reports on many phases in recreation. Outstanding among its contributions to the professional field has been its financing and sponsoring of national workshops. Out of these work sessions, attended by national leaders and teachers, have come some fine articles in the field, as well as programs of action. The Institute also serves as a catalyst for the merging of interests among the several professional organizations. It operates a correspondence and information service and has recently started a field service. It is a potent force in the advancement of the profession and the movement.

Recreation Interest Groups

In addition to the professional *fellowship* and professional *service* organizations, there are countless organizations which provide resources for the development of recreation in relation to specialized interests or problems. The number of such organizations would easily go into three and perhaps four figures. For purposes of illustration, *selected* examples of such groups (*not* previously here listed) are as follows:

Academy of Model Aeronautics
Amateur Athletic Union of the United
  States
Amateur Skating Union of the United
  States
Amateur Softball Association of
  America
American Baseball Congress
American Bowling Congress
American Contract Bridge League
American Federation of Arts
American Lawn Bowling Association
American Library Association
American Nature Association
American Philatelic Society
American Power Boat Association
American Shuffleboard Leagues
American Theater Wing
American Water Ski Association
American Youth Hostels
Fish and Wildlife Service
Hobby Guild of America
Izaak Walton League of America
Little League Baseball
Model Yacht Racing Association
  of America
National Archery Association of the
  U.S.
National Association of Angling and
  Casting Clubs

Amateur Badminton Association
Amateur Bicycle League of America
Amateur Fencers' League of America
National Audubon Society
National Collegiate Athletic Association
National Conference on State Parks
National Council of State Garden Clubs
National Federation of Music Clubs
National Field Archery Association
National Golf Foundation
National Horseshoe Pitchers Associa-
  tion of America
National Philatelic Society
National Shuffleboard Association
National Skeet Shooting Association
National Ski Association of America
National Softball Congress of America
National Wildlife Federation
Outboard Boating Club of America
Professional Golfers Association of
  America
Professional Lawn Tennis Association
  of U.S.
U.S. Amateur Roller Skating
  Association
U.S. Floor Tennis Association
U.S. Handball Association
U.S. Lawn Tennis Association
U.S. Table Tennis Association
U.S. Volleyball Association

THE WORKSHOP

1. Interview a professional recreator and secure his reactions to the values of
   professional organization.
2. Attend a local or district meeting of a professional organization and evaluate
   its worth.
3. Explore the differences and similarities between a professional *fellowship*
   organization and a professional *service* agency.
4. Invite a professional recreator to speak to your group on "How you will
   benefit from belonging to a given professional organization."
5. Examine the program and activities of a professional group and compare
   them with the purposes for which it was founded.
6. Prepare a plan for organizing a student chapter of one of the professional
   recreation organizations.
7. List the characteristics of a profession.

8. Compare the status of the recreation profession with a few of the older established professions.
9. Report on a state voluntary registration program for recreation personnel.
10. Discuss the advantages and disadvantages of unifying all of the professional groups into one organization.

REFERENCES AND COMMENTS

All professional groups have printed material available on the purposes, organization, functions, services, and benefits of their groups. A number of these organizations also provide directories and rosters of their membership. Such information can be secured directly by communicating with these organizations.

In Appendix B—there is an excellent listing of national non-governmental agencies and organizations interested primarily in Recreation from a professional specialty approach.

Get a listing of state Recreation and Park Societies from the National Recreation and Park Association. Each will have professional information. Many of them print a professional journal.

The National Recreation and Park Association should be contacted for information.

Many recreation text books have chapters devoted to professional developments—check them.

22

Administration

Thus far, in this volume, attention has been given to the historical, philosophical, and theoretical background of recreation, play, and leisure, as well as to the settings, conditions, and problems with which recreation is involved. Organized recreation, however, requires planning, management, and direction. It calls for the securing and use of certain tools—money, personnel, facilities, methods, and the like—applied intelligently. This chapter sets forth the important highlights and considerations in administering organized recreation services. Administration refers to the *organization, direction, management, and control of all matters related to providing recreation services.*[1]

PLANNING AND RESEARCH

If effective recreation services are to be established, there must be careful and intelligent planning. A community study or survey should be made to bring to light the recreation needs and interests of the people, the resources—laws, facilities, personnel, funds, and the like—available to

[1] Although the basic principles and considerations of administration are common to *all* organized recreation services, those mentioned here are presented in terms of local public recreation. Attention is given to the *major factors* involved in recreation administration and *not* to their *detailed application,* which is the basis for special volumes devoted to Recreation and Park Administration.

help meet the need, and an appropriate, workable plan of action. In this way, not only are the needs and problems discovered, but the resources for meeting them are also mobilized and used, and a course for future action is charted.

Depending upon the situation, the study of recreation in the community may be limited or quite extensive in scope. Often it includes information on:

1. Population (number, age, sex, race, trends, and the like).
2. Characteristics of the community (historical, geographical, climatic, economic, cultural, sociological).
3. Government (type, status, powers, finances, departmental resources).
4. Laws (local and state) related to recreation.
5. Residential data (housing, real estate developments).
6. Social problems (health, delinquency, accidents, relief case rate).
7. Facilities, personnel, equipment, finances, programs, and services of:
   A. Public agencies, such as parks, beaches, forests, golf courses, schools, playgrounds, libraries, museums.
   B. Voluntary agencies, such as the Boy Scouts, Girl Scouts, Boys Clubs, Jewish community centers, settlements, Y.M.C.A.'s, Y.W.C.A.'s.
   C. Commercial agencies, such as the motion pictures, bowling lanes, amusement parks.
   D. Employee associations and organizations.
   E. Religious organizations and groups.
   F. Private and civic clubs and organizations.

A study of the need for local public recreation services might begin, for example, by discussing *recreation—as a basic human need*. This might be followed by a narrative on *recreation—a function of government* and a setting forth of the *guiding principles for public recreation and park services*. Next, there would be a presentation of the *standards for public recreation and park areas and facilities*. If there were a facilities emphasis in the study, at this point there would be included, perhaps, a discussion of *the important factors to be considered in design and layout of the recreation and park areas and facilities*. Depending upon the situation, *principles and factors in programming*, or in providing recreation services, also would be presented. Finally, it is often customary to include in the study *information on administration*, including material on the governmental pattern of the community, the financial considerations, the choices and types of managing authorities, the leadership, organization and management aspects, the community and neighborhood organization elements, and the agency-organization-departmental relationships.

Tables, charts, diagrams, and pictures are often used to illustrate the problems, conditions, and needs. After the above and similar information are secured and assembled, an analysis is made of the data, and the needs, gaps, and deficiencies are evaluated. This evaluation may be made in connection with accepted professional standards related to the adequacy of facilities and space, program, funds, and personnel, for communities similar in size and make-up, or simply assessed in terms of local conditions. The survey may undertake to define the major areas of need and services and allocate responsibilities for them. It may serve as a basis for meeting immediate needs or long-range needs over a period of years. In any event, the study or survey includes a list of recommendations and findings based upon principles set forth in the study and may even include a priorities schedule, indicating the problems and needs and the order in which they should receive attention. Some surveys and studies include suggestions on implementing the recommendations.

Studies and surveys do not always include all aspects of community recreation. In some instances they may be concerned only with those programs which are tax-supported. In other cases they may be aimed at alleviating a given social problem, such as increased juvenile delinquency. In still other situations, the study may be concerned only with providing facts helpful in the building or construction of recreation facilities. The initiative for starting surveys and studies comes from different sources—perhaps a municipality, a community chest, or even a civic group, such as the Chamber of Commerce or Rotary Club. But effective recreation services must always be preceded by careful study of the situation.

The making of a recreation survey, however, is only one element in the planning process. The survey or study is the device which presents the picture of things as they are and the blueprint for things as they might be. The problem of actually improving conditions through planning—getting the best results in the most efficient way—calls for knowledge of, and ability to bring into systematic and effective action, all of the other elements upon which discussion is to follow. What is more, planning is not static. It is a continuing process involving careful and extensive thought, deliberation, and action. A most important part of planning is *research*—research in every phase of recreation.

Research results in the development of a scientfiic body of knowledge based upon intelligent and objective study and exploration. It means a continuing search for information not only on the techniques, methods, and tools for getting the job done, but also on the basic needs, purposes, values, and potentials of recreation as they bear upon the well-being of the individual, the group, and the community.

Research in recreation, up to now, has been largely of the *survey* type—making inventories of recreation facilities, making interest studies, compiling statistics on resources, and the like. These are important, but there is also a real need for more basic research. We refer to the kinds of research which would enlighten us on the question of what recreation can do for people. Of course, planning need not be delayed until everything is proven. But research is needed to help develop, modify, and test principles. Research is an essential tool in the administration of recreation services.

The patterns in the development of research studies are rather routine and usually take the outline of something comparable to the following:

Statement of the problem.
Purpose of the study or investigation.
Hypothesis (suppositions, unproved theory).
Need for the study or research.
Scope, range, and limitations of the undertaking.
Definition of terms.
Methods and techniques of research which are used.
Analysis of the data.
Findings.
Conclusions.
Recommendations.

LEGISLATION

All local recreation programs, services, and facilities supported with tax funds have their foundations of authority in local and state laws. Much of organized recreation, whether under governmental auspices or not, is at least indirectly influenced by law. For example, a nonprofit, voluntary youth-serving agency secures its permission to incorporate through the state government which, in turn, has laws governing the incorporation of such bodies. Again, the seating capacity of a motion-picture theater must conform to state and often local regulations born of state laws and municipal ordinances. Tax supported recreation systems are even more directly related to public laws inasmuch as their very functions and operations are specifically defined and authorized by law.

Local and state laws are not the sole legislation which governs public recreation. Where national interests are involved in tax-supported recreation, there are also laws of the federal government. These laws relate to recreation in the public domain, to parks and forests, to the propagation and protection of plant and animal life, to the conservation of natural resources, to the regulation of interstate commerce, to public health and safety, to public education involving federal funds, and to many other phases of recreation in which the federal government has an interest.

As far as local, public recreation services are concerned, however, we are concerned with laws at two levels of government—(1) local or *community laws* and (2) *state laws*.

Local Laws

The local law authorizes the provision of recreation services. Such legislation must conform to (1) the *state recreation enabling laws* or (2) to the local *charter* where home rule applies (community charters are approved by the state). If the former, the local legislation is known as an *ordinance*.

The purpose of the local recreation law is to define the organization, powers, duties, functions, and responsibilities of the group selected to manage the recreation system, such as the recreation commission or board. In some instances, the law may authorize the provision of recreation services through an existing agency of government—as a board of education or a school board—without establishing a new body to perform these services. Local recreation ordinances are usually prepared and passed by the governing body of the community. When units of government such as park departments and school boards are financially and legally independent of the remainder of city government, they may establish their own ordinances. Generally, the local recreation ordinance or law refers to:

1. The state laws which authorize the establishment of local recreation services.

2. The local body or managing authority which shall be responsible for local public recreation services. If a recreation commission, for example, is established, the ordinance indicates the number of members, how and by whom appointed, what officers shall serve, basis upon which members are to serve (usually without pay), representation on the commission, and the terms of service for the members.

3. Responsibilities and functions of the commission (determining policies, rules, and regulations; employing personnel; submitting reports; receiving gifts and bequests for recreation; levying fees and charges, and the like).

4. Authorization for the commission to work cooperatively with other departments and agencies, and, in some instances, other communities.

5. Geographical jurisdiction of the managing authority.

6. Authorization for the provision, conduct, and supervision of broad programs, services, and facilities.

State Laws

The laws of the state which govern recreation in its many settings are usually more varied and more extensive than those of the local community. References to recreation will be found in the laws which authorize the establishment of local, district, and regional park systems, in laws related to the operation of school systems, in laws concerned with such activities as camping, the use of school property, the conservation of resources, public health and safety, the use of fairground facilities, the establishment of civic community centers, and countless other concerns directly or indirectly connected with recreation.

State recreation laws may well be thought of in terms of these classifications:

1. *Laws which authorize the establishment of local recreation programs, services, and facilities (Enabling Laws).* These include laws found in the state park code of laws, in the state school code of laws, and in the *state recreation* enabling legislation. For example, state park laws may say that, under certain conditions, a park department may levy a tax for recreation programs up to a given amount and may employ personnel and establish facilities for such purposes. Or, the state school laws may say that, with the permission of the board of education, schools may be used for community recreation purposes when they are not being used for school purposes, or, that boards of education may spend portions of their appropriations to employ recreation personnel. (The state recreation enabling legislation, because of its importance, is explained in detail later.)

2. *Laws which authorize state agencies and departments to provide services and sometimes operate programs and facilities for the people of the state (Service Laws).* These laws authorize the work of state agencies which have recreation as their primary interest and responsibility. Examples are a state recreation commission or a state board of recreation. Such laws also authorize the operations of state departments and agencies which include recreation in their services but which have other major and primary interests and functions. Typical of these would be the recreation services provided by state boards of education, park and conservation department, welfare departments, highway commissions, youth authorities, and the like.

3. *Laws which are enacted for the purpose of regulating, controlling, licensing, censoring, or supervising recreation activity in the best interests of the public's health, safety, and welfare (Regulatory Laws).* Examples of such laws can be found in the laws which make it mandatory for films to be reviewed and approved by a state board of censors before being shown in public theaters. State laws of this kind are also found in the setting aside of certain seasons for hunting game, in limiting the number of fish which an angler may catch in a single day, in approving the sanitary conditions of a swimming pool or motel, in regulating the speed of motor boats on lakes, and in hundreds of other ways.

4. *Laws enacted by the state authorizing the expenditure of funds, or action, for projects of interest only to a given locality, and for which general, state-wide authority is neither requested nor required (Special*

Project Laws). A community may need the consent of the state, for example, to use a watershed area as a day camp, or to develop a portion of the land at an airport for recreation. In this instance, only the community involved, and not other communities in the state, is concerned; thus, a special law authorizing the specific use or project is sought.

Enabling Legislation

Of all of the state laws which influence local, tax-supported recreation, none is more important than the state *recreation enabling legislation.* All of the states now have such laws and efforts are being made to broaden and liberalize them. Enabling legislation, in a single act, empowers the communities to establish, organize, administer, and conduct recreation programs under one of several authorities such as recreation boards and commissions, park departments or school boards. If it were not for the enabling legislation, the legislature would have to pass a law each time a community wanted to establish a recreation system. The enabling act gives blanket approval, provided the community follows certain steps in establishing the service. The enabling legislation is "permissive" and not mandatory upon the communities in the sense that they are not *required* to establish recreation systems. Usually state recreation enabling laws authorize:

1. Assignment of responsibility for managing the recreation system to an existing agency such as a park department or school board, or the creation of a new unit such as a recreation board or commission.
2. Joint and cooperative action among the public departments and agencies of a community.
3. Employment of trained and qualified recreation personnel.
4. Equipping, operating, and maintaining areas and facilities.
5. Acquiring properties through purchase, lease, donation, transfer, or condemnation.
6. Expenditure of public funds—or the levying of a tax—for recreation.
7. Collective action between two or more communities.
8. Method of appointment of officers, number of officers, type of representation, and terms of officers.[2]

District Legislation

Public services are sometimes administered more efficiently if they can be paid for and provided on the basis of where the population is centered, rather than upon long-established municipal boundaries. Recent migra-

---

[2] If the legislation requires approval of the electorate through a referendum, details are provided regarding the methods of placing the proposal on the public ballot.

tion of families from the cities to the suburban areas has focused attention upon the need for legislation which makes possible *district* organization of services. The public school *district* is a fine example of machinery which has been provided to meet this need. Illinois, for example, has had excellent state laws relating to the establishment and operation of park districts for a long time. Recently, comparable provision has been made in some of the states for recreation districts. A great advantage of the so-called *district* organization is that it not only places both the financial support and the service where the people are, but it also enables neighborhoods, areas, and unincorporated as well as incorporated communities to do collectively (through pooling their resources) what they might not be able to do individually. District laws—which are state-enacted laws—usually include information on:

1. Minimum number of legal residents required and population limitations within the district.
2. Methods of annexing additional territory for the district.
3. Methods whereby petition may be made for a district.
4. How the managing authority shall be established and composed (members are usually elected rather than appointed).
5. Financial possibilities, methods, and limitations (usually including a minimum and maximum tax levy).
6. Powers in acquiring, developing, and maintaining areas and facilities, providing services, employing personnel, and accounting for stewardship.

Liability

Another point at which recreation law becomes significant is in relation to the protection and safety of children and adults and in the protection of property rights. It is in this connection that the matter of liability comes into the picture. If someone is injured, if property rights are infringed upon—who is liable and to what extent? These questions call for answers which involve not only the laws but also the court's interpretation of them. Generally speaking—and it is only generally, the outcome of lawsuits frequently hinges heavily upon the circumstances of the case—the municipality appears to run less risk of liability in those instances when the courts of the state consider recreation to be a *governmental* function (i.e., the municipality is considered as an agent of the state, and recreation is held to be a governmental service essential to the health, morals, and general well-being of the people) rather than a *proprietary* function (i.e., the municipality is looked upon as an organization to care for local needs in a private or proprietary capacity). Where the function is interpreted as *governmental,* unless gross negligence on the part of the municipality can be proved, or the municipality has made more than a nominal charge for the service, liability risks are small. Naturally, the interpretations of the courts greatly influence the matter of insurance coverage.

ORGANIZATIONAL MANAGEMENT

Organized recreation, as the term implies, requires an organizational structure. It is only in this way that the work can be managed and the service effectively provided. Some person or group must be given official responsibility for looking after the affairs of the agency, department, or organization. It is the purpose of over-all organizational management to plan, organize, manage, direct, supervise, operate, and evaluate recreation programs, services, and facilities, to administer funds, to employ and use personnel, and to interpret and give an accounting of its efforts. As far as personnel is concerned, organizational management in recreation usually has several levels of management or administration. Depending upon the circumstances and the size of the operation, there are times when the functions of these management levels are combined.

Organization management is directly responsible to the public which supports the program. When the work is tax supported, as it is in a public recreation or park department, the responsibility is to *all* of the taxpayers, the total electorate. If the service is supported by voluntary contributions, the responsibility is to the contributors and the agency's constituency.

Going beyond the public, then, as a part of the organizational management, we find three levels of management: (1) the governing group or authority, (2) the executive, and (3) the staff, which includes supervisors and leaders, as well as clerical and maintenance personnel.

The Governing Group

In public recreation, more often than not, primary responsibility for management is placed in a board of directors or a board of commissioners. This might be a recreation board, a recreation commission, a board of park commissioners, a school board, or similar group. Persons who serve on such boards are in the vast majority of cases unpaid. They are interested, civic leaders appointed to the board by the chief officer of a municipality, such as the mayor, or elected at the polls by the electorate, as is often the case for those who serve on park boards and school boards. In some cases, the governing functions are assumed entirely by the chief executive officer of the recreation department or agency as the head of a municipal department. In these situations an *advisory* committee of citizens may be used to counsel the executive. The primary and major function of the governing group or board is *to develop the policies, establish the regulations, provide the guideposts, and generally chart the broad course of action.* A competent governing body can be helpful in creating and reflecting public opinion, interpreting objectives, and in negotiating advantages.

The Executive

The chief executive officer of a recreation or park and recreation department is often known as the superintendent. In some places he is called the director, and in a few instances, the general manager. In a Y.M.C.A., for example, this person would be known as the general secretary, or in a boys' club, the director. The executive is directly responsible to and appointed by the governing board. His major function is to *carry out or execute the policies and plans* adopted by the governing board. The executive is also the administrator. He provides the data, information, and professional counsel to the governing board upon which action can be taken in adopting policies and general procedures. He bridges the gap between policies on one hand and recreation services on the other, thereby translating top level opinion into action. His time is given to planning, organizing, supervising, and generally promoting the work and interests of the department. He is also responsible for the selection and development of his staff, for preparation of the budget and handling the finances, for relationships with other agencies and groups, for program expansion, for the development and maintenance of the physical plant, and for public relations.

The Staff

As far as recreation leadership is concerned, the staff consists of the *supervisors* and the *recreation leaders.* Other staff personnel consist of clerks and stenographers, maintenance and custodial help.

The major function of the supervisor is to *lead, guide, stimulate and counsel the recreation leaders.* He also checks to see if regulations, policies, and procedures are being followed. He helps to identify and correct problems before they become acute. He evaluates the work of the leader and generally assists in the growth and development of the staff and the program. Much of the supervisor's time is given to the matter of general program planning and making recommendations of all kinds to the executive. It is clear that the supervior must be adept at giving leadership, in its best and broadest sense, to the corps of recreation leaders. Supervisors may be assigned responsibilities on the basis of "function" or "area of specialization" (e.g., supervisor of athletics and sports, supervisor of women's and girls' activities, supervisor of camping, supervisor of drama or music, supervisor of aquatics, supervisor of playgrounds, supervisor of community centers) or, upon a geographical basis (i.e., regional, district).

The major function of the recreation leader is to *plan, organize, conduct, and evaluate recreation programs, services, and opportunities.* In this role, he must discover the recreational interests of the people he serves and have the technical knowledge and capacity to serve these needs. He has responsibility for carrying out policies and regulations and working with people, face-to-face.

All personnel from recreation leader to board member are involved in administration. Administration is related to people—what they do and how they do it in the structural organization. Staff responsibility is upward from leader to supervisor to executive to governing board, but responsibility for successful administration belongs to everyone.

Organizational Structure in the Combined Recreation and Park Department

The levels of management (1. governing authority, 2. executive, and 3. staff) remain essentially the same in *any* recreation system. The functions and titles of personnel in those instances in which there are both *program* and *physical plant* responsibilities may be different, but the categories of management remain.

For example, the management structure of a combined recreation and park department might appear (briefly) as follows:

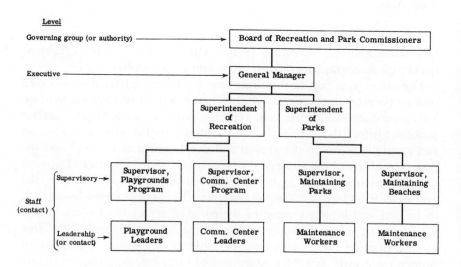

Figure 3.

Organization Methods

The patterns for organizing local public recreation and park services vary among communities. Local conditions, needs, and practices often govern the form or organization. The power and limitations of government, state, and local laws, financial resources, the availability of property for recreation use, public opinion, and the attitudes and interests of public officials and civic leaders, all influence the type of administration selected to get the job done.

Many communities prefer to establish a recreation board or commission whereby recreation is administered as an independent function by a governing body that has recreation as a major responsibility. Others see wisdom in assigning the recreation function to a park department, a school department, or, as is increasingly the case in many parts of the nation, a combination such as a recreation and park department. Under any condition, the following principles of organizing for recreation are sound:

1. All resources—physical, financial, and human—should be mobilized and used.
2. A broad, well-balanced program designed to meet the interests of all ages and groups should be provided.
3. Responsibility for management of the system should be clearly and definitely fixed.
4. Cooperative relationships among all concerned and interested organizations, agencies, and departments should be encouraged.
5. Management should have represented in it the public interests and resources of departments which have a major contribution to make to recreation developments.
6. Trained and professionally qualified executive, supervisory, and staff personnel is essential.
7. Effective service should receive priority consideration over convenience of administration, preservation of organizational identity, or vested interest.
8. Recreation should be organized in a way that will allow unhampered freedom of action, growth, and development.
9. Recreation should be given assurance of continuing and adequate financial support through funds which cannot be diverted for other purposes and the expenditure of which will allow the public to clearly judge recreation, including the *human use* of physical resources, on its own merits.

STEPS IN ORGANIZING A LOCAL PUBLIC RECREATION SYSTEM

1. Survey and appraise existing and potential physical, human, and financial resources, as well as the recreation problems, needs, and deficiencies of the community.

2. Publicize the conditions and findings.

3. Check state enabling or similar legislation to determine legal authority, possibilities, and limitations.

4. Check existing local legislation relating to recreation and allied fields.

5. Prepare plans as related to budget, areas and facilities required, personnel needed, program and services desired.

6. Enlist support of civic and social organizations and agencies.

PROGRAM

The recreation program which includes all of the activities and services from which people secure satisfaction is the end product of organized recreation. All resources—the laws, money, leadership, facilities, and management—are valuable only insofar as they can be used to provide and improve opportunities for recreation.

If recreation programs and services are to satisfy those who engage in them, they must provide an outlet for persons of varying interests to enjoy, to create and express, to have adventuresome new experiences, and to achieve. Persons, young and old, must find in the recreation program opportunities for sociability and fellowship, for physical and emotional release and development, for beauty and for service. Some phases of the recreation program must also take into consideration the desire for occasional relaxation.

Program Range

Attempts have been made to classify recreation activities in a number of ways—according to the forms which recreation takes (physical, mental, social), according to the satisfactions derived (creativity, achievement, service), according to the facilities required (playgrounds, community centers, water areas)—but no classification can be "absolute," because the range of people's interests is unlimited, because the characteristics of human expression are so interrelated, and because the common denominators of activities are so broad. It is the *range* of recreation opportunities which is important. Thus, organized recreation includes, but is *not* limited to, such areas as arts and crafts; dancing and rhythmic actions; drama; music; games, sports, and athletics; outdoor recreation, including nature recreation and all forms of camping; activities related to oral or written communication and social activities in all of their many forms. Hobbies of all kinds, special activities and events, and the opportunities for voluntary services in recreation are all a part of the total program.

It is clear that each area is not exclusive to itself. For example, music is often a part of camping, a baseball game has its social characteristics, crafts are the hobbies of many people, and so on.

Type of Organization

The recreation program, or parts of it, may be organized to serve the interests and needs of the *individual,* the *group,* or the entire *community.* As is the case in the provision of beaches and picnic areas, perhaps only the facilities, equipment, and custodial care need be provided. As far as the organized program is concerned in this instance, little is required, and program leadership is not necessary. On the other hand, in the operation of playgrounds and community centers or the conducting of athletic leagues, not only are facilities and equipment needed, but there is also a need for much organization and program leadership. In still other instances, as in the case of friendship groups and clubs whose main satisfactions grow out of group experience, an even greater degree of organization and leadership may be required. Very often, the amount and complexity of organization required to provide recreation programs and services increases with the number of persons and interests involved.

Influencing Factors in Individual Recreation Interests

The interests, needs, and capabilities of people in recreation are governed and influenced by many factors which must be considered in planning and organizing the recreation program. Among these considerations are:

1. Age (early childhood, later childhood, youth, young adults, adults, older people)
2. Sex
3. Educational, cultural, and nationality backgrounds
4. Economic and social advantages
5. Traditions and customs
6. Geography and climate
7. Home life
8. Incidence of social need
9. Health status
10. Previous recreation experiences and skills

Basic Considerations

To be adequate and effective, the recreation program must take into account (1) the people who are to be served by the program, (2) the leadership to plan and conduct the program, (3) the physical plant necessary to house the program, (4) the money needed to finance the program, and (5) the range and depth of the program itself.

In serving the people, all of the influencing factors mentioned above must be carefully weighed and acted upon. The extent to which this is successfully accomplished largely determines whether the goals of the program are achieved. In this connection, the people themselves should be brought into the planning of the recreation program.

The assistance of qualified and trained leadership, professional and volunteer, is the hub around which the recreation program revolves. A recreation program is only as good as the quality of its leadership.

Recreation in any form requires space. Successful recreation programs have been provided with only a minimum of recreation facilities, but the chances for success are much greater when an adequate physical plant is at hand. Equipment and supplies are also required. Facilities should be designed, oriented, and located in terms of functional recreation use. Their importance to the recreation program cannot be overemphasized.

The organized recreation program is a legitimate charge on the public treasury. The program calls for a sound, continuing basis of fiscal support. Some activities—those which require little in the way of facilities, supplies, and instruction—can be provided at minimum costs. In other instances, funds are necessary to make even the basic services available. The costs of providing recreation activities should be considered in terms of their values and public interest in them. More often than not, appropriations made from taxes, or funds solicited from the community, are supplemented with charges and fees and other forms of revenue.

The activities of the recreation program must be geared to the needs of those they are intended to serve. The program must be broad, varied, and well balanced in the sense of serving the largest cross section of interests. The recreation program should also be available year round and not just upon a seasonal basis, serving all regardless of age, sex, race, creed, economic or social status.

Tests for the Adequacy of a Recreation Program

Evaluating the adequacy of a recreation program may be accomplished by asking the following questions:

1. Does it take into consideration the varied and diversified interests, needs, and capabilities of those it serves?
2. Does it take into consideration the physiological and psychological capacities and characteristics of the participants?
3. Does it consider the cultural, economic, and social characteristics of the people?
4. Is it cooperatively planned and conducted, involving participant and leader, interested groups, agencies, and associations?

5. Does it involve the use of accepted program standards?
6. Does it provide for various levels and progressions of skills and proficiency?
7. Is it soundly supported in leadership, facilities, and finance?
8. Does it mobilize and use all available resources?
9. Does it provide for equality of opportunity for all individuals and groups?
10. Is it flexible enough and can it be modified to meet changing needs and conditions?
11. Does it protect the health and safety of the participant?
12. Does it encourage a high plane of personal behavior and conduct?
13. Does it take into consideration long-range as well as immediate program needs and interests?
14. Is the cost of the program in line with the values derived from it?
15. Does it avoid exploiting the individual or group?
16. Do the participants receive basic satisfactions?
17. Does it lend itself to and provide for a sound, continuous evaluation?

FACILITIES

Outdoor recreation areas, indoor recreation facilities, property, equipment, and supplies are needed to provide a community recreation program. Not all recreation activities require special facilities, but many of them do. Hiking, for example, can be carried on anywhere at anytime without thought of special facilities, but golf requires a golf course and tennis requires a court. Sometimes, recreation activities can be provided by using facilities established for other purposes, such as a school, an armory, or a library. *All* recreation activities require space. A recreation program is most successful when an adequate physical plant, planned, designed, and developed for recreation is available. The projection of plans for community recreation must give serious consideration to the question of facilities. Areas, facilities, equipment, and supplies are a means to an end and not an end in themselves. They should be considered not as physical exhibits, but rather as tools necessary to providing recreation opportunities for the population. Moreover, the number and kinds of facilities required are determined by the interests to be served, the program to be conducted, and the opportunities to be offered.

Many times outdoor recreation areas can be used in their primitive or natural state, as in the case of forests, reservations, and natural lakes. In other cases, considerable modification is necessary—for example, in developing a playfield wherein the topography must be modified, the landscape changed, and the area oriented and developed for playing-field use.

Recreation areas and facilities must be planned to meet special needs. If the area is a children's playground, it must be safely and conveniently accessible to children of a certain age. If it is a day camp, a sailboat house, or a rifle range, it must be planned in a way that will serve the special program purpose.

Types of Areas and Facilities

Keeping in mind that recreation areas and facilities are supposed to serve people's interests and the program's purposes, it follows that the kinds and types of facilities have a wide range. Among the more common types of facilities found in community recreation are: [3]

Outdoor Areas	Indoor Facilities
Athletic fields	Armories
Beaches	Auditoriums
Bridle paths	Bathhouses
Camps	Boathouses
Forests	Bowling lanes
Golf courses	Clubhouses
Hiking trails	Clubrooms
Historical monuments	Community centers
Marinas	Dance halls
Parks	Field houses
Playfields	Game rooms
Playgrounds	Hobby shops
Play lots	Libraries
Picnic areas	Museums
Reservations	Recreation buildings
Stadiums	Schools
Swimming pools	Shelters
Tennis courts	Swimming pools
Wading pools	Theaters
	Youth centers

The Bureau of Outdoor Recreation has classified (nationally) outdoor recreation areas into six major types:

1. *High-Density Recreation Areas.* These areas are intensively developed and managed for use by large numbers of people. They are usually located close to major centers of urban population and are most often in municipal, district, county, or state ownership and managed exclusively for recreation purposes. Such facilities as beaches, marinas, playing fields, artificial lakes, eating and sanitary accommodations are included. Examples would be the Cook Forest Preserve in Illinois and Jones Beach in New York.

2. *General Outdoor Recreation Areas.* These areas are subject to development for a wide variety of specific recreation uses. They are in public and private ownership and include portions of public parks and forests

[3] This is not a complete list of facilities for community recreation programs.

as well as facilities for camping, picnicking, fishing, water sports, nature activities, and outdoor games. Ski areas, trailer parks, hunting preserves, and resorts are all included.

3. *Natural Environment Areas.* These areas of various types are suitable for recreation in a natural environment, usually in combination with other uses. These lands are found throughout the country and are very high in acreage. Grazing, lumbering, and mining are among the other uses made of such areas. They may be part of a national park or national forest, and in some instances, state parks and forests. Opportunities can be found in them for hiking, hunting, fishing, camping, picnicking, canoeing, and sightseeing.

4. *Unique Natural Areas.* These are areas of outstanding scenic splendor, natural wonder, and scientific importance. They may be found in the national and state parks and forests. Yosemite Valley in California, Grand Canyon in Arizona, and Old Faithful in Yellowstone National Park are examples.

5. *Primitive Areas.* These are undisturbed, isolated, roadless areas, characterized by natural, wild conditions, including "wilderness areas." These undeveloped areas have high inspirational, aesthetic, scientific, and cultural values. There are no man-made recreation or permanent habitation facilities in these places, nor are they desired.

6. *Historic and Cultural Sites.* These are sites of major historic or cultural significance, either local, regional, or national. Examples are Mount Vernon, the historic Indian dwellings in Mesa Verde National Park, and the Civil War battle areas.

STANDARDS

There is much discussion currently as to standards for recreation areas and facilities. Economists, demographers, land-use planners, foresters, conservationists and many others are concerned in one way or another about the effects of an accelerated population increase along with an increased leisure on the already burdened recreation resources of our nation. The definitions of the problem and proposed solutions are as varied as the colors of the rainbow and indicate the diverse interest orientations of those involved.

Population projections, demand analysis, user origin studies, economic projections, and capacity formulas are but a few of the methods utilized and/or promoted in efforts to arrive at standards for recreation areas and facilities.

The quality-quantity dichotomy is frequently referred to in these studies. Also, it is argued that the number and use of recreation facilities and areas are a function of various combinations of the following:

geographic location; population density; accessibility; purpose and philosophy of development and operation; quality of management, maintenance, and operation; age level and skill level of the participant.

Due to the above remarks it is deemed inadvisable to list in this publication a set of suggested standards for general application in the field of recreation. This position is further reinforced by the belief that such a listing of suggested standards would be not only misleading but would tend to promote the standardization of programs.

Facilities and areas exist for the sake of program. When areas and facilities are standardized, programs become standardized, thereby negating efforts at innovative and creative programming.

It is recommended that each community establish its own standards based upon its own stated goals, aspirations and needs. This should come after careful study of the community and with the constant goal of providing the best possible program of activities and opportunities.

Where interest is high in one activity, this interest should be maintained and encouraged with adequate leadership and facilities. The goal should be to add to and broaden interest and participation in a diversified program by providing leadership and facilities to expand the opportunities of the citizen.

Areas and facilities should first be developed as an expression of the specific felt needs of the community they serve. They should then be added to and developed further to provide for both breadth and depth of programming.

Adequacy of Facilities

Whether or not facilities for the community recreation program are well planned and adequately provided may be determined by applying certain principles in terms of the following questions:

1. Are the facilities planned, located, and laid out, or modified and oriented, for functional recreation use? Are they geared to program needs?
2. Is the recreation facilities planning integrated with comprehensive city planning?
3. Does the facilities planning consider long-range as well as immediate recreation needs? Is there included a schedule of priorities for acquiring property and improving it?
4. Are standards applied intelligently? Is space sufficient?
5. Are the facilities accessible to those who use them?
6. Are they planned to keep to a minimum costs of construction, improvement, and maintenance?
7. Are the facilities aesthetically attractive and comfortable?
8. Are supervision, control, and leadership made easy?
9. Are the facilities designed for multiple use?

10. Can maximum use be obtained around the clock and calendar?
11. Are the health and safety of the users protected?
12. Does pedestrian and vehicle traffic flow freely and are adequate accommodations provided without hazard?
13. Are natural resources used to the best advantage?
14. Are the facilities planned and operated so as not to constitute a nuisance to adjacent property owners?
15. Do the facilities lend themselves to maintaining cleanliness and proper sanitation?
16. Are the "service" facilities well arranged?
17. Are acoustical conditions good?
18. Are crowding of facilities and over-use of equipment avoided?

FINANCE

Sound and effective community recreation programs require broad, continuing fiscal support. It is a mistake to assume that recreation services can be provided without spending money. Funds are needed to purchase land and property, to construct, operate, and maintain facilities, to buy equipment and supplies, to pay salaries and wages, and to pay the many other costs involved in operating a recreation system.

Expenditures for Recreation

The amount of funds necessary for recreation varies among communities because their needs, resources, and conditions are different. A satisfactory answer as to how much a community should spend for recreation can be found only in the needs and resources of the community. Some communities are wealthier and better managed than others. Some have large tax revenues from real estate property and other sources of tax income. Both the state and local laws which authorize and limit expenditures for public recreation are more liberal in one locality than in another. There are large differences in the prevailing rates for salaries, wages, services, and materials. Geographical boundaries, climate, location, and population density influence the amount of money needed for recreation, as does the extent to which people are able and willing to make voluntary contributions of their time and money. A national suggested standard for *public* park and recreation services is a *minimum* of $10.00 per capita ($5.00 for programs and services—and of this $2.50 for leadership—and the remainder for facilities maintenance and other costs). Expenses for acquiring property and making capital improvements are over and beyond operating costs, and additional funds are needed for these purposes.

Methods of Financing

Public recreation services can no more be self-supporting than can public education. The basic floor of services must be financed through tax funds if they are to be adequate and continuing.

The two most common ways of supporting local public recreation are (1) *appropriations from the general funds of the municipality* and (2) *special tax levy.*

In the former, the municipal authorities, upon receiving a budgetary request from the recreation department, allocate a certain amount of money for recreation for one year just as they assign funds for the operation of the fire department, police department, or street department.

When the special tax levy is used (this depends upon state and local laws), a certain percentage (within a range established by state and local law) of the taxes collected is earmarked for recreation and can be used only for this purpose. The special tax levy method is preceded by a public referendum through which public approval is given to such action. The main advantage of this method is that it guarantees a source of income not dependent upon the attitude of those responsible for over-all government. But it has the disadvantage of not being able to relate income to changing needs beyond the range of the levy fixed by law.

There are other methods of financing public recreation. Among them are:

Bond Issues—With the consent of the electorate at the polls bonds are sold on the open market, the principal and interest on which are paid out of taxes collected over a period of years. Funds secured from bond issues are used for capital improvements.

Charges and Fees—Nominal charges are paid by those who participate in a given recreation activity or attend a recreation function. Athletic teams pay entry fees to participate in a league (this money may be used to pay for supplies or officials); persons pay a small charge to use a swimming pool or a golf course; individuals may pay a fee to go to a camp, and so on. The use of charges and fees as a means of supporting recreation must be applied carefully and equitably and not be used as the main basis of fiscal support.

Special Assessments—Property owners for whom certain facilities are made available or services provided are assessed with their consent to pay for the accommodations. This method has hazards in that it tends to encourage development on the basis of ability to pay rather than upon need.

Supplementary Assistance—Under certain circumstances and conditions of need, communities may receive financial assistance from higher levels of government. This is accomplished through grants from Federal and state governments along, in most cases, with matching funds. Reference has already been made regarding these possibilities. From year to year the concept of grants-in-aid, to further recreation programs along many lines of administrative needs, is gaining popularity. New York State provides supplementary financial assistance through its Youth Commission to help develop recreation opportunities for young people. The Pennsylvania Department of Public Instruction assists local boards of education in financing adult education and recreation.

Other Methods—Other methods of financing public recreation include *special taxes*—using taxes derived from the sale of merchandise, from parking meters, commercial amusements, and the like, for recreation; *contributions*—civic-minded people endow the operation of a community recreation center, through wills and bequests give titles to properties, and the like; *leases, rentals, and transfers*—the temporary—sometimes for long periods—use of property is acquired in exchange for a stipulated sum of money or other advantage to the owner; and *excess condemnation*—property needed in the public interests is condemned and acquired, and a fair price, determined by the court, is paid to the owner. Property acquired in excess of what is actually needed is resold to obtain additional income.

Budgeting and Accounting

Equally as important as sound financing are the matters of sound budgeting and accounting in recreation. Budgeting refers to the *method of making financial estimates for a given period—usually one fiscal year—based upon need and allocating funds for various purposes.* It is through the budget that expenditures are resolved with income and from which sound planning and services result. Accounting is the administrative companion of budgeting and means simply an *orderly procedure of numerically explaining and reporting income and expenditures.* It indicates the quality of financial stewardship and responsibility and is indispensable in the financial picture.

Methods of budgeting and accounting vary among the municipalities and in recreation conform to established local practices, particularly if the recreation department is not fiscally independent from the remainder of local government. Although budget classifications differ, a sound budget will include information on:

1. Justification and explanation of the various items based upon need.
2. Estimates on expenditures and income for the previous, current, and ensuing years.
3. Breakdown of estimates on a unit cost basis showing how they were made.
4. Major categories of expenditures (e.g., personal and contractual services, commodities, current charges and obligations, properties, debt payments, and the like).

Some budgets are prepared on the basis of line items (indicates what the money will buy). Other budgets are based on "performance" (indicates what services will be provided).

The accounting system must be accurate and clear if it is to serve as a basis for evaluating expenditures, meeting legal requirements, and providing a sound picture of the financial operations. It involves the careful keeping of records and ledgers which at any time can accurately reveal the financial status of the operation. Included are records of official actions, receipts, expenditures and encumbrances (operating and capital), and materials, stores, and supplies.

LEADERSHIP

The key to the success of a recreation program is the quality of its leadership. The recreator is to recreation what the teacher is to education.

Persons with many kinds of talent, abilities, and interests are needed to operate successful recreation systems—laymen, civic leaders who serve on boards and committees, the executive or superintendent who provides the highest level of professional leadership, and supervisory leaders responsible for leading and supervising the work of others on a geographical or functional basis. There are also specialists in sports, drama, music, and crafts. A large share of the leadership responsibility rests in those professional workers who direct the programs at given outdoor and indoor recreation centers and the many recreation activity leaders who work under their direction. The number and types of leaders in a recreation system depend upon the size and scope of the program. The importance of leadership in the recreation program is emphasized by the recommendation that three-fourths of the total expenditures for recreation might well be spent on leadership. To this corps of professional leadership must be added the volunteer leaders who can contribute so much in time, energy, and service.

Importance of Qualified Leadership

Recreation leadership at its best requires a thorough understanding of people, their interests, desires, and needs. It also calls for technical knowledge of methods and techniques in helping to serve these needs and interests on a broad recreation plane. It is a mission in human relations, in bringing out the best creative capacities in varied personalities. Therefore, recreation leadership calls into play a philosophy as well as ability and knowledge in the planning, organization, conduct, and evaluation of recreation methods and techniques. Moreover, the recreation leader must possess the qualities of an effective teacher—which means he must possess technical skills—a competent salesman, and an efficient administrator. Recreation leadership also requires knowledge of laws, community organization, program planning and operation, facilities, equipment and supplies, personnel training and supervision, the securing of financial support, and public relations. The recreation leader must of necessity possess many desirable personal characteristics, among them intelligence, a democratic point of view, and soundness of character. He must also be personable, imaginative, resourceful, dependable, and enthusiastic.

When viewed as a whole, the recreator must have a sound philosophy, well-developed skills, and values—the right values.

Leadership Functions

The functions of a recreator vary with his degree of responsibility, his place in the organization, and his assignment. Specifically, however, recreation leadership functions and duties include all or some of the following:

1. *Administration* of program, funds, equipment, supplies, staff, and volunteer personnel.
2. *Supervision* of personnel (professional and volunteer), program, funds, equipment, and supplies.
3. *Organization* and conduct of programs, services, and facilities.
4. *Evaluation* of programs, services, and facilities.
5. *Promulgation* of standards of programs, leadership, and the like.
6. *Application* of policies and regulations.
7. *Stimulation* of public relations.
8. *Solicitation and exploration* of financial and legislative support.
9. *Representation* with related interests, agencies, and organizations.

The Professional Recreation Field

There are many kinds of professional opportunities in the recreation field. Positions as recreation leaders, directors and supervisors, managers, specialists, technicians, and superintendents—in fact, positions with varying degrees of responsibility and difficulty with corresponding levels of salaries are found in a large number of settings. These positions are available in local agencies and their counterparts at county, state, and national levels. Included in these groups are:

Recreation, park, and school departments.
Voluntary agencies such as the Boy Scouts, Girl Scouts, Boys' Clubs, Settlements, Y.M.C.A.'s, Y.W.C.A.'s.
Industries and business concerns.
Hospitals (neuropsychiatric, general, tuberculosis, and children's) and rehabilitation centers.
Institutions (for the aging, handicapped, dependent, and delinquent).

Religious groups and organizations.
Camps of all kinds.
Commercial recreation (resorts, hotels, motels, ship lines).

COMMUNITY ORGANIZATION

Recreation positions can also be found in housing developments, in the armed forces, in colleges and universities, and in organizations engaged in rural work. Often recreation positions are on a part time, or combination, basis. Some of these are:

Recreation and physical education.   Recreation and conservation.
Recreation and coaching.   Recreation and counseling.
Recreation and therapy or rehabilitation.   Recreation and planning.

Most recreation positions today are open on the basis of selection through merit. Local residence is seldom required. Job benefits such as retirement, vacations, and sick leave are liberal, and salaries range from $6000 to $25,000 annually. The recreator is on the job, however, when others are at leisure. The recreation job calls for working at odd times. It demands devotion to the service, but has many compensations and rewards. From all indications, the demand for professionally prepared recreators is likely to exceed greatly the supply for a long time to come.

Volunteers

No field of public service has greater potential for the use of volunteers than does recreation. Indeed, the chance to be of voluntary help is in itself a form of recreation.

Volunteers can help in teaching skills, in organizing and assisting in the organization of activities, in serving as officials, in giving counsel and assistance, in acting as hosts and hostesses, in carrying out the business and clerical details of the organization, in public relations efforts, and in hundreds of other ways in the recreation program. The important things to keep in mind in using volunteers are:

1. Volunteers supplement and do not substitute for or supplant professional workers.

2. Volunteers must be carefully selected, oriented, trained, assigned, and supervised.

3. Volunteers must understand, accept, and be willing and able to abide by the policies and practices of the agency.

4. The job of the volunteer must be purposeful and consistent with his skills and abilities.

5. The work of the volunteer must be evaluated and its worth recognized.

Preparation

Recreation, as a profession, has its own history, theory, and philosophy, its own methods, skills, and techniques, and its objectives and purposes. For years recreators received training only as they were able to get it through experience on the job. Many people who have been in recreation for a long time either received their training completely on the job or were enrolled in other disciplines—physical education, general education, the social sciences, the arts—while in college. Early attempts to provide training for recreation personnel were in the Normal Course in Play, started by the Playground Association of America in 1909, and the National Recreation School (National Recreation Association), established in 1926. Neither of these, however, gave students recognized collegiate credit. Today, however, many universities and colleges offer courses in recreation, a sizable number offer undergraduate degrees in recreation, and some offer graduate study in recreation leading to the masters and doctoral degree.

Academic preparation attempts to give the student a solid background of general education and also helps him develop a philosophy and understanding of the significance, function, and place of recreation, as well as teach certain skills and provide knowledge in methods of organizing and administering recreation programs. Graduate study provides the opportunity for the gaining of further knowledge and perhaps assists the student in becoming more competent in a given area. Opportunity is also provided in undergraduate and graduate study for students to major in recreation and minor in an allied field.

A large part of recreation training is nonacademic. Such training is provided for both professional and volunteer recreation leaders. All kinds of conferences, institutes, clinics, demonstrations, and workshops make up a large part of such preparation. Training sessions are held to help orient new workers with respect to their assignments and agency policies and procedures, to teach new activity skills and methods of organization, or to prepare for a particular program, such as a summer playground program, a camping program, or an arts and crafts program.

In-service training, or, better, *staff development* programs are standard among most recreation departments and agencies today. Opportunity is provided for the worker to grow professionally while he carries on with his work. This type of training is accomplished through staff meetings and conferences, supervisory interviews, correspondence and extension courses, home study, professional conferences, inspection tours, and in many other ways.

Training for recreation is continuous throughout the career of the professional. Able recreators are perpetual students. They must be if they hope to keep abreast of rapidly changing conditions, needs, problems, and practices in this fast-changing and vital public service.

Identification

A major problem which the recreation profession faces is that of establishing some official system of public identification of recreation personnel. Teachers are certified by the state before they are allowed to teach in public schools. Doctors, dentists, and other professional people must pass state examinations and be licensed before they can practice. There is a comparable need for certifying, licensing, or in some other way giving official, professional recognition to recreation personnel. Efforts to accomplish this are already under way in some states. California, Illinois, and North Carolina are among the states which have voluntary registration plans in operation. New Jersey and New York require legal certification of recreators if they are employed by school systems. Georgia has created, by law, a Board of Recreation Examiners—House Bill No. 849, passed in the 1967–1968 session of the state legislature.

The National Recreation and Park Association has a committee working on national and state plans for accreditation. Accomplishment here will mean much to the professional status of the recreator and the academic status of recreation curriculums and departments in institutions of higher learning. The therapeutic recreation section of the NRPA has a national registration plan for recreators in the field of services to the ill and disabled.

PUBLIC RELATIONS

A sound and fruitful public relations program is essential in recreation administration. *Public relations,* as a function, aims at *establishing, preserving, and strengthening the "goodwill" of the public.* It is a duty and responsibility of everyone—from the governing board and the executive to the recreation leader, stenographer, and custodian—to establish and improve good public relations. It is a task that has no end, no boundaries, and no limitations in the forms it takes. It includes planning, reporting, informing, interpreting, and many kinds of publicity media.

Objectives

The purposes of public relations efforts are to acquaint the public with the services, methods, opportunities, objectives, and values of the program; to give an acounting of the stewardship which the public entrusts to the agency and which it financially supports; to enlist participation, attendance, and interest, and secure maximum use of the facilities and services; to correct misunderstandings, false impressions, and ill-founded conceptions; to condition and inform the public of plans, policies, and regulations, or let the public know of changes; to popularize activities which need to be supported, and to enlist support for the enterprise generally.

Media

As mentioned earlier, public relations operates for good or bad continuously. It involves not only *what* is said, but also *how* it is said and *when* it is said. The manner in which a secretary answers the phone, the speed with which replies are made to correspondence, the way in which employees conduct themselves on the job—all are a part of public relations. Handling complaints expeditiously and tactfully, employing and dismissing workers fairly, and handling bothersome disciplinary cases discreetly are just as important in public relations as publishing interesting articles in the newspapers. The attitudes and manners of all recreation employees cannot be discounted. Therefore, an all-inclusive list of public relations media is not possible.

Among the more commonly used media for carrying on public relations in recreation are:

Newspapers (news, sports, society, editorial, and feature pages)
Printed materials (pamphlets, reports, bulletins, folders, directories, guides, posters, and the like)
Visual and audio aids (television, radio, motion pictures, filmstrips and slides, stationary and mobile amplifying systems, sound recorders)
Magazines and periodicals (popular and professional)
Speeches, discussions, forums, and conferences
Clubs, councils, and committees
Inspection, exhibitions, and demonstrations
Relationships with other organizations, agencies, and departments
Contests, special events, and observances
Employee contacts

The programs and services of a recreation agency are, in themselves, its best media for public relations. If they are sound and effective, the chances are that the public relations will be, too.

Public Relations Effectiveness

To some extent, the effectiveness of a public relations program can be judged by the answers to the following questions:

1. Is the public relations program planned?
2. Is the public generally aware of what the department is trying to accomplish? Its goals and objectives? Its services and the opportunities it provides?
3. Can the public secure information quickly, easily, and accurately?
4. Is the public relations effort geared to the policies and objectives of the department?
5. Are all employees aware of their public relations responsibilities and do they have the benefit of clearly established policies to follow?
6. Does the public relations program give appropriate attention to *all* of the aspects of recreation opportunities?
7. Are facts presented as they *are?*
8. Are a large variety of media used?
9. Are the representatives of the several major publicity media (e.g., press, radio, television) treated equitably?
10. Is the public relations effort continuous?
11. Does the agency attach importance and significance, including the appropriation of time, energy, and money, to public relations?
12. Is public relations in proper balance with all other efforts?

COMMUNITY ORGANIZATION

Closely related to recreation *administration* is the matter of *community organization*. This involves the use of community resources and the organization of such forces for recreation development. It also includes the use of certain devices to accomplish the task and bring into play relationships with people and organizations. Community organization for recreation assumes no single set pattern—the approach depends on what needs to be done and what community resources and forces are at hand with which to do it.

Types

Among the more common types used in recreation are:

Committees and Task Forces: This consists of two or more persons appointed or elected to carry out a given assignment or perform a given task. Such groups may be temporary or permanent. Committees are used for hundreds of purposes in recreation. Examples are a drama and music committee and day camp committee. Committees vary greatly in size, function, representation, and purpose.

Community Recreation Council: This consists of a group of representative and interested persons who act as an advisory group on matters pertaining to community-wide recreation. In the absence of a legal authority, the council often is responsible for raising funds, making policies, and generally guiding the development and operation of recreation services.

4. *People will have more money to spend.* The per capita income, as well as the *real* income, of the individual will rise. The purchasing power to "spend in leisure" will continue to expand.

5. *People will be more mobile* than ever before.

6. *People will be better informed* and more highly educated in a world of seething unrest, conflicting interests, and political turmoil.

7. *Urbanization, projecting into metropolitan areas and regional patterns, can be expected.*

8. *Personal values, personal interests, personal skills, and personal competencies will become more significant* in relation to leisure.

All of these predictions have already begun to come true. Reference was made to them in the early chapters of this book. In one sense, they are simply a continuing trend which started a long time ago.

Trace economic trends and discover that a nation's lines of production (since the Industrial Revolution, especially), its standard of living levels, and the amounts of leisure its people enjoy, parallel one another. When production is *up,* the standard of living is *up,* and so is the quantity of leisure. Similarly, when production is *down,* so are the standard of living and leisure. The only exceptions to these parallels are during a war, when production and the standard of living and leisure are *down;* or, when the economy is dislocated, as is the case during an economic depression. Under these circumstances, production is *down,* the standard of living is *down,* and the amount of leisure people have on their hands is *up!* This however, is an *enforced* rather than a true leisure. It is the kind of leisure which nobody wants.

These developments then, which have long since begun, and which we can look forward to experiencing in larger quantities in the future, will bring new challenges in the recreative use of leisure. They will have to be met imaginatively, resourcefully, and intelligently to help prevent the shredding of our social fabric.

These challenges of leisure will cast recreation in a new role. If earning a living is going to be only a part-time job for many people, they will have to find in their leisure many of the satisfactions they heretofore found in their work. Leisure will have to be used in more lastingly satisfying ways than simply to provide entertainment, amusement, and comfort. Somehow it will need to be used for self-fulfillment, for creative and cultural development. Can the recreative use of leisure equal or better the incentives which are built into work? As Norman Cousins has observed, if it were only a matter of teaching a person a hobby, the task would be easy. But it is a matter of building a new kind of man!

These are the challenges, and they are not laid at the feet of the recreation profession alone. They become the responsibility of all professions, the increasingly important recreation profession among them.

WHAT THE RECREATION MOVEMENT NEEDS

Every public service, every profession, every movement needs supports upon which it may advance and upon which its future depends. The recreation movement is not an exception. It has made rapid gains in the past. But these are little in comparison with the fertile ground of opportunity which lies ahead. Among the things the recreation movement needs are these:

Recreation Needs a Policies Center

Unlike public education, which can look to the Educational Policies Commission of the National Education Association for the establishment of national policy, the recreation movement has no source to which to turn for stimulation and guidance. For a short time during the late 1940's, there was an informally organized National Recreation Policies Committee. It went out of existence, partly because it lacked financial assistance and partly because it lacked the enthusiastic support of the national professional organizations and service agencies. Possibly the attempt to establish this committee came too early.

The Federation of National Professional Organizations for Recreation, organized in 1953, served as a means of exchanging views among representatives of the national professional organizations interested in recreation. This organization helped unify efforts and effect better understanding of each other's work. But it was not constituted to perform the functions of a national policies unit and could not serve the need for a *rallying point.*

The recreation movement needs a high level, professionally distinguished National Recreation Policies Commission whose task it would be to prepare, publish, and disseminate statements of proposed policy regarding recreation. This commission would explore recreation needs, examine recreation developments, and identify recreation problems before they became acute. It would also share its majority and minority views and make its recommendations known. The commission might be supported by the professional organizations and governmental and nongovernmental agencies working in the field of recreation. Preferably, however, such a commission should be separately endowed. While some of its membership might be nominated by national professional and service groups, the remaining members being elected "at large" by the commission members themselves, no member of the commission should represent *anyone* or *any group.* The quality of membership should be the highest. The success of a National Recreation Policies Commission would stand largely upon the quality, soundness, and convincingness of the policies it developed.

This kind of national device is essential to the future of the recreation movement and it is hoped that the National Recreation and Park Association may spearhead a move in this direction.

A Federal Government move in this direction was made in March 1968 through an Executive Order from the White House creating a President's Council and a Committee on Recreation and Natural Beauty. The Council and the Committee are composed mostly of Cabinet Officials and Federal Agency Heads.

A Federal Recreation Service Is Needed

In a leisure-conscious and perhaps leisure-centered society, recreation needs a permanent place in the federal government to concern itself primarily with the over-all recreative needs of every segment of the population.

The United States has made provision for recreation services of one kind or another during national emergencies, as described earlier in this book, and to alleviate social problems (e.g., help solve problems of unemployment, delinquency, lack of fitness). The establishment of the Bureau of Outdoor Recreation was an important step in the right direction—a long-needed vehicle for *outdoor* recreation. But it is not enough. The Federal Government needs to provide recreation services on a *permanent* basis as an opportunity for personality growth and development, and in *all* of man's settings.

Public recreation in the community and in the state needs its counterpart in the federal government as is the case in health, education, welfare, law enforcement, and conservation.

Relationship of the Public and Voluntary Recreation Agency Needs To Be Cleared and a Division of Labor Achieved

A discussion of the future of recreation in the United States would be incomplete without consideration of the basic question of the relation between public and voluntary recreation. Now and for the immediate future, there is a wide-open field of unserved recreation interests. Both public and private recreation resources also face common enemies—lack of understanding of the importance of recreation in modern life, the age-old attitude of *laissez faire,* let each one seek and pay for his own recreation, and the interpretation of recreation as being limited to play for children. Public and voluntary resources are allied against these common enemies.

The argument is properly made that to strengthen recreation at any one point is to strengthen it all along the line. Consequently, public and voluntary agencies, and commercial interests, too, should stand together in the battle to persuade people of the importance of recreation in determining the kind of national life we build. The unmet needs are so vast, it is correctly claimed, that sameness of functions and expenditures is not too disastrous. The gaps and disparities in service which still remain are far more serious than duplications which may exist. Even so, planning and correlation of functions and resources are required.

Every community should set up a process by which planning and execution of programs and expenditures will be cooperative and in terms of two major premises:

1. The obligation of public recreation—as in the areas of health and education—is to see that all people in all communities have access to varied and wholesome recreation and that the basic floor of recreation opportunities is provided. Not all of these opportunities have to be a charge upon tax funds, but it is the obligation of public recreation to set up and/or support the agencies which can most properly, effectively, and economically provide the recreation opportunities which will meet the varied recreation needs and interests of diverse peoples. Thus there is upon public recreation leaders an unqualified obligation to support and promote the totality of recreation.

2. The obligation of voluntary recreation interests is to: (a) provide those services and contributions which meet the highly specialized needs, religious, racial, cultural, or economic, of the individuals who voluntarily associate themselves with voluntary auspices; (b) avoid competition and duplication with other voluntary groups; and (c) support the plans and work of all voluntary and public groups, united in the common aim of making available to the people those recreation opportunities which are required to lift our personal and national life to the level of wholesome development and satisfaction.

As services increase, budgets will conflict and erstwhile allies may become potential competitors. The recreation public should be warned of this situation.

The initial premise is that if recreation opportunities develop as they should to the point where all people in all communities have access to varied and multiple recreation facilities and activities, public and private agencies will ultimately clash in their pursuit of the final available tax and philanthropic dollar. The solution to this problem lies primarily in an increasingly clear definition and acceptance of the specialized and limited services of the voluntary groups.

There will always be a need for both public and private recreation agencies, even when and if recreation opportunities for all people are achieved. At that time, however, the so-called voluntary groups will have been restricted to a highly specialized function and contribution which cannot be met under public auspices. The Catholic Church, for example, may always need a program of recreation activities in connection with its major and basic religious program. Correspondingly, other voluntary groups will have their own contributions to make to the leisure interests and needs of people, but each contribution will have to be justified in terms of, and limited to, the original and historic purpose of the administering group, avoiding duplication of the activities of any other group.

To the responsibilities of the public and voluntary agencies need to be added two other considerations:

a. Neither the public nor voluntary recreation agency should be expected to provide for the individual what he can, in his and society's best interests, provide for himself.
b. The commercial enterprise, whose destiny is determined mainly by its profits, should go on its way unrestricted except when it violates the *public* interest.

Research Must Develop

The extent to which recreation progresses in the future will depend, to a large degree, upon the quantity and *quality* of research undertaken in it. No public service goes far these days in the absence of a developing body of scientific information and knowledge. As indicated earlier, research in recreation in the past has been largely mechanical—inventorying space, attempting to determine the recreation interests of people, comparing one community with another recreationally, and so on.

The future will bring an expansion of research in recreation both in scope and depth. Principles and concepts, already established and to come, will need to be substantiated and, perhaps, modified. This can be done not only through experience but also through research. Recreation research of the future will be directed toward shedding light on such perplexing issues as (1) the effects of various forms of recreation upon the physiological and psychological well-being and behavior of individuals, (2) the relationship of the recreative use of leisure to the community and to the general social fabric, (3) the comparative effectiveness and values of recreation in relation to different age groups, (4) the testing, discovery, and development of more effective uses of leisure, (5) the discovery and evaluation of leisure habits, interests, and demands of the public, (6) the potentials of recreation in preventive and remedial medicine, as well as in rehabilitation, (7) the relation of recreation to the economy, especially as concerns land use, and (8) the discovery of factors related to public policy with respect to sharing and allocating responsibility for recreation opportunities among public, voluntary, and commercial interests.

Inequalities Need To Be Erased

Much of the future of recreation in the United States, and, indeed, the future of the nation itself, depends upon erasing the inequalities of recreation opportunities which exist between geographical areas, including inequalities in communities, between neighborhoods, and in neighborhoods—between income groups, age groups, and racial groups. The extent to which these opportunities are available largely determines recreation's contribution to our national life. It is important that the men and women of the United States and their families have a chance to enjoy abundant recreation, regardless of their social or economic status, their religious beliefs, or the color of their skin. The fact that the income of one state or county is high and another's low is no valid reason for permitting recreation inadequacies to continue. The deficiencies must be remedied without regard to geographical boundary lines or economic status.

Likewise, recreation inequalities based upon racial discrimination must be corrected. Wholesome recreation attempts to stimulate personality growth and should not be denied for reasons as invalid as color, religion, or nationality. If recreation is to contribute to democratic living, it must eliminate discrimination and smother bigotry. Its future can be bright only if the inequalities are eradicated.

Government at All Levels Must Accept Its Responsibilities

Earlier, the need for establishing a Federal Recreation Service was mentioned, but the municipalities, counties, and states, as well as the federal government, cannot escape their responsibilities for recreation. Recreation is a function of government. It rests upon the municipalities and counties to provide the foundation of public recreation services and opportunities for the people. The state and federal governments are obligated to help the communities help themselves. Government must take the lead. Recreation is an entirely defensible claim on the tax dollar. It is not extravagant to say that the day is not far off when a permanent service, whose major purpose is the promotion and fostering of recreation, will become a basic part of the federal government's general welfare program. State government also will provide for the recreation needs of its political subdivisions as it now does in such fields as education, health, welfare, and social insurance. Progress along these lines may at times seem slow and unsatisfactory, but this is because the people as a whole, and consequently their governments, have been slow to learn the business of human development, which really should be their main concern. Recreation is winning new ground daily in its struggle for governmental adoption, and when recreation takes its rightful place among the essential services, its goals will be more quickly reached. As far as federal provision is concerned, it need not be blocked or delayed until such time as all of the state services are organized. If the cry of states' rights is raised, the autonomy of states and communities can be protected in the legislation authorizing federal recreation services.

Accent on Leadership

The whole question of leadership is paramount in the consideration of recreation's future. The problem involves two kinds of leadership, both necessary to progress. One type is broad, courageous, and imaginative but practical. This is the leadership which is needed on a national scale. It is the kind of leadership which is first and always concerned with *total* recreation needs and our whole national life. It is the kind of leadership which will sacrifice the preservation of agency identity to total objectives. It emphasizes the general well-being of humanity and does not allow itself to be retarded by pettiness. It is more concerned with recreation as a way of life than it is with whose interests shall be the longest lived. The recreation movement needs imaginative leaders. It needs creative direction of the type which will look more to the way recreation should be in the future and less to what it has been in the past. It also needs new blood, refreshing points of view, and precise thinking.

The second type of leadership must meet the need for highly qualified recreation personnel to organize, supervise, and operate the increasing number of recreation services throughout the nation. Recreation tomorrow will only be as strong as its leaders. They must be of the highest caliber to meet the exacting requirements of a profession whose aims and potentials are second to none. They must understand the richest philosophies, know at first hand the lasting principles of meeting the leisure needs of people, appreciate the limitless range of opportunities, and be capable of administering programs efficiently. Whether recreation can attract this kind of leadership will depend to some degree upon the challenges it can evidence and the records it can provide, including salaries. Salaries will have to be much higher than they are now. As public understanding of the importance of organized recreation grows, the income of recreation workers will increase. Salary ranges in the recreation profession are already considerably higher than they were a decade ago, and the increase is by no means due entirely to the higher cost of living.

The quality of leadership, and hence, the progress of the recreation movement, will depend, in no small way, upon the excellence of professional preparation in recreation. This places a heavy responsibility upon our colleges and universities. Added to the need for their helping to educate *all* young people for "living in leisure" is their obligation to prepare young men and women for careers in recreation.

University and college recreation curriculums in the future will begin with general education and remain close to the liberal arts and the humanities. To these will be added the behavioral sciences, and in some areas of specialization such studies as physiology, anatomy, and chemistry (for recreation therapy), and botany, zoology, and ecology (for outdoor recreation). Breadth of philosophy, pinpointing recreation in relation to human development and the *totality* of living, and depth in one or two skills (e.g., sports, crafts, music) will be encouraged.

There will be an unlimited number of professional opportunities in recreation tomorrow. As this is written, the demand for qualified recreators in a variety of settings, at home and abroad, and of varying degrees of responsibility, is *far* in excess of the supply. As the recreation explosion continues, the shortage of recreators will become more pronounced.

Professional preparation, nevertheless, will be extended both in the number of institutions offering it, and in the length of study time required. The number of persons seeking *advanced* degrees in recreation will increase.

Registration and then legal certification of recreation personnel will become more widespread.

Competent, imaginative, resourceful recreators will be needed in larger and larger numbers.

Need for Professional Unity

Because recreation is inherently broad and diversified, it is natural that there should have grown up around it a variety of professional interests. There are, today, a number of professional organizations and service agencies actively engaged in helping to advance recreation on many fronts.

In 1966, five of these agencies—the American Recreation Society, the American Institute of Park Executives, the National Recreation Association, the American Association of Zoological Parks and Aquariums, and the National Conference of State Parks—joined into a merger forming the National Recreation and Park Association—a real step toward professional unity. This merger has been mentioned a number of times throughout this volume. Two fine bodies of professional leadership cannot be a part of the merger, the American Association of Health, Physical Education and Recreation, and the American Association of Group Workers—the first is a part of the National Education Association and the second a part of the National Social Welfare Assembly. There are, however, other groups that could unite with NRPA and it is hoped that further merger will continue. Certainly, all groups can coordinate and cooperate, thus developing a unity of professional concern and purpose. The recreation movement would benefit greatly from a single, national organization spearheading its interests. There is good reason to expect that the tide is running toward unity of action, if not yet unification of organization. If and when the latter comes, it will be on the path of compromise, each existing group giving up something and each not getting everything it wants.

ROUND-UP FOR TOMORROW

It is often difficult to identify a trend; nevertheless, there are certain observable developments which appear to be shaping the destinies of recreation. Careful consideration, based upon a close examination of events of the past and present, seems to make the following a reasonably accurate forecast of what might be expected recreationally in the future:

1. As indicated earlier in the chapter, barring nuclear war, the people of the United States and Canada will have more free time, more leisure. This will be true because of the shorter work week (it will drop from 40 to 30 to 20 hours and below for some, and result in total unemployment for many). Work time will shrink mainly for those with low educational backgrounds. It will thus be shortened first for the blue-collar worker, especially for those who perform manual tasks. Some fathers will work fewer hours than their children are in school. Professional, semi-professional, and skilled workers will be the last to have a large amount of leisure on their hands.

2. The attitudes of people toward leisure will change. They will look upon it as something desirable—as an opportunity for personal enjoyment and release from the rigors of a highly organized, complex, and crowded existence. The desire *for* leisure will continue up to the point where people encounter *enforced* leisure, at which time their attitudes toward leisure will be governed largely by their personal values (what they believe life is for), how well prepared they are to use their leisure in recreative and self-fulfilling ways, by the status of their health, and their purchasing power.

3. The arrival of a new leisure for more people will eventually focus more attention on the fact that the delights of work and recreation are tied together. Neither can stand alone; one is dependent upon the other, and too much of one at the expense of the other results only in problems. The great unanswered question of the new leisure is whether it will contribute to or detract from the goal of human equilibrium, of balanced living.

4. The concept of recreation will broaden in the future. It will not be defined and interpreted as narrowly as it has been in the past. The relation of recreation to the shaping of personality, to physiological and psychological development, and as a means of helping the individual adapt to his changing environment will become better understood. More attention to the role of recreation in the future will be buttressed by a more thorough examination of its role in the cultural past.

5. More people will become more literate, recreationally. But this will not come quickly any more than can becoming educated. People, nevertheless, will acquire new recreation interests and skills. These, in turn, will bring new experiences and values. Hopefully, more people will come to understand the importance of the *recreative* existence and why it is the *right* way. There will be increased emphasis upon *participation,* although vast improvements in communication and transportation will also sustain the immense number of opportunities in recreation to witness and listen to the performances of others.

6. As indicated earlier, the trend toward urbanization will continue. The struggle to maintain urban centers and design them primarily for man rather than machines will continue. Despite the advances of city and regional planning, urban renewal programs, and the like, there will have to be waged a real campaign to claim and protect open space for recreation.

7. The more population increases, and the more living space becomes crowded, the greater will be the premium placed upon opportunity for relaxation, contemplation, privacy, and solitude, for reducing pressures to always be "on the go"—for achieving the *lesisurely.*

8. If for no other reason than that the forces of modern living tend to pull the family apart, recreation, in its countless forms, will be used increasingly to hold the family together.

9. Recreation will hold an increasingly important place in the international pattern. This is already evident in the increased volume in travel, in the increasing similarity of the recreation habits of the people of different nations, and in the new international organizations which concern themselves with international recreation affairs (e.g., International Recreation Association, European Recreation Society).

10. In the future there will be more attention given to helping the individual help himself, recreationally. This will mean the development of individual recreation skills so that a person will be able to use his leisure satisfyingly without having to depend upon others for planning the use of his leisure. It will also mean enlisting the support of and developing the skills of the individual in order that he may serve others. There will be a larger need for the trained, available, competent amateur. The volunteer will supplement the professional in larger numbers in helping to serve community recreation needs.

11. There will be more public concern for an effort to plan, develop,

use, protect, and conserve land and water areas in the public domain for recreation and other human purposes. Patterns will develop for using our lands recreationally, but in ways which will best conserve and protect them. Those things which threaten our public lands and waters— overgrazing, soil erosion, range fires, lack of land retirement, absence of reforestation and proper wildlife management, unfavorable weather conditions, industrial pollution, and over-extended industrial and population use—will be better controlled.

12. There will be gains made in research in recreation. Research will move out of the survey-questionnaire-inventory stage and into the area of trying to discover what happens to people when they engage in various forms of recreation. The research will first have to be directed toward people's recreation and leisure habits, then to observing and assessing behavioral aspects. Methods and techniques best suited for research in recreation will have to be adopted, tested, and validated. These investigations will have to be undertaken by persons adept in research methods and knowledgeable in recreation, often in concert with researchers in other social sciences. From them will emerge the body of knowledge, the principles and concepts, and, finally, the policies upon which the future of recreation will be determined and from which it will advance.

13. Recreation programs will be better balanced and more carefully related to the physiological and psychological needs, interests, satisfactions, and capabilities of individuals and groups.

14. Attempts will be made to determine how much recreation a community should provide, and gains will be made in dividing labor between public and voluntary agencies. Coordination between them will improve. More attention will be given to what community recreation services are indispensable, essential, or simply desirable if the community can afford them.

15. There will be more widespread understanding, appreciation, and acceptance of recreation as a function to be supported by the resources of society.

16. Recreation for industrial and business employees will increase, although there may not be a corresponding increase in the development of plant-managed programs.

17. The number of new, local, tax-supported recreation systems will increase. At the point where public recreation services are available to the entire population, the number of managing authorities will decrease. This will come about by the consolidation of authorities, giving a smaller number of them wider geographical jurisdiction.

18. There will be an increased number of mergers in local park and recreation systems.

19. The states will increase their support of and interest in state recreation services.

20. The federal government will establish some kind of permanent,

national service program for the promotion and development of recreation.

21. Recreation as a therapy, particularly in mental hospitals, physical rehabilitation centers, and in camps for the handicapped, will make undreamed-of progress.

22. The armed forces will establish "career" programs in recreation for officer personnel.

23. Added financial support will be given to the development of our state and national parks and forests. Some of the burden of supplying these funds will be put on the user.

24. Recreation will be more carefully weighed in relation to the conservation of our national resources, including the development of water power.

25. Professional recreation literature will expand greatly, and the behavioral sciences, generally, will make increasing contributions to the areas of recreation and leisure, and vice versa.

26. Recreation personnel will receive some form of recognized professional identification.

27. There will be greater cross-fertilization of interests between recreation on one hand and such areas as education, health, regional planning, and welfare on the other.

28. There will be much program emphasis upon corecreation, the aging, the needs of young married couples, and outdoor living of all kinds.

29. Legislation will enable cities to solve "fringe-area" problems by widening the tax base for recreation services. Such legislation will be comparable to that which currently authorizes the establishment of *park districts* or *school districts*. It will also have the effect of allowing municipalities and towns to pool their resources.

30. State recreation-enabling legislation will be liberalized but will remain permissive. *Eventually,* states may have laws requiring minimum standards of provision for public recreation, just as there are now state laws requiring minimum standards in public health and public education.

31. There will be wider use and development of community facilities for recreation, including the projection of outdoor resources such as watersheds, forests, and reservations for functional recreation use.

32. A new type of professional recreation specialization will develop in the form of recreation counselors. Such counselors will be attracted to industries, hospitals, clinics, schools, and perhaps public recreation departments.

33. Recreation as a method of teaching will find its way into the elementary and secondary systems. Indeed, recreation will be accepted in many school systems as a *teaching* subject.

34. All kinds of outdoor recreation facilities, public and commercial, will be illuminated for night use.

35. All forms of the arts, cultural and performing, will become more popular and more accessible.

36. More satisfactory methods for appraising and evaluating recreation programs, services, and facilities will be developed.

The projections made here with respect to the future of recreation will certainly not be accepted unanimously. Nor do the authors expect them to be received without question. The future, as always, is unpredictable, if predictability is equated with *absolute* certainty. The best that can be said of these predictions is that they have their roots in the past and in the observable present. The foundations and beginnings of many of these trends and expectations are a matter of fact at this moment. The odds favor their coming into full bloom, if for no other reason than that they are cloaked in man's eternal search and struggle to attain the "full life" —a state of being which will have to be very much realized in his hours of leisure in the future.

These, then, are among the important milestones recreation will pass as it gains stature and makes an ever-increasing contribution to mankind. Its role will become larger, its range wider, and its challenge greater. Progress will not be made in the absence of reversals and setbacks, but while recreation's progress may at times be impeded, its potential contributions to the well-being of people are so great as to make impossible a complete halt to its forward march.

We are experiencing a change in the structure of our lives in relationship to the content of time and the pace and values of living. The contemporary leisure mode is rooted in a unique partnership of scientific research, engineering skill, and mass production.

These forces present to us four contributions:

1. Increasing amount of *disposable time,* which may be defined as those hours which are available for off-the-job living.

2. Increasing amount of *disposable human energy,* which is defined as those powers which are unleashed by automation, better health and longer life, and which are not expended in earning an existence wage.

3. Increasing amount of *disposable income,* defined as the financial resources which are greater than what is required for an existence level of living.

4. The fourth condition is that of the greater variety and *depth of Recreation skills* and of the more overtly expressed readiness for their employment.

As a result, enjoyment once reserved for a privileged elite is becoming widely distributed. The new concept of man in relation to time, in an age whose tempo has been quickened by the application of atomic concepts and electronics gives promise of the flowering of a great culture. Already there is emerging a new role for the family, a new concept of neighborhood, a new sense of community, and a new vigor of participation. Leisure, as we experience it, becomes a function of an unseen but very real and enormously fruitful configuration of scientific concepts and theories which over arch and undergird our complex era.

We plunge into the tomorrows, confident of our contribution through recreation for a better life. In that belief: May we dare to think ahead, plan ahead, and move ahead.

The challenge here is to earnestly plead with those of you who are devoted to this profession to become a crusader of its potentials—a creative master of this art, the inventor for the road ahead, the interpreter of its objectives and values, the analyst of its procedures, the scientist of human relations, the researcher for its proofs, the explorer of its hidden possibilities and the ambassador of its worth.

REFERENCES

Bell, Norman, and Ezra F. Vogel, eds., *A Modern Introduction to the Family.* New York: Free Press of Glencoe, Inc., 1960.

Bernstein, Peter L., *The Price of Prosperity.* New York: Doubleday and Company, Inc., 1962.

Brightbill, Charles K., *Educating for Leisure Living.* Harrisburg, Pennsylvania: The Stackpole Company, 1966.

Brightbill, Charles K., *Man and Leisure—A Philosophy of Recreation.* Englewood Cliffs, New Jersey: Prentice-Hall, Inc., 1961.

Brown, Harrison, James Bonner, and John Weir, *The Next Hundred Years.* New York: The Viking Press, Inc., 1961.

Clawson, Marion, *Land and Water for Recreation—Opportunities, Problems, and Policies.* Chicago: Rand McNally & Co., 1963.

De Grazia, Sebastian, *Of Time, Work, and Leisure.* New York: The Twentieth Century Fund, 1962.

Editors of *Fortune Magazine,* "The Exploding Metropolis." New York: Doubleday and Company, 1958.

Feinstein, Otto, *Two Worlds of Change.* New York: Anchor Books. Doubleday and Company, 1964.

Galbraith, John K., *The Affluent Society.* New York: Mentor Books, 1958.

Kaplan, Max, *Leisure in America—A Social Inquiry.* New York: John Wiley & Sons, Inc., 1960.

Kleemier, Robert W., ed., *Aging and Leisure.* New York: Oxford University Press, 1961.

Larrabee, Eric, and Rolf Meyersohn, eds., *Mass Leisure.* New York: Free Press of Glencoe, Inc., 1958.

Michael, Donald N., *The Next Generation—The Prospects Ahead for the Youth of Today and Tomorrow.* New York: A Vintage Book, Division of Random House, 1965.

Morphet, Edgar L. and Charles O. Ryan, eds., *Designing Education for the Future—Prospective Changes in Society by 1980*. New York: Citation Press, Scholastic Magazines, Inc., 1967.

Mumford, Lewis, *The Story of Utopia*. New York: Compass Books, 1962.

Philipson, Morris, ed., *Automation—Implications for the Future*. New York: Vintage Books, 1962.

Pieper, J., *Leisure, The Basis of Culture*. New York: New American Library, 1964.

Smigel, Erwin O., ed., *Work and Leisure—A Contemporary Social Problem*. New Haven, Conn.: College and University Press, 1963.

Sorenson, Ray, *Tomorrow in Today's Community*. Excerpts from unpublished papers. New York: Community Research Associates, 124 East 40th Street, 10016, 1967.

Comments

In addition to the books listed in References, current magazines and special features in newspapers carry many articles relating to Recreation, Leisure, and the Future. It will be worthwhile to develop a scrapbook of this material.

One of the most significant pieces of literature on this subject is the book, *Dynamics of Change*, a series of six chapters published by the Kaiser Aluminum News, Kaiser Center, 866 Oakland, California 94694. This volume is a MUST for the best understanding of important factors of the future. Chapter 5 is titled "The Leisure Masses" 1967.

The National Recreation and Park Association has a number of documents on the subject. Note—"Recreation and Park Manpower—Supply and Demand Workbook."

The Bureau of Outdoor Recreation is also publishing excellent material. Note a reference catalog of *Outdoor Recreation Research,* 1967, Department of the Interior and Smithsonian Institution, Science Information Exchange. This is the second catalog published. The two volumes of *An Index of Selected Outdoor Recreation Literature* is a valuable document from the Bureau of Outdoor Recreation; Volume I published in 1967 and Volume II in 1968.

Trends in American Living and Outdoor Recreation published by the Outdoor Recreation Resources Review Commission is a very fruitful volume for future concern in determining a chart of progress for Recreation.

Determine to *Keep Up*—think ahead, plan ahead, and develop programs of action for bringing to all our people more abundant and wholesome Recreation.

Appendix

GLOSSARY

Selected terms from a Bulletin published by the North Carolina Recreation Commission—*A GLOSSARY OF PUBLIC RECREATION TERMS* by H. Douglas Sessoms, Chairman, Curriculum in Recreation Administration, University of North Carolina. (Prepared originally by Douglas Sessoms as an unpublished master's thesis at the University of Illinois.)

Activity: A medium through which individuals satisfy their recreation needs and interests. Recreation activities are performed during leisure and may be of a passive or active nature.

Administration: Determined action taken in pursuit of conscious purpose; its components are planning, organizing, staffing, directing, supervising, coordinating, reporting, and budgeting.

Camping: A form or recreation in which living-out-of-doors in a more or less close relationship with the natural environment is significant. The use of a portable shelter is usually involved.

Community: Includes people, geographical territory, and a common purpose. The people are held together by psychological, sociological, and economic bonds and may act together consciously or unconsciously in their chief concerns of life. The community creates, as a result of its common interests, certain institutions of legal, protective, educational, economic, recreation, and religious character. A community includes factors of interdependence and belonging and a sense of usefulness through contributing to the common good.

Entertainment: A relatively passive form of recreation arousing interest and

439

pleasurable emotions emanating from activities which engage the attention agreeably, amuse, or divert, whether in private, as by conversation, or in public, as by attending the theater.

Governmental Functions: Those services performed by a municipality or other governmental unit, such as a school board or county, which are for the public welfare, such as education, health. Frequently this is a mandatory duty such as welfare, prescribed by the state. Services which are not definitely proprietary or governmental may be declared one or the other by the legislature or supreme court.

Leadership: The ability of one person or a group of people to influence others to recognize goals of common interest and to stimulate them to act cooperatively to achieve their goals.

Leisure: Time, free from work and free from fulfilling the basic obligations and necessities of life, available for pursuits freely decided upon by the individual.

Managing Authority: An agency such as the recreation department, board of education, park department, or park district established under proper legislative authorization to manage and administer certain recreation areas and facilities, programs and services for the general public.

Master Plan for Recreation: A long term guide for the systematic and orderly selection and development of recreation facilities and services over a given period of time. It might be composed of such elements as goals, organization structure, activity program, areas, facilities, personnel, and financial support.

Park District: A subdivision of state government exercising within its jurisdiction the authority of a municipality. It may operate and maintain parks, recreation programs, police forces, airports, and other such facilities and programs designated in the act of establishing the district.

Program: Recreation opportunities which result from the organization and planned use of community recreation resources such as finances, facilities, and leadership. The activities of a program may be planned or unplanned, organized or unorganized, active or passive, and include individual or group participation. Program may also refer to a specific phase of the total program such as nature program, drama program, and community center program.

Proprietary Functions: Those services performed by a municipality, school, county, or other governmental unit for the specific benefit of the inhabitants of that unit, rather than for the general public.

Recreation: The natural expression of certain human interests and needs seeking satisfaction during leisure. It is an individual or a group experience motivated primarily by the enjoyment and satisfaction derived therefrom. It takes many forms and may be a planned or spontaneous activity.

Recreation Board or Commission: An appointed or elected body of laymen, serving on a salaried or volunteer basis, usually responsible for determining the policies of a public recreation agency and/or advising the chief executive. It convenes from time to time and is generally required to act collectively according to powers derived from enabling legislation, charter, and similar jurisdictions.

Recreation, Church: A recreation program conducted for and/or by the church, its organizations, members, and their friends.

Recreation, Commercial: Recreation services and activities, such as dance halls, bowling alleys, theaters, amusement parks, and carnivals, organized primarily for profit and provided by business enterprises.

Recreation, Community: All recreation services and activities provided by public, private, and commercial agencies for persons who have in common a geographical, psychological, or institutional bond, and a community of interest.

Recreation Areas: Land and water space set aside for recreation usage, such as parks, playgrounds, lakes, and reservations.

Recreation District: A subdivision of state government exercising within its jurisdiction the authority of a public recreation agency. It may include incorporated and/or unincorporated territory and have corporate responsibility and powers such as taxation, bond issuance and eminent domain.

Recreation Facilities: Buildings and other physical features and provisions, such as swimming pools, community recreation centers, stadiums, and outdoor theaters, designed and constructed for recreation use.

Recreation, Federal: Recreation programs, activities, and consultative services administered by an agency of the Federal Government such as the Department of Interior, the Department of Agriculture and its Extension Services, the Department of Health, Education and Welfare, and the Tennessee Valley Authority.

Recreation, Industrial: Recreation programs designed for the employees of industrial and business firms and their families. These programs are usually administered either by the firms, their employees, public recreation agencies, labor unions, or a combination of any or all the above mentioned groups. Often referred to as Employee Recreation.

Recreation, International: Recreation activities, programs and consultative services administered by various public and private agencies on an international basis. The work of the Recreation Committee of the International Labor Office and the cultural programs of UNESCO, along with the activities of the Olympic Games, are examples of International Recreation.

Recreation, Institutional: A recreation program operated for or by an institution designed to meet many of the recreation needs and interests of its inmates whether they be delinquents, defectives, or dependents. Institutions often provide a program of recreation activities for their employees as well as for their inmates.

Recreation, Municipal: A program of public recreation provided by the corporate body for persons residing in any one of the several types of governmental units having the power of local self-government.

Recreation Objectives: A frame of reference that provides measuring rods for use in reaching goals. Objectives may be for one event, a program within a specific setting, or the expression of the philosophy of the recreation profession.

Recreation, Organized: The provision of supervised and unsupervised recreation programs, services, areas, and facilities by a recreation agency or agencies for a specific clientele or community at large.

Recreation Principles: Generalized and abbreviated statements with respect to recreation about which competent recreation authorities are in agreement. These principles are generally used as guides for action.

Recreation, Private: A recreation program and/or services established under the auspices of an agency or organization supported by other than governmental funds such as the Community Chest, private donations, and membership fees. Private agencies usually serve a particular constituency and often limit their services to a given area of a city. Recreation is often a technique rather than the primary purpose in private agencies.

Recreation Profession: A vocation in which one has acquired some special knowledge to guide others in recreation activities. It is usually characterized by a high degree of technical skill in the conduct of organized recreation. It entails specialized preparation, generally at institutions of higher learning, special vocation identity, a strong sense of vocational honor and solidarity, membership in professional associations, and a code of ethics.

Recreation, Public: Governmental provision of recreation opportunities and services available to all people. It is financed primarily by taxation and includes the establishment, operation, conduct, control, and maintenance of program, services, areas, and facilities.

Recreation, Rural: Recreation services and programs conducted for inhabitants of unincorporated places of approximately 2500 or less and for inhabitants of open country or unincorporated areas.

Recreation, School: A recreation program, operated as an essential part of the educational program, teaching the arts of leisure and/or providing recreation opportunities for individuals and groups of the community along with the total school program.

Recreation, State: A recreation program or service offered by a state agency such as the State Recreation Commission, Conservation Department, or Welfare Department on a state-wide basis. Services may include the operating of a public area and facility such as a state park, the carrying forth of statewide research, the planning and promotion of new recreation programs, and/or advising local groups on various problems relating to recreation.

Recreation Therapy: The use of recreation activities as a means to aid in the cure and correction of individual deviations from the normal or healthy condition.

Referendum: A method by which the people bring a legislative measure to a direct vote of the electorate.

Recreator: Any person giving full-time service of professional quality to the field of recreation; a recreation worker. (See Recreation Profession)

Recreology: The science of man's recreative use of leisure, dealing with the acts, states, and agents of recreation, and investigating the forces and effects of recreation; that body of knowledge concerned with the past, present, and future of the recreation movement, with man's use, misuse, and/or abuse of leisure. It is examined attentively by those endeavoring to educate formally for the worthy use of leisure.

Social Group Work: A technique of social work in which the worker promotes the social adjustment of individuals through their participation in guided corporate activity.

Therapeutic Recreation: Those activities designed or adapted for an ill or handicapped person by a professional recreator. The activities and the patient's participation in them are structured to be therapeutic in addition to providing each individual with an opportunity for the recreation experience.

NATIONAL NON-GOVERNMENTAL AGENCIES AND ORGANIZATIONS

Amateur Athletic Union of the United States, 233 Broadway, New York, New York 10000

American Association for Health, Physical Education, and Recreation, 1201 Sixteenth Street, N.W., Washington, D.C. 20000

American Association of Museums, Smithsonian Institution, 2306 Massachusetts Avenue, N.W., Washington, D.C. 20000

American Bowling Congress, 2200 North Third Street, Milwaukee, Wisconsin 53200

American Camping Association, Bradford Woods, Martinsville, Indiana 46151

American Conservation Association, Inc., 30 Rockefeller Plaza, New York, New York 10020

American Council on Education, 1785 Massachusetts Avenue, N.W., Washington, D.C. 20000

American Country Life Association, Room 228, 327 LaSalle Street, Chicago 4, Illinois 60600

American Federation of Arts, 41 E. 65th Street, New York 10000

American Federation of Labor-Congress of Industrial Organization, AFL-CIO Building, 815 16th Street, N.W., Washington, D.C. 20000

American Forest Institute, Inc., 1835 K Street, N.W., Washington, D.C. 20006

American Forestry Association, The, 919 17th Street, N.W., Washington, D.C. 20006

American Legion, 700 North Pennsylvania Street, Indianapolis, Indiana 46200

American Library Association, 50 East Huron Street, Chicago, Illinois 60600

American National Red Cross, 17th and D Streets, N.W., Washington, D.C. 20000

American Nature Association, 1214 Sixteenth Street, N.W., Washington, D.C. 20000

American Psychiatric Association, 1700 18th Street, N.W., Washington, D.C. 20000

American Psychological Association, 1200 17th Street, N.W., Washington, D.C. 20000

American Public Health Association, 224 E. Capital, Washington, D.C. 20000

American Scenic and Historic Preservation Society, Federal Hall Memorial, Wall and Nassau Streets, New York, New York 10005

American Society of Planning Officials, 1313 East 60th Street, Chicago, Illinois 60600

American Sociological Society, 1001 Connecticut Avenue, N.W., Washington, D.C. 20000

American Youth Foundation, 3460 Hampton Street, St. Louis, Missouri 63100

American Youth Hostels, Inc., 1400 L Street, N.W., Washington, D.C. 20000

Association of College Unions, Willard Straight Hall, Cornell University, Ithaca, New York 14850

Association of the Junior Leagues of America, Waldorf Astoria, 305 Park Avenue, New York, New York 10020

Athletic Institute, Room 850, Merchandise Mart, Chicago 5, Illinois 60600

Boy Scouts of America, National Council, New Brunswick, New Jersey 08903

Boys' Clubs of America, 771 First Avenue, New York 17, New York 10000

Camp Fire Girls, Inc., 65 Worth Street, New York, New York 10000

Catholic Youth Organization, 112 S. Wabash Avenue, Chicago, Illinois 60600

Chamber of Commerce of the United States of America, Community and Regional Resource Development Group, 1615 H Street, N.W., Washington, D.C. 20006

Child Welfare League of America, 44 E. 23rd Street, New York, New York 10020

Civitan International, 115 N. 21st Street, Birmingham, Alabama 35200

Cooperative League of the United States of America, 1012 14th Street, N.W., Washington, D.C. 20006

Cooperative Recreation Service, 500 State Route 203, Delaware, Ohio 43015

Folklore Associates, Hatboro Industrial Parks, Hatboro, Pennsylvania 19040

Future Farmers of America, 330 Independence Avenue, S.W., Washington, D.C. 20000

Garden Club of America, The, 598 Madison Avenue, New York, New York 10020

General Board of Education of the Methodist Church, P.O. Box 871, Nashville, Tennessee 37200

General Federation of Women's Clubs, 1734 N. Street, N.W., Washington, D.C. 20006

Girl Scouts of the United States of America, 830 Third Avenue, New York, New York 10020

Girls Clubs of America, 22 East 38th Street, New York, New York 10020

Institute of Adult Education, 525 West 120th Street, New York, New York 10000

International Association of Altrusa Clubs, Inc., 332 S. Michigan Avenue, Chicago, Illinois 60600

Izaak Walton League of America, 1326 Waukegan Road, Glenview, Illinois 60025

Junior Achievement, 51 West 51st Street, New York 10019

Junior Chamber of Commerce, Merchandise Mart, Chicago, Illinois 60600

Kiwanis International, 101 East Erie Street, Chicago, Illinois 60600

Lions International, 209 North Michigan Avenue, Chicago, Illinois 60600

National Association of County Officials, 1001 Connecticut Avenue, N.W., Washington, D.C. 20036

National Association of Social Workers—Group Work Division, 2 Park Avenue, New York, New York 10020

National Audubon Society, 1130 5th Avenue, New York, New York 10020

National Association for Mental Health, 10 Columbus Circle, New York, New York 10020

National Catholic Community Service, 1312 Massachusetts Avenue, N.W., Washington, D.C. 20006

National Committee on Housing, Inc., 512 Fifth Avenue, New York, New York 10020

National Conference on Social Welfare, 22 West Gay Street, Columbus, Ohio 43215

National Congress of Parents and Teachers, 700 North Rush Street, Chicago, Illinois 60611

National Council on the Aging, 315 Park Avenue, S., New York 10010

National Council of the Churches of Christ in the United States of America, 475 Riverside Drive, New York 10027

National Education Association of the United States, 1201 Sixteenth Street, N.W., Washington, D.C. 20000

National Federation of Business and Professional Women's Clubs, 2012 Massachusetts Avenue, N.W., Washington, D.C. 20000

National Federation of Music Clubs, Bankers Trust Building, Norfolk, Virginia 23500

National Federation of Settlements and Neighborhood Centers, 226 West 47th Street, New York, New York 10020

National Geographic Society, 1145 17th Street, N.W., Washington, D.C. 20036

National Governor's Council, 1735 DeSales Street, N.W., Washington, D.C. 20036

National Grange, 1616 H Street, N.W., Washington, D.C. 20006

National Industrial Recreation Association, 20 N. Wacker Drive, Chicago, Illinois 60600

National Jewish Welfare Board, 145 East 32nd Street, New York, New York 10016

National League of Cities, 1612 K Street, N.W., Washington, D.C. 20006

National Parks Association, 1300 New Hampshire Avenue, N.W., Washington, D.C. 20036

National Planning Association, 1606 New Hampshire Avenue, N.W., Washington, D.C. 20036

National Public Relations Council for Health and Welfare Services, Inc., Park Avenue, S., New York 10010

National Recreation and Park Association, 1700 Pennsylvania Avenue, N.W., Washington, D.C. 20006

National Research Council, 2101 Constitution Avenue, Washington, D.C. 20036

National Rifle Association, 1600 Rhode Island Avenue, N.W., Washington, D.C. 20036

National Social Welfare Assembly, 345 East 46th Street, New York, New York 10020

National Wildlife Federation, 1412 16th Street, N.W., Washington, D.C. 20036

Nature Conservancy, 1522 K Street, N.W., Washington, D.C. 20006

Optimist International, 4494 Lindell Boulevard, St. Louis, Missouri 53100

Outboard Boating Club of America, 333 N. Michigan Avenue, Chicago, Illinois 60601

Play School Association, 120 West 57th Street, New York, New York 10020

Public Administration Service, 1313 East 60th Street, Chicago, Illinois 60601

Rotary International, 1600 N. Ridge Street, Evanston, Illinois 60201

Resources for the Future, Inc., 1755 Massachusetts Avenue, N.W., Washington, D.C. 20036

Society of State Directors of Health, Physical Education, and Recreation, 1201 16th Street, N.W., Washington, D.C. 20036

Sport Fishing Institute, 719 13th Street, N.W., Washington, D.C. 20005

Twentieth Century Fund, Inc., 460 W. 54th Street, New York, New York 10000

United Community Funds and Council of America, 345 East 46th Street, New York, New York 10000

United Service Organizations, 237 E. 52nd Street, New York, New York 10000

Wildlife Management Institute, 709 Wire Building, Washington, D.C. 20005

Young Men's Christian Association of the United States of America, National Council, 291 Broadway, New York, New York 10020

Young Men's Hebrew and Young Women's Hebrew Associations, 145 E. 32 Street, New York, New York 10020

Young Women's Christian Association of the United States of America, National Board, 600 Lexington Avenue, New York, New York 10000

TYPES OF LOCAL PUBLIC AGENCIES ENGAGED IN RECREATION
Suggestive, not complete

Recreation Departments, Commissions, Districts, Boards, Committees, and Councils

Park Departments, Commissions, Districts, Boards, and Committees

Recreation and Park Departments, Commissions, Districts, Boards, and Committees

Departments of Parks and Public Property or Buildings

School Boards, Departments, Districts, and Other School Authorities

City Managers, Borough Councils, and County Boards

Departments of Public Works

Departments of Public Welfare

Beach, Bath, and Swimming Pool Commissions

Golf Boards, Commissions, and Departments

Public Service and Public Affairs Departments

Also: Libraries, Museums, Institutes, and so on

TYPES OF LOCAL PRIVATE AGENCIES ENGAGED IN RECREATION
Suggestive, not complete

Boy Scouts	Jewish Welfare Board
Boy Rangers	Junior Achievement
Boys' Clubs	Red Cross
Camp Fire Girls	Salvation Army
Catholic Youth Organization	Settlements
4-H Clubs	Youth Hostels
Churches	Y.W.C.A.
Girl Scouts	Y.M.C.A.
Girls' Clubs	Y.M.H.A.
Granges	Y.W.H.A.

Also: Miscellaneous religious, educational, patriotic, political, fraternal, industrial, labor, rural, interracial, civic, and institutional organizations.

Other helpful aids:

Of public recreation systems:
  Recreation and Park Yearbook, National Recreation Association, 8 West
  Eighth Street, New York 11, New York. Issued Yearly.
Of school systems:
  Educational Directory, United States Office of Education, Washington, D.C.
  Latest Issue.
Of youth-serving organizations:
  Youth-serving Organizations, National Nongovernmental Associations, Ameri-
  can Youth Commission—American Council on Education, 1785 Massachu-
  setts Avenue, N.W., Washington 6, D.C.
Of all types of organizations, governmental and nongovernmental:
  Social Work Year Book, National Association of Social Workers, Group Work
  Division, 95 Madison Avenue, New York, New York. Latest Issue.

RECREATION FILMS

Many fine films are available on all phases of community recreation. These
and other audio-visual aids are most helpful in understanding recreation, its
implications and potentials. It is impractical to list here even a small portion
of the films which can be obtained, hence only a few are included for purposes
of illustration.

Information on complete title listings, rental and purchase prices, film descriptions, booking dates, transportation arrangements and charges can be obtained
from the film catalogues and listings of the distributors, libraries or institutions
handling the films.

Special Publications Listing Recreation Films and Slides
  Films (A Listing of Free and Inexpensive Films)—Vermont State Board of
  Recreation, Montpelier, Vermont
  Film Catalogue—New York State Youth Commission, 66 Beaver Street, Albany,
  New York
  Here's How To Do It—Department of National Health and Welfare, Ottawa,
  Canada
  Sound Slidefilm Service—Athletic Institute, Merchandise Mart—Room 805, Chi-
  cago, Illinois 60654
Other Sources of Information on Film, Filmstrip Producers, Distributors and
  Libraries
  American Library Association, 50 East Huron Street, Chicago, Illinois. Has
  available for distribution a mimeographed list of all public libraries offering
  film services.
  The Department of Audio-Visual Instruction, National Education Association,
  1201 16th Street, N.W., Washington, D.C.
  Educational Film Library Association, 1600 Broadway Street, New York, New
  York. Information available concerning affiliated film libraries in schools,
  universities, and college and public libraries.

Film Council of America, 600 Davis Street, Evanston, Illinois. Information available concerning local film councils, film information centers, film discussion programs, film preview centers.

International Council of Religious Education, Department of Audio-Visual and Radio Education, 203 North Wabash Avenue, Chicago, Illinois. Will supply information on affiliated local and state religious organizations offering film loan services.

National Audio-Visual Association, 2540 Eastwood Avenue, Evanston, Illinois. Publishes a "Directory of Accredited Retail Dealers in Audio-Visual Equipment, Materials, Supplies and Films."

The United States Office of Education, Visual Education Services, Federal Security Agency, Washington, D.C.

H. W. Wilson Company, 950 University Avenue, New York, New York. Publishes, as part of its annual Education Film Guide, a directory of producers, distributors and sponsors of 16 mm films listed therein. Also carries a list of filmstrips producers and distributors in its annual Educational Film Strip Guide.

Note: The visual aid centers of state colleges and universities are an excellent source of information and procurement of films and slides on recreation.

LIST OF FILMS

This is a selected list of films of special interest to recreators. There are hundreds of other films available—note addresses given above. All of these films are of 16 mm sound.

It is suggested that you write to the National Recreation and Park Association for information and procedure relative to obtaining the use of the films. Many of the films may be obtained from the Association—such as "A Chance to Play," "Classrooms in the Park," "People, Parks and Recreation," "Rx-Recreation," "This is Our Land" and others.

Here are further listings:

General Interpretation and Administration

Leaders for Leisure, Color, 21 min., Athletic Institute
$1,000 for Recreation, Color, 12 min., Athletic Institute
Playtown U.S.A., Color, 25 min., Athletic Institute
When All the People Play, Black and White, 25 min., National Film Board of Canada
You and Your Time, Black and White, 11 min., Association Films
They Grow Up So Fast, Color, 23 min., Athletic Institute
Better Use of Leisure, Color, 11 min., Coronet
Careers in Recreation, Color, 25 min., Athletic Institute
My Own Yard to Play In, Black and White, 7 min., Edward Harrison

Better Bulletin Boards, Color, 13 min., Indiana University
Film Tactics, Black and White, 21 min., U.S. Navy
Heritage of Splendor, Color, 18 min., Alfred Higgins Productions
Is There Communication When You Speak?, Black and White, 19 min., McGraw-Hill
Marshland is Not Wasteland, Color, 14 min., Roy Wilcox Productions
Of Time, Work and Leisure, Black and White, 28 min., National Recreation & Park Assn.

Program Areas

ABC of Puppet Making, Black and White, 10 min., Bailey Films
Adventuring in the Arts, Color, 22 min., Girl Scouts of the USA
Adventure in Conservation, Color, 14 min., Indiana University
Art from Scrap, Color, 5 min., International Film Bureau
Craftsmanship in Clay, Decoration, Color, 11 min., Indiana University
Dolls, Puppets, Diversions, Black and White, 28 min., Girl Scouts of the USA
Fun Fathoms, Color, 27 min., Aetna Life Affiliated
How to Make a Mask, Color, 11 min., Bailey Films
How to Make a Puppet, Color, 12 min., Bailey Films
Masks and Imagination, Black and White, 28 min., Girls Scouts of the USA
Music and Musical Instruments, Black and White, 28 min., Girls Scouts of the USA
Techniques of Paper Sculpture, Color, 11 min., Allen-Moore
Therapeutic Camping, Color, Deveruex Foundations

Special Settings

Adventure in Maturity, Color, 22 min., Oklahoma Department of Mental Health
Class for Tommy, Black and White, 20 min., Los Angeles City Schools
Comeback, Color, 28 min., Association Films
Proud Years, Black and White, 28 min., Columbia University Education Films
Recreation Center for the Handicapped, Inc., Color, 21 min., Stanford University
Someone Who Cares, Black and White, 28 min., Indiana Association of Mental Health
This is Girl Scouting, Color, 30 min., Girl Scouts of the USA
Time for What? Secret of the Later Years, Black and White, 12 min., Greater Miami Jewish Community Center.

Index

Abrahams, Joseph, cited, 362
Accounting. *See* Finance
Activity therapies. *See* Therapeutic recreation
Adjunctive therapies. *See* Therapeutic recreation
Administration
  community organization. *See* Community organization
  contrasted, 287–89
  defined, 97
  employee recreation, 270–71
  the executive, of, 399
  facilities. *See* Facilities
  finance. *See* Finance
  governing group in, 398–99
  legislation of, 393–98. *See also* Legislation
  managing authorities of, 97–104
  office management of, 419–20
  organizational management of, 398–402
  planning and research of, 390–93
  program of, 402–5
  and public relations. *See* Public relations
  purpose of, 96–97
  rural recreation types of, 109–10
  staff of, 399–400
  in the state, 124–30
  variety of types of, 97–99
Administration on Aging, 26, 59, 145, 352, 353, 354n

Adult education, 223–24
Age groups, 74
Aging, 335–54
  needs of, 337–38
  organization and administration of, 339–42
  program for, 343–48
Agriculture, Department of, 59, 75, 120–21, 135, 141–44, 209, 252, 299
Albemarle Committee on Youth Service, 173
American Association of Group Workers, 430. *See also* National Association of Social Workers
American Association of Health, Physical Education, and Recreation, 213n, 215n, 229, 332, 385, 430
American Association of Zoological Parks and Aquariums, 378, 380–82, 430
American Camping Association, 300–301, 310–11, 384–85
American Home Economics Association, 209
American Institute of Park Executives, 378–81, 430
American Junior Red Cross, 253–54
American Library Association, 157, 388
American National Red Cross, 22, 157, 160, 253, 326, 386
American Recreation Society, 20, 165, 318n, 330n, 332, 378–82, 430
American Youth Hostels, 386, 388